ORIENTAL RUGS
ANTIQUE AND MODERN

Walter
A. Hawley

DOVER PUBLICATIONS, INC.

NEW YORK

1304   301

Published in Canada by General Publishing Company, Ltd., 30 Lesmill Road, Don Mills, Toronto, Ontario.
Published in the United Kingdom by Constable and Company, Ltd., 10 Orange Street, London WC 2.

This Dover edition, first published in 1970, is an unabridged republication of the work originally published by John Lane Company in 1913.

Standard Book Number: 486-22366-3
Library of Congress Catalog Card Number: 79-105665

Manufactured in the United States of America
Dover Publications, Inc.
180 Varick Street
New York, N.Y. 10014

PREFACE

INCE the appearance, in 1900, of the excellent work of Mr. John Kimberly Mumford on Oriental Rugs, the public interest in these fabrics has so largely increased that the author feels warranted in offering this monograph, which aims to treat the subject in a way that will not only appeal to the general reader but be of value to the student.

In the chapter entitled "Rug Weaving Before the XVIII Century" is a brief review of some of the notable achievements in this branch of art; and in order that the public may as far as possible have access to the masterpieces described, the carpets on exhibition in the Metropolitan Museum of Art in New York have been given unusual prominence. The chapters on "How to Distinguish Rugs" and on "Purchasing Rugs" should prove serviceable to those who are collecting or are buying for use; and the chapter on "Weaving" contains many details which have not previously received from connoisseurs the consideration they deserve.

The descriptions of all but the least important classes of rugs in the Persian, Asia Minor, Caucasian, and Central Asiatic groups include not only a general statement of their most striking features, but also a technical analysis that is termed "Type Characteristics." It should be understood, however, that these characteristics are not invariable, but are remarkably constant. They may interest chiefly those who aim to acquire expert information, yet they will doubtlessly prove valuable to every owner of a rug as a means for its identification.

It would be difficult to acknowledge all the assistance received by the author since he began the study of rugs; for sometimes a mere suggestion has started a line of investigation resulting in interesting discoveries. He has freely consulted well-known authorities, who are quoted in the body of the work; and has received valuable suggestions and assistance from Messrs. T. S. Hawley, of Santa Barbara, Cal., George Harootunian and Frank Loftus, of

Los Angeles, Cal.; George Stevenson, of New York; G. Graf, of the Persiche Teppiche Gesellschaft, of Tabriz; and P. de Andrea & Co., of Constantinople. He gratefully acknowledges the permission of Messrs. C. F. Williams, of Norristown, Penn., and James F. Ballard, of St. Louis, Mo., to study their valuable collections; and the permission of Dr. Wilhelm R. Valentiner, Curator of Decorative Arts in the Metropolitan Museum in New York, to examine the carpets of the museum and to take photographs of them. He also wishes particularly to mention the kindness of the following collectors and firms who have allowed their rugs to be used for illustrations: Miss Emily Davis, of Buffalo, N. Y.; the Misses Palache, and Messrs. Nathan Bentz and T. S. Hawley, of Santa Barbara, Cal.; Mr. R. Y. Struble, of Fredericktown, Ohio; Mr. E. L. Pierce, of Syracuse, N.Y.; Mr. H. C. Merritt, of Pasadena, Cal.; Mr. J. F. Ballard, of St. Louis, Mo.; Mr. C. F. Williams, of Norristown, Penn.; Major L. B. Lawton, U.S.A., of Seneca Falls, N.Y.; Messrs. Mihran & Co., of Los Angeles, Cal.; Messrs. B. Altman & Co., Benguiat & Keresey, Wm. Baumgarten & Co., Jones & Brindisi, Jos. Wild & Co., W. & J. Sloane, and the Tiffany Studios, of New York City. He is also indebted to Vincent Robinson & Co., Ltd., of London, for the use of the colour plate of the Royal Garden Carpet, now owned by them, and to the Royal Victoria and Albert Museum, South Kensington, London, for permission to obtain a colour plate of the Holy Carpet of the Mosque of Ardebil.

WALTER A. HAWLEY.

NEW YORK, June, 1913.

CONTENTS

ILLUSTRATIONS

Colour Plates (following page 54)

Halftone Illustrations

ORIENTAL RUGS
ANTIQUE AND MODERN

ORIENTAL RUGS

CHAPTER I

INTRODUCTION

IT is not altogether surprising that in a most materialistic age many of a race distinguished more for its utilitarian than artistic accomplishments should fail to see in Oriental carpets high artistic expression; yet during the last twenty years choice specimens have been sold for sums which not only are very large, but show a tendency to increase with each succeeding year. In 1893 a woollen rug, known as the Ardebil carpet and regarded, on account of its beautiful designs and exquisite colours, as one of the finest products of Oriental art, was purchased for the South Kensington Museum. Since it had a length of thirty-four and a half feet with a breadth of seventeen and a half, the price of £2500, which was the sum paid, was at the rate of twenty dollars per square foot. At an auction sale in New York in 1910,* a woollen rug five and a half feet long by three and three quarters wide was sold for the sum of $10,200, or at the rate of four hundred and ninety-one dollars per square foot; and a silk rug seven feet and two inches long by six feet and four inches wide was sold for the sum of $35,500, or at the rate of nine hundred and thirty dollars per square foot. As it was the general opinion of connoisseurs that the prices paid for these two rugs were low, and as it is well known that these rugs are not more valuable than some others of equal size, it is not unreasonable to assume that many of the best judges of Oriental rugs would declare that at the present time the sum of five hundred dollars per square foot is a fair price for some antique woollen rugs, and the sum of one thousand dollars per square foot a fair price for some antique silk rugs.

* The Yerkes sale.

If these judges were asked on what they based their opinion of the value of these old pieces, which are less serviceable for wear than new rugs that can be bought of an American factory at twenty cents per square foot, they might with reason reply that they are works of art, woven in those days when Michelangelo, Titian, Rubens, and Rembrandt were busy in their studios; that they are as scarce as the paintings of these masters; and that they might justly be compared with them in beauty and artistic execution. Though granting that the technique of weaving makes it impossible to represent a design as perfectly as can be done with a brush, they would claim that the drawing of dainty vines, scrolls, and arabesques was often represented by lines that in abstract beauty of form are unsurpassed, and that no artist had ever produced from his palette colours which equalled in brilliant sheen and marvellously changing hue those of the woven masterpieces.

Whoever is inclined to disagree with these judges and with those art critics of Europe and America who assert that in an æsthetic sense the people of the Orient are cultured to a standard beyond the comprehension of the Western world, should remember that the taste for any kind of art is based on convention and is largely a matter of cultivation. The Occidental, who for generations has cultivated the taste for paintings and statuary, looks to the painter and sculptor for the highest expression of artistic genius; but the Oriental takes greater delight in his marvellous creations of porcelain or woven fabrics. There is, too, a marked difference in treatment. The Occidental demands that in art "everything should be stated with the utmost fullness of a tedious realism before he can grasp its meaning" * and fails to recognise the more subtle beauty of various forms of Oriental art. The Oriental, on the other hand, is far less realistic and is better satisfied if his subject suggests abstract qualities that depend for their fullest appreciation on those quickening experiences that at different times have touched the soul of the observer. Moreover, as Buddhism, which prevails in many of the countries of Asia, teaches that a universal spirit is manifested in each form of nature, determining its character, and a similar idea pervades other religions of the East, the highest aim of Asiatic art is to express that inner spirit. It is largely this difference in artistic cultivation that accounts for the difference in taste. Whoever then would fully appreciate these rugs must view

* Stewart Dix, in "Arts of Old Japan."

them not only with an eye trained to see the beautiful harmonies of colour and design, but with the artistic temperament of the Oriental.

By study and cultivation the European as well as the American is growing to value more highly the products of Oriental art. When the old sea captains carried on trade with Japan, they imported into Europe large quantities of Imari ware, which the Japanese purposely decorated with crude and vulgar colours to meet the less refined taste of the Europeans, who regarded many of them as fine specimens of ceramic art and studiously copied them in their factories. But so great has been the change in artistic taste since then that now they are valued principally as objects of curiosity. Likewise, many beautiful Japanese Makimonos, in which a few strong lines gave but a hint of the essential thought, formerly passed before the eyes of Europeans as the paintings of semi-barbarians. But now we begin to see, as did Whistler, that they are often the products of great genius and that they express thought and feeling with marvellous power. There has been a similar growth in the appreciation of Oriental rugs. Even within the last generation this growth has been apparent, so that the few who wisely bought those old worn pieces which thirty years ago hung at doors of little shops where dark-faced foreigners invited acquaintance, are now the envy of the many who, too late, have learned that to-day they can scarcely be bought at any price.

The more we study the several fields of art in the Orient, the better we realise the wonderful creative genius of its people and learn to value the products of any one field. Japan has awakened the admiration of the highest art critics for its bronzes, some of which exceed in size any other castings in the world, and for its netsukés, which are the smallest of carvings. Its blades of steel are superior to those of Damascus and Toledo; and its lacquer, which is the most wonderful of its artistic products, displays genius of a very high order. To China, a country that we often regard as barbarous, we owe the invention of silks, the printing press, and gunpowder; yet it is in porcelain, that was manufactured even in those days when Cæsar was marching with his legions against the barbarous races of Central and Northern Europe, that China has surpassed the world and set a standard that probably will never again be reached. In the land where glide the Indus and the Ganges stand temples, erected by the descendants of the house of Tamerlane, be-

fore which the beholder, even if familiar with the wonders of St.
Peter's, is lost in admiration of the intricate delicacy of detail, the
majesty of proportions, and the gorgeous splendour of colour with
which some of the spirit of the East is expressed in material form.
When we realise that in these different lines of artistic effort the
genius of Asia has rivalled and surpassed that of Europe and
America, we become the better prepared to believe that choice
specimens of woven fabrics, in weaving which every class of every
country of Asia has been engaged from time immemorial, are to be
regarded as works of the highest art.

However pleasing the design or elaborate the detail, it is principally in the colouring that these rugs claim our interest and admiration. The colours which are derived from vegetable or animal dyes
grow more mellow and beautiful with passing years, and applied
to wools of finest texture acquire a lustre and softness which in
the choicest specimens are like the radiant throat of a humming
bird, or tints at the close of an autumn day. The different shades
have different moods, expressing peace, joy, pensiveness, sorrow,
the deep meaning of which the Oriental mind with its subtle and
serious imagination has grasped as has none other. Moreover,
in all truly fine pieces there is perfect harmony of tone. It is in
this richness, suggestiveness, and harmony that the greatest artistic value lies.

That all do not appreciate these qualities is not because they do
not exist; for the keen perception of colour, like the keen perception of music, is a faculty granted to one person but denied to another. Even to those who take delight in colour there are different
degrees of appreciation. "The fact is," said John Ruskin, "we
none of us enough appreciate the nobleness and sacredness of colour."
But as the ear can be cultivated to a higher taste for music, so can
the eye be cultivated to a higher taste for colour; and to fully appreciate the beauties of Oriental rugs it is necessary to develop this
faculty to its fullest extent.

And yet it is not alone as works of art that Oriental rugs interest
us. They suggest something of the life and religious thought of
the people who made them. Some seem redolent with the fra-
grance of flowers, others reflect the spirit of desert wastes and
wind-swept steppes. So, too, in the colours and designs of some
appear the symbols of that mysticism with which the minds of the
followers of Zoroaster in their effort to commune with the unseen

forces of the universe were imbued; and though the original meaning of many of these symbols has been forgotten, the study of
others leads to a better understanding of the life-thought of the
weavers.

Realising, then, that Asia has been the cradle from which has
come the highest expression of many forms of artistic achievement,
and that the Western mind is now assigning to its woven fabrics
their proper place in the galleries of art, we may begin the study
of Oriental rugs with the assurance that the further it is pursued the greater will be the appreciation and delight. It will take
us among strange and interesting people, and over fields that were
historic grounds before the walls of Rome were built. It will lead
beyond the dome of St. Sophia to the land of the Arabian tales,
where the splendour of former days is reflected in tomb and mosque,
and where, perhaps, when the Western world grows old, there will
rise again from crumbling ruins another nation that will revive the
poetic and artistic genius of the East with all the majesty and creative power of the past.

CHAPTER II

PHYSICAL FEATURES AND HISTORY OF THE RUG–PRODUCING LANDS

HE artistic character of Oriental rugs, like every other artistic impulse, is subject to the influence of physical environment. This influence is not alone that to which an individual weaver has been subjected, but is the transmitted effect of the accumulated experiences of many generations. It appears in the colours which simulate tones displayed by varying phases of nature, and also in the designs or symbols which, derived from older types by a long process of evolution, partially reflect feelings engendered in a people of highly imaginative and poetic temperament by long contact with elemental forces. Moreover, the quality of material used depends almost exclusively on the climate and physical conditions of countries where it is produced. Accordingly, the artistic and essential characteristics of rugs are better understood by a knowledge of the salient physical features of the countries where they are woven.*

The principal Oriental countries that continue to produce rugs are China, India, Afghanistan, Beluchistan, Persia, Turkestan, Caucasia, and Asia Minor. As all of them are contiguous, they may be regarded as a geographic unit; and though there is much diversity of detail, there is also much in common. From near the western boundary of Asia Minor a vast plateau stretches eastward into Central Asia, increasing in altitude towards the east.

---

* The influence of the physical aspects of a country on its art as expressed in architecture is nowhere more clearly shown than in Egypt, and there is little doubt that, likewise, the character of the native rugs was influenced by the spirit of the sluggish Nile and the boundless desert wastes. But as Egypt long ago ceased to be a rug-producing country, and none of its ancient rugs remain, it will only be briefly referred to in this work, though symbolic designs which had their origin there during the Caliphate or even earlier were adopted by foreign weavers and occasionally appear with modified form in modern rugs.

Its mean elevation in Asia Minor is from two thousand to three thousand feet, and as it extends beyond the Zagros Mountains and crosses the northern half of Persia, it rises from four thousand to five thousand feet. Continuing eastward through Southern Turkestan and Afghanistan it increases in altitude until it has risen to nearly twelve thousand feet in the lofty tablelands of Central Asia, where it begins to descend as it extends farther into the desert of Gobi. From the western part of this plateau a spur extends northward between the Black and Caspian seas, to form the high tableland of Caucasia, which has a mean elevation of about seven thousand feet.

The general topographic features of this plateau include great stretches of comparatively level land, broad tracts from which there is no drainage to the sea, and sandy desert wastes. On almost every side it is bounded by mountain chains and is intersected by transverse ridges that lift still higher peaks where rests the perpetual snow. Throughout the deserts and large parts of the tablelands the rainfall is slight, so that there are but few important river courses.

The cultivated portions of this vast area are relatively small, and consist largely of strips of land in fertile valleys, through which flow perennial streams. From time immemorial these streams have been used for irrigation, and the inhabitants of the districts have prospered by abundant harvests. In one or another of these valleys have been built the principal cities, within the walls of which were imposing temples that stimulated religious fervour, schools of learning to quicken the intellect, and gardens where perfumed flowers and the songs of birds delighted the æsthetic senses. In these cities science, philosophy, religion, and art received their highest development. In them lived the most skilled artisans and artists of the Orient; and the products of the loom were of the finest quality.

Beyond these valleys are great stretches of uncultivated tracts consisting of plains, hills, and mountains. Some of these tracts are naturally fertile and could be made productive, but at present are used only for pasturage, and over them numberless tribes of fierce nomads drive their flocks of sheep. On the other hand, where the land has no drainage to the sea, so that the streams and rivers that flow into it empty into small lakes or are finally absorbed, the soil becomes impregnated with alkali deposited from the waters, and the grass is scanty. There are also sandy wastes of great extent where scarcely any animal life can exist. Moreover in many parts of the country the rain falls only during a few months of the year, and more abundantly in the higher altitudes, so that the nomads are constantly searching for fresh pasturage, and moving from the lowlands, where the grass dies after the rainy season, to the higher altitudes, from which they return again at the approach of winter. So numerous are the flocks that in the struggle for pasture the weaker tribes are driven to the poorer land.

The pastoral life, the necessity of moving from place to place, the strife resulting from the difference in quality of pasture, have affected the temperament and character of the people. The boundless stretches of land, the clear atmosphere, the burning desert sands, the delicate mirage, and the starry heavens, have made men hospitable, thoughtful, devotional; constant wanderings have made them independent; the struggle for pasturage has made them lawless and cruel. These qualities are reflected to some extent in their woven fabrics, which lack the high artistic finish of those woven in cities. A large proportion of them are prayer rugs and contain symbols of the sun and fire worship. The designs are barbaric, and many are doubtless the same as those used hundreds of years ago. The colours of the old pieces, woven on upland plains or in mountain fastnesses, blend less harmoniously than those woven by more cultured weavers; but they frequently possess rich, pure tones, which are no longer seen in the modern rugs. As even a partial expression of the thoughts and feelings of a people, there are no rugs from the Orient more worthy of study than the rare old pieces woven by nomadic tribes.

Not only physical environment but the conquests of foreign enemies, as well as political struggles at home, have had an important influence on all art. It will be of interest, therefore, to briefly review the histories of Central and Southwestern Asia, where rugs have been made for over three thousand years, in order to understand the different racial influences which have affected their artistic development.

In the rich valleys near the mouths of the Tigris and Euphrates dwelt in the remote past a race of unknown origin called Sumerians, and to the north of them lived another people known as the Accadians. These races built canals, cultivated the soil, established towns, and invented the cuneiform writing. They lived in harmony

PLATE 1. KHORASSAN RUG

PLATE 2.   MESHED RUG

with one another, and continued to prosper until about 3000 B.C., when the Semitic race of the Chaldees, appearing from an unknown land, subdued them. The Chaldees, however, allowed the conquered races to retain part of their lands, adopted their civilisation, and about the year 2500 B.C. built the city of Babylon, the foundation of which biblical students claim was laid by the mighty hunter Nimrod. By cultivating the surrounding country, by developing its trade and commerce, the Babylonians became a wealthy and powerful nation; and by encouraging manufactures, art, and science, they became noted for their delicate fabrics, magnificent temples, and knowledge of mathematics and astronomy.

About the year 2000 B.C. a number of tribesmen, among whom was Abraham, migrated with their flocks to the upper valleys of the Tigris and founded Nineveh. A century later the land occupied by colonists who settled about Nineveh was known as Assyria. It increased in numbers and in power until, in 1300 B.C., it gained its first victory over Babylon; and during the next four hundred years, though meeting with occasional reverses, it extended its rule over Babylonia, Asia Minor, and Assyria, and received tribute even from Egypt. It thus became the first great conquering power in Southwestern Asia. In their magnificent palaces of Nineveh, surrounded by luxury, the rulers of Assyria were resting in supposed security when a powerful and unexpected enemy appeared from the land now known as Persia.

When the valleys of the Tigris and the Euphrates were inhabited by Sumerians and Accadians, Iran, which included modern Persia, was similarly inhabited by races of unknown origin. Subsequently, but at an exceedingly remote period, from the region about the Oxus river in Western Asia two branches of the great Aryan family migrated to Iran. One of these, which settled in the northern part, was known as the Medes; the other, which settled in the southern part, was known as the Persians. Both Medes and Persians subdued the native races and in the course of centuries constructed powerful empires. The former were the first to extend their conquests, and forming an alliance with the viceroy of Babylon they attacked Nineveh in the year 606 B.C. and destroyed it. Babylon now became the mistress of all Mesopotamia, and under Nebuchadnezzar it was enlarged to cover an area of one hundred square miles, and surrounded by walls three hundred feet high. These walls enclosed parks, orchards, gardens, and a city that soon be-

came famous for its palaces, its temple of Bel, and its Hanging
Gardens.

While Babylon was rising in power changes were occurring
in Iran. Cyrus, leader of the Persians, instigated a revolt against
the Medes and conquered them. But not satisfied with making
the Persians rulers of Iran he extended his conquests westward,
and in the year 538 B.C., by diverting the waters of the Euphrates,
surprised Belshazzar in his banquet hall and became master of
Babylonia. The complete subjection of all Asia Minor followed,
and for the next two centuries the warlike Persians were the dominant power in Western Asia. But in the year 331 B.C., when
Alexander the Great defeated their armies under Darius, the Persian Empire melted away.

Whether in Egypt or China or by the Tigris the art of weaving
first took definite form, it was in this land of Babylon and Nineveh,
of the Medes and the Persians, of Abraham, Belshazzar, and Cyrus,
where a few remaining monuments attest the delicate textiles of
those early days, that in more recent ages have been woven the
most perfect carpets of which there is any knowledge.

During the succeeding five hundred years Persia, Asia Minor,
Caucasia, and Syria became the prey of the Parthians, Greeks,
and Romans, to whom petty tribes, recognising no sovereign power
and secure in their mountain fastnesses, bade occasional defiance.
About the year 226 A.D. an able leader of one of the Persian tribes
founded the dynasty of the Sassanides, which during the reign of
Chosroes (531–579 A.D.) and his grandson Chosroes II (590–628 A.D.)
ruled over the country from the Oxus on the north to Arabia and
Egypt on the south, and from India on the east to Assyria on the
west. This was a period of prosperity and luxury, the glory of which
continued until the middle of the VII Century, when it was over-
thrown by a new power rising from a most unexpected quarter.

In the inhospitable land of Arabia, noted for its coffee, dates,
and myrrh, for its dreary, sandy, waterless wastes, a land hitherto
almost unknown in history, Mohammed promulgated the religion
which, suited to the temperament and desires of the Bedouins,
united them into a fanatic, militant body of conquerors. After
his death his successors, known as the Caliphs, extended his
conquests. Their successful armies quickly overran Persia and over-
threw the Sassanian rule; then marching northward into Turkestan and as far east as the Indus they overcame all resistance.

From the Greeks, by whom they were known as the Saracens, they snatched Palestine and Syria, and invading Egypt, conquered it after the long stubborn siege of Alexandria. A little later the Arabs became masters of Northern Africa, and settling there intermarried with the native races. Near the Straits of Gibraltar their African descendants, known as the Moors, crossed to Spain, where in the year 711 they vanquished a powerful army that opposed them. During the following year they subdued all of that country and began an invasion of Northern Europe. But on the rich pasture lands near Tours, where the infantry of Charles Martel met the Mussulman cavalry in one of the most decisive battles of history, they were defeated with terrible slaughter and Christian Europe was saved.

These conquests of the Mohammedans had not only a political and religious significance, but also an important influence on art at a time when Europe was sunk in ignorance and barbarism. Fond of magnificence and luxury, the Caliphs founded great capitals in Assyria, Egypt, and Spain, and built palaces that have histories which sound like fairy tales. Bagdad on the banks of the Tigris, with its sixteen hundred canals, one hundred and five bridges, and nearly a million people, with its countless baths, its many thousand mosques, and its royal palace, where was collected the best of Asiatic taste, elegance, and splendour, possessed more grandeur than any other city in the world. Gibbon states that within the palace, furnished with Oriental luxury, hung thirty-eight thousand pieces of tapestry, one third of which were of silk embroidered with gold, and that on the floors lay twenty-two thousand carpets. In Cairo and in Cordova, likewise, the Caliphs surrounded themselves with similar splendour, of which, unfortunately, but few traces now exist; but the Castle of the Alhambra still remains as a powerful reminder of their taste and artistic genius. It is largely to the influence of this race that were due many of the beautiful Spanish rugs such as Queen Eleanor in the XIII Century took to England from Cordova and Granada, as well as those of other periods. Moreover, in some of the choicest pieces of Asia Minor and Persia, woven during the XVI and XVII Centuries, are traces of this early Saracenic art.

For about five centuries the militant power of these Mohammedans was dominant in Southwestern Asia when another conquering race appeared. The great wall of China, which was built over two hundred years before Christ by the famous Che-Hwang-te, to protect it against the invasions of the Tartars, turned westward many wandering hordes from the more fertile pastures and valleys of Southeastern Asia. One of these hordes was of Turks, who, leaving their homes near the sources of the Irtish and Yenisei rivers in the Altai Mountains, settled in Turkestan. Many centuries afterwards, to escape from other hordes pressing westward and to reach fresh pastures, different branches of them migrated southward and westward. About the year 1000 A.D. one of these branches known as the Seljukian Turks gained a foothold in Persia, and under Malek Shah, in 1072, made Ispahan its capital. About the same time it extended its power over Asia Minor and overran Georgia, where it destroyed the capital Tiflis after slaughtering the inhabitants. To this Turkoman race should probably be accredited the earliest Mongolian influence on Persian textile art.

Somewhat later a people numbering forty thousand tents were ranging that part of Mongolia which lies north of the desert of Gobi in search of pasture and water. One of their number gathered about him a few followers, and by his own genius gained the ascendency over his tribes. He then allied himself with another powerful tribe, and reducing to obedience all the Mongolians who dwelt north of the desert of Gobi, in 1206, in the presence of his chiefs, he assumed the title of Genghis Khan. After becoming the ruler of millions of nomads of the great central plateau of Asia and conquering part of China, which was then enjoying a period of great wealth and prosperity, he invaded Western Asia. Bokhara offered no resistance and might have been spared, but learning that some of the Sultan's garrison were concealed he ordered the city to be burned. Samarkand, which surrendered after three days' siege, was pillaged and the inhabitants were slaughtered. Herat appeased his anger by opening its gates. Even his death did not stop the ravages of the Mongol horde that captured and sacked Bagdad, and, crossing the Tigris and Euphrates, pillaged all Asia Minor. In 1258, Hulaku Khan, grandson of Genghis, conquered Persia and established his capital in the province of Azerbijan, where his descendants ruled for over a century.

With these invasions another wave of Mongolian influence was felt in Western Asia. Whatever may have been the effect on local art by the settlement of the Seljukian Turks in Persia and Asia Minor during the early part of the XI Century, it was

inappreciable as compared with that of Genghis Khan and his followers. For the influence of Bagdad over Southwestern Asia was
like that of Rome over the empire of the Cæsars, and when in the
middle of the XIII Century it was plundered for forty days, and
other important cities of Asia Minor and Persia similarly treated,
there was no longer the same incentive to work, so that art for a
time languished. But in some cities the artistic spirit of the people
prevailed over the loss of independence, and the more skilled workmen were encouraged by their new masters, who, recognising the
beauty of the Persian carpets, sent many Persian artists to China
and brought many Chinese artists to Persia, that the different
races might derive advantages from the instruction of one another.
It is therefore not surprising that from this time the influence of
Chinese art has been recognised in the woven fabrics and metal
work made in the southwestern part of Asia. In fact, the Chinese
motive known as the "key pattern," as well as other less familiar designs of distinctly Mongolian origin, appeared for the first time in
some of the carpets and metal work of this period.

Like Turkestan, Asia Minor has been one of the great battle-
grounds of the world. During parts of the XI, XII, and XIII
Centuries not only Seljukian Turks, but Mongols and Ottoman
Turks under Murad and Bajazet, rose in influence until all Asia
Minor, as well as Thrace and Macedonia, was subject to them. But
still another power from the far East was to overrun Asia and divert Bajazet from the walls of Constantinople.

Under Tamerlane, the descendant of Genghis Khan, the Mongol
hordes were again united and again attempted the conquest of the
world. From the walls of China to the Mediterranean Sea, and from
the Steppes of Turkestan to the Arabian deserts, his victorious
armies overcame all opposition. Never was conqueror more rapa-
cious, more bloodthirsty. At Ispahan, seventy thousand inhabitants
were slain. Georgia was laid waste and the people were massacred. In 1401, Bagdad was besieged and, when taken, a pyramid
of ninety thousand human victims was raised as a monument
to the Tartar conqueror. In the following year, when the armies
of Bajazet and Tamerlane met on the plains near Angora, the
Turks were defeated and Bajazet was captured. But now the tide
of Mongol invasion receded; and laden with spoils Tamerlane returned to his capital at Samarkand, where he enjoyed the remaining years of his life by surrounding himself with a brilliant court and

by building palaces and temples, which he adorned with royal splendour. With all his atrocious barbarities he had a higher appreciation of art than his Mongolian predecessors. At his capital were assembled skilled artisans from Eastern and Western Asia; and there at the beginning of the XIV Century European travellers saw innumerable art treasures, including carpets of wonderful workmanship and beauty.

The Mongol power also gained an important foothold in India. This country, like Iran, had been subjugated by a branch of the Aryan race, which conquered the native Dravidians, and remained dominant until the VII and VIII Centuries. Then the Mohammedans invaded it, and were still in ascendency when Tamerlane crossed the mountains and attacked Delhi. After the lapse of more than a hundred years his descendants, Baber, Akbar, and Shah Jahan, rose to power. The magnificence of their courts and the splendour of the temples which they built stimulated Indian art; and under the instruction of Persian artisans, who were induced to settle in that country, the natives attained their highest skill in weaving.

With the death of Tamerlane, in 1405, the Ottoman power in Persia and Asia Minor rose again, and Turkish victories followed in quick succession until in 1453 Constantinople fell and the church of St. Sophia became a mosque.

After the lapse of half a century Shah Ismael of the family of the Safavids defeated the Turkomans in 1502, and founded a new dynasty in Persia. With his rise began one of the most splendid periods in its history. Within a few years victories extended his empire from the Euphrates river to Afghanistan and from the Oxus to the Persian gulf. This was the land of ancient Iran, over which from his court at Ardebil he ruled until his death. In the early part of the reign of Shah Tamasp, which lasted from 1524 to 1576, the new dynasty was threatened by the Turkish ruler, Soliman the Magnificent, after he had taken Rhodes from the Knights of St. John and invaded Southern Europe. In 1534 he captured Bagdad and Tabriz, as well as conquered Shirvan and Georgia.* But the lost territory was soon regained and the new Persian capital was established at Tabriz where, as will be seen later, were woven many of the greatest masterpieces of Persian textile fabrics. Much as these

---

* It is said that he carried Persian weavers as captives to Asia Minor and Constantinople.

monarchs had accomplished, it was Shah Abbas the Great who, after ten years of internal strife, succeeded by expelling the Turks from Persia, restoring tranquillity, and establishing commerce, in elevating his country from one of devastation and confusion to one of greatness such as it had not known for many ages. He transferred his court to Ispahan, where, while adding to the magnificence of the city, he encouraged art even to the extent of sending to Italy, for study, a number of the most skilled artists of Persia. These in time returned and exerted an influence that appeared in the more elaborate designs of carpets of a subsequent period. It is also probable that he rendered valuable assistance to Akbar of India in founding carpet-weaving in that country. He ruled from 1586 to 1628. This period, during which America was a wilderness and England under Queen Elizabeth was still struggling with the feudal system, was the golden age of Persian history and Persian art; but with his death the Safavid dynasty declined and art decadence began.

In 1722, the Afghans conquered Persia and for a number of years ruled it with horrible cruelty; but they were finally defeated by Nadir Shah, who captured Herat in 1731, extended his dominion into Georgia, and recovered some of the lost territory from the Turkish Empire in the West. After his death the sovereignty of Persia again waned, until in time it was confined to its present limits.

It thus appears that from the earliest times recorded in history the southwestern part of Asia has been subject to invasion, and to constant struggles between the different races of the East for supremacy. Even from the desert of Gobi, the flanks of the Altai Mountains, and the deserts of Arabia have poured forth armies to devastate the land. One victorious power after another has extended its sway from the banks of the Indus to the shores of the Mediterranean. The result is that the present Oriental textile art is of a composite character, which can be understood only by taking into consideration the value of these racial influences that have contributed to it some of its most interesting and subtle charms.

CHAPTER III

THE MATERIALS

S was the case with the earliest shepherd weavers, many nomads living in unfrequented parts of Asia spin the wool taken from their own flocks, then colour it with dyes brewed from roots and herbs that they have personally gathered, and finally weave it according to well-known patterns into fabrics. But in large, enlightened communities the manufacture of an Oriental rug involves a division of labour. From the shepherds the professional dyers obtain the wool, which, after colouring, they sell to weavers; and these in turn often receive their patterns from others. A knowledge of these separate steps involving the industries of producing the different materials and the crafts of dyeing, weaving, and designing is essential to a full understanding of any Oriental woven fabric.

The materials that were formerly used in weaving were generally of animal origin, such as the wool of sheep, goats, and camels. To a more limited extent silk and cotton also were used, and occasionally hair of the yak, cow, and even human hair. In later years, when there arose a western demand for eastern fabrics so that the aim of the weaver was to produce an article as cheaply as possible, flax, hemp, jute, and larger quantities of cotton were sometimes substituted. Since all of these materials are indigenous to the country where they are used, and are affected by its climate, altitude, humidity, and fertility, they acquire qualities that frequently give to rugs a distinctly local character.

The wool of sheep constitutes the warp and weft of at least half the Oriental rugs and the pile of over ninety per cent. To be sure, in Japan the pile is largely jute and cotton; in a few of the districts of Asia Minor and Persia it is mercerised cotton or silk; and in districts where the camel is still a beast of burden its wool and fine hair are often substituted for other kinds; but throughout all the rug-

PLATE 3. KIRMAN RUG

PLATE 4. SHIRAZ RUG

weaving countries of the East the wool of the sheep has been and still is preferred to all other materials for the pile of rugs. This is due not alone to its warmth, to the facility with which it can be spun and twisted into knots, but also to the fact that from the remotest times the inhabitants of these districts, like Abraham of old, have been shepherds, who followed their calling because over the steppes of Tartary and the great plateaus that extend through Asia Minor, Persia, Afghanistan, and Turkestan spread vast pasture lands that seem better suited than any other parts of the world for the nourishment of sheep with fine fleeces. In fact, a part of these districts seems to be the natural habitat of the sheep; for among the crags of some of the lofty mountain chains of Central Asia, and farther west where Eastern and Western Turkestan meet in the lofty plateau of Pamir, called the "Roof of the World," still wander great bands of magnificent native sheep with enormous horns and brownish grey wool, from which it is believed sprang the vast flocks that now browse on every hill and mountain slope of Western Asia.

Centuries of care have effected an important evolution in this native stock, for in no other part of the world are there sheep with longer and more silky fleeces. Nevertheless there are different grades, as the quality depends in a measure on the climate and pasturage as well as on the care of the sheep. Thus in the hot, sandy lands the wool shows some deterioration; but in the cold, dry climates of the many high lands of Western Asia and in the pastures of particular localities the wool is long, fine, and lustrous. For instance, in parts of Khorassan, on the flanks of high mountains near Kirman and Shiraz, on the shores of Lake Niris in Farsistan, among the rolling uplands of Asia Minor, are produced uncommonly fine and beautiful fleeces. When, moreover, the sheep of these localities receive the care that is given by some of the nomadic tribes, as the Uzbeck Tartars, who not only shelter them but cover them with blankets, the wool acquires a soft and silky quality that is unsurpassed. The wool produced in many parts of India, on the other hand, is poor; for not only are the serrations, on which largely depends its value for textile purposes, less numerous than in better varieties, but it is harsh and contains many long hairs that do not well unite with it and that take up very little dye.

The wool of the goat is much less extensively used, yet appears in some rugs, not only as warp and weft, but also as pile. The goats of Kashmir, which live in the cold climate of a tableland three miles above the ocean level, produce the finest and most beautiful wool; but as it grows near the skin, and beneath wiry hairs from which it can be removed only with tedious care, it is too precious to be used excepting for the most beautiful shawls and choicest carpets. Of next importance and finest texture is the wool of the Angora goat, known to commerce as mohair. Formerly there was not much demand for it, but now, on account of the consideration that it has received in the carpet factories of recent Sultans, it is found in many of the rugs of Asia Minor. As it grows to an average length of five to six inches it is easily spun; and its soft, lustrous sheen gives to the rugs in which it is used a silky and brilliant appearance. Some of the Bokhara goats, also, yield fine wool that is used in rugs. Yet, as a rule, yarn made from the fleece of the goat is not regarded with favour by weavers, since it is apt to be coarse and to pack closely. Nor does the wool of the goat mix well with the wool of the sheep. There is, however, a much finer grade growing next to the skin, which may be removed with a knife when it is exposed by combing the longer fleece in a direction reverse to that in which it lies. The tougher grades are preferred to any other material by weavers of the Afghanistan, Beluchistan, and some Turkoman rugs for selvages at the sides, as they afford excellent protection against hard usage. Goat's hair is also sometimes used in these rugs for warp. Unless mixed with wool it is very rarely used for weft, as it is not sufficiently pliable.

Of more frequent use than the wool of the goat is the wool of the camel which grows close to the skin beneath the long hair. In the tropical countries, as in Soudan, the camel has no wool, but in more northern latitudes it yields a crop which increases in quantity and improves in quality as the climate grows colder. Thus in Arabia, Asia Minor, and in most of Persia and Turkestan the yield is small, in the tablelands of Eastern Persia and Afghanistan it is much larger, and on the lofty plateaus of Turkestan and Chinese Tartary as much as ten pounds of wool is obtained yearly from each beast. The clip is taken at the usual moulting season during the spring of the year. The wool of the older camels is coarse and dark, what is taken from the young is finer and lighter, and the most silky and valuable of all is what is obtained from the unborn. The best grade has been more highly esteemed than the wool of any other animal, and rugs in which it constitutes the pile are more valuable than those in which the wool of sheep is used. It is seldom woven in modern rugs, but dyed wool or goats' hair of similar colour is often substituted for it.

The wool or underhair of the yak is used only among the mountain tribes of Tartary, and is never found in any of the choicer grades of rugs. Occasionally the hair of the horse or cow is employed to a limited extent in the pile of nomadic rugs, where it may be distinguished by its coarse and wiry character. In old rugs of which the pile is much worn cows' hair will now and then protrude like the hairs of small bristle brushes. Only very rarely is human hair seen in a rug.

Natural colours of the several kinds of wool, which have made it possible to dispense with their dyeing, have always been taken advantage of by weavers. The only black yarn on which the wear of time has left no impress is from the fleece of the proverbially despised black sheep. Shades of white, ivory, brown, grey, rufus, and even a plum are obtained from different varieties. Likewise a wide range of rich chestnut colours are furnished by the camel.

It is but natural that the nomad should depend on the wool of his flocks and herds for warp, weft, and pile; but people of fixed habitations have employed other kinds of material also. Where the sensuous luxury of the East called for magnificent carpets, they were often woven almost entirely of silk, which was easily obtained, as silkworms thrive on the mulberry trees that grow wild on the plains of Central and Southwestern Asia. Silk rugs are still woven in a few cities of Asia Minor and Persia. For the cheaper grades of rugs flax, hemp, and jute have been sparingly used; and during recent years cotton has been widely adopted, particularly in Persian, Indian, and Chinese rugs, on account of its cheapness as compared with wool. It is, however, almost entirely as warp and weft and rarely as pile that it is used. Though much less durable than wool, its white colour is far less likely to darken with age; yet there is a poorer variety which, after being thoroughly wet, acquires a dark colour.

In the preparation of these different textile materials wool requires the greatest care. In some parts of the Orient it is not washed, and the lustrous hues of the pile are attributed to the fact that it is dyed in its naturally greasy state; but in other parts the grease and dirt are carefully removed. This cleansing is a craft that has been transmitted from parent to child, and is practised according to different methods in different parts of the country. One of the chief essentials is an abundance of clear running water free from alkali; for when the water is hard, as is often the case in the more arid parts of the country, it loses some of its cleansing properties, and potash or other chemicals are required to counteract this unfavourable quality. After the wool has been thoroughly washed it is carefully dried in the sun and open air.

The next important step is the proper sorting, picking, and combing. The sorting consists of the separation of black and light wool, or of an inferior from a better grade; and the picking consists of the removal of burrs or foreign particles. The object of combing is to effect an orderly arrangement of the wool so that it is ready for spinning. One method, corresponding to carding, is to draw the wool repeatedly between rows of upright spikes set in a wooden frame until every matted particle has been separated and all the fibres are disentangled. The older method, still employed in nearly every part of the Orient, consists of "teasing" with the cord of a heavy bow, which is suspended or held firmly by the left hand over the wool, while with the right hand the cord is made to vibrate either by striking it with a wooden instrument or plucking it, so that the fibres of wool are separated and assorted by the vibrations.

When the wool has thus been prepared, it is wound about the distaff and then spun into yarn. In many parts of the Orient the common spinning-wheel has been introduced and adopted for both wool and cotton; in other parts are crudely made spinning-wheels of different design and about the height of a man. The natives of districts more remote from civilisation still cling to the primeval spindle, which sometimes consists of no more than a rounded stick half an inch in diameter and a foot in length with a ball of clay at one end. Many of the nomadic tribes of Asia Minor and Mesopotamia use in place of it a small stone of convenient shape, to which is tied a strip of linen a few inches in length. A few fibres of wool are attached to the end of the linen by twisting them about it, and a few more fibres are similarly attached to these when the stone is suspended and twirled. As the fibres become closely twisted together more fibres are added until on account of the length of the thread thus formed the stone reaches the ground. The thread is then wound about the stone and secured by a couple of loops so as to leave a piece only a few inches in length, to which more wool is attached in continuing the spinning. When a large ball of thread has been spun, it is removed from the stone and the process begun again.

One advantage of these simple devices is that they can easily be carried anywhere. Even to-day a not unusual sight is a half barbaric shepherd following his flock, while he spins with simple distaff and spindle or stone, as did his ancestors thousands of years ago. On the end of the distaff, that rests beneath his left arm, is the ball of wool from which he selects and twists the fibres, while he deftly turns the short spindle or twirls the stone with thumb and forefinger of the right hand. The threads spun by professional spinners on spinning-wheels are of small diameter and are the most regular in size and texture, those spun with the small spindle are of larger diameter and less regular, and those spun by twirling a stone are made of the coarsest diameter in order to insure sufficient stoutness, since they are the most irregular in size and texture; yet yarn so made is the most highly valued by all weavers.

Only very rarely, indeed, is one of these single threads used for yarn, since it would be apt to part. Two of them, therefore, are twisted together to form a double thread. A simple device used by many nomadic tribes for this purpose consists of two short sticks crossing at right angles, and another piece with end like a crochet needle perpendicular to them. The threads which are attached to this piece pass through a hole at the intersection of the crossed sticks and are twisted by twirling them. It is very seldom that three single threads are twisted to make a triple thread, and when such is the case it is the work of a professional spinner who uses a large spinning-wheel, and never the work of a nomad. For the weft of many rugs, and for the pile of a few rugs such as Sarouks and Kashans, a double thread alone is used; whilst for the pile of most rugs the double thread is again doubled, trebled, or quadrupled, so as to form yarn of two, three, or four ply, and even yarn of six ply is sometimes used. A distinction also exists in the manner of twisting together double threads to make yarn of two or more ply, since according to the custom of different tribes they may be twisted so loosely that in the length of an inch they do not describe more than a single revolution or so tightly as to describe several.

Until the introduction of the modern spinning-wheel wool was spun in the Orient exactly as it was ages ago. It is this almost incredible disposition to adhere as with religious fanaticism to methods transmitted from father to son and to resist as pernicious every attempt at innovation that makes a precise analysis of rugs possible. Accordingly, the evenness or unevenness of single threads, the looseness or tightness with which double threads are twisted together to form yarn of different ply, as well as the number of the ply used, are a few of the important indices for distinguishing between rugs of different districts.

Even after the yarn is spun it is not always ready for the dyer, and in order that it may properly absorb the dye it is often washed and rewashed. In some parts of the Orient it is first soaked in warm water and carefully rinsed in cold water. It is then placed in a copper pot or vat containing boiling water to which has been added carbonate or sulphate of soda and potash, and stirred for about an hour. After this thorough cleansing it is again washed very carefully in soft water and thoroughly dried in the sun.

The wonderful sheen of many old rugs is due almost entirely to the materials of which they are made. This material, as a rule, is unsurpassed by similar products of any other part of the world, and is prepared by patient races who know little of the value of time. The simple labour required is in itself prosaic enough, yet without a doubt the earlier spinners and weavers, while following their flocks with minds free from all conventions and limitations of art, discerned the elemental forces of nature in all their freshness and power, and from them drew inspiration that bore fruit in the exquisite colouring and delicate tracery of the woven carpets.

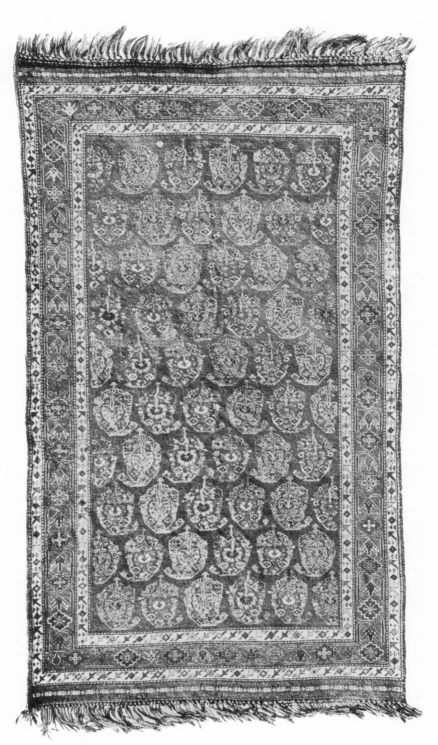

PLATE 5. NIRIS RUG

PLATE 6. FERAGHAN RUG

CHAPTER IV

DYEING

OWEVER remarkable the achievements of Oriental art in any field, their most pleasing effect has always been associated with colour. Without it the beauty of the lustre tiles of Persia, the marvellous porcelains of China, and the delicate textiles of Western Asia would fade into insignificance. It is indeed the wonderful harmonies of exquisite tints chosen by the touch of genius from a palette of many thousand pigments that awaken the appreciation of the luxurious splendour of the East. This love for colour is inherent in every rug-producing race of Asia and is older than history. It is but natural, then, that the earliest carpets should be radiant with glorious tints, which in a lesser measure are reflected in modern fabrics.

If high praise is due to the artist who, by a skilful association of different colours of co-ordinate tones, creates the picture that delights the sense, a fair measure is also due to the artisan who not only controls the secrets of the dyes, but has mastered the difficult knowledge of their proper application; for the beauty of the finished woven product depends on the judicious dyeing of the yarn more than on anything else. From father to son for many generations has been transmitted a knowledge of those particular vegetable and animal products of root, leaf, fruit, and insect, and the manner of their use, by which the imperishable lustrous sheen and colour of the finest woven fabrics are produced. Indeed, this art requires to-day more technical knowledge than any other branch of rug weaving, since modern designs are no longer more than the imitation of those in older carpets; and so important is it regarded that a successful dyer is a man of distinction in his tribe.

The sources from which are obtained many of the dyes that give the innumerable carpet colours are recorded. A few of them are received from remote countries, but most of the plants from which they are extracted grow in marshes and on hills and plains where the nomads wander with their flocks. Many of them are used without blending, but even some of the seven primary colours are derived by proper blending; and from a number of dyes of different strengths and qualities are produced an infinite number of rich and delicate shades.

The principal blues of Oriental rugs are obtained from indigo. This is derived from colouring matter in the leaves of plants of the genus *Indigofera*, that grow to a height of four to six feet in the East Indies, when they are cut and placed in a vat containing water. In about twelve hours fermentation ensues; and after this subsides the liquid is drawn off into another vat, where after one or two hours of agitation the indigo forms as a precipitate. Many different species of this plant grow wild throughout Asia, and from the earliest times have been used to produce dye-stuff. Indigo is one of the most valuable of all dyes, as by using it in conjunction with others an infinite variety of shades result.

Some reds are obtained from the plant madder (*Rubia tinctorum*), that grows abundantly in Central and Southwestern Asia. Its colouring properties were known to the ancients; and for a long period it has been cultivated in Asia Minor, where the succulent roots of the second and third years' growth are regularly dried and prepared for use. Other reds are derived from the insect cochineal (*Coccus ilicis*) that lives on oaks of the countries bordering the Mediterranean, and was known among the Arabs as "kermes," signifying Red Dye. After the discovery of America another species (*Coccus cacti*) was found that was more productive of dyeing qualities. The females, which alone are valuable, are plucked from the trees and killed by exposing them to vapours of acetic acid, or placing them in hot water, or in an oven. From their dried bodies, of which over fifty thousand are necessary to make a pound, the dye is produced. As both these dyes are noted for their fastness, they are constantly used, but when silk or wool is to be dyed cochineal is preferable to madder.

The yellow dyes are obtained from several sources. Some are from the berries of plants of Western Asia. Others are from the leaves of the sumach bushes, that are indigenous to nearly every part of the world. An orange tinge is derived from the turmeric extracted from the short root stocks of a plant of the genus *Curcuma*. From time immemorial a beautiful yellow has been obtained from saffron. It is the product of the stigmas of the fragrant crocus, which are so small that over four thousand are necessary to furnish an ounce of dried saffron; yet the dye is so powerful that it will give a distinct tint to seven hundred thousand times its weight of water. As saffron has something of a stimulating effect on the human system, it has been taken by the Persians when mixed with their rice.

With none of these three basic colours was any national feeling associated, yet the Persians excelled in the use of blues. The Turkomans of Turkestan and Asia Minor produced better reds than any other colour, and the best yellows, even if generally inferior in positiveness to blues and reds, were those of the Chinese.

Though other primary and secondary colours sometimes result from the application of a single dye, the many thousand different tints can only be produced by the blending of two or more. Moreover, the qualities of the same dye vary greatly, as they depend on the soil where the plant grew, the time of year when it was removed, and the weather and other conditions prevailing during the dyeing.

In nature green is one of the most pleasing colours, but in carpets it is most unsatisfactory, as it has generally a faded appearance, due probably to the fact that one of the dyes of which it is formed by blending is less permanent than the other. The Chinese greens obtained from the buckthorns are generally the best.

Greys and browns are sometimes derived from gall nuts, and reddish brown from henna. For very dark browns and black, iron pyrites has been largely used in both old and modern rugs; but unfortunately the dye has a corrosive effect on the wool, so that the black knots of old rugs are often worn to the warp.

In parts of India flowers of the bastard teak (*Butea frondosa*) make a favourite dye, from which are produced, by blending with other dyes, a large number of shades ranging from deep yellow to brownish copper tones. Another well known dye is *Butti lac*, obtained from an insect, *Coccus lacca*, that lives on the twigs of trees. It is a substitute for cochineal and produces different shades of red, crimson, terra cotta, and purple, according to the other dyes and the mordants with which it is blended.

Besides these few dyes are innumerable others that are used either singly or in combination. Furthermore, different colour effects are produced by the application of different mordants, which it is necessary to use for the reason that without them many fibrous materials are unable to absorb a large number of the dyes. The most valuable of all mordants is alum; and the sulphate of iron and tin are largely employed in the case of red colours. Of the vegetable mordants, pomegranate rind, which contains some yellow colouring matter, is the best known. Valonia also is some-times used; as well as limes, lemons, the fruit of the tamarind, and the mango.

In the monograph of Mr. Harris on the "Carpet Weaving Industry of Southern India" are a number of directions from an old manuscript owned by a dyer who stated that he was the de-scendant of twenty generations of dyers who originally came from Tabriz, and that he had made his copy from a Persian book of dyes which had belonged to his grandfather. A few of these are given below, because they show not only the dyes and mordants, but also the methods employed.

"Birbul's Blue. Take cinnabar, indigo, and alum, grind and sift lighter than the light dust of the high hills; soak for ten hours; keep stirring it; put in the wool and soak for many hours. Boil for three hours; wash in kurd water, water in which kurds and whey have been well beaten up; leave for three hours, and then wash and beat again in water.

"A Fine Indigo Blue. Take indigo, soak it in water for twelve hours, grind it to a fine paste in a mortar, add some *Terminalia citrina*, pomegranate peel, and alum; and mix thoroughly. Boil; put the water into the hot bath and keep stirring till cold. Now mix in some iron-filings water, and boil steadily for another two and a half to three hours; wash with a beating and dry.

"Ruddy Brown Grey. Take sulphate of iron, *Terminalia citrina*, oak galls, and alum; mix well; dry; then steep for twenty-four hours. Put in the wool; soak it for twenty-four hours, then boil for two or three hours. Dip in a soda-bath, wash, and dry.

"Cinnamon. Take oak galls, acacia bark, cinnabar, and alum, and steep for a night. Put in the wool, and soak for twenty or thirty hours; boil the water for two or three hours and give a soda-bath wash; dip in acidulated water; and wash again with beating.

"Crimson. Take lac colour and cochineal. Steep for from four to six days in the sun, in hot weather for the lesser time, stirring constantly till a rich deep colour comes where some has stood for a few minutes in a thin glass bottle and settled. Then strain through two cloths, and put in pomegranate rind and good iron-filings water.

Add mineral acid; steep wool for thirty-six hours, then boil for three hours, wash well, and dry.

"Pale Greyish Green. Take copper rust, asburg,* and alum. Mix well with any hot water, not boiling; soak wool for eighteen hours, then boil for three hours. Give a bath with water acidulated with some limes, and dry in shade.

"Old Gold and Rich Yellow. Take turmeric and asburg, cinnabar and alum. Soak all night. Steep wool for twenty-four hours, boil for four and a half hours, wash with a beating, and dry in shade.

"Dark Grey. Take of the fruit of *Cupressus sempervirens*, seeds and seed pods of babul (*Acacia arabica*), iron-filings water, and alum. Steep over night. Now add the water and let it soak for twenty-four hours, then boil for two or three hours, until the colour is right, then wash and dry in the sun.

"Rose Colour. Take ratanjot (*Onosma echioides*), a thought of cochineal, manjit (*Rubia cordifolia*) or lac colour a very little, and cinnabar. Add water, soak them for twelve hours, put in wool, and steep for thirty-six hours; cook it for three hours, then bathe the wool in alum and wash nicely; afterward dry in the shade.

"Persian Scarlet. Take lac colour, and if you choose a little cochineal for richness, and soak from four to six days; strain it in two cloths and add alum and a little turmeric; let it stand for three hours. Put wool in and steep for twenty-four hours, then boil for two hours. Take out the wool and add mineral acid; re-enter wool and boil an hour more. Wash fifteen minutes when cold, and dry in the shade.

"Saffron Yellow. Take turmeric, cinnabar, and soda, add water and keep for a full day. Then add some alum, make the dip, and soak the wool for thirty hours. Cook it for several hours, and dry in the shade after beating and good washing.

"Rich Yellow. Take asburg and turmeric, soak for a night in water, steep the wool for twenty-four hours, add alum, shake out, and dry in shade."

Identical shades of a number of colours are not produced in all parts of the Orient, not only for the reason that soil, moisture, and climate affect the colour values of dye-stuff, but because each family of dyers preserve inviolable the craft secrets transmitted from their forefathers. Thus it happens that different parts of the

* This is a product of flowers of the genus *Delphinum* that grows in the Himalayas. It is also obtained as a powder from Afghanistan.

rug-producing countries adhere to particular tones that help to identify the locality where the fabrics were woven.

Unfortunately the Western aniline dyes, which were introduced about the year 1860 and quickly adopted because they are cheaper and less complicated in their application, have to such an extent transplanted some of these fine old vegetable dyes that a number of the richest and most delicate colours found in the rugs of a former century are no longer produced. Thus the superb blue of the fine old Ispahans, as well as of lustre tiles and illuminated manuscripts, belongs to a lost art. The disadvantages of the aniline dyes are several: they have a tendency to make the fibres of the textile fabric brittle, and when it is wet the colours will frequently run. Some dyes also fade more readily than others, so that if a colour be the product of two or more dyes, the resultant tint may be totally unlike the original. On the other hand, not all vegetable dyes are fast; but as they fade they mellow into more pleasing shades. Efforts have been made to encourage the use of old vegetable dyes; but unless the laws which have been enacted in parts of Asia to restrict the importation of aniline dyes be more stringently enforced than in the past, the cultivation in the garden patch of the dye-producing herbs and plants will soon cease to be the time-honoured occupation it was in days gone by.

Almost as important as the art of preparing the dyes is that of properly applying them to the yarns. It is an art that demands infinite pains in its technique, as well as a lifetime to acquire. It is in itself a separate profession practised by artisans who guard with jealousy the sacred secrets that transmitted from generation to generation occupy their thoughts to the exclusion of almost everything else. The homes of these professional dyers in the larger villages and cities are located on a stream of water which possesses mineral properties that long experience has proven especially suitable as solvents for the different kinds of colouring matter. Ranged about the walls of their low dwellings are jars or vats containing liquid dye of various colours. Suspended above them, from hooks driven into beams, are the yarns from which, after immersion in the proper vats, the liquids are allowed to drain. After this the yarns are exposed for the proper length of time to the dry air and burning sun. It is, therefore, the suitable mordants, the preparation of the proper dyes for the vats, the immersion of the yarn in correct sequence and for the correct length of time, as well as the exposure to the glare and heat of the sun for a definite period to be gauged to the exact moment, on which the colour results depend. This complicated process by which, for instance, the infinitely different shades of a red, a blue, or a brown may be conveyed to yarn by using the same dyes but by slightly modifying the steps requires the greatest precision, for which no rule but an experience amounting almost to instinct is the guide.

There was a time when the Oriental had not learned the meaning of *tempus fugit* or seen the glitter of Western gold, when his dyeing and weaving were proud callings, in which entered his deepest feelings. Then the old vegetable dyes that mellow, grow softer and more lustrous, were almost exclusively used; but now throughout all weaving countries the dyer has deteriorated so that he can no longer produce some of the rich colours in use half a century ago. Yet remote from the principal lines of travel, on the edges of the desert, in lonely valleys, among rugged mountains, half-tamed tribes are still dyeing their hand-spun yarn as did their fathers' fathers.

CHAPTER V

WEAVING

EAR the tents of some nomadic tribes may occasionally be seen crude looms on which are woven some of the most interesting rugs that now reach the Western markets. In all probability they are not dissimilar to what were used thousands of years ago, for it would be impossible to construct a simpler loom. Where two trees suitably branching are found growing a few feet apart, all of the upper branches are removed excepting two, which are so trimmed as to leave a crotch at the same height in each tree. In each crotch is rested the end of a pole or beam, and parallel to it is placed another extending at a short distance above the ground from trunk to trunk. Or, as is more frequently the case, roughly hewn posts are firmly implanted in the ground and horizontal beams are stretched between them. In the upper one is a groove with a rod to which one end of the warp, consisting of strong threads of yarn numbering from ten to thirty to the inch, is attached, while the other end is tightly stretched and firmly secured to the lower horizontal beam. Sometimes the beams to which the warp is attached are placed perpendicularly, so that the weaver may stand and move sideways as the work progresses. But among a very large number of those tribes that are constantly wandering in search of new pastures for their flocks and herds, it is customary to let the loom lie flat on the ground, while the weaver sits on the finished part of the rug.

Under more favourable circumstances, when the tribes live in villages or cities, the looms are so made that the weavers are not compelled to bend in order to tie the first row of knots or stand erect to finish the last rows of a long rug. Of the several devices by which the weaver may remain seated while at work, the crudest consists of a plank used as a seat, which rests on the rungs of two ladders placed parallel to each other at the sides of the rug. As

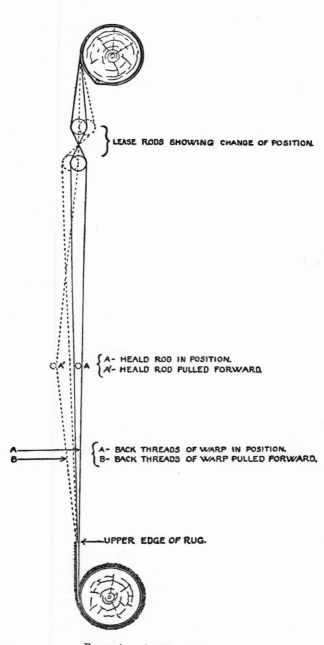

LEASE RODS SHOWING CHANGE OF POSITION.

A- HEALD ROD IN POSITION.
A'- HEALD ROD PULLED FORWARD.

A- BACK THREADS OF WARP IN POSITION.
B- BACK THREADS OF WARP PULLED FORWARD.

UPPER EDGE OF RUG.

PLATE A. — AN UPRIGHT LOOM

the work progresses, the plank is raised and rested upon the higher rungs. More frequently, however, both upper and lower beams of the frame have the shape of cylinders of small diameter, which revolve between the upright posts. The lower ends of the threads of warp are attached to the lower beam, and the other ends may either be wound several times around the upper one or else pass over it and be kept taut by weights attached to them. Such a loom is generally used for weaving very large rugs, which are rolled up on the lower beam as the work progresses.

In Plate A (Page 45) is represented a loom commonly used in many parts of the Orient. When preparing it for weaving two stakes are driven in the ground at a suitable distance apart, and about them the warp is wound in the way a figure eight is formed. The warp is then carefully transferred to two rods that are attached to the upper and lower beams. If it has been carefully wound, none of the threads should be slack; but if desired the tension may be further increased by different devices. Two other rods, known as "Healds," are then attached to the front and back threads of warp; or in the case of a single rod, it is attached to the back threads, as shown in the Plate. A lease rod is next inserted between the threads of warp that cross below the upper beam, and another is placed below it where, if necessary, it is supported in position by loops. When the weaving begins, a short web is generally woven at the lower end to protect the knots from wear. After the first row has been tied, the shuttle carrying the thread of weft is passed between the front and back threads of warp; the heald rod attached to these back threads is then pulled forward, so that they are now in front of the others, and the shuttle is passed back. If the rug is narrow, only one shuttle is used; but if the rug is wide, or if the weft consists of two threads of unequal thickness, a shuttle is passed across from each side. Every thread of warp is in this way completely encircled by the thread of weft as it passes and repasses. When weaving large rugs, there is an advantage in having two heald rods, as by their use the distance between the front and back threads of warp may be increased. The object of the lease rod is to prevent any slack caused by drawing forward the threads of warp, and is accomplished in a very simple manner, as will be seen by studying the drawing; since when the tension of the back threads is increased by drawing them forward, the tension of the front threads is also increased by displacing the lease rods which thereby stretches them.

PLATE 7. FERAGHAN RUG

PLATE 8. HAMADAN RUG

The products of the loom are divided according to their weave into three separate classes. The simplest of these are the kilims, which are without pile and consist only of warp and weft to which a few embroidered stitches representing some symbol are occasionally added.

A more elaborately made class are the Soumaks. They consist of warp covered by flat stitches of yarn and of a thread of weft which extends across and back between each row of stitches in the old rugs and between each second and third row of stitches in the new rugs. In the narrow, perpendicular lines that define both borders and designs the stitch is made by the yarn encircling two adjacent threads of warp; but in other parts of the rug it is made by the yarn passing across two adjacent threads of warp at the front, and after encircling them at the back, recrossing them again at the front. It is then continued across the next pair of adjacent threads of warp. The result is that at the back of these rugs each of the two threads of warp encircled by the yarn appears as a separate cord, while at the front the yarn passes diagonally across four threads of warp. As this diagonal movement is reversed in each succeeding row, the surface has an uneven appearance sometimes termed "herring bone" weave.

By far the largest class of rugs are those with a pile. When making them, the weaver begins at the bottom and ties to each pair of adjacent threads of warp a knot of yarn so as to form a horizontal row. A thread of weft is then passed, as often as desired, between the threads of warp and pressed more or less firmly with a metal or wooden comb upon the knots, when they are trimmed with a knife to the desired length. Another horizontal row of knots is tied to the threads of warp; again the yarn of weft is inserted; and so the process continues until the pile is completed. In tying the knots, work almost invariably proceeds from left to right and from the bottom to the top. It is but rarely that the warp is stretched horizontally and that the knots are tied in rows parallel to the sides. It is still more infrequently that a rug is found in which the knots are tied by working from the centre to the right and left, and to the top and bottom. These interesting exceptions may easily be discovered by rubbing the hand over the pile, when it will be noticed that the knots lie on one another so as to face the same direction, which is the opposite to that in which the work of tying advanced, or as is generally the case, from top to bottom.

The compactness, durability, and value of a rug depend somewhat on the number of knots in any particular area. Yet if the yarn is coarse, the rug may be compact even though the number of knots be small; and if the yarn is fine, the rug may be loosely woven, either because the rows of knots have not been firmly pressed down, or because there are several "filling threads" of weft, and still the number of knots be large. A square inch is a convenient size for measurement; but since all parts of a rug are not woven with equal compactness, the measurement should be made in several places if exactness be required. In loosely woven pieces, such as the Oushaks and some of the Genghas, there may be less than twenty knots to the square inch; but among the more closely woven, as the Kirmans and Bokharas, are frequently several hundred.

These knots are of two classes, the Ghiordes and the Sehna. The Ghiordes are found in all rugs of Asia Minor and Caucasia, in some of the rugs of India, and in most of the rugs of Persia. They are named after the town of Ghiordes in Asia Minor, where some of the finest Asiatic pieces were made, and which tradition states was once the ancient Gordion, noted even in the days of Alexander. In tying the knot, the two ends of yarn appear together at the surface included between two * adjacent threads of warp around which they have been passed, so that the tighter the yarn is drawn the more compact the knot becomes. The three different ways of tying this knot are shown in Plate B, Figs. 1, 2, and 3 (Page 49), of which the second is known as a "right hand" and the third as a "left hand" knot. The Sehna knots, which are used in the Turkoman, Chinese, many of the Persian, and in some of the Indian rugs, take their name from the city of Sehna in Persia. In tying them, a piece of yarn encircles a thread of warp and is twisted so that its ends appear at the surface, one at each side of the adjacent thread of warp, as is shown in Plate B, Figs. 4, 5, and 6. According as this thread of warp is to the right or the left of the one they encircle, the knots are known as "right-hand" or "left-hand" knots,† but in the appearance of the carpet there is no distinction. If the pile of a rug is carefully parted, the two ends of yarn forming a Sehna knot can be separated; but with the Ghiordes knot this is impossible, as will be understood by studying Plate B, in which Figs. 1, 2, 3, 7, 8, and 9 are Ghiordes knots, and Figs. 4, 5, 6, and 10 are Sehna

* In a few rare instances a knot is tied to four threads of warp.
† Most Sehna knots are right-hand knots, but the Sehna knots of a large proportion of Khorassan rugs are left-hand knots.

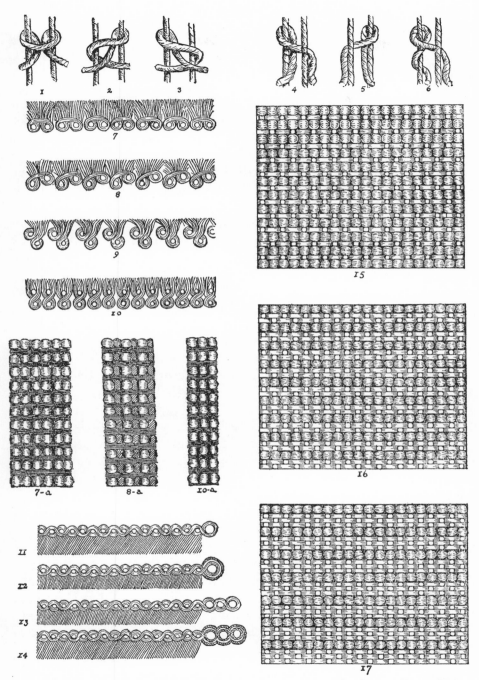

PLATE B. — Nos. 1, 2, 3, 7, 8, 9, Ghiordes knots. Nos. 4, 5, 6, 10, Sehna knots. No. 11, Weft-overcasting. No. 12, Double-overcasting. No. 13, Weft-selvage. No. 14, Double-selvage. Nos. 15, 16, 17, illustrate one, two, and three threads of weft passing between two rows of knots.

49

knots.   As a rule, the Sehna knots, which permit of closer weaving and clearer definition of pattern, appear in rugs of shorter nap.

The nice distinctions in the technique of weaving are rarely understood even by those who are familiar with Oriental rugs. The general pattern, which next to colour is the characteristic that most quickly arrests the attention, is often the sole guide by which novices guess the class.   The more experienced will observe if the knot be Ghiordes or Sehna, and examine the finish at the sides and ends; but few give the peculiarities of the weave the consideration they deserve.   This, perhaps, is because only those who have made a special study would believe the constancy with which members of a tribe or locality have followed the same method of tying the knot and inserting the weft.   The different methods of treatment by separate tribes are sometimes only slight, but they afford a most important clue for determining the place of origin of doubtful classes. In fact, nearly every class has a typical weave differentiating it from all other classes.   To be sure, there are exceptions to the established type which are inevitable; since, for instance, a man from the Feraghan district might marry a woman from the adjoining Hamadan district, who, to please her husband, might weave a rug with pattern common to his district but follow the style of weaving that she has been familiar with from childhood.   Nevertheless, weavers of a particular district adhere more closely to a typical style of weaving than they do to any other characteristic of a rug.   Nor is this surprising, since weaving is learned in earliest childhood; and as it contains no elements calculated to stimulate the imagination, it is mechanically followed with stereotyped precision.   An innovation in pattern, by copying some strange designs that strike the fancy, is far more likely.   These distinctions in weaving may be conveniently divided into those that affect the knot, the warp, and the weft.*

THE KNOT. — Not only may a knot be tied as a Ghiordes or a Sehna knot, but it may have other distinguishing peculiarities; as, for instance, it may be of fine or coarse wool.   This is most conveniently observed at the back, where it will be seen that the knots of rugs such as the Bokhara, Kirman, Joshaghan, and Bergamo are tied with fine yarn; while the knots of other rugs, as the Sam-

---

* As far as the writer is aware, no one has hitherto called attention to the many precise distinctions there are in weaving, and to the fact that each class of rugs follows a distinct type of its own.   For this reason this branch of the subject is treated more fully than would otherwise be necessary.

arkand, Bijar, Gorevan, Kurdistan, Yuruk, and Kazak are tied with coarse yarn. Whether the yarn be fine, medium, or coarse, all specimens of any class will show a remarkable conformity. Also in some rugs the knots are drawn very tight against the warp, while in others the yarn encircles the warp loosely. Any one who has examined the back of many Sarouks, Kashans, Kirmans, or Daghestans, and rubbed the finger-nail against them, could not possibly mistake them for a Shiraz, Kulah, Yuruk, or Karabagh, which are less tightly woven. Again, as a result of using yarn in which the double thread that forms two or more ply has been very loosely or very tightly twisted together, there is some difference in the direction or slant of the strands forming the yarn, where it shows at the back, though this feature is not pronounced. For example, in most Afghans, Yuruks, Bijars, and others the strands of yarn where it crosses the warp in forming the knot lie for the most part in a direction parallel to the weft; while in other rugs, as Mosuls, Kurdistans, and Kazaks, the strands of yarn slant irregularly. Furthermore, in some rugs, as the Melez and Yuruks, as a result of the threads of yarn being strung rather far apart, each half of a knot encircling a thread of warp stands out at the back distinctly from the other with clear cut edges; while in many rugs, as the Shiraz or Sehna, each half is very closely pressed together. Also in some rugs, as Sarabends and Afshars, each of these half knots where they show at the back have the same length, measured in a direction parallel to the warp, as width, measured in a direction parallel to the weft; while in such rugs as the Kazaks, since the yarn generally consists of several ply, the length exceeds the width; and in a few rugs the length is less than the width.

THE WARP. — The appearance of the back of a rug is partly due to the relative positions of the two threads of warp encircled by a knot. If, for instance, in any Kazak a pin be thrust through the nap wherever a single perpendicular line of one colour appears at the surface, it will be seen that each of the two threads of warp encircled by a single knot lie side by side with equal prominence. This is shown in Plate B, Figs. 7 and 7a (Page 49), in which the former represents a section of a rug cut transversely to the threads of warp, and the latter the appearance of the rug at the back. The same will be found true of Beluchistans, Feraghans, Yuruks, and many others. If, however, a Kulah, Persian-Kurdish, or Karabagh be similarly examined, it will be seen that one thread of warp to each knot is depressed, so that the back has a slightly corrugated appearance (as in Plate B, Figs. 8 and 8a). And in the case of a Bijar or Sarouk it will be seen that one thread of warp, included in every knot, has been doubled under so as to be entirely concealed from view; with the result that the foundation of warp has a double thickness, which makes the rug much stronger, as in Plate B, Fig. 9, representing a Ghiordes knot, and Fig. 10 representing a Sehna knot. To be sure, it occasionally happens that in rugs of a particular class some may have each thread of warp included in a knot equally prominent and others may have one slightly depressed; or that in rugs of another class some may have one thread of warp depressed and others may have it entirely concealed; but as a rule these tribal features show a remarkable constancy. These relative positions of the two threads of warp encircled by a knot are partly due to the degree of closeness with which the threads of warp are strung, also partly to the method of inserting the threads of weft or "filling" between the rows of knots; but more than all else they are due to the way one end of the knots is pulled when they are tied.

THE WEFT. — In the character and arrangement of weft are technical differences that are more serviceable than any other feature for distinguishing between the rugs of different tribes and districts. So subtle are some of them that they can be learned only by long and painstaking study, and are appreciated by few except native weavers. Nevertheless, to any one who will carefully examine almost any well-known classes, it will be apparent that these differences in the weave are real, and that they are sufficiently constant to differentiate one class from another. The fine brown weft of the Bokhara, or equally fine bluish weft of a Sarouk that is almost concealed between firmly tied knots; the fine thread of cotton weft passing but once between two rows of knots and covered only by the transverse warp of the Sehna; the coarse thread of cotton weft similarly passing but once between two rows of knots in the Hamadan; the coarse thread of cotton weft that once crossing and recrossing appears irregularly between appressed rows of knots in Kerman-shahs; the bead-like appearance of the threads of weft that, as a rule, pass many times between two rows of knots in Genghas; the crudely spun weft of coarse diameter crossing and recrossing once between the rows of knots in modern Mosuls; the very fine reddish brown weft that entirely conceals from view the warp in old Ber-gamos, — are features peculiar to these separate classes with which every rug expert is familiar. The weft of many other classes is equally distinctive, though there are exceptions to the types. It should be remembered, however, that the weave of many rugs woven over a hundred and fifty years ago is different from the weave of rugs woven only fifty years ago; and that many modern pieces cheaply made for commercial purposes are more crudely woven than were the same classes thirty years ago.

These distinctions in the weft relate to the material of which it is made, its colour, the size of the diameter, the way in which it is spun, to its loose or compressed condition between separate rows of knots, as well as to the number of times it crosses the warp between them, and to whether it is inserted with much or little slack. Most rugs are woven with woollen weft of a natural colour, but occasionally it has a reddish brown, a blue, or a yellow tint. When cotton, jute, or hemp are used, they are almost invariably of natural colour; only in a very few pieces, as some of the Kulahs, are both wool and jute ever used in the same piece. The weft of some classes, as Bokharas, Sarouks, and Bergamos, is of a very small diameter, and of others, as the Hamadans and Kurdistans, it is of relatively large diameter. In some classes, as the Karajes and Genghas, the weft is tightly spun like twine; while in the Beluchistans, Mosuls, and Kurdistans it is loosely spun, so that the projecting fibres of wool give a rough appearance to its surface.

Also the weavers of some districts invariably compress very firmly the yarn of weft between every two rows of knots, while other weavers compress it only to a slight degree; as, for instance, in the Afghan, Tabriz, and Kirman the rows of knots are pressed down so firmly that the weft is almost concealed at the back and the transverse threads of warp are entirely covered; whilst, on the other hand, in the Karabagh or Kazak between every two rows of knots the weft and part of the transverse threads of warp are exposed to view. According as the rows of knots are pressed down upon the threads of weft or not, one of the two halves of each separate knot, as shown at the back, may extend slightly or very much beyond the other in the direction of the length of the rug, or each of them may lie in a straight line at right angles to the warp. Comparing Kazak, Kutais, and Tiflis rugs, for example, it will be noticed that as a rule the line thus formed in Tiflis rugs is nearly an even, clear cut line at right angles to the warp, that in the Kutais part of one knot extends beyond the other, while in Kazaks this unevenness is even more

conspicuous. Or again, if typical Shirvans, Kabistans, and Daghestans be compared, it will be noticed that in Shirvans the half-knots,
or parts of the knot encircling the two adjacent threads of warp, are
often inclined at an angle of at least thirty degrees to the line of
weft so as to present a serrated appearance, but that the alignment
formed by knots of Daghestans is nearly even, and that of Kabistans
is intermediate. To be sure, there are exceptions to this rule, but
these features are remarkably constant.

The number of times that a thread of weft is inserted between
two rows of knots varies with the practice of different localities, but
is almost constant in each locality. Weavers of Sehna rugs insert
only a single thread of weft between every two rows of knots, which
winds in front of and behind alternate threads of warp, with the
result that the back of these rugs have a checkered or quincunx
appearance, caused by minute portions of exposed warp and weft
crossing each other at right angles. In Hamadans a much heavier
thread of weft passes only once before and behind alternate threads
of warp, so that the appearance of the weave is very similar to that
of Sehnas.* In almost all other rugs the weft crosses twice, that is,
across and back once, between every two rows of knots so as to completely encircle each thread of warp. The weave of a few rugs, as
some Anatolians, shows the weft crossing three times, that is, twice
in one direction and once in the opposite direction. In the Genghas,
Tcherkess, Bergamos, and in many rugs over one hundred and fifty
years old, the threads of weft frequently cross many times; and it is
not unusual for the number to vary in different parts of the same
rug. In Plate B, Figs. 15, 16, and 17 (Page 49), is illustrated the
appearance of the back of rugs in which a thread of weft crosses
once, twice, and three times between two adjacent rows of knots.
There are likewise rugs in which the number varies with methodical
regularity; for instance, in Khorassans it is usual to find an extra
thread of weft inserted at intervals of every few rows of knots;
in many Herats the threads of weft cross twice between several
successive rows of knots, then three times between the following
several rows, and so continue to alternate; and in some of the
Kulahs a thread of woollen weft that crosses twice alternates with
a single coarser thread of jute.

* A few of the weavers about Gozene in Asia Minor make rugs with a double
foundation, in which a single thread of coarse weft crosses twice between parallel
rows of threads of warp. Only rarely is this method followed in other districts.

COLOR PLATES

COLOUR PLATE I — OUSHAK CARPET

The colours and pattern of this antique Oushak are similar to those of the best examples that remain of the carpets woven in Asia Minor during the XV and XVI Centuries. The deep blue of the central field, the rich red of the medallions, and the golden yellow of the leaves are entirely unlike the more subdued hues found in Persian rugs. Strongly contrasting with them are the more delicate tones of the tendrils and leaves, which display in their drawing a keen sense of refinement. In the formal pattern of the field are stateliness and elegance; in the narrow borders are simplicity and grace. Such colours and drawing show that the early Asia Minor weavers had an intense appreciation of the ennobling qualities of beauty and harmony.

Loaned by Mr. James F. Ballard

COLOUR PLATE II — MOSUL RUG

Long before the commercial instinct had been felt among the weavers of the Orient, one or more of them dwelling in the Mesopotamian valley tied the knots of this old Mosul. The central field is of camel's hair that shades from a rich dark chestnut at one end to lighter tones at the other, and is enlivened by bright flowers representing those found on the river's banks. This variation of ground colour, the small geometric designs at the extreme ends of the fields, the eight-pointed stars of the main stripe of the border, and some of the drawing are nomadic characteristics. The dainty vine and flower of the narrow guard stripes, on the other hand, show Persian influence. This piece represents a type of which few now remain.

Property of the Author

COLOUR PLATE I

COLOUR PLATE II

COLOUR PLATE III

COLOUR PLATE III — BERGAMO RUG

The weaver of this interesting Bergamo followed the early Asia Minor traditions in the use of rich, deep blue and red of field and border, yet in respect to pattern showed his freedom from conventionality by departing from types peculiar to his district and adopting many nomadic designs prevalent throughout Anatolia. Reciprocal latch-hooks form the background of the central field, on which are three upright panels containing octagonal discs; and latch-hooks surrounding lozenges and forming what may originally have been intended to represent the tree of life appear almost as conspicuously in the border. There are also combs, knots of destiny, and innumerable S-forms. The panels at the upper and lower ends of the field and the reciprocal vandykes are most suggestive of Ladiks, but in the place of pomegranates at the ends of the upright stalks are small checquered squares. Bergamos with such patterns are now rarely seen.

Loaned by Mr. Hulett C. Merritt

COLOUR PLATE IV — GHIORDES PRAYER RUG

Only now and then is seen a prayer Ghiordes that represents such a high type of artistic skill. The weaving follows more closely the fine technique of the Persian than that of the Asia Minor weaver. Yet it is the drawing and colouring that claim attention. The delicate tracery of the spandrel, the minute delineation of tendril and leaf in the border, and the perfect balance of every part of one side with a corresponding part in the other, resemble the finest workmanship of old Iran. Not only so, but the beautiful border pattern of rosette and leaf is so suggestive of the well-known Herati design that it seems not improbable that here is shown the influence of those Persian weavers that Solyman the Magnificent took with him to Asia Minor after his capture of Tabriz. The colour also displays dainty tones and careful shading found in no other class of Asia Minor rugs. Such pieces are usually regarded as products of the XVI Century.

Property of the Author

COLOUR PLATE IV

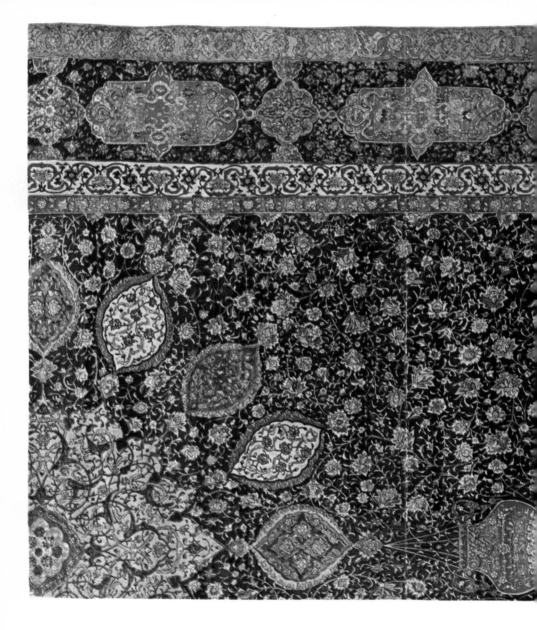

COLOUR PLATE V
SECTION OF THE HOLY CARPET OF THE MOSQUE AT ARDEBIL,
Size: 34 ft. 6 in. by 17 ft. 6 in.
Described on pages 83 and 84
FORMERLY IN THE POSSESSION OF VINCENT ROBINSON & CO., LTD.,
34 WIGMORE STREET, LONDON, W.,
And Sold by them in 1892 to
THE ROYAL VICTORIA AND ALBERT MUSEUM. SOUTH KENSINGTON, LOND

TRANSLATION OF INSCRIPTION.

I have no refuge in the world other than thy threshold,
My head has no protection other than this porchway;
The work of the Slave of this Holy Place.

       Maksoud of Kashan.

        946 A.H. = 1540 A.D.

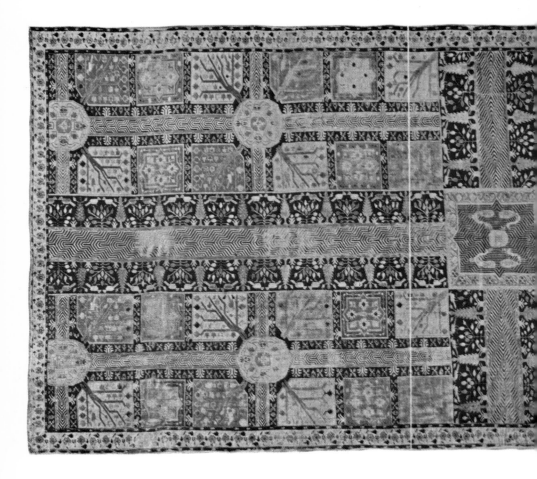

COLOUR PLATE VI

A 16TH CENTURY PERSIAN ROYAL " GARDEN "CARPET.

(Reputed to have been made for Sháh 'Abbás for Sefavi Palace.)   Date 1587-16..

31 ft. 0 in. × 12 ft. 3 in.

[*Statement of the owner*]

IN THE POSSESSION OF VINCENT ROBINSON & CO., LTD.

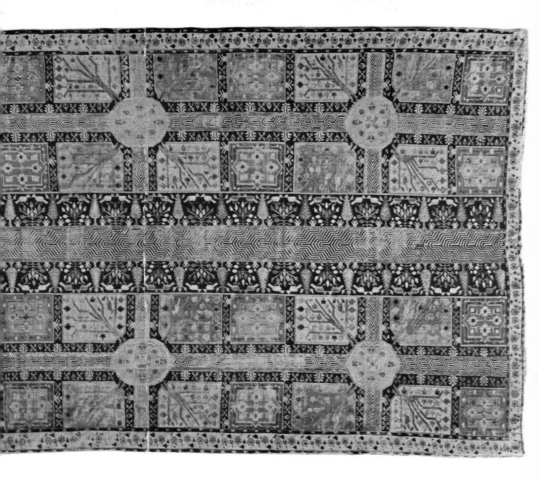

This carpet and the one at the Naesby House, Sweden, which it resembles
in pattern but not in colouring, are, so far as known, the only complete carpets of this type. The Naesby carpet has been assigned to the middle of
the XVIII Century; this is undoubtedly much older.

The pattern represents a Persian garden divided into four sections by two
intersecting streams, which are bordered by rows of cypress trees, alternating
with bushes on which are birds. These sections are similarly divided by
smaller streams, that meet at the four pavillions of each side, into plots containing trees and flowering bushes. Four peacocks rest above the central basin.
The colours are harmonious, and show the mellowing influence of time.

COLOUR PLATE VII—LADIK PRAYER RUG

The rug here represented conforms in every particular to one of the best types of Ladik prayer rugs. It contains the beautiful border stripe of Rhodian lilies, the pomegranates and vandykes in the panel below the central field, and the queer designs of scrolls and serrated leaves so peculiar to these rugs. It is interesting to see how the pattern of the innermost stripe, which consists of a row of S-forms at the top and sides, is changed so as to resemble a ribbon at the bottom, to note the eight-pointed stars resting on octagons in the lower panel, so suggestive of nomads, and also the designs which have been placed near the two corners on the left, between the rosettes and Rhodian lilies of the main stripe, as if to divert the spell of the "evil-eye." Such irregularities, denoting the idiosyncrasies of the weaver, add to the charm of Oriental rugs.

Loaned by Mr. Hulett C. Merritt

COLOUR PLATE VII

COLOUR PLATE VIII — SOUMAK RUG

The shape, colouring, and particularly the pattern of this interesting Soumak, which was probably woven seventy-five or more years ago, not only are unusual but belong to a higher type than is often seen. Arranged in diagonal rows on a field of red are flowering bushes, that for the most part are blue and pink, but at one end are green, yellow, and brown. The accurate drawing of these bushes and of the reciprocal trefoils of the guard stripes, the care with which the stitches have been inserted, and the fine texture of the wool, as is shown even in the cream-white warp at the knotted ends, alike proclaim the excellent quality of this rare piece.

Loaned by Mr. Theodore S. Hawley

COLOUR PLATE VIII

COLOUR PLATE X

COLOUR PLATE XI

COLOUR PLATE X — CHINESE RUG

Perfect technique of weaving, accuracy of drawing, and subdued rich colouring are the characteristics of this unusual piece. The knots of the fine woollen yarn are tied with a precision not frequently seen in Chinese rugs, and the shortness of nap discloses the faithfulness with which an artist of no ordinary ability has represented plants and flowers. Their soft tones stand out in relief against a background now darkened and enriched by the mellowing influence of time. Moreover, the motives of the upper and the lower half of the field, even to the minutest detail, show an exact balance. Many old Chinese rugs are of uncertain age, but this piece has been attributed, not without reason, to the Kang-hi period.

Loaned by Mr. Nathan Bentz

COLOUR PLATE XI — CHINESE RUG

This large Chinese carpet represents some of the best workmanship of the Keen-lung period. In it are shown the graceful drawing of leaf, fruit, flower, and butterfly, and the dainty colouring of blue, yellow, brown, and apricot on a field of ivory that are so characteristic of this time. The usual balance of designs throughout the field is maintained with precision; but, as is not always the case, different motives occupy corresponding positions. Thus a cluster of leaves and fruit may be balanced with a cluster of leaves and flowers. The conventional drawing of the corners and the somewhat formal panel that surrounds the central medallion give to the pattern strength of character while they detract nothing from its beauty.

Loaned by Mr. Nathan Bentz

As the shuttle passes back and forth, the thread of weft may be allowed considerable slack, so that when it is pressed down by the comb it will fit about the sides of the warp; or it may be drawn tightly across, so that it has a tendency to displace the threads of warp. If, for instance, a Hamadan and one of the Feraghans which, unlike the majority of them, has only one thread of weft crossing between the rows of knots, be examined, it will be seen that in the Hamadan the weft crosses with hardly any slack, so that the warp stands out clearly and well defined at the back; but that in the Feraghan the weft crosses with much slack, so that it folds about the warp, which accordingly seems slightly imbedded in it at the back. In some rugs the weft is passed across once with very slight slack, and as it recrosses it is allowed much slack. These features of the weave, which are followed with remarkable constancy in the same class, can be observed to advantage in a fragment of a rug cut transversely to the direction of the warp. If, for instance, the weft which crosses and recrosses between the rows of knots be carefully removed so as not to disturb its mould, it will be noticed in the case of many rugs that each thread of yarn has a similar shape of moderately deep undulations, which show how it conformed to the warp and indicate how slack it was when inserted. In the case of a few rugs, as the Luristans, each thread will likewise have similar undulations, but they will be very prominent. If, on the other hand, the weft be removed from some classes, as the Tabriz, Sarouk, and Kashan, one of the two threads will be almost straight or have slight undulations, while the other thread will have deep undulations. The weft of the Herez, Herats, old Khorassans, and Koniehs have the same peculiarities, excepting that the thread with very slight undulations is of three or four ply, while the other is of a single ply.

The only instruments employed in weaving are the knife, comb, and scissors. The first is used, after each row of knots has been tied, to cut the ends of yarn to nearly the proper length; the second, to press firmly each row of knots; and the last, to trim the nap with care, so that the finished product may present an even and compact appearance.

FINISH OF SIDES. — As the sides are constantly exposed to wear weavers of different districts strengthen them in different ways, which may be designated as Weft Overcasting, Double Overcasting, Weft Selvage, Double Selvage, and Added Selvage. Each of these terms, though not euphonious, suggests the method employed.

In Weft Overcasting (Plate B, Fig. 11, Page 49) the thread of weft, after encircling the threads of warp to which the knots are tied, is wound about a much heavier cord that is strung at the side of the rug for a space equal to the thickness of the knots. It then partly encircles the threads of warp between the next two rows of knots as it passes to the other side, when it is wound about the heavy cord there. As this process continues, the cords at the sides are completely overcast with the thread of weft. When the sides have a Double Overcasting (Plate B, Fig. 12), heavy yarn is wound about the cord that has previously been encircled by the weft. Frequently several threads of yarn take the place of a single heavy cord. Weft Selvage (Plate B, Fig. 13) is made by placing two or more heavy cords instead of a single one at the side of the warp, and encircling them by the weft in figure-eight fashion. As they extend beyond the rows of knots they form a plain flat selvage. The Double Selvage (Plate B, Fig. 14) is used among nomadic tribes such as the Beluches and Afghans, whose rugs receive an unusual amount of hard wear, so that an extra selvage is necessary. In adding this extra selvage the threads of weft are carried about the heavy cords, as in weft selvage, and then the extra yarn is wound over it in figure-eight fashion so as again to encircle the heavy cords. In Added Selvage the heavy cords are not encircled by the weft, but are attached to the side of the rug by the extra yarn that winds about them figure-eight fashion, and also encircles two or more adjoining threads of warp. Sometimes also the selvage is "Mixed," or made by the weft encircling only one or two of the heavy cords, and then an extra yarn is wound about these and the remaining cord or cords. Moreover, the Double Overcasting and Double Selvage may be "attached" more firmly to the sides of the rug by the yarn passing in figure-eight fashion about the adjacent thread or threads of warp between the two rows of knots. When a Double Overcasting is thus "attached," it is somewhat similar to a two-cord Double Selvage.

These are the principal methods of finishing the sides, though they are sometimes modified by tribal customs. Simple as they seem, skill is required in both overcasting and making the selvage; for if carelessly done the sides are frequently made to curl. This is occasionally found to be the defect of old rugs, the worn sides of which have been recently overcast by inexperienced weavers. When such is the case, removing the stitches and overcasting with more care will remove the defect.

PLATE 9.   SAROUK RUG

PLATE 10. SARABEND RUG

FINISH OF ENDS. — The ends, which receive more attention than the sides, are treated in several different ways; and in many rugs a distinction exists between the treatment of each end. The simplest finish is where the warp and weft are woven like the threads of a kilim, and extend beyond the pile as a web, which may be exceedingly short, or, as in Beluches and Afghans, several inches long. Frequently the ends are finished by a selvage formed by cords heavier than the weft braided into the warp; or the upper end may be doubled back and hemmed. It is not unusual to find both web and selvage; but though the finish be web, selvage, or web and selvage, the warp of the end finished last generally forms a fringe, and often each end will have a fringe. Sometimes each separate thread of warp hangs loose; sometimes a number a foot or more in length are twisted together in cords; and again they are knotted or are tied to one another diagonally so as to form a network from which hang the loose ends. Very frequently the loops formed by the warp that encircled the rod extend beyond the web at the lower end of the rug, or else are braided about the ultimate thread of weft in the web. Though the warp and weft are generally undyed in the body of the rug, the web of the ends is very frequently coloured. Some of the webs, particularly those of the Beluches, are embroidered; and through others, as the Kurdistans, a parti-coloured cord runs transversely; still others, as Bergamos, are adorned with shells, beads, or other articles to avert the evil eye.

In the study of rugs it should be remembered that the effect of rough usage is so considerable that in old pieces the webs of the ends have frequently disappeared, leaving short fringes composed of the ends of warp from which some rows of knots have been removed, and that recent overcasting of the sides may take the place of former selvage.

The many characteristics of knot, warp, weft, sides, and ends, with all the variations made by innumerable tribes, remarkably constant in their methods, are technical peculiarities that are uninteresting to those who feel only an æsthetic interest in rugs, yet they demand the most careful consideration of whoever would learn to differentiate accurately between the many classes. Though admitting of exceptions, these peculiarities are real and definite, yet their analyses often require the subtlest perception of small though exact distinctions, without which expert understanding would be impossible.

CHAPTER VI

DESIGNS AND SYMBOLS

OWEVER well woven, however resplendent in rich modulations of colour, Oriental rugs would quickly lose their fascination if in patterns and designs there were not at least some partial expression of the simple lives of the people, of their religious feelings, and of that veiled mysticism which pervades the thought of every Eastern race.

In all nomadic rugs as well as in many others are innumerable reminders of common life. It may be only crude outlines of the goat or camel, or realistically drawn rose and lily; but even these are suggestive of associations.

Religion, too, exercised on the character of rugs an important influence, which is expressed in the symbolism of both designs and colour. Without a doubt, some of these well-known designs have been transmitted from the earliest times, and were once associated with different forms of idolatry. Thus, among the old Babylonians the sun and moon, which are sometimes seen in the old pieces, represented particular deities; and very many of the oldest Chinese rugs that remain also contain symbols of their deities. In the early religion of Iran, which over 1000 years B.C. was reduced to a system by Zoroaster, the elements were worshipped, so that designs representing these elements would likewise represent the divine forces they personified. This ancient fire worship of the Parsees, which even to-day has a few devotees in parts of Persia, and the kindred sun worship have added much to the symbolism of Oriental rugs. Buddhism also has contributed its share; and with the spread of Mohammedanism appeared a Saracenic influence that is frequently recognised. Even the two great sects of Mohammedan followers, the Shiites and Sunnites, have had distinct effects in the use of designs, as the former employed animal figures and the latter prohibited them.

There was, moreover, a symbolism that in a manner expressed the vague philosophic teachings of the ancient races. It was but natural that the early weaver engaged in tedious sedentary work, often requiring many months of constant application to complete, should endeavour to express therein not only artistic taste, but also the spirit of his innermost thoughts. So as he wove he sometimes left the result, though poorly defined and little understood to-day, of that struggle to interpret the great mysteries of the visible and unseen universe, from which arose the crude beginnings of philosophy.*

The patterns, however, of many Oriental rugs are chiefly decorative. Even a casual examination shows that in all of them the coloured knots of the surface represent a border surrounding a central field. The former serves much the same function to the latter as a frame to a picture; yet its office is in no wise subordinate. Nor is there any part of the pattern more useful in determining the place of its origin. For this reason it is well to clearly define the special names which in this work are applied to its different parts. The lineal divisions are designated "Stripes," though they are frequently spoken of as separate borders. At or near the centre of the border is the main stripe, which is generally accompanied by a much narrower pair, one on each side, known as "Guard stripes." Very narrow stripes are sometimes called "Ribbon stripes," and those of only one or two knots in width are called "Lines." The latter are of solid colour or have the simplest geometric device. The decoration of the ribbon stripes is also necessarily simple; but in the main stripe of artistic rugs the patterns are often exceedingly elaborate, of exquisite colours, and co-ordinate in character with those of the field.

The fields display even greater diversity of pattern than the

* Sir George Birdwood has made the statement that "A deep and complicate symbolism, originating in Babylonia and possibly in India, pervades every denomination of Oriental carpet. Thus the carpet itself prefigures space and eternity, and the general pattern or filling, as it is technically termed, the fleeting, finite universe of animated beauty. Every colour has its significance; and the design, whether mythological or natural, human, bestial, or floral, has its hidden meaning. Even the representatives of men hunting wild beasts have their special indications. So have the natural flowers of Persia their symbolism, wherever they are introduced, generally following that of their colours. The very irregularities either in drawing or colouring, to be observed in almost every Oriental carpet, and invariably in Turkoman carpets, are seldom accidental, the usual deliberate intention being to avert the evil eye and insure good luck."

borders. Frequently they are covered with a heterogeneous mass of detached and unrelated figures, as in many of the nomadic rugs; or, on the other hand, are entirely covered with repetitive patterns, as in the Turkomans; or with intricate and correlated designs, as in the diaper and floral patterns of so many of the Persian and Indian rugs. Others consist of a background of solid colour on which appear isolated formal designs, as in some of the Khorassans, or medallions on which are represented smaller figures, as in some of the old Sehnas and Feraghans. Occasionally the medallions are so large as to extend to the sides and ends of the fields, and thus separate the corners into nearly triangular shaped sections, such as are characteristic of a number of Persian and one or two Caucasian rugs. In a few of the latter, also, the fields are covered with large geometric figures suggesting the medallions. It is only within comparatively modern times that weavers have used solid colours for large portions of the fields. The intent no doubt was a saving in labour and pains, but the effect is frequently most gratifying; as when, for instance, the space beneath the arch of Asia Minor prayer rugs is of a uniform red, blue, or cream, relieved only by a gracefully suspended lamp, the tree of life, or some other emblem of immortality.

The patterns of prayer rugs are not only pleasing, but have a peculiar importance, as weavers of certain sections of the country adhere so strictly to time-honoured traditions that the shape of the arch, or mihrab, which is the principal feature, often denotes the class, as well as the group, to which they belong. Some of these arches are illustrated in Plates C and D (Pages 61 and 63), from which it will be seen that in Persian rugs they are formed by gracefully curving lines, but that in rugs of other groups, with the exception of a very few old Ghiordes pieces, they are geometric. The peculiarities of the arches of the several classes, also, are observable; as those of the Beluchistans, which are rectilinear and relatively high, and those of the Bokharas, which are tent-shaped, flat, and small. In the Caucasian group they have a marked resemblance to one another and also to those of the Turkoman rugs, but are larger than the latter. Again, the arch of almost all Asia Minor rugs rises higher than those of any others, excepting the Persian, and extends from one side of the field to the other. In many of them a panel is placed above the spandrel, and occasionally a second panel is placed beneath the field. Above the niche of some Asia Minor and Caucasian prayer rugs

PLATE C. — PRAYER ARCHES OF PERSIAN, CAUCASIAN, AND CENTRAL ASIATIC RUGS

No. 1, Antique silk.   No. 2, Kermanshah.   No. 3, Khorassan.   No. 4, Sarouk.   No. 5, Persian, XVI Century.   No. 6, Kashan.   No. 7, Feraghan.   No. 8, Shiraz.   No. 9, Daghestan, Kabistan, Shirvan, Chichi, Kazak, Karabagh.   No. 10, Kazak.   No. 11, Shirvan.   No. 12, Karabagh (not usual).   No. 13, Beluchistan.   No. 14, Bokhara, Tekke.   No. 15, Khiva.   No. 16, Beshire.

is woven a small rhomboidal figure, where the suppliant plants the pebble or bit of earth that he has brought from Mecca; and at the sides of a few arches are crude figures, where are placed the hands during the act of worship. More than one arch is the exception; but now and then are seen two and even four, one above the other, or several parallel to one another. These and other special features associated with prayer rugs will be considered more fully in subsequent chapters.

The smaller designs that appear in rugs and compose the general pattern are distinguished as geometric and floral ornamentation. The former is adopted in those countries where the population is principally nomadic; and the latter is the accepted style in countries where exist numerous towns and cities in which the arts have been cultivated and where a large percentage of the population have enjoyed an advanced state of society. Thus in Caucasia, Turkestan, Afghanistan, and Beluchistan geometric designs are characteristic of the rugs; but in China, India, Persia, and part of Asia Minor floral designs prevail. Sir George Birdwood, an eminent authority on Oriental rugs, has made the statement that the geometric designs are found among the lower Turanian and the floral among the higher Aryan. But it seems most probable that the adoption of the geometric or floral style of ornamentation is due not so much to racial distinctions as to the state to which the textile art had advanced among the different peoples and to the waves of influence that at times spread over the countries. Thus the early rugs of Asia Minor had patterns that were more geometric than those of later times, and during the period when the Mongols ruled in Persia geometric patterns were more frequently employed in the rugs of that country than subsequently.

In all rugs, however, some trace of the floral design appears. Even in the Turkoman weavings, the pattern of which is strictly geometric, some vestige of the tree of life is manifest. In the fields of Caucasian rugs, in which are represented squares, octagons, triangles, diagonals, lozenges, stars, etc., the weavers have depicted designs that are almost as geometric as those of the Turkoman rugs by which they have been influenced; but, on the other hand, large numbers of the border designs are distinctly floral. In the rugs of China and Asia Minor are found both geometric and floral ornamentation, the latter predominating in pieces woven during the last two centuries, and the former in those of earlier date. Among

PLATE D. — PRAYER ARCHES OF ASIA MINOR RUGS

Nos. 1, 2, 3, 4, Ghiordes. Nos. 5, 6, 7, Kulah. No. 8, Ladik. Nos. 9, 10, Bergamo. Nos. 11, 12, Melez. No. 13, Kir-sehehr, Mudjar. Nos. 14, 15, Konieh. No. 16, Anatolian.

63

the woven fabrics of India and Persia, however, few traces of the geometric pattern remain; but vines, leaves, and flowers form the favourite theme for decoration.

The floral patterns are the result of many centuries of growth, that reached its highest development in the Persian carpets of the XVI and XVII Centuries; and since then till the present time they have continued as the most characteristic features of the rugs of that country and India. They represent the highest technique of the weaver. In the borders are generally represented vines from which are pendant rosettes, palmettes, or flowers; and in the fields, particularly those of the fine antique rugs, are a profusion of floral forms realistically portrayed. On long, gracefully twining and intertwining stems is often the rose, pink, violet, lotus, crocus, narcissus, or daisy. But if the rug is more modern, in its field of uniform colour may be represented a central medallion covered with delicate tracings enriched by bright-coloured conventionalised flowers.

In the general pattern of all rugs are interwoven particular designs or motives that give them a distinctive character and render the greatest assistance in distinguishing the groups and classes. Thus the serrated leaf and wine cup (Plate I, Fig. 1, opp. Page 226) is found only in Caucasian and old Armenian rugs; and the design represented in Plate H, Fig. 10 (opp. Page 194), suggestive of some Chinese character, is found almost exclusively in Kulahs. Not only are all designs important as aids in classification, but they have a special interest, as it is maintained by writers of the highest authority that when employed by the earliest weavers each had a symbolic meaning. To be sure, the origin of many has been lost in the remote past and is unknown even to those who now employ them; but others still represent definite ideas, as they did centuries ago, and portray to some extent the thought of the weaver. They therefore deserve the most careful study.

Few of these designs have been transmitted from a more remote past or have been more universally employed than has been the figure S or ↄ. It appears in each of the groups of Oriental rugs excepting the Chinese; and two of the forms it assumes are exceedingly like the arms of the swastika and parts of the fret as occasionally seen in Chinese designs. In Indian rugs it is rarely found except in the borders, which may have been copied from those of other countries. It is very commonly seen in the Beluchistans,

PLATE 11.   CARPET FROM NORTHWESTERN PERSIA

Loaned by C. F. Williams, Esq., to the Metropolitan Museum of Art, New York

PLATE 12. CARPET FROM NORTHWESTERN PERSIA

Loaned by C. F. Williams, Esq., to the Metropolitan Museum of Art, New York

Tekkes, and Beshires, of the Central Asiatic group; and in the rugs of the Persian group that show nomadic influences. There is probably not a single class of the Caucasian group, nor any of the Asia Minor group, with the exception of the old Ghiordes, in which it is not sometimes represented. It may be seen near the corner of the Asia Minor "Dragon and Phœnix" carpet of the XIV Century, illustrated in Plate 20 (opp. Page 87); and appears in some of the old Armenian carpets, which are believed to be even older. That it was associated with sun worship and regarded as an emblem of light and the deity is the accepted belief. It is possible, however, that it was intended by some weavers to represent the serpent, which among many different races is emblematic of superhuman knowledge.

Probably no other design has been more universally employed than the swastika, which appears in the textile fabrics of North American Indians, on the Maya ruins of Yucatan, among the monuments of the Nile, and on the temples of India. Widely as is its distribution, its most usual form of intersecting right angles is found in each of these countries. It is not improbable that it originated in China, where it is a most common decorative motive, and was almost invariably represented in the borders and in many of the medallions of rugs woven before the beginning of the XVIII Century. It is also very frequently seen in the rugs of Samarkand, and occasionally in those of Caucasia. It seldom appears in the rugs of Persia, Asia Minor, or Turkestan. The universality of the design indicates its great antiquity, yet its primitive symbolic meaning of abundance, fertility, and prosperity has never been lost. Some of its different forms are shown in Plate O, Figs. 5a, 5b, 5c, 5d, 5e, and 5f (Page 291).

The reciprocal trefoil (Plate F, Fig. 17, opp. Page 158) is a very usual design in Caucasian and Persian rugs; it is often found in some of the rugs of India and in Beluchistans, but is very rarely seen in other classes of the Central Asiatic or in the Chinese and Asia Minor groups. Its origin is uncertain, but since it appears in the "Polish Carpets" and other antique Persian carpets of strictly floral pattern, where its drawing is more elaborate than in modern rugs, it is not improbable that it is the conventionalised form of the lily or a spray bearing three leaves, and that it has the emblematic significance of the tree form.

Among all primitive races the sun, moon, and stars have been associated with their religion, so that it is surprising that so few

emblems of them are recognised in rugs. In the theology of the
Chaldees, from which the earliest weavers must have received inspiration, the sun was regarded as one of their principal deities
and the moon as another. The sun is generally represented by a
plain circle, a circle with diameters intersecting at right angles,
or a circle with small ovals intersecting at right angles; the moon
is represented by the crescent. Of much more frequent occurrence
is the eight-pointed star, another inheritance of those ancient times
when all primitive races worshipped the heavenly bodies. It represented the female principle of the Chaldean sun god; and it is
believed, too, that it represented the deity to the Medes, ancestors
of many of the present Persians. There is a tradition among some
Eastern races that King Solomon wore a ring of diamonds arranged
in the form of an eight-pointed star, and also a crown containing
a large star of which the eight points and centre were composed of
precious stones of different colour. A star now and then seen in rugs
with colours so arranged is known as "Mohammedan's jewel design."
The six-pointed star, a Jewish symbol for the "shield of David,"
was adopted as a talisman by some of the Moslems. All of these
stars are chiefly nomadic symbols, they rarely if ever are seen
in the rugs of China or India, they are only occasionally found
in those of Persia, and are of most frequent occurrence in the Caucasian pieces.

Another design is an octagonal-shaped disc (Plate O, Fig. 10,
Page 291), usually about two and a half inches in diameter, on the
face of which and extending the full width are figures somewhat
like hour-glasses placed at right angles to one another. It seems not
improbable that it is of the same origin as the large designs that appear in the field of the Holbein rug of the XV Century, illustrated in
Plate 21 (opp. Page 92). It is a very old motive, and is sometimes
regarded as a dial symbolising the diurnal motion of the earth. It
is of very frequent occurrence in nomadic rugs; and is found in
Beluchistans, in nearly all Caucasians, in some rugs from Asia
Minor, and in only a very few from Persia.

The zigzag line, known as the water motive, is found in many of
the rugs of China, India, Persia, Caucasia, and Asia Minor, as well
as in the Beluchistans and Beshires of the Central Asiatic group,
though in some instances it appears as little more than a serrated
line. It is represented in the narrow guard-stripes of some of the
Western Asia Minor carpets of the XV Century. According to Mr.

John Mumford, "even in the oldest Egyptian symbolism a zigzag line stood for water and by implication for eternity; and a succession of these arranged to represent the sea has long been a recognised carpet design in India, China, and Persia."

One of the most common designs is what has been called the "latch-hook." When there is a long succession of latch-hooks with the straight ends resting on a line and the hooked ends inclined in the same direction, as in Plate K, Fig. 20 (opp. Page 230), they are called "running latch-hooks." Since they appear in the Dragon and Phœnix rug (opp. Page 87), that was probably woven about the end of the XIV Century, they are evidently a very old design, which not improbably was derived from the Chinese fret. The hook is of different shapes, and is sometimes perpendicular, sometimes inclined. Its particular function is to shade or subdue the harsh effect of a sudden transition from one colour to another that is entirely different. As such a device is unnecessary in artistic rugs of intricate designs, it is rarely seen in any Indian or Persian piece, excepting the modern Shiraz that frequently adopts geometric patterns; but it is found in all the rugs of Caucasia, Central Asia, and in most of those of Asia Minor. It is in fact as universal as the reciprocal trefoil.

In rugs of geometric patterns are occasionally found both Greek and Roman crosses. The latter are represented in most of the Soumak rugs, and appear profusely in old Asia Minor or Armenian rugs, in which they were probably woven with the intent to convey a religious significance; but in many instances crosses are not used symbolically.

The design of a comb (Plate O, Fig. 11, Page 291) is a Mohammedan emblem suggestive of cleanliness, yet it is not improbable that it is sometimes intended to represent the instrument employed in pressing the threads of weft closely against the knots. It is found mostly in Caucasian rugs, and rarely in those of other groups.

In a large number of the finest carpets woven in Persia three or four centuries ago was represented what is known as the Chinese cloud-band (Plate O, Fig. 7). It appeared in Persia about the middle of the XV Century, and was conspicuous in the carpets of Herat, Tabriz, and Gilan, as well as in many of the "Polish Carpets." Later it was introduced into Asia Minor, but was never represented in any of the strictly nomadic weavings. It appears in only a very few of the modern rugs, and these are mostly Persian. Nor is it recognised in its usual form in any of the Chinese rugs that now exist; though without a doubt it originated with the Chinese, since their early mythology placed the abode of the Supreme Ruler in the Constellation of Ursa Major, of which the stars of the Big Dipper were represented in early art as enveloped in a band of clouds; but in more conventionalised ornamentation the stars are omitted and the band remains. As a motive, then, it is symbolic of heaven and the deity.

In almost all rugs are found expressions of vegetable life, as a twig, vine, flower, or tree. Sometimes they are most naturalistic, again they are partly conventionalised, or so disguised, as in nomadic rugs of geometric designs, that only by study and comparison of many forms in a series can their origin be established. This universal adoption of floral form was due to something more than an æsthetic love for the beautiful, since in every country of the East some part of the tree or plant was emblematic. Moreover, a tree form known as the Tree of Life had a religious significance among many races. The Jews were told that in the Garden of Eden grew the "Tree of Knowledge of Good and Evil;" and in the Book of Revelation the Apostle John speaks of "The Tree of Life which bore twelve manner of fruits and yielded her fruit every month, and the leaves of the tree were for the healing of the nations." From this passage may have been borrowed the belief of the Mohammedans in the Tree of Life which grew in Paradise, and spread its branches that true believers might rest beneath them and enjoy its fruits and the companionship of beautiful houri. In the ancient lore of China is the Taoist tradition of the Tree of Life, growing by the Sea of Jade, that confers immortality on the fortunate who may gather and eat its fruits; also the tradition of the mountain top where grows the sacred tree on which the elect may climb and mount to heaven. Even among the ancient Chaldees was a story of a tree that grew to heaven and sheltered the earth. In different countries the Tree of Life is represented by different kinds; in Yarkand of Eastern Turkesta 1 it takes the form of a cedar; in Persia it is generally the cypress. Wherever employed it is symbolic of knowledge, resurrection, immortality.

No other form of vegetable life was so universally employed in Oriental symbolism as the lotus flower (Plate O, Figs. 16a, b, and c), since the Egyptian, Assyrian, Indian, Chinese, and Persian alike did it reverence. It was, perhaps, first employed emblematically in the valley of the Nile, but later it was held in high esteem by the inhabitants of India where the floating blossom is regarded as an emblem of the world. It was inseparately associated with Buddha, and its religious significance must have extended with the spread of Buddhism. Professor Goodyear regards a large number of designs that apparently are not related in form as derived from it through a long series of evolutions. During the highest development of the textile art in Persia it appears most realistically drawn in a large number of the carpets, especially the so-called Ispahans, or Herats, and the so-called Polish. It is also most artistically represented in the fabrics of India, and is a favourite design for Chinese weavers. But in other modern rugs it is seldom used as a motive, and is so conventionalised as often to escape notice.

If the lotus was the first flower to be represented in early woven fabrics, as seems not improbable, several others have met with greater favour among modern weavers. Of these the rose, which is cultivated extensively in the gardens of the East, appears in a large number of the rugs of Persia and Asia Minor. Moreover, a pattern frequently seen in many old Persian rugs is an all-over pattern of small bushes with flowering roses. Almost equally popular is the lily, which is characteristic of many of the rugs of India and of a few of Western Asia Minor. The "Euphrates flower," which grows by the river banks of the Mesopotamian valley, is also occasionally found as an all-over pattern in some of the rugs of Western Iran and Southern Caucasia. Less frequently seen and still less frequently recognised, as they are generally woven in small figures, are the daisy, anemone, crocus, narcissus, pink, and violet. All are depicted chiefly on account of their associations and beauty, and whatever emblematic meaning they are intended to convey is generally no more than that of their colours. There are, however, in a few old Persian carpets designs of sunflowers, which were accepted by the Zoroastrians and the earlier sun and fire worshippers as symbols of the sun and emblems of light.

Of the fruits of the earth none is more highly esteemed than the pomegranate, which was sculptured in temples of Mesopotamia and embroidered on the robes of Assyrian and Jewish priests. In the days of King Solomon it was cultivated in Palestine, where the Israelites, like modern Persians, made a sherbet by mixing its juice with sugar and spices. At the time of Homer it was cultivated in Phrygia. Now it grows wild over vast tracts of Syria, Persia, and Asia

Minor. Yet it rarely appears conspicuously in any woven fabrics excepting the Ladik prayer rugs, in which it is invariably seen. Since the weavers of these, whether Christian or Moslem, would probably be familiar with many of the old Jewish and Assyrian rites, it is not unlikely that it refers emblematically to its religious associations rather than symbolises, as has been suggested, the idea of fruitfulness as expressed in the Turkish wedding custom where the bride throws a pomegranate at her feet that the scattered seed may foretell the number of her children.

In almost every rug of Persia, India, and Asia Minor there is in some part of the border a vine with pendant leaves, flowers, rosettes, or palmettes; and even in many Caucasian rugs of geometric pattern the vine with its appendages is seen in conventionalised form. In a few of the more sumptuous carpets, where the drawing is elaborate, delicate tendrils bearing flowers or the more formal designs of the Herati border take the place of the vine, from which they were evolved. In such borders the designs generally convey no symbolic meaning, but the simpler vine encircling the field without beginning or end represents symbolically the continuity of purpose and permanency.

One of the most interesting designs (Plate O, Fig. 6, Page 291) is known as the Cone, Palm, Mango, Almond, River Loop, and Pear. By some it is believed to represent no more than the closed palm of the hand, since there is an old tradition in Persia that a weaver once asked his little son to devise for him a new design, whereupon the boy thrust his hand into a pot of dye, then placed it sidewise upon a piece of white linen, on which became impressed the "palm" design formed by the hand and incurving small finger. By some it is regarded as a cluster of old Iranian crown jewels. To others, who point to the well-known pattern of the Kashmir weaving, it denotes the bend of the river Jhelum above Srinagar in the valley of Kashmir; and to Sir George Birdwood it symbolises the flame sacred to ancient fire worshippers. In this work it will be called the Pear, the name now generally applied to it. In the course of the many centuries that have elapsed since its origin, and in its migration through India, Persia, Turkestan, Caucasia, and Asia Minor, it has adopted more strange shapes than any other device. In the rugs of Sarabend it is represented in its best-known form of simple curving lines, in the Bakus its identity is almost lost on account of its geometric appearance, and in the fabrics of India it is often very

PLATE 13. COMPARTMENT CARPET IN THE METROPOLITAN MUSEUM OF ART,
NEW YORK

PLATE 14. PERSIAN ANIMAL CARPET IN THE METROPOLITAN MUSEUM
OF ART, NEW YORK

ornate. Though its origin is hidden in the mists of the past, when its antiquity is considered, and also the devotion of the early races to the glowing orb of the sun and to terrestrial fires, it is not surprising that it has been regarded as a relic of the Zoroastrian faith of old Iran, symbolising the eternal flames before which the Parsees worshipped.

If the floral designs are more beautiful, others are more truly symbolic, and when appearing in rugs of barbaric patterns they are more interesting. Of these the creeping things are represented by the serpent, scorpion, turtle, crab, and tarantula. Among a few races of Asia the serpent, which is found in a few old Persian carpets, has been regarded as emblematic of immortality, but has been more frequently considered as the symbol of knowledge. The scorpion, also, was supposed to represent the idea of knowledge. It does not often appear in woven design, but is sometimes drawn with careful precision in Caucasian fabrics. The turtle or tortoise stands for constancy. What is called the "turtle border" (Plate E, Fig. 3, opp. Page 156), which was probably derived from interlacing arabesques, occurs most frequently in Feraghans and also in some other Persian rugs, as Muskabads, Sarabends, Serapis, and even the Sehnas. The tarantula and crab designs are found exclusively in borders of Caucasian rugs. As their resemblance to the animals they are supposed to represent is remote, it is most probable that they are simply the conventionalised forms of the star and palmette.

Among the designs seen in Chinese rugs are several not found in any others. Of these the dragon, originally intended as a symbol of the infinite, denotes imperial power; the stork, long life; the duck, conjugal felicity; the bat, happiness; and the butterfly, a spirit. These designs will be noticed in the chapter on Chinese rugs.

With few exceptions the only modern rugs in which birds are represented are the Persian. The drawing as a rule is far from natural; but in the fine old carpets it is often so accurate as to show unmistakably the order to which they belong. Several of them were used symbolically, as the bird of paradise, suggestive of felicity; the peacock, symbol of fire; the eagle, emblem of power. The attitude, to be sure, in which they appear, affects in a measure their symbolic meaning; as an eagle in flight denotes good fortune, but one in the act of descending denotes ill luck.

As the Mohammedan religion interdicts portraying birds and beasts as well as human forms, they are rarely seen in any rug of

Western Asia Minor, which is inhabited by the Sunnites, the strict conformists to the law of the Koran; but in Mohammedan countries lying farther to the east, where the Shiites or nonconformists live, animal designs are very common. In modern rugs of Persia and Caucasia, dogs, goats, and camels are the most popular animal subjects, but the drawing is often so poor that the identity is in doubt. In the old carpets, on the other hand, animals and human beings were most realistically drawn, and were intended to represent symbolically the weaver's thought.   In fact, those masterpieces of Persian art known as the "Hunting Carpets" would lose much of their interest if their many forms of animal life were without symbolic meaning. In them the lion is a symbol of victory, power, the sun, and the day; the antelope and unicorn are symbols of restfulness and the moon. The lion destroying an antelope would mean, then, the victory of day over night, or of a powerful over a weak foe. Leopards and hounds likewise symbolise success and fame.   There are also mythological creatures, as the phœnix, emblematic of life and resurrection, and the winged *djinni* or Persian spirits, that often adorn the fields and borders of some of the elaborate antique carpets of Iran.

Not only the forms of vegetable and animal life and their relative attitudes to one another were intended to convey a symbolic meaning, but among almost all ancient races colours had a special significance.   To the Moslems no colour was more sacred than the green, which, though difficult to produce in beautiful tones, they have placed in the fields of many of their prayer rugs. To them, also, blue was the emblem of eternity, and in the spandrels above the arches it was the symbol of the sky. Though to the Hindoo it denotes ill luck, it was the chosen colour of the Persians, as well as one of the imperial colours of the Chinese. Among all nations yellow, another imperial colour of China, and red are suggestive of joy and happiness. Such colours, when used in conjunction with other emblems, expressed not only beauty, but also different shades of thought.

These are but a few of the many motives that are employed by the weaver. Some of them represent objects intimately associated with his daily life. Some of them reflect his thoughts and emotions.   Others are the still unsolved hieroglyphics of his craft. When, then, we examine some old worn rug, we may see only an exquisite pattern resplendent in the deep rich colours of an art now lost; but if to an æsthetic taste be added an interest in a symbolism that expresses something of the thought and life of the weaver, we may find in the study of the various designs another charm that increases with the discovery of any previously hidden meaning.

CHAPTER VII

RUG WEAVING BEFORE THE XVIII CENTURY

HERE are no records to definitely indicate in what land the art of rug weaving originated, or to disprove that it developed independently in different lands. It would be unreasonable, then, to assume that rugs were not woven in northern regions as early as in southern. In fact, during the Neolithic age the Lake-dwellers of Switzerland grew and spun flax, and it is believed that they had looms. Moreover, it is probable that the savages of cold climates soon learned to weave garments with the long wool of their sheep or goats; and the similar process of weaving mats for the floors of their huts would naturally follow. Nevertheless, such evidence as now remains points to the civilisations of the Euphrates or the Nile, as the birthplace of this art.

Though we do not know when the first rugs were made, without a doubt they existed before the pyramids of Egypt or the palaces of Babylon had risen from the plains. Among the rock-cut tombs of Beni-Hassan in Egypt, that date from about 2500 B. C. are pictures of men with spindles, of looms and weavers. There is also unmistakable evidence of the antiquity of a high state of the textile art among the ruins in the valleys of the Tigris and the Euphrates. On carved walls of the palaces of Nineveh, where dwelt the rulers of Assyria over three thousand years ago, are elaborate drawings indicating that carpets of remarkable workmanship were then in use. In the borders of some of the robes worn by the rulers are designs of rosettes and latch-hooks, and on one is depicted the tree of life, similar to what may be seen in modern rugs. Nor are ancient writers silent. In the Old Testament are frequent references to woven fabrics. Homer, also, speaks of them in his Odyssey. Herodotus, Diodorus, Pliny, Strabo, in fact almost all classic writers have mentioned them. Moreover, designs on pottery, bowls, tiles, and walls, similar in appearance to those found in the oldest existing carpets, carry contributory evidence to their antiquity and character.

This art, that necessity created, comfort nourished, and luxury matured, has been a process of slow development. To the mind of some dark tribeswoman of the desert contemplating the rushes gathered from a sluggish stream and strewn upon the floor of her master's hut several thousand years ago, may have been suggested the first idea of a mat. Indeed, from earliest times mats of reeds, straw, bamboo, or other pliable material have been constantly made. At first they were doubtless without ornament; later they were coloured with dyes obtained from roots and herbs to increase their attractiveness; finally designs symbolic of nature or the deity were embroidered on them. As wealth and luxury increased the ornamentation became more elaborate, until during the rule of the Caliphs the mats rivalled in beauty the carpets for which, during the summer months, they were substituted. "On these mats," wrote the eminent authority, Dr. F. R. Martin, "the artist found free scope for displaying as much artistic skill as on the real carpets, and gold threads were intertwined to make them as precious as the most expensive silk and gold carpets." Long, however, before they had reached such a high state of perfection, they would have suggested the idea of making warmer and more durable floor coverings. The first of these was a simple web of warp and woof; later they assumed a character not dissimilar to the kilims now made in the lands of their origin. With further advance, more elaborate carpets and tapestries were made; but it was not until the art had been developing for a great many centuries, that there appeared those most perfect products of knotted pile that were similar in kind but superior in quality to the modern pieces.

Slow as was this development, as early as the Christian era, the work of the most skilled weavers of the Orient deserved to be classed as a fine art. During the time of the Sassanian kingdom (extending from about 226 A. D. to 632 A. D.) carpets of elaborate design and finish were produced in Mesopotamia and Syria. Most of them were of the wool of sheep or goats; and in them were represented designs of trees, birds, animals, and other figures. Other pieces were made of silk richly embroidered with silver and gold. Moreover, authentic evidence from the VI Century A. D. not only gives us positive knowledge of the marvellous workmanship of that time, but enables us to conjecture through what a long period of progression the artisans had been labouring to arrive at such results. Dr. Karabacek, director of the Imperial Library of Vienna, in his monograph "Die Persische Nadelmalerei Susandschird," gave the following description of the "Spring of Chosroes" carpet:

"When Ctesiphon, the residence of the Sassanides, fell into the hands of the Arabs in the year 637 A. D., they found in the royal palace, the ruins of which still remain, a colossal carpet of 1051 square metres,* which was originally made for Chosroes I. His successor, Anoschar (531–579 A. D.), used it also, but only during the stormy weather, when remaining in the gardens was impracticable. The festivities were then transferred to the palace, where a garden with the beauty of springtime was represented by the pattern of the carpet. This was the Winter Carpet that was called in Persia the Spring of Chosroes. Its material, which was marvellous and costly, consisted of silk, gold, silver, and precious stones. On it was represented a beautiful pleasure ground with brooks and interlacing paths, with trees and flowers of springtime. On the wide borders surrounding it were represented flower-beds in which precious stones coloured blue, red, yellow, white, and green denoted the beauty of the flowers. Gold imitated the yellow-coloured soil and defined the borders of the brooks, where the water was represented by crystals. Gravel paths were indicated by stones of the size of pearls. The stalks of trees were of gold and silver, the leaves and flowers of silk, the fruits of many-coloured stones."

As the value of this carpet was estimated at about three quarters of a million dollars, it was regarded as too precious to fall to the lot of a single captor, and was accordingly divided into segments to be distributed as booty among the soldiers. Even if during this period there was no other fabric so valuable and elaborate, it represented the importance of the textile art during the dynasty of the Sassanides.

During the Caliphate (632 to 1258 A. D.) the Moslem rulers, devoted to luxury, preserved the art treasures of their conquered subjects and encouraged them to renewed efforts. This is particularly true of the Caliphs and sultans of Syria and Egypt. A carpet that adorned the banquet hall of the Caliph Hisham of Egypt, who died 743 A. D., was of silk interwoven with strands of gold, and had a length of three hundred feet and a breadth of one hundred and

* The equivalent of 106 feet square.

PLATE 15.   PERSIAN ANIMAL CARPET IN THE METROPOLITAN MUSEUM OF ART,
NEW YORK

PLATE 16. PERSIAN ANIMAL CARPET IN THE METROPOLITAN MUSEUM OF ART,
NEW YORK

fifty feet. All of the rooms of the Egyptian palaces, occupied by the sultans, contained carpets of silk and satin; and the mosques of Syria were similarly furnished. In the year 1067 A.D. one of the Caliphs was forced to sell his accumulated treasures, which consisted, besides jewels and works of art, of about four thousand bales of carpets. Dr. Martin states that a single one of these bales contained several hundred perfect carpets, which were woven in silk and gold, and that some of them contained portraits of entire royal families. One of them, valued at about $300,000, was made for the Caliph el Mirz li alla in the year 964 A. D. It was of blue silk, on which were represented the heavens and the earth, seas and rivers, as well as the holy cities Mecca and Medina. Such was the character of some of the carpets woven during the days of the Caliphs.

As the imperfect records which have been left us indicate that the finest carpet collections of this period were in the mosques and palaces of Syria and Egypt, it has been assumed that they were woven by the native artisans. To some extent this is doubtless true, as rug weaving was one of the oldest industries of these countries. But it is more probable that most of them were made elsewhere and were acquired as presents or by purchase. Some were made in Armenia, Assyria, and Turkestan; but the largest number, as well as the most costly and elaborate, doubtless came from the same hills and towns of Persia where many of the finest pieces are woven to-day. In several of these towns as many as three or four hundred looms were constantly at work; and since the carpets consisted of warp and weft only, it is probable that they were produced far more rapidly than modern rugs in which knots are tied to the warp. But if they lacked the richness of deep, heavy pile, they were elaborately woven with threads of gold and silver, and were often embellished with precious stones.

ANTIQUE PERSIAN CARPETS

To the tendency of overestimating the age of art objects to which antiquity adds value, there is no exception in the case of Oriental rugs, yet there is good reason to believe that a few pieces still exist that were woven in Persia as early as the XIII or XIV Century. Indeed, we cannot positively affirm that there may not be religiously preserved some relic of the Seljukian dynasty, which ruled in Persia till about 1150 A.D., for we have little knowledge of what some of the old mosques which no Christian has ever entered may contain; but it is more probable that the oldest remaining pieces belong to the Mongolian period, which began with the invasion of the armies of Genghis Khan in the first half of the XIII Century. This conclusion is based partly on the facts that their archaic patterns indicate a very remote period, and that they suggest early Mongolian influences. Moreover, as the age of rugs of a somewhat later period can be determined by the evidence of similarity of their designs with those of early tiles, metal work, pottery, and miniatures, of established age, it is possible to infer the relative age of these older pieces by comparison of patterns showing a progressive development.

One of the oldest Persian pieces now existing, the property of C. F. Williams, Esq., of Norristown, Pa., is in the Metropolitan Museum of Art of New York (Plate 11, opp. Page 64). It is also one of the most interesting. In it are found Persian, Armenian, Caucasian, and Mongolian characteristics, which serve to determine the district where it was woven and to suggest its age. Its Sehna knot, cotton warp and weft, as well as much of the drawing, are typical of Persia. The tri-cleft leaf and stem seen in the two lower corners, in the main stripe, and in parts of the field are found in almost all Armenian rugs. The reciprocal sawtooth of the outer border stripe and the geometric inner stripe are Caucasian features. Certain colour tones, the octagonal discs at each end of the large central palmettes, and more particularly the tendrils or scrolls of the main stripe of the border which resemble the foliate forms as they appear in Chinese rugs and porcelains of the late Ming and Kang-hi periods, are Mongolian. The combination of these characteristics indicates that it was made in the most northwesterly part of Persia where in 1258 Hulaku Khan established his capital, and his successors ruled for over a century. Here undoubtedly the craft of weaving flourished for a long period, and exercised an important influence on the surrounding countries. To judge by the colours; the formal character of the border; the rigid lines of the large palmette motives of the field, which are not seen in carpets of a much later period; and the stiff, archaic character of the bushes with foliage and blossoms arranged mechanically on the thick trunks, it is not unreasonable to place this piece as early as the middle of the XIV Century, during the interval between the overthrow of the Seljukian dynasty by the followers of Genghis Khan and the later invasion of the

Timurids. In fact, it may be even older, since those graceful lines that belong to the highest art of a subsequent period are entirely lacking. But in the drawing is strength, and in the colours, a few of which have faded, are beauty and harmony.

Such old pieces are very rare, yet a similar one, belonging to Prof. W. Bode, is in the Kaiser Friedrich Museum at Berlin. Its drawing is more regular, and the trunks of the trees are broader. These two carpets represent the art of weaving at a very early period.

Of equal interest and higher artistic merit is another carpet (Plate 12, opp. Page 65), belonging to C. F. Williams, Esq., and at present in the Metropolitan Museum of Art but formerly in the possession of J. Böhler of Munich. It has a length of nearly seventeen feet and a breadth of nearly twelve. There are about three hundred knots to the square inch. Though much of that stiffness of drawing found in the earlier pieces remains, the more pliant branches and less regular setting of the flowers indicate a later date; so that it is not improbable that it was woven about the first of the XV Century. Dr. Martin regards this piece as one of the oldest of the Timurid period if not from the Mongolian, and says that the trees resemble those in a Mongolian miniature in the Musée des Arts Decoratifs in Paris, and in a manuscript from the year 1396. At any rate, they display more formal drawing than the trees of more recent carpets. The character of pattern and the colouring suggest that it was woven in Northwestern Persia.

The field is skilfully divided into three subfields by beds of flowers, from which slender trees rise and partly screen from view more stately cypresses. The subdivisions are further indicated by pairs of palmettes, of which the upper pair mark a transition between the lower pair and those more elegant forms commonly seen two centuries later. There are likewise palmettes of simpler form in the two guard stripes. But the principal ornamentation of the rich border is the interlacing arabesques of three different colours, which are decorated with a slender wreath of leaf and flower. There is, moreover, a particular interest in the grouping of the arabesques since they form a design which may be the prototype of the so-called turtle borders so frequently seen in Feraghans and Gorevans, and is itself derived, according to Dr. Martin, from a still older form in which branching arabesques extend across the whole field. It may not be unreasonable to assume that this pattern has been handed down from that earlier period when a Saracenic influence was felt in all the weavings.

If the chief interest in this piece is centred in the pattern, its greatest charm lies in its soft, dainty colours, some of which are exquisitely beautiful. They are expressed in delicate shades of orange, ivory, light green, sable brown, and light and dark blue on a background of pinkish red. This pattern and colouring suggest an Eastern wood when the first frost of autumn has left its touch on the leaves. The border contains the same colours as the field but is strong and effective, since the soft tones are in the narrow guard stripes and the deeper colours appear in the broad central stripe in larger masses and in immediate contact.

If this carpet was woven about 1400 A.D., as seems not improbable, the drawing of the trees, palmettes, and border designs becomes by comparison an important guide for determining the age of other antique Persian carpets.

Very different, indeed, from the preceding is a woollen piece (Plate 13, opp. Page 70), sixteen feet four inches long by eleven feet two inches wide, that was formerly in the collection of Mr. Vincent Robinson of London, but is now in the Metropolitan Museum of Art, New York, which bought it at the Yerkes sale in 1910, for $19,600. It has about six hundred knots to the square inch, and is woven with warp of cotton and silk, and with weft of silk. The pile is velvety, and the texture, drawing, and colouring display a high grade of artistic craftsmanship. Another of similar character is represented in the Vienna Publication of Oriental Carpets of 1889, at which time it belonged to the Countess Clotilde Clam-Gallas of Vienna; and a third belongs to the Palais de Commerce at Lyons.

In no other rugs from Iran is the effect of Mongolian tradition on design more noticeable; but that this was due to the Timurid invasion at the end of the XIV Century is doubtful, and it is not improbable that more immediate intervention with China determined the motives. Nor is the Saracenic influence obscured, since in every part of the field and border is seen the perfect rhythm of graceful arabesques. Such carpets represent, in fact, the transition from those earlier pieces to the higher products of Persian looms.

One of the simplest ways of studying the pattern is to regard it as consisting of a number of units formed by a large rounded octagon encircled by eight heart-shaped escutcheons, and with a

PLATE 17. SO-CALLED POLISH OR POLONAISE CARPET IN THE METROPOLITAN
MUSEUM OF ART, NEW YORK

PLATE 18.   SO-CALLED ISPAHAN IN THE METROPOLITAN MUSEUM OF ART, NEW YORK

smaller rounded octagon at the centre of the diagonal lines connecting them.   On the large octagons, which are of dark blue crossed
by narrow bands of sable brown, is represented the fight of dragon
and phœnix so common in the ornamentation of the Ming dynasty;
and in the smaller octagons, which are plum colour, are four running
lions in red, blue, and green.   The eight escutcheons alternate in
crimson and blue, and have arabesques and Chinese ducks.   The
large pentagonal-shaped areas of the ivory field are covered with a
most symmetrically drawn tracery of tendrils and flowers in red,
yellow, and blue; and in the smaller hexagonal-shaped areas are
cloud bands of similar colours.

The border shows a marked advance over that of the preceding
piece.   The main stripe, which follows a pattern that with slight
modification is adopted in many of the carpets of this and a later
period, consists of a chain-like series of octagons similar to those of
the field, separating elongated panels with crenated edges.   The
latter are adorned with cloud bands in yellow interlaced with delicate tendrils supporting flowers in red, yellow, green, and white, on
a dark blue field; and surrounding them on a red ground is also a
delicate tracery of leaves and flowers.   The outer and inner stripes
have arabesques and tendrils bearing flowers in red, green, and
blue on a ground of golden yellow.   All the colours of both field and
border have mellowed into rich, beautiful hues in which is the most
perfect harmony.

The intricacy and character of design, the delicacy of drawing,
and the tones of colour indicate that this piece was woven near the
beginning of the Safavid dynasty, in the early part of the XVI Century.   Mr. Robinson ascribes its origin to Bagdad; but it seems far
more probable that it came from the northwestern part of Persia,
which was an important centre of textile art only a few years later.
This piece and the two others described on the pages just preceding
are among the most interesting carpets now existing; for they represent not only a very high standard of the textile craft, but also
most important steps in its development.

There is no evidence to indicate how early animal carpets were
woven in Persia.   Dr. Martin found a piece with archaic drawing,
that from its resemblance to an old tile of established age, he placed
at about the year 1300 A. D.; but it was about the beginning of the
XVI Century that were woven the first of those masterly pieces
which displayed animals surrounded by a maze of floral life.   Lions,

leopards, boars, deer, and hounds were the principal motives. To each of these was ascribed some principle or quality, so that it has been assumed that the aim of the weaver was to give expression to some theme of interest.

A number of these carpets represent the chase and are called "Hunting Carpets." The best of them are regarded by Dr. Martin as belonging to the latter half of the XVI Century for reasons indicated in the following extract from his work: "The manuscript of Nizami, one of the pearls of the British Museum, which was executed in Tabriz 1539–1542 for the Shah Tamasp, has the most wonderful designs on the margins. Although the manuscripts and the miniatures are signed by Persia's most renowned masters, there is nothing to give a hint as to who has drawn these magnificent borders. This manuscript, which at the time it was written, was considered one of the most remarkable 'the like of which the eye of time never beheld,' plainly proves that the large carpets with hunting scenes must be relegated to a later time or to about 1560–1570. Both animals and trees are of a far more stately and earlier character in the manuscript."

One of the best of these pieces with animals (Plate 14, opp. Page 71) is in the Metropolitan Museum of Art, in New York, by which it was purchased at the Yerkes sale in 1910, for $15,200. It has a length of ten feet eleven inches with a breadth of five feet ten inches, and an average of four hundred and eighty knots to the square inch. Both warp and weft are of silk, and the pile is of wool. As it was confidently believed by Mr. Edward Stebbing * that this piece belonged for a long time to the Mosque of Ardebil, where Ismael had established his capital, and from which Tamasp subsequently moved; it is not improbable that it belongs to the early period, between the closing years of Ismael's reign and the first part of the reign of Tamasp.† Nor is there anything in the technique of colour or design to convey a different impression, as the general colour of the field is a claret red, and that of the border a dark blue characteristic of this period.

The most noticeable feature of the carpet is the display of animal life amid the carefully balanced arrangement of floral figures. Four-fifths of the field can be divided into two perfect squares with sides equal to the breadth of the field; and the remainder will be equiva-

* See his work, " The Holy Carpet of the Mosque at Ardebil."
† Ismael reigned, 1502–1524; Tamasp reigned, 1524–1576.

lent to one-half of one of these squares.   Each quarter of a square
contains animals, probably intended to represent a lion, leopard,
and boar, that are perfectly balanced with those of the adjacent
and alternating quarters.   Moreover, the same balance exists in
the case of the smaller animals and floral forms.   Thus it appears
that each square forms a perfect unit in which is shown a remarkable
relation between all parts.   Such mathematical exactness indicates
the highest artistic skill.   The repetition of pattern also accentuates
the predominant idea of animal life, which is rendered even more
noticeable by the strong golden yellow of some of the group.   Whoever has studied the early Iranian monuments remembers with
how slight variation some of the drawing has been copied during
subsequent generations; so that it is not surprising that Mr. Stebbing should call attention to the resemblance of some of the animals
in this carpet to those of the rock-carved sculptures of Tak-i-Bostan
near Kermanshah.

    As is the case with most modern Persian rugs, there is no corre-
spondence between the size of the animals and the flowers.   Nevertheless the lack of harmony is not felt, as the animal and the floral
life are intended to be regarded separately.   The principal flowers
of the field are peonies, some of which are woven with silver threads.
They also appear in the border arranged with perfect precision
within the folds of symmetrical cloud-bands and interlacing arabesques.   The latter form a well-executed repetitive figure that
suggests an origin for the reciprocal trefoil or lily pattern, as it is
sometimes called, which received its highest development in the
silk rugs of a later century.

    On the whole, this piece is not far short of the highest sumptu-
ary standard of a subsequent period, and is an excellent example
of the artistic development of the earliest part of the Safavid dynasty.   In few other carpets is combined such intricacy of design
with richness and simplicity of colour.

    Of still greater interest than the last is the Arbedil Carpet, now
in the South Kensington Museum.   It has a length of thirty-four
and a half feet with a breadth of seventeen and a half; the texture
shows about three hundred and twenty-five knots to the square
inch; and the pile is of wool tied to warp and weft of silk.   It has
been very carefully studied by Mr. Edward Stebbing, from whose
description the following extracts are taken:

    "The body ground is blue, covered with a floral tracery of

exquisite delicacy and freedom of treatment. A central medallion
of pale yellow terminates on its outer edge in sixteen minaret-
shaped points from which spring sixteen cartouches; four green,
four red, and eight light cream; and from two of these again, as it
were, suspended and hanging in the direction of the respective ends
of the carpet, two of the sacred lamps of the mosque.

"Quarter sections of the central medallion also on a pale yellow
ground, relieved by tracery, form the angles; while a broader
border completes the glorious design, a border of the alternate
elongated and rounded cartouches filled with floral and other tracery,
the former on a base of red, the latter on a rich brown ground flanked
on the inner side by a broad band of cream seven inches wide, relieved
by a variation of a so-called cloud pattern, and a narrower band of
crimson near the body of the carpet; and on the outer side by a
single broad band, also seven inches wide, of tawny hue, shading
from dark to light, and relieved by a bold design in blue."

But however exquisite the tracery, however delicate the colouring, the greatest interest centres in the fact that in a panel adjoining
the border of the upper end is the following inscription:

"I have no refuge in the world other than thy threshold;
"My head has no protection other than thy porchway;
"The work of the slave of the holy place, Maksoud of Kashan,
in the year 942."

Here is revealed the age of the carpet, which not only determines
the character of workmanship of a particular period, but affords a
standard for determining by comparison the relative age of other
pieces. The year 942 corresponds with our year 1539 A. D., and
the position of the date indicates that it was inscribed a little before
the completion of the fabric. Accordingly, it would not be unreasonable to assume that the carpet was begun during the closing years
of the reign of Ismael, who died at Ardebil in 1524, and that it was
finished during the reign of Tamasp I.

To infer that at this period were many such carpets would be a
mistake; since this was doubtless woven by the order of the court,
and by one of the most skilled artisans, who may have made it the
crowning labour of his life. It indicates the highest technique acquired in the early part of the Safavid dynasty.

Besides the mosque carpets, other pieces such as small prayer
rugs were used for devotional purposes. When the first of them
were made is unknown, though they existed in the days of the

Caliphs, when the words of the Prophet were still fresh in the memories of his followers; and they were also used at an early period among Turkomans. The oldest that remain belong to the early part of the Safavid rule. One that was formerly in the collection of Stefano Bardini of Florence and is now owned by Mr. Benjamin Altman, appeared at the exhibit of the Metropolitan Museum of Art in 1910. It is a woollen piece with a length of nearly five and a half feet and a breadth of three and a quarter. In the central field is a prayer arch resembling some of a later period, with outlines gracefully recurving near the base and broken on each side by a pentagonal-shaped flower. All parts of each of the two trees that rise from the bottom of the field are reversely duplicated in the other. Some of the stiffness of drawing of the earlier carpets remains, but the blossoms are clustered more naturally and the whole treatment is more skilful. The effect of the scroll-work on the red ground of the spandrel; of the suspended lamp with its bright flowers of red, yellow, and pink; and of the blossoming trees beneath, is most pleasing; but the chief interest centres in the outer border stripe, where appear features that are more interesting than harmonious, features derived from Persia, Assyria, Mongolia, and Arabia. The rounded octagons have Cufic lettering that recalls early Mesopotamian civilisation; the cartouches at the bottom with their cloud-bands suggest Mongolian conquests; and the upper cartouches contain the following verses from the Koran:

"Iman the victorious and expected Mahdi, the Lord of the Age.

Zalsi and Hason; and bless the standing proof.

Oh Lord bless Mohammed the chosen one. Ali, the elect, Fatimeh the Immaculate.

Jofer Sadik, Mooza Kazin, Ali Riza Mohammed Taki, Mohammed Nakee, Ali.

The two branches Harson and Hussein Bless Ali Zaimulubbad Mohammed Bak'r."

These verses, the archaic lamp, and the green of the field, a colour sacred to Moslems, all indicate the religious character of the carpet. Similar features also appear in another antique piece of about the same age, but the Cufic characters of the border are within squares surrounded by circles that resemble Chinese seals as they appear in early manuscripts. Both of these pieces were probably woven in Northwestern Persia about the middle of the XVI Century. Few such prayer carpets remain, though without doubt they were used by devotees during succeeding periods, and it is not unusual to see, even in modern Kermanshahs, prayer arches of the same pattern.

Of totally different character but of about the same age is an animal rug (Plate 15, opp. Page 76) that belongs to the Metropolitan Museum of Art. It was bought at the Yerkes sale in 1910, for $5,600, and had previously belonged to the collection of Vincent Robinson of London. It has a length of about seven and a half feet with a breadth of about five and a half, and consists of woollen pile tied to cotton warp crossed by woollen weft. The weave is not unlike what is seen in many modern Sarouks; as the knot is Sehna, one thread of warp is doubled under the other in each knot, and the coloured thread of weft, which crosses twice, is partly exposed at the back.

Like so many of the old Persian pieces, the ground colour of red appears in the main field, and is strongly contrasted with the dark blue of the medallion and dark green of the corners. Red and green also appear in the border contrasted with yellow. This association of colour is not usual, nor is the repetitive pattern of the border with its sharp cusps at many of the angles, nor the trapeziform corners, and the nearly rectangular medallion. Likewise the mechanically formed bushes with their quince-like fruit, on which sit birds of disproportionate size, show a departure from the accepted traditions of the Safavid schools. Yet these very features awaken new interest, and suggest that it was probably woven in some part of Northern or Western Persia where the influence of the court was not paramount. Nevertheless the accurate balance of the different halves, and the drawing of the palmettes show that it is distinctly Iranian.

If this last piece be compared with the animal rug (Plate 16, opp. Page 77) that was presented to the Metropolitan Museum of Art by Mr. Cochran, the wide contrast will at once be noticeable. As the latter has a length of about eight and two-thirds feet with a breadth of nearly six, the difference in size and proportions is not great; nor is there any particular difference in the number of animals; nor in the balanced relation of upper and lower, right and left halves; nor in the red ground of the main fields. But here the resemblance ends. Whereas in the former the animals are one of the most prominent features, in the latter they are subordinate to the rich assemblage of floral and palmette forms, that occupy not only the field but also the border. It is, indeed, a piece that marks

PLATE 19. ARMENIAN CARPET IN THE METROPOLITAN MUSEUM
OF ART, NEW YORK

PLATE 20. ASIA MINOR DRAGON AND PHOENIX CARPET IN THE KAISER
FRIEDRICH MUSEUM, BERLIN

a transition from the animal rugs, so prominent in the early part of the XVI Century but rarely woven later than its end, to the more elegant pieces, so characteristic of the court of Ispahan, which belong almost exclusively to the XVII Century. It accordingly seems not without reason to assign it to about the year 1600.

Not only do these different elements that denote a transition add interest; they also give a most pleasing effect. The main border stripe of a rich green with its well-drawn palmettes surrounded by vines and foliated stalks, on which rest naturally drawn birds of handsome plumage, and the chaste floral designs of the narrow guards, serve as a tasteful frame to the central picture. Here again the outer field, with artistic effect, brings into greater relief the central medallion, where on a ground of greenish yellow, standing and seated amidst blossoming shrubs in red, blue, and green, as in a garden, are richly dressed human forms. Apart from these, yet perhaps intended in some way to reflect the tenor of their thoughts, are four ducks, emblematic of matrimonial happiness. Whatever may have been the original shade of the central medallion, it is now slightly out of harmony with the surrounding colours, and is perhaps the only jarring note in this exquisite piece of workmanship. Not improbably the present shade is due to the unfriendly hand of time, since the artistic genius of the weaver is fully displayed in the masterly arrangement of other colours and in the delicacy and precision of the drawing of the perfectly balanced floral and animal forms.

The difficulty of determining the locality where the antique carpets were woven is often greater than in the case of modern rugs, but this piece was probably one of the last of those fine old animal carpets that were woven in the northwestern part of Persia.

Though modern silk rugs fail to awaken the interest of woollen pieces, the old silk carpets were formerly regarded as the choicest products of weaving. As a rule, they were the work of the most skilled artists employed in the imperial factory under the direction and patronage of the court. It was during the reign of Shah Tamasp that they received special attention. Following a custom that had been in vogue of sending carpets as presents to foreign courts, in 1566 he sent to the Sultan of Constantinople a number of pieces on which flowers, birds, and animals were woven with silk on threads of gold. But it was doubtless after his successor Shah Abbas I had begun to embellish his capital at Ispahan, that were made the famous "Polish" silk or "Polonaise" carpets about which there has been so much controversy. It is true that Mr. Robinson in his "Eastern Carpets" claims that they were woven in Poland by Persians taken there by a Pole named Mersherski; but it seems far more probable that they were woven under the supervision of the Persian court and were either sent as presents to European sovereigns or purchased by wealthy connoisseurs of art.

How many of these pieces may be hidden away in the palaces and mosques of the far East it is impossible to determine, but two hundred would be a very conservative estimate of the number owned by the different courts of Europe and by private collectors of that country and America. One of them was presented to the Danish court as late as 1639; and it is believed that all that reached Europe arrived there between the years 1604 and 1650.

Their beauty is exquisite and chaste. To the threads of silver and gold is tied silken nap that often displays a striking brilliancy. Unlike the earlier Persian carpets which had more subdued hues, these pieces have light tones such as salmon, rose, and green, which are arranged with perfect harmony. Moreover, there is an elegance of design representing the highest types of Iranian, Saracenic, and Mongolian influences combined. Here in perfection are dainty floral forms, the rhythmic tracery of arabesques, and delicate cloudbands. In them the textile art of the East reached a perfection that probably has never been surpassed.

One of these (Plate 17, opp. Page 80), that has a length of about nine feet and a breadth of five and a half, belongs to the Metropolitan Museum of Art. In many respects it is typical of its class, though threads of yellow and grey are substituted for the usual gold and silver of the foundation. On a field of rose are outlined palmettes, leaves, and scrolls in green, blue, brown, and salmon, that harmonise with the light blue of the border. All of these colours blend with pleasing effect and soften lines that in a print seem harsh. Furthermore with all its complexity of detail, every part of the pattern is arranged with mathematical precision. That a carpet with such perfect balance of every part, such intricacy of elaborate detail, such graceful curves of the heavy foliate leaves should be woven without copying some older pattern or a carefully executed drawing, seems improbable.

In this piece and in others of the same class can be recognised what is probably the prototype of more conventionalised and less elegant designs so often seen in modern Persian pieces, since the palmette with encircling lancet leaves in its borders is most suggestive of the borders of modern Herats; and the rhomboidal-shaped figure connecting four palmettes at the centre is equally suggestive of the Herati or fish pattern seen in the field of innumerable Feraghans.

It was also during the reign of Shah Abbas * and his immediate successors that most of the so-called Ispahans were woven, though some of them appeared as early as the XV and some as late as the close of the XVII Century. As in the case with the Polish silk carpets, within recent years some difference of opinion has existed regarding the place of their manufacture. After careful research, Dr. Martin believes that they came from Herat and with this idea some other authorities concur. It is true that Herat belonged to the Persian Empire during the reign of the Safavid dynasty, and that even in the days of Shah Ismael magnificent carpets were woven there. It is also true that during the time of Tamasp and Abbas it was as important an art centre as Tabriz, and that the weaving of carpets was a leading industry there. Furthermore, there has not been found the same evidence to show that Ispahan was at this period an equally important centre of weaving. On the other hand, it is well known that the splendid industrial and art products of this period were largely due to the direct encouragement and favour of the court, and that the court was for most of the time at Ispahan. It is also known that skilled artisans were repeatedly removed from one district to another at the command of a sovereign, so that carpets of similar character might be woven contemporaneously in remote parts of Persia. It accordingly seems not improbable that the original type of these carpets was evolved at Herat and that many of them at least were made at Herat, but that others were also made at Ispahan. At any rate they were made to a great extent under the influence that emanated from Ispahan.

Almost without exception they are pieces of large size and oblong shape. The ground colour of the field is usually red, the border blue; but blue is occasionally used in the field and green in the border. Their distinguishing feature is the use of the palmette, that was probably derived from the lotus, so frequently associated with the Buddhist cult of India and China. In the field it gener-

* 1586–1628.

ally occurs in pairs that slightly vary in size. Of almost equal importance are the Chinese cloud-bands and the scrolls or arabesques. These three designs were constant motives in almost all the Ispahans; but they were subject to modifications in size and shape, which appearing in chronological order furnish some guide to the time when the carpets were woven. For instance, the palmettes were at first small and distributed plentifully over the field; later they became larger, until in a few instances they were a yard in diameter. Dr. Martin says that in the first part of the XVII Century the palmettes began to be very large and the richness of the interior design to disappear; until at the end of the XVII Century only a few were sufficient to cover the ground that one hundred years before was almost hidden by innumerable designs of small palmettes, cloud-bands, and scroll work. He also states that towards the middle of the XVII Century the borders began to lose their importance and that the palmettes were surrounded by two long, narrow leaves.

Though most of the antique Iranian carpets that remain were woven in the Northern provinces, it is well known that even from earliest times carpets of elaborate design and skilful technique were also woven in Southern Persia. In fact, many of the wonderful pieces that adorned the palaces and mosques of the Fatimid Caliphs of Egypt came from the districts of Fars and Kirman. The latter, notwithstanding invasions of Seljukian Turks, Mongolians, and Afghans, has continued almost uninterruptedly as a centre of the textile industry; yet comparatively few pieces exist that were woven there three or four centuries ago. Their colour scheme harmonises more with that of the carpets of Western Persia than with the more sombre tones of the old animal carpets and Ispahans, or with the brighter hues of the so-called Polish. Their patterns also show a distinction from those of northern textile fabrics. The fields are often artificially divided, by foliate stalks or lance-shaped leaves with serrated edges, into rhomboidal figures that contain mechanically drawn shrubs, palmettes, or flowers. In the main stripe of the border are generally represented interlacing arabesques adorned with flowering vines or arabesques and a subpattern of vines. Mongolian designs are rarely seen in any of these pieces, which probably represent more closely than any other Persian carpets native art unaffected by foreign influences. Almost all of them are now owned in Europe.

Of the early rugs, those woven in Armenia are far less known than those from Persia. Nevertheless, it may reasonably be assumed that the high culture that was manifested in Bagdad and Ctesiphon during the sway of the Caliphs was felt among the mountainous districts to the north; and that the Seljukian rulers, who left such artistic monuments in the old Armenian capitals, appreciated and encouraged the manufacture of fine woollen fabrics. In fact, Marco Polo, who travelled through that region during the latter part of the XIII Century, referred to them as being remarkably handsome.

Probably the oldest remaining pieces are the so-called Dragon carpets, which, it is believed, were produced from the XIV to the XVII Century and possibly even earlier. Not infrequently the length is at least twice the breadth; the very narrow border occasionally consists of only a single stripe; and the field is occupied by a trellis-like pattern of narrow, conventionalised leaves, within which are designs containing archaic flowers and dragons. The ground colour of the field is generally some shade of red, that of the border white, and the leaves are yellow, blue, or green. In the borders of many of them appear an S motive from which undoubtedly was derived the design so frequently seen in panels of more recent Asia Minor prayer rugs.

In the Metropolitan Museum of Art of New York is a XV Century carpet (Plate 19, opp. Page 86), which, though widely differing from these pieces in general pattern, so closely resembles them in the essential characteristics of weave and colour that it is unquestionably of the same class. The field is occupied by concentric diamonds with stepped sides. The encircling bands, that are mostly red, yellow, and violet, and the corners, that are white, contain numerous archaic forms, including palmettes, trees, birds, and animals. There are also numerous small designs of the tri-cleft leaf so common to the Circassian and Soumak rugs; and the ray-like edges of the central lozenge, as well as the four palmettes that rest upon it, suggest the origin of the effulgent stars of old Daghestans and Kabistans. An effort has been made to balance similar designs in corresponding parts of the field, though its centre is at one side of the geometric centre of the diamonds. The palmettes show distinctly a strong Persian influence and the animal forms likewise show that it was not woven by a sectarian Sunnite of Western Asia Minor.

Part of a very unusual carpet (Plate 20, opp. Page 87), from a district in Eastern Asia Minor, is in the Kaiser Friedrich Museum at Berlin. Its principal interest lies in the fact that it is very old and that its approximate age has been determined. In the hospital at Siena, Italy, a similar rug is represented in a fresco called the "Wedding of the Foundling," painted by Domenico di Bartolo about the year 1440, so that it is reasonable to conclude that this particular piece was woven not much later. In fact, its character would indicate that it or some other from which it has been copied was much older. Each of the nearly square compartments contain octagons, within which on a yellow field are represented the mythical fight of the dragon and phœnix that was adopted as the Ming coat of arms. It is interesting to note that the chain pattern of the brownish-black main border stripe is not unlike what is seen in modern pieces, but the running latch hooks of the corners and the small S designs are unusually stiff. This disposition to formal drawing, which is conspicuous in all parts of the rug, shows an archaic style noticeable only in the very earliest carpets.

In the celebrated painting of Georg Gyze (Plate 21, opp. Page 92) which hangs in the Berlin Gallery, is represented a rug of a class so frequently seen in the paintings of Hans Holbein that they are known as "Holbein rugs." Their marked dissimilarity to those previously described indicates that they were woven under different circumstances if not in different regions. Neither in the fields nor borders is any trace of Mongolian or Persian influences; and the absence of all floral, leaf, and animal forms so usual in most antique carpets is noticeable. Indeed, the fact that animal forms rarely appear in the art of the Sunni Mohammedans aids in determining the place of their origin. They came from Asia Minor or Western Armenia.

It has generally been assumed that they were woven in Western Asia Minor, because they were purchased there in former centuries and taken thence to Europe; but they possess many features that indicate they may have been woven farther to the east, whence many could easily have been transported westward in caravans. Their borders contain the well-known pattern derived from Cufic letters which, more conventionalised, appears in later years only in such rugs as the Kabistans and Daghestans of Eastern Caucasia. Most of them also contain the small octagonal discs and larger octagonal figures with Greek crosses at the centre that suggest forcibly the designs of Southeastern Caucasia. The narrow stripes

PLATE 21.   PORTRAIT OF GEORG GYZE BY HANS HOLBEIN, SHOWING A HOLBEIN
RUG WITH CUFIC BORDER

PLATE 22. OUSHAK CARPET

Loaned by C. F. Williams, Esq., to the Metropolitan Museum of
Art, New York

of ribbon and chain pattern found in many of them also are very common in Caucasian rugs; so that it seems not improbable that these Holbein rugs were made within the boundaries of that greater Armenia which, embracing the upper Mesopotamian valley, extended over the eastern part of Asia Minor and the southern part of modern Caucasia.

These rugs claim the attention not only because they have borders of such interesting origin, but by the fact that the age when they were woven is ascertainable. As Holbein lived between the years 1497 and 1543, and some other rugs of this type appear in the works of early Flemish and Italian painters, it may reasonably be assumed that some of them were made before the end of the XV Century.

A very excellent example of this class, owned by Mr. C. F. Williams, is now in the Metropolitan Museum of Art. It has a length of about five feet with a breadth of three and a half. The ground colour of the field is an olive green and that of the main stripe of the border is red. The prevailing colours of the designs, which are entirely geometric, are blue, green, and ivory. All of these rugs are small or of moderate size, and are slightly oblong. Some of them have a ground colour of green; and yellow is frequently found in the pattern. The weaving is rather loose; and compared with Persian rugs they have fewer knots to the square inch.

Another carpet from Asia Minor that also belongs to Mr. C. F. Williams appears in Plate 22, opp. Page 93. It is the only entire rug with this pattern that is known, though a piece of a similar rug is in the Victoria and Albert Museum at London. On fields of blue and red are outlined three large four-pointed stars separated by smaller diamonds. Within these figures and in the surrounding field is a network of tracery supporting conventionalised leaf and floral forms. Between the field and the main stripe of the narrow border is a close co-ordination of pattern, but the simple ribbon of the inner guard seems alien. It appears without modification in many later Asia Minor and Caucasian rugs.

An important feature are the double knots at the corners of the stars, since they are identical with designs found in a manuscript made for one of the Shahs in 1435, and thus assist to determine the age of the rug. For this reason and on account of its general character, it seems not unreasonable to place it as early as the middle of the XV Century.

Similar carpets were woven during a long period, and it is probable that in the latter half of the following century they were largely influenced by the weavers that Solyman the Magnificent, after capturing Tabriz in 1534, transported to his own country. The same general features still remained, but the detail was more elaborate and ornate. Arabesques, palmettes, and floral forms, both of field and border, resembled more nearly the Iranian character. But at a later period, after the beginning of the general decadence to which every industry and art were subject, the patterns became much simpler, and the colours were reduced almost exclusively to red and blue with a little green. At length, both pattern and colours assumed the type of modern Oushaks, that by a slow process of devolution originated from these antique pieces.

In Armenia and Asia Minor it is probable that weaving existed before the Christian era, and that the earliest carpets which remain, though affected by more eastern influences, are largely the product of an indigenous art. But in India it was otherwise. It is true that Sir George Birdwood is authority for the statement that the Saracens introduced carpet-weaving there; but it is most probable that at the time of the invasion of the armies of Tamerlane and during the lives of many of his successors, whatever carpets were woven were very crude. Even when the Moguls began to build and embellish palaces, they obtained their carpets from Persia. But at length Shah Akbar established manufacturies at Lahore about the year 1580, and invited Persian weavers to settle there. From them the native workmen acquired much of their knowledge of patterns and technique.

It was during the reign of Shah Jahan (1628–1658), builder of the famous peacock throne and Taj Mahal, that most of the choicest pieces that now remain were woven. In delicacy of texture they rival those of any other country, and it is not unusual to find pieces with nearly eight hundred knots to the square inch; moreover, all their designs are depicted with remarkable clearness of definition. One of the most noted of these carpets is the woollen piece, about eight yards long by two and a half wide, that was made at the royal factory at Lahore and presented to the Girdlers Company of London in 1634. The mingling of leaf and floral forms, as well as the Herati designs of rosette and crumpled leaf, on a field of red, shows unmistakably its relation to Persian carpets. At the same period were woven large numbers of others with fields covered with an imposing display of superbly drawn flowers, of which every part from root to leaf tips was represented with astonishing realism. Another class included the animal or hunting carpets, which unlike their Persian prototypes seem intended not so much to portray symbolically some historic event or abstract idea, as to convey a correct impression of an actual event.

One of these, a woollen piece with a length of eight and a quarter feet and a breadth of five and a quarter, is in the Boston Museum of Fine Arts. The inspiration was from some old Persian piece, but the rendering is peculiarly Indian. In this representation of an Oriental jungle is a strange mingling of the real and unreal. The struggle of a monster bird with a winged beast, half lion, half elephant, and the demoniac faces of the border suggest the inspiration of early pagan mythology; but the movements of the running gazelles and the stealthily creeping tiger, the attitude of the driver of the cart and his attendant, are most natural. The drawing as a whole is exceedingly delicate. The ground colour of the field is the red of most Ispahans and Herats of this period, but the border is a cream colour, a combination not in accord with Persian tradition. The other colours are fawn, blue, pink, grey and brown. It is probably the only Indian hunting carpet of its kind.

Few strictly antique carpets from other countries of the Orient are known. Of the innumerable pieces that were surely woven in Caucasia and Western Turkestan before the end of the XVII Century, scarcely a vestige can be found. Nor are there many from the looms of Syria, though in the days of the Caliphs every mosque was adorned with magnificent carpets. It is true a few sterling pieces of Saracenic character, that have been ascribed to the region about Damascus, still exist. There are also a few rare and beautiful pieces that have come to light in China.* But of the countless thousands that in almost every country of the Orient once covered floors of palaces and mosques, representing one of the most refined arts, now nearly lost, only an insignificant fraction remains.

* These will be considered in a later chapter.

CHART INDICATING PERIODS WHEN ANTIQUE CARPETS WERE MADE

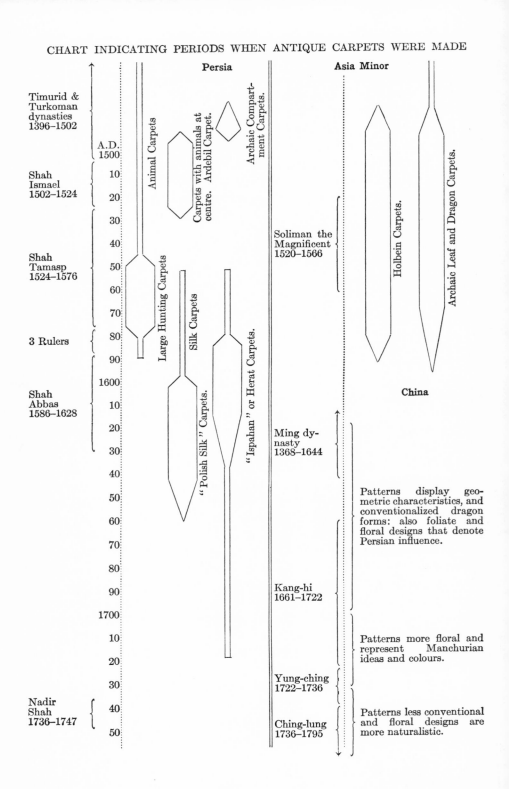

CHAPTER VIII

CLASSIFICATION OF MODERN RUGS

UGS contribute to the comfort of the nomad more than any other fabric. With them he closes the entrance to his tent or covers the floor and couches on which he sits and sleeps. Thrown over other objects they form the table, made into saddle bags they take the place of trunks. The followers of Islam when at prayer kneel on a rug, and in token of affection spread one over the grave of a friend. To dwellers in cities, also, rugs contribute largely to the comfort and luxury of the home. Indeed, without them the splendour of Oriental life would seem incomplete, since they are the principal furnishings of every house, where stout woven pieces with long pile are spread as floor coverings, and lighter ones are hung as portières and tapestries. Yet it is in the assembly or dining hall that the finest rugs are used, though here the most valued are exposed only on great occasions.

In the East a rug receives a particular name according to which of these special purposes it is adapted. The large, almost square piece that is used to cover the centre of the assembly hall is known as the "Khali;" and the narrow strips or "runners" that are placed at its sides and ends are known as the "Kenares." It is on the Kenares that the servants are required to walk and the less honoured guests to stand, for they are rarely of such fine quality as the former. Before the divan, that generally surrounds three walls and is covered with fine cloth and velvet, are seats on which are placed carpets called "Sedjadeh." They are nearly twice as long as broad, and since they are of moderate size and excellent quality they are frequently used for many other purposes. The hearth rug, termed "Odjalik," can generally be distinguished from others, as each end of the field is of triangular shape with the apex at the extremity. However much any of these may be valued, the one that to every worshipper of Allah has the most sacred association is the "Namaz-lik," or prayer rug, at one end of which is an arch in token of the mosque. At call for prayer the faithful Moslem spreads his rug with arch directed towards Mecca, and kneeling with the palms of his hands at each side of the centre he bows his head till it touches the rug. As the Mohammedans of Persia are unwilling that a Namazlik be trampled by the foot of an infidel, few from there can be bought; but the Mohammedans of other countries are less scrupulous, so that many of the prayer rugs sold in America have been made solely for trade and have never been used in worship. They may be beautiful, but special interest attaches to old pieces of which the well-worn nap shows where the knees of both father and son for over half a century have often pressed. In addition to these are other rugs with technical names, but a classification of much greater importance is that which depends on the country or district where they are woven.

When the Oriental rugs first appeared in the market of the United States, they were spoken of as "Turkish," for the reason that import-ers purchased them from Turkish merchants of Constantinople. But when it became known that they had been taken there by caravans from countries farther to the east, and that large numbers of them came from Persia, the name "Persian," that to the mind of many conveys ideas of splendour, was at once applied; even to-day all classes of Ori-ental rugs are often spoken of as Persian. As objects of ornament or utility, their value is independent of their place of origin; yet it is known that the wool of the nap and the dyes used in some dis-tricts are superior to those in others, and that in consequence the beauty of some rugs will improve with age far more than that of others. It is also known that because in certain districts the material of warp and weft, as well as the workmanship, is of a superior quality, the rugs made there will wear better than others. The knowledge, then, of where a rug is made is important in determining the quality and value, which otherwise only a critical examination, that few people are able to make, would show.

Furthermore, the knowledge of where a rug is made, suggesting the class of people who wove it, adds immeasurably to our interest. When, for instance, we look at an old piece of Kurdish weave with its nomadic designs and shaggy nap, on which a Moslem savage as an Apache often rested fully half a century ago, there is called up a picture of the dark-visaged tribesman, fearless and untamed as were his ancestors who contested the march of Xenophon over two thousand years ago. We see him wandering with his flocks over the hills while he watches for a chance to fall upon an unsuspecting stranger. We picture to ourselves the hut of brush upon the mountain side where a slender barbaric girl bends to tie, with wonderful patience, the knots one by one. So if we would enjoy our Oriental rugs, we should know what people made them, and whence and how they journeyed, before they reached our fireside.

At the request of a purchaser the vendor is ever ready to classify a rug, but his statements are not always reliable. This is partly due to the fact that even the great importing houses are often deceived. Throughout Asia Minor, Persia, Turkestan, even farther east, great fairs are regularly held. Here gather the representatives of tribes from far distant quarters to enjoy for a few days or weeks the gay life and abandon of the East while bartering the products of their different crafts. Here come the purchasing agents looking for rugs; and the pieces that may be brought from afar are bought and shipped by camel and rail to such great marts as Tabriz, Tiflis, and Constantinople, where the bales are unpacked and the rugs assorted, classified and labelled, before they are resold to the importing houses of Europe and America. Thus both in the buying from the itinerant agent of rugs assembled from different quarters and in the reassortment at the exporting cities there is frequent opportunity for errors of classification.

The characteristics of the different groups and classes of rugs are given in later chapters, but it should not be presumed that these are infallible guides to the locality where they were made. Often a ruler, by fostering art, has drawn to his capital artists and artisans from other districts. Thus designs and quality of workmanship characteristic of one district would be adopted in another. So, too, the great caravans that pass along regular routes eastward and westward, and the annual pilgrimages to Meshed and Mecca, have been most potent influences for the dissemination of designs. Yet taking into consideration the general pattern and smaller designs; the material of warp, weft, and pile; the knot; the dyes; the finish of sides and ends, and the peculiarities of the weave, it is possible with a reasonable amount of certainty to determine in what districts almost all Oriental rugs are woven.

It should be borne in mind, however, that the names by which some of the rugs are known in America are not the same as those by which they are known in Asia. For instance, the rugs made by some of the tribes of the Tekke Khanate are known in the Orient as "Tekkes;" but as the great depot for Turkestan carpets was formerly the city of Bokhara, they are generally known in this country as "Bokharas."   On the other hand, there are local distinctions in the eastern countries not known in the western. The accompanying classification, therefore, is slightly arbitrary, but should be convenient for reference; since the classes represent the cities or districts where are woven the several different kinds, excepting the Chinese, which are divided chronologically. The names of the groups are not in each instance entirely satisfactory, but are probably the best that can be chosen. The fourth group, for example, has frequently been called the "Turkoman;" but as it includes some of the rugs of Afghanistan, and also those of Beluchistan, which is remote from Turkestan, that name is not sufficiently comprehensive. The district where these rugs are made is, strictly speaking, the western and southwestern part of Central Asia; but the term here employed has the authority of some German writers of note. So, too, the rugs of Herat, though it is now a city of Afghanistan, are included with the Persian group; but it should be remembered that Herat, as well as the districts of Mosul and Kurdistan, was once part of the old Persian Empire.

GROUP I. PERSIAN.

(a) Khorassan district:
　　Herat, Khorassan, Meshed.
(b) Shiraz district:
　　Ispahan, Kirman, Yezd, Shiraz, Niris.
(c) Feraghan district:
　　Feraghan, Hamadan, Kara-Geuz, Bibikabad, Iran, Sarouk, Kashan, Sarabend, Burujird, Sultanabad, Muskabad, Mahal, Joshaghan, Gulistan, Teheran.
(d) Sehna district, or Adelan province:
　　Sehna, Bijar, Kermanshah, Persian Kurdistan, Karaje.
(e) Tabriz district:
　　Tabriz, Gorevan, Bakshis, Serapi, Herez, Suj-Bulak, Karadagh, Afshar.
(f) Kurdistan district:
　　Western Kurdistan, Mosul, Gozene.

GROUP II. ASIA MINOR OR TURKISH.

(*a*) West Asia Minor district:
Bergamo, Ghiordes, Kulah, Oushak, Ak-Hissar, Demirdji, Kutayah, Smyrna, Melez, Isbarta, Rhodian, Broussa, Hereke.
(*b*) Central Asia Minor district:
Konieh, Ladik, Kir-Shehr, Anatolian, Karaman, Sivas, Mudjar, Nigde, Tuzla, Kaisariyeh, Zile, Yuruk.

GROUP III. CAUCASIAN.

(*a*) North Caucasian:
Daghestan, Kabistan, Kuba, Derbend, Lesghian, Chichi, Tcherkes.
(*b*) Trans Caucasian:
Baku, Shirvan, Soumak, Shemakha, Tiflis, Kutais, Kazak, Karabagh, Shusha, Gengha.

GROUP IV. CENTRAL ASIATIC.

(*a*) West Turkoman sub-group, Western influence:
Royal Bokhara, Princess Bokhara, Tekke, Yomud, Khiva, Afghan, Beshir.
(*b*) East Turkoman sub-group, Eastern influence:
Samarkand, Kashgar, Yarkand.
(*c*) Beluchistan.

GROUP V. INDIAN.

(*a*) Northern India:
Srinagar, Amritsar, Lahore, Multan, Agra, Allahabad, Mirzapur, Zabalpur, Patna, Jaipur.
(*b*) Southern India:
Madras, Mysore, Bangalore, Warangal, Malabar, Hyderabad, Marsulipatam.

GROUP VI. CHINESE.[1]

(*a*) XVII Century:
Late Ming 1600–1643 and Early Kang-hi (1662–1700).
(*b*) XVIII Century:
1. Late Kang-hi (1700–1722). 2. Yung-ching (1722–1736). 3. Keen-lung (1736–1795).
(*c*) Early and Middle XIX Century.
(*d*) Late XIX Century or Modern.

[1] This group includes both antique and modern rugs.

CHAPTER IX

PERSIAN RUGS

I N the grouping of Oriental rugs, it is not always desirable to follow the present political divisions of territory, since great and frequent changes in national boundaries have occurred without corresponding changes in the traditional style of weaving. Thus it happens that with the rugs made in Persia, which is still called Iran by its inhabitants, it is desirable to group those made within that former Iran that included the valley of Mesopotamia on the west and part of Afghanistan on the east. The woven products of all this territory have characteristics that are similar to one another and that differentiate them from those of other countries. Their patterns are distinctly floral, representing leaf, bud, and flower, and show a tendency to naturalistic drawing with graceful and often intricate lines. Moreover, their colour schemes of delicate tones are not only beautiful but in perfect harmony. In marked contrast with them are the rugs of Caucasia, Asia Minor, and Central Asia, which have patterns of geometric shape or highly conventionalised flower forms, and colours that often appear in bold contrast. In the Chinese rugs, also, is generally less harmony of colour, as well as less co-ordination of design, than in the Persian. The scroll and floral patterns appear on the field in isolated figures, or else imitate with more formal drawing the diaper pattern of some Iranian carpets. Only in the rugs of India is there a similarity to the patterns and colour tones of those of Persia; but the designs are more realistically drawn, less artistically arranged, and less profuse.

The similarity in the rugs of the Persian group is due to past political influences as well as to common ties of race and religion. From the time when Ctesiphon and Babylon vied with the cities of Persia in the splendour of their capitals, all of this territory was repeatedly under one and the same dominant power, which at different times was held by Saracens, Seljukian Turks, Timurids, and Safavids; and even after the end of the Safavid dynasty the influence of Nadir Shah was felt over Mesopotamia as well as Western Afghanistan. A still stronger influence is that of race; for Aryans, Arabs, Armenians, and Turks have blended with the early people of the whole territory, until not only do all resemble one another, but their craftsmanship is similar. Furthermore, with the exception of a few rapidly disappearing Parsees, who still cling to the early Zoroastrian faith, all are Mohammedans; and in their frequent pilgrimages to the same shrines is a constant interchange of ideas and exchange of fabrics. It is true Asia Minor, Caucasia, and India have shared to some extent the same influences, but to a much less degree.

A resemblance, also, exists between many of the physical features of the entire country that affect the habits and industries of the people. To be sure the Euphrates and Tigris, that wind sluggishly through the great Mesopotamian valley, and the great ranges of the Elburz and Zagros, that extend from Mt. Ararat easterly and southeasterly through Persia, have no counterpart; but on the other hand in Mesopotamia, Persia, and Western Afghanistan are great stretches of sandy wastes where there is little vegetation, high tablelands where during rainless summer months the earth is parched, and little valleys of fertile soil that are watered by streams from the encircling mountain ridges. Throughout this territory, wherever physical conditions are similar, the people follow similar pursuits. In the deserts the impoverished Bedouins live; in the higher lands some two millions of nomads follow their sheep and goats, pitching their tents wherever there is pasture; in the valleys are several millions of people, who, with the placid contentment of the East, irrigate their garden patches, fashion simple articles of metal, and weave artistic rugs.

A general decadence in social, political, and industrial life pervades the whole country; yet due partly to the inheritance of a past associated with the glories of Persepolis and Ecbatana, Babylon and Nineveh, Bagdad and Ctesiphon, and to the more immediate influence of the textile masterpieces of three centuries ago, rugs are still produced that in delicacy of weave, beauty of design, and harmony of colours surpass those of any other part of the world. In the weave of the best examples is displayed a technical skill only approached by a few of the Royal Bokharas. In the fine rhythm of lines and in the colour scheme of harmonious and delicate tones, with which a few of the best products of India alone compare, is united the touch of both artist and artisan. The fields of the old pieces are lavishly covered with intricate designs of buds and blossoms supported by vines or tendrils, and frequently encircled by arabesques that interlace so as to form an harmonious whole. The fields of the modern pieces are frequently of solid colour, with central medallions and triangular corners defined by graceful lines. Again, the ground colour of the field, which is either uniform or slightly shading from one end to the other, is covered with realistically drawn or conventionalised floral designs that are arranged with studied precision, and are now and then relieved by some nomadic design. Surrounding the fields are borders of several stripes, some of which contain an undulating vine with pendent flowers or palmettes co-ordinate in drawing and colouring with the main pattern. It is, however, principally in the colours, which are delicate yet rich, subdued yet lustrous, that these rugs surpass all others. Their most distinctive tones are blues, reds, browns, and greens, so arranged that the ground colours of border and field generally contrast yet remain in perfect harmony; as where there is some moss green in border and wine colour in field, each being subordinated to other superimposed colours representing floral detail.

The best known of the floral patterns, repeated with formal precision throughout the field, is the Herati pattern, which is of uncertain antiquity and origin. It consists of a central figure that generally represents a rose, but sometimes a peony or rosette, about which are grouped other figures like crumpled or lance-shaped leaves. Probably both the central and encircling figures are of Persian origin, though the latter have been regarded by some authorities as representing fish and attributed to Egypt or to China; in fact, they are occasionally drawn so as distinctly to show eyes and fins. Very frequently four of these figures are arranged about a lattice-shaped design with pendants and a central rosette, as in Plate O, Fig. 4 (Page 291). This Herati or Fish Pattern, as it is frequently called, appears in many of the old Persian rugs and in most of the modern pieces, particularly the Feraghans and Herats. A less frequently seen floral pattern, which has been used from a very remote time and is still represented in modern rugs, is the Guli Hinnai, or Flower of Hinnai (Plate O, Fig. 3). Of this plant Mohammed was so fond that he called it the "chief of this world and the next."

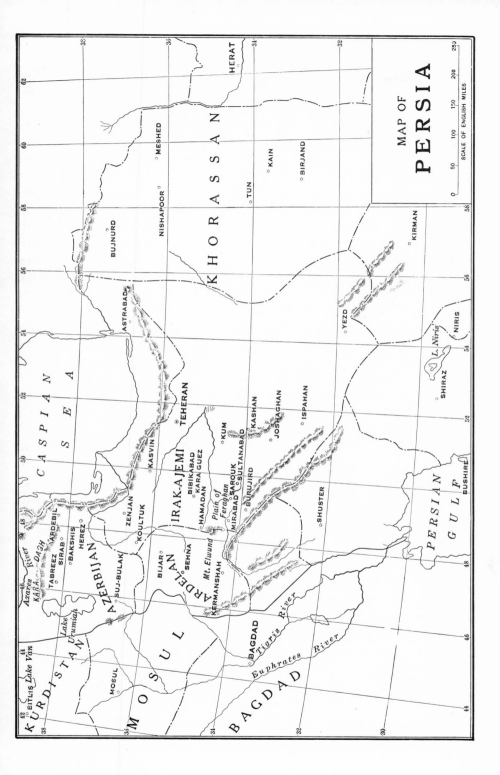

MAP OF

PERSIA

SCALE OF ENGLISH MILES

0   50   100   150   200   250

HERAT

MESHED

K H O R A S S A N

BUJNURD

NISHAPOOR

TUN

KAIN

BIRJAND

KIRMAN

ASTRABAD

YEZD

NIRIS

L. Niris

SHIRAZ

C A S P I A N

S E A

TEHERAN

KASVIN

KOULTUK

ZENJAN

HEREZ

BAKSHIS

SIRAB

TABREEZ

ARDEBIL

KARA DAGH

Axares River

Lake Van

BITLIS

K U R D I S T A N

Lake Urumiah

A Z E R B I J A N

SUJ-BULAK

MOSUL

M O S U L

BIJAR

SEHNA

A R D E L A N

KERMANSHAH

Mt. Elwund

Plain of Feraghan

BAGDAD

Tigris River

Euphrates River

B A G D A D

I R A K - A J E M I

BIBIKABAD

KARA GUEZ

HAMADAN

SAROUK

MIRABAD

SULTANABAD

BURUJIRD

KUM

KASHAN

JOSHAGHAN

ISPAHAN

SHUSTER

P E R S I A N

G U L F

BUSHIRE

62

60

58

56

54

52

50

48

46

44

42

38

40

44

46

48

50

52

54

56

58

34

36

32

31

32

30

PLATE 23. SEHNA RUG

It occurs as a formal pattern in many of the Feraghans, and in several other rugs in which its bright five-petalled flowers are scattered informally over the field. Another floral pattern frequently seen is the Mina Khani, illustrated in Plate O, Fig. 2, that was named after Mina Khan, a former Persian ruler. It is particularly characteristic of Persian Kurdish pieces in which a dark blue field is covered by a network of intersecting olive-coloured vines. At the intersections are placed large flowers that alternate in regular series according to their different designs and colours; and between them often appear other flowers, such as the smaller and brighter coloured Hinnai, so as to destroy too great stiffness of design. As the flowers are relatively large and sufficiently separate to show the intervening blue field, this is one of the most effective of the formal repetitive floral patterns. A still more formal pattern (Plate O, Fig. 1), which appeared in some of the Persian rugs of the XVI and XVII centuries, was named after Shah Abbas. It is not unlikely that it was suggested by the Mina Khani design, to which it bears a slight resemblance; but the principal motive is so conventionalised that it has lost much of the floral character. Between the large and formal palmettes, that are arranged with mathematical precision, are grouped with similar regularity smaller palmettes, connected by angular vines and leafy branches.

Only a few Persian rugs have the formal repetitive patterns, such as the Herati, Guli Hinnai, Mina Khani, and Shah Abbas. Others have the repetitive pattern of bushes, flowers, or the pear, on a field of rich colour. The remainder have patterns consisting largely of scrolls, vines, or tendrils, drawn with exquisite art and decorated with leaves, flowers, and buds in beautiful profusion; also birds, beasts, human beings, demons, and other imaginary shapes, sometimes associated with the foliage but frequently bearing no apparent relation to it, appear as special motives. Since many of these forms, which originated in the remote past, have been transplanted from one country to another, and conventionalised to meet the new environment, it is interesting to observe the designs in the different classes of rugs and trace as far as possible the influences to which they are due.

HERATS. — On great lines of travel between India, Turkestan, and Persia, the city of Herat in Northwestern Afghanistan for centuries occupied commercially a most important position, so that its people long since became familiar with the best fabrics of the surrounding countries. During the XV Century it reached its greatest prosperity, and exerted an important influence on the art and culture of Western Asia. Before the art decadence that followed the capture of the city by Nadir Shah in 1731, and the removal of many of its artisans to Persia, its looms were producing some of the best rugs of the Orient, which excelled in delicacy of drawing and in perfect harmony of colours. The fields contained patterns of serrated leaves entwined with flowing arabesques, scrolls, and Chinese cloud-bands. Conspicuous among this tracery were palmettes and such flowers as the lotus and peony, which were often most realistically drawn.* These rugs are of further interest, as they contained in field and border the design that, slightly changed, appears in many of the later rugs of Persia as the Herati pattern.

The modern rugs are as unlike other Afghans as were the antique pieces and show a close relationship to those of Persia. Nor is this surprising, as the weavers, though falling far short of the high standards of the time when Herat was part of Persia, are still mindful of the early traditions. Moreover, many of the rugs are made across the border in Khorassan, and have the silky pile peculiar to the rugs of that province; but their tones of colour, consisting principally of red or blue in the field, and light green, yellow, and ivory in the border, as well as most of the patterns, are dissimilar. In one type the fields are covered with pear designs; but their bent narrow ends always turn in the same direction, whilst those of other rugs turn in different directions in alternate rows. Another type suggests the Feraghans, because their fields are covered with the Herati or Fish pattern; but the borders of the Feraghans usually have the well-known turtle pattern, while the borders of these adhere to the traditional Herati design. It is also not unusual to see a large central medallion, in which blue or red predominates, separated by a field of lighter colour from the triangular patterns of the corners. Now and then, a nomadic influence is seen in the small adventitious figures of the field.

One of the most characteristic features of this class are the borders, that generally have three stripes, of which the central

* Robert Kerr Porter, a well-known traveller, stated that the floor of the audience hall of the governor at Tabriz, whom he visited in 1818, "was entirely overspread with Herat carpets, those of that manufacture being the richest that can be made."

PLATE 24. BIJAR RUG

PLATE 25. KERMANSHAH RUG

consists of a continuous vine of crumpled leaves so convention- alised as to be merely bent, thorny stalks partly enveloping formal rosettes. The other stripes are narrow, and have some simple undu- lating vine. This typical border, the stout, closely woven warp and weft of cotton, their large, almost square shapes and rather coarse weave, are important aids in distinguishing this class from all others. Some of the rugs recently made are coarse; but the older rugs have excellent dyes, lustrous nap, and matured tones of well- blended colours.

*Type Characteristics.** *Colours,* principally red and blue with minor quantities of green, yellow, and ivory. *Knot,* Ghiordes, rarely Sehna. Knots to inch horizontally, eight to eleven; perpendicularly, nine to twelve. A half knot, as it appears at back, is about as long, measured in direction of length of rug, as wide.† The rows of knots are firmly pressed down so that the warp is concealed at back. *Warp,* of cotton, rarely wool; one of the two threads encircled by a knot is generally doubled under the other, sometimes it is only de- pressed. *Weft,* wool, occasionally cotton; of coarse diameter. For a short space a thread of weft crosses twice, that is across and back once, between every two rows of knots, then three times, and so alternates every several rows. *Pile,* wool of medium length, soft, and silky. *Border,* three to five stripes, and frequently an outer edging of uniform colour. *Sides,* a double overcasting. *Both ends,* narrow web and loose warp fringe. *Texture,* stout and firm. *Weave* at back is of coarse grain. *Usual length,* eight to twenty feet. *Usual width,* three fifths to three quarters length.

KHORASSANS. — Among Iranians, Khorassan is often spoken of as the Land of the Sun. In its northern part are long ranges of mountains where herds and flocks find excellent pastures, and intervening valleys where the soil is cultivated. But the remainder of the province, with the exception of scattered oases, where small towns and villages are located, is almost entirely a desert, from which in classic times the Parthians advanced to harass the armies of Greece and Rome, then retreated to seek the protection of its vast salt marshes and inhospitable wastes.

* By "Type Characteristics" is meant the characteristics of such types of the class as are most frequently seen. There are exceptions to these types.
† As this is the case with most rugs, only the exceptions to this feature will be noticed in the type characteristics of other classes.

Nevertheless, in the little villages surrounded by a dreary wilderness have been produced as beautiful rugs as in those more favoured spots where prevailed cultured influences that could develop an Omar Khayyam and produce the sacred shrine of Meshed. Even before the Mongolian invasion several hundred looms, each employing four or five women, were busy in the town of Toon in Central Khorassan. Lying farther to the east is the district of Kain, which was once renowned for its beautiful rugs of Herati pattern, but of later years has produced coarser pieces with inferior designs and bad colours. Still better known was Birjand, in the southeastern part of the province, where formerly were woven pieces of superior workmanship that contained from two hundred to three hundred knots to the square inch. Their colours were of delicate shades; and it was not unusual to employ ivory or other light tones for the ground, with which was contrasted the darker tones of the Herati or pear patterns. Over a century ago many such towns in Khorassan were weaving rugs of artistic design and beautiful colours, but as a rule the present products fall far below the early standards.

Most of the Khorassans now seen were made almost fifty years or more ago and rival the best of modern Persian rugs. As a rule, they are of large size and have closely woven texture. They can be distinguished from most others by the silkiness of their moderately long nap, which is often due to the fact that it is from the fleece of a yearling lamb as well as because it is cut long and unevenly. Another characteristic is the use of some shade of red, as a pink, rose, or wine colour. Very frequently it is magenta or even purple, which are rarely found in other Persian rugs. Blue and cream are also largely employed. Their colours are generally softened by age, yet are warm, and at times brilliant, as when a large field of bright rose red or blue surrounds a central medallion.

The diversity of pattern in Khorassans is partly due to copying designs of rugs brought from other provinces by the pilgrims who yearly visit Meshed, and to the remoteness from one another of different centres of weaving in a province occupying one fourth of all Persia. One pattern, however, based upon the treatment of the pear design, which is employed in many of these pieces, at once distinguishes them from rugs of other districts. It consists of large pears arranged in regular order on a field of dark colour with their principal axes inclined diagonally in the same direction, and of two or three much smaller pears partly resting on them and partly projecting beyond their edges. Unlike the pear designs in other Persian rugs, which are oval, these are elongated like those of Indian rugs; and within them, as well as in the field, are often small floral figures. This distinctive pattern is rendered more effective by the colour scheme; since frequently pears of red or magenta, defined by lines of yellow and containing white petalled flowers, rest upon a ground of dark blue. The Herati design is also frequently employed, and in very old pieces are occasionally represented birds and animals naturalistically drawn. It is not unusual to see a central medallion or large vase of flowers surrounded by a field of bright uniform colour, and in some rugs are two medallions. When the centre contains a medallion, the triangular-shaped corners are set off by lines that are much simpler than those in Sarouks and Kermanshahs.

Few other rugs have more noticeable borders; for not only are they very wide, but in the main stripe, which is as wide as several guard stripes, is some characteristic pattern. Occasionally it contains the Herati design, but more frequently it consists of a heavy undulating vine with incipient flower forms, that at times almost assume the appearance of a bird's head resting on a sub-pattern of double floral vine. This stripe, illustrated in Plate E, Fig. 2, (opp. Page 156) is so frequently met with in Khorassans as to be characteristic of them. The narrow guard stripes usually contain some simple vine or ornate reciprocal figure.

Type Characteristics. Colours, principally rose, blue, and ivory, with minor quantities of yellow and green. *Knot,* Sehna. Many are "left-hand." Knots to inch horizontally, eight to thirteen; perpendicularly, twelve to twenty. The rows of knots are firmly pressed down, so that the warp is concealed and the weft is partly hidden at back. *Warp,* cotton; one of the two threads encircled by a knot is doubled under the other. A few short lengths of threads of warp hang loose at the back of some pieces. *Weft,* almost always cotton, occasionally wool of fine diameter and usually dyed blue. A thread of weft crosses twice between two rows of knots, excepting at intervals of every six or eight rows of knots, where it crosses three or more times. *Pile,* wool of medium length, silky and unevenly clipped. *Border,* three to six stripes, and generally an outer edging of uniform colour. *Sides,* a double overcasting of same colour as edging. *Both ends,* a narrow web and short warp fringe. *Texture,* moderately firm. *Weave* at back is of moderately fine grain. *Usual length*, five to twelve feet. *Usual width*, three fifths to three quarters length.

MESHEDS. — In few parts of the East have the weavers received greater inspiration from sacred and historic association than those of Meshed. To Shiite Mohammedans it contains the most holy spot in Persia; for within a mosque resplendent with façade of blue and white tiles, and with gilded minarets of exquisite design, lie the remains of Ali Riza, the eighth Imam or Moslem priest, in a tomb that is viewed yearly by nearly one hundred thousand pilgrims. It was for a short time the capital of Shah Abbas, who beautified its mosques; and here Nadir Shah, whose remains lie in the mausoleum, held his court after the capture of Delhi. Within its walls was born Firdousi, the Homer of Persia; and not far away, among the mountains to the west, was the home of the poet and astronomer, Omar Khayyam. Not only devotees but large numbers of merchants regularly visit the city in the caravans from Khiva, Bokhara, Herat, Yezd, and Teheran, so that it is also a city of commercial importance.

It is possible that a few of those matchless pieces which were attributed to Herat before its destruction by Nadir Shah were made in the district near Meshed, since according to an Arabian traveller * who visited it during the XIV Century many fine carpets then lay on the floor of its mosque. It is also believed that within the shrine, which has never been entered by an unbeliever, still remain some of the most magnificent carpets of the Orient. But for more than a century the textile industry has been declining, and the rugs now seen are generally of recent manufacture.

As a rule, these rugs are of the Khorassan type, and have the same silky appearance of nap, though it is shorter and more evenly clipped. The pattern, however, is generally different, as seldom is the field completely covered with the pear design, but whenever used, it is of elaborate drawing and frequently very large. Nor is the characteristic Khorassan border stripe, illustrated in Plate E, Fig. 2 (opp. Page 156), employed. On the other hand, it is not usual to see large central medallions, with floral designs in tones of rose or pink on fields of blue or ivory, and borders with undulating floral vines, in which appears evidence of Herati influence. Most of the rugs that now exist were made within the last fifty years, and are of large

* Ibn Batutah.

size and almost square shape. The colour scheme inclines to light and often brilliant tones, which at times are strongly contrasted with small masses of much darker shades. The wool is excellent, and the warp and weft are rarely coarse.

Type Characteristics. Colours, principally rose or pink, blue and white, with minor quantities of yellow and green. *Knot,* generally Sehna, rarely Ghiordes. Knots to inch horizontally, eight to fifteen; perpendicularly, twelve to seventeen. The rows of knots are pressed down, so that the warp is concealed and the weft is partly hidden at back. *Warp,* generally cotton, occasionally wool; one of the two threads encircled by a knot is doubled under the other. *Weft,* wool or cotton, of fine diameter and usually dyed blue. A thread of weft crosses twice between every two rows of knots. *Pile,* wool of fine quality and medium length. *Border,* usually from three to six stripes, occasionally as many as eight, and generally an outer edging of uniform colour. *Sides,* a double overcasting of same colour as edging. *Lower end,* a narrow web and warp fringe. *Upper end,* a web and warp fringe. *Texture,* moderately firm. *Weave* at back is of slightly coarse grain. *Usual length,* six to fourteen feet. *Usual width,* two thirds to seven eighths length.

Ispahans. — Still imposing in the ruins of its former splendour, surrounded by orchards, vineyards, and groves of trees that shade a broad, well-watered plain, is the ancient city of Ispahan. Under the Caliphs it became the capital of Persia; and though sacked by Tamerlane, who slew seventy thousand of its inhabitants, it rose to such importance that in the XVII Century it contained within its walls several palaces, one hundred and sixty mosques, over two score of colleges, nearly two thousand caravansaries, and about three quarters of a million people. Now the population has dwindled to about sixty thousand; and the few stately mosques and colleges that remain amid miles of deserted streets, abandoned bazaars, and ruined homes but feebly reflect the magnificence of the former capital.

Here was the royal court of Shah Abbas, who sent to Italy, for the purpose of studying decorative art, a number of the most experienced artisans, to whom are accredited some of the gracefully drawn designs of many of the early carpets. Here, in the days of its greatest prosperity, were founded many industries, and on its looms were undoubtedly woven some of the best of old Persian carpets.

Though Herat is now regarded by some authorities as the centre
where the so-called Ispahan rugs were made, it is improbable, as
previously pointed out, that all of them came from there.   But
after the death of Shah Abbas the rug industry began to decline;
and with the removal of the capital to Shiraz, in 1760, Ispahan ceased
to be a rug-producing centre of consequence.   There may be a doubt
whether such enormous carpets, as the one with length of sixty
feet and breadth of thirty that Sir Purdon Clark in his monograph
on Oriental Carpets mentions as lying in the hall of Chehel Sutoon
at Ispahan, were made there or were imported from other cities;
but the weaving of rugs has never entirely ceased; and so great
is the fame of the former glory of the city that even now Oriental
dealers will often apply to rugs the term " Ispahan " as an epithet of
superiority.

The few modern pieces which reach the western markets bear
little resemblance to their prototypes; and even among themselves
show little similarity of pattern, though the pear and Herati designs
are not uncommon.   In some rugs a century old the field is almost
covered with what is known as the Persian crown jewel, and in others
the field contains diamond-shaped medallions arranged in regular
order with small foliate and floral forms placed between them.
Small figures of animals are also occasionally represented.   The
border is generally narrow and lacking in impressive individuality,
so that the character of the rugs depends largely on the pattern of
the field and the well-seasoned colours, which are always rich and
harmonious.   Some shade of red or blue is usually chosen for the
ground; and in the designs are green, yellow, and white.   The
weave has variations rarely found in other rugs; for the warp, which
is usually cotton, may also be wool, or wool and cotton twisted together; and the weft may likewise be wool or cotton, and may
cross between the rows of knots either once or twice in different rugs,
or even once or twice in the same rug.

*Type Characteristics.** *Colours*, principally red and blue, with
minor quantities of green and yellow. *Knot*, Ghiordes.   Knots
to inch horizontally six to nine; perpendicularly, eight to fourteen.
The rows of knots are firmly pressed down. *Warp*, usually cotton,
occasionally wool; in a few pieces wool or cotton are twisted together.
Each thread of warp is equally prominent at back. *Weft*, wool or
cotton.   A thread of weft crosses once or twice between two rows of

* Of modern Ispahans.

knots. If it is wool, it generally crosses twice; if of cotton, two threads are generally placed side by side and cross together once as a single thread. *Pile,* wool, of short or medium length. *Sides,* a double selvage of two or three chords. *Lower end,* a web. *Upper end,* a web and fringe. Occasionally the web is turned back and hemmed. *Texture,* firm. *Weave* at back is moderately coarse. *Usual length,* six to fourteen feet. *Usual width,* two fifths to two thirds length.

KIRMANS. — On account of the isolated position of Kirman in Southeastern Persia, where the almost impassable saline and sandy deserts by which it is surrounded on the north and east, and the mountain ridges that separate it from the fertile valleys of Persia on the west, in a measure protected it from the repeated invasions that disturbed the political and industrial conditions of Northern Persia, it has continuously for over a thousand years been an important centre for the manufacture of rugs. Moreover, during all this period it has been noted for the excellence of their quality. As early as the Mohammedan conquests its fabrics were taken to furnish the floors and divans of Caliphs' palaces. When Marco Polo visited Persia in 1270 he wrote of the beautiful shawls and carpets made by the women of Kirman; and the noted French traveller Chardin, who lived in that country during part of the XVII Century, also spoke most favourably of them. Even after Nadir Shah removed many of the most skilled weavers to the northern part of Persia subsequent to ascending the throne in 1739, and Aga Mohammed Khan pillaged the city and massacred many of the inhabitants in 1794, the rug industry continued to prosper, and to-day that district is producing the best of modern pieces.

To this isolation is also largely due the excellence of the weave and dyes, since the artisans have in a measure escaped the pernicious influences of market demands and aniline colours. And to it must be attributed the fact that the old Iranian textile art appears nowhere else in greater purity; for of all the rugs on the market to-day these conform more nearly in texture, colour, and design to the masterpieces of earlier times, and show none of the foreign influences appearing in pieces woven in the north. And yet in Kirman is complexity of race as well as religion; for the Beluches who have wandered across the desert mingle with the Persians; and the Guebres, still practising in secret their fire worship, meet with the Mohammedans.

For long ages silkworms have been cultivated in the district about Kirman and fed on the mulberry trees that grow wild among its hills, so that it is not surprising that small quantities of silk are sometimes used in the rugs; but as a rule the pile is entirely of wool, yet of such fine quality and so well woven that many of the old pieces have a lustrous and silky appearance. This wool, which is white and of unusually fine texture, is partly the product of the native sheep and partly the product of a variety of goats that live among the ridges and yield fleeces almost as fine as those of Kashmir.

It is probably because of the fondness of the people of Kirman for roses, which they cultivate for the attar, that they depict them so profusely in their rugs. Sometimes they represent them as filling vases set in rows, or again as formal bouquets arranged in regular order upon the field. They also weave them in the borders among green leaves, as placed there tenderly and not hanging from such stiffly formed vines as are seen in other Persian rugs. Nor are they conventionalised like the flowers of most modern rugs; but petal, leaf, and stem are drawn with a precision that suggests the work of Indian weavers. Usually they are red contrasting with a ground colour of soft, ashy grey in the field, and of golden yellow in the rich, harmonious border. Sometimes, instead of a profusion of roses, there are other flowers, such as the sunflower, suggesting the old Zoroastrian faith, the cypress, or the sacred "cocos." Again, the general design may be modified from one strictly floral, and amid the foliage may be introduced birds, animals, or human beings; but the naturalistic drawing is always noticeable. In modern pieces the central medallion is often adopted, yet the general resemblance to older pieces is evident. As a rule the border has five stripes, of which the main one is twice the width of any other, and surrounding the outer is a narrow edging that is usually pinkish red; though now and then, according to the general colour scheme, a very pleasing effect is obtained by substituting an edging of moss green.

Type Characteristics. Colours, principally grey or ivory, with minor quantities of faun, yellow, rose, and blue. *Knot*, Sehna. Knots to inch horizontally eleven to twenty; perpendicularly, eleven to twenty. The rows of knots are pressed down so that the warp is concealed and the weft is partly hidden at back. *Warp*, cotton; one of the two threads encircled by knot is doubled under the other. *Weft*, generally wool of fine diameter, occasionally cotton, and frequently dyed blue. A thread of weft crosses twice between every

PLATE 26. KURDISTAN RUG WITH MINA KHANI PATTERN

PLATE 27. GOREVAN RUG

two rows of knots. *Pile,* wool, short, soft, and silky. *Border,* usually of five stripes and an outer edging of uniform colour that is generally pink but sometimes green. *Sides,* a double overcasting of the same colour as edging. *Both ends,* a narrow web and short warp fringe. *Texture,* very firm. *Weave* at back is of moderately fine grain. *Usual length,* five to seven feet. *Usual width,* three fifths to two thirds length.

YEZD. — In the centre of a sandy plain, midway between Kirman and Kashan, is the city of Yezd, where almost the last of the Iranian fire-worshippers, now a small part of the total population, still follow the ancient faith. Though partly shut off from the great desert of Khorassan by a mountain range, the city is only an oasis, where the drifting sands that buried the old city ever suggest to the inhabitants the dread spirit of desolation which finds an echo in ruined walls within. At the present time very few piled rugs are woven there and they are rarely seen in Western markets; yet on account of the historic interest in its people, the name is sometimes applied to modern products made in other districts. At one time it was noted for its silk rugs, and also for its felt "namads," which are generally too heavy to be transported, since some of them have a thickness of two inches and a superficial area of ten thousand square feet.

SHIRAZ. — Near the centre of a small, well-cultivated valley encircled by mountains is Shiraz, capital of Farsistan. During the reign of Kerim Khan, from 1760 to 1779, it was the capital of Persia; but since then it has suffered from earthquakes and neglect until now much of its former glory has departed. And yet there still remain associations to kindle the imagination, for without the gates are the gardens that Persian poets have extolled in verse; the tombs of Saadi and Hafiz; and not far away are the spots where Cyrus, Darius, and Xerxes lived, and the ruined palaces that Alexander destroyed in a night of drunken revelry.

As early as the time of the Caliphs this district produced large numbers of carpets; though few, if any, remain that were woven before the XV Century. As is the case with modern pieces, all of them were distinguished for their soft and beautiful wool, which is to be attributed to the climate and pasture of the surrounding mountains and valleys. One of the oldest existing rugs of this district which displays the characteristic wool is referred to by Dr. F. R. Martin in the following words:* "As soon as I had touched it, I was certain that we had to deal with a very rare kind of carpets which were made at Shiraz, or at least with the brilliant Shiraz wool. Most of the carpets made of that wool are lost, because the material was such a soft one that it was easily worn out. I know of very few which are older than the eighteenth century. No wool in all Persia takes such rich and deep colour as the Shiraz wool. The deep blue and the dark ruby red are equally extraordinary, and that is due to the brilliancy of the wool, which is firmer and, so to say, more transparent than silk, and makes one think of translucent enamel. As a piece of colour this carpet is certainly one of the finest, and there are very few carpets that have greater charm, which even the best reproduction could not give. In its colours there is something of an early Gothic stained-glass window, where the dust of ages has so covered the design that it has become obscured and the imagination of the spectator must complete it. Certainly the Persians for whom this carpet was made used to sit and dream for hours over the beauty of its colours, beautiful as the wonderful landscape surrounding Shiraz."

On account of the design and workmanship of this remarkable piece it is referred by Dr. Martin to the XV Century. During the two following centuries the carpets of Shiraz attained the high standard of excellence prevalent in the principal cities of Persia; but most of those pieces are now extremely rare, as they were woven chiefly for imperial use or for exchange with foreign rulers. This city experienced the art decadence that began with the XVIII Century, yet under the patronage of Kerim Khan imperial factories for weaving were again established there.

Though some of the rugs made eighty or even sixty years ago are certainly beautiful, these modern pieces, as a rule, lack the excellent qualities of early rugs, and those more recently woven are still poorer. On a few of them are depicted designs that are strictly Persian; but they generally depart widely from the early traditions, and floral forms are very much conventionalised. In a large number of this class the field is covered with pear designs which are described by straight lines and angles. Sometimes they are as small as in the Sarabends,

* "Burlington Magazine," December, 1909.

occupying the whole field as the principal motive; or they may be placed less prominently within diagonal or perpendicular stripes. Again, they may be as large as in Khorassans and grouped with other designs. Another very common pattern, known as the "pole-medallion," consists of a narrow perpendicular bar connecting two or more large diamond-shaped figures on which are grouped conventionalised floral forms and geometric designs. In other pieces the pattern is as geometric as that of any Caucasian rug, and it is not unusual to see both field and border profusely adorned with latch-hooks enclosed within and surrounding geometric figures. Nor is it unusual to see small figures of men and animals scattered through the field. Indeed, there is no other Persian rug in which the pattern is so heterogeneous. The borders usually consist of a number of narrow stripes, or a wide one with narrow guard stripes. One of them, at least, almost invariably contains some form of vine and leaves, and not infrequently the row of small X figures that also appear in Shirvans. In fact, the rugs are sometimes mistaken for Shirvans on account of the resemblance in geometric designs.

Though there is such variety in the patterns, these rugs are not difficult to recognise. There is something distinctive about the dark blues and reds contrasted with smaller areas of ivory and yellow. They are, as a rule, loosely woven, and many of them have a trait of lying unevenly on the floor. Not infrequently an extra band of pile is woven between the border and the broad embroidered webs of the ends, from which hang a loose fringe. The sides are overcast with heavy strands of wool varied like a barber-pole at regular intervals; and, as is not the case with any other class, they are often ornamented at intervals with coloured tassels.

There are also large numbers of Shiraz saddle-bags, which are superior to any others made. They resemble the Caucasian, as the patterns are geometric; but they may be distinguished from them by the finer wool and a slightly different colour scheme.

Not infrequently the term "Mecca" is applied to Shiraz rugs, and the impression is conveyed that they were made there. Nor is the statement always entirely devoid of truth; for each year caravans aggregating some two hundred thousand souls enter that city to make their devotions to Allah, to walk around the sacred stone within the Kaaba, and leaving behind their forgotten sins to return homeward with a bit of sacred earth or a strip of the temple's covering. Each of these pilgrims bears offerings for propitiation, of which a large proportion are rugs; and whatever their size, they are invariably the choicest the devotee can offer. Since the Mohammedan priests regard the best interests of their religion and themselves as conserved by a disposition of all articles not directly available for their use, they sell large quantities of such rugs, that find their way to Cairo, Damascus, and Constantinople. Furthermore, the pilgrims carry many pieces which are sold or exchanged along the routes of the caravans or at Mecca, and ultimately reach the same markets. Such a large number of the pieces that years ago came from these sources were of the well-known type of Shiraz rugs that they and similar pieces which had never left Persia were called Mecca rugs. This deception is still encouraged by some dealers, because for many buyers a special interest is attached to a piece that they are persuaded has been carried on this pilgrimage as an offering.

Type Characteristics. Colours, principally blue, red, and ivory, with minor quantities of yellow and green. *Knot*, generally Sehna, frequently Ghiordes. Knots to inch horizontally seven to twelve; perpendicularly, eight to twelve. At back one of the half knots is generally smaller than the other and pressed to one side. The other half knot is about as long as wide, and the yarn is not drawn tight against the warp. The rows of knots are pressed down, so that their alignment is slightly irregular, and the warp is concealed at back. *Warp*, almost always wool; in a few modern rugs goats' hair is used. Each of the threads encircled by a knot is almost equally prominent at back, or occasionally one to each knot is depressed. *Weft*, wool of medium diameter, frequently coloured red. A thread of weft crosses twice between every two rows of knots. *Pile*, wool, short to medium, and silky. *Border*, three to five stripes. Beyond the borders, at each end, is frequently a narrow band of pile. *Sides*, a heavy double overcasting in a barber-pole stripe or in short lengths of different colours, which generally consist of two of the following colours: red, yellow, green, and blue. In some pieces small tufts of wool protrude from the sides at regular intervals of one or more feet. *Lower end*, a broad web of coloured stripes, through which may run a dovetailed coloured cord, and warp loops. *Upper end*, a broad web of coloured stripes, through which may run a dovetailed coloured cord, and warp fringe. *Texture*, loose. *Weave* at back is of slightly coarse grain. *Usual length*, five to nine feet. *Usual width*, three fifths to four fifths length.

NIRIS. — A resemblance exists between the rugs that take their name from Lake Niris and those of Shiraz, which is distant only fifty miles to the westward; for many of each class are woven with the same silky wool, obtained from sheep that graze in the intervening mountain ranges, and the shepherd weavers about the lake have acquired ideas from the old capital. This resemblance exists mostly in the soft, floccy appearance of the nap, and in the barber-pole or parti-coloured overcasting of the sides. The webs of each end are broad and have long fringes; but generally those of the Shiraz are embroidered and crossed with one or more parti-coloured cords, whilst those of Niris pieces are, as a rule, flatly woven in stripes of different colours. There is also an occasional resemblance in pattern, but the best known pattern of the Niris is rarely seen in the Shiraz. On the other hand, they are more firmly woven; and there is a slight difference in the character of their weave, since one of the two threads of warp encircled by a knot is depressed below the other, and the weft is of wool coloured red, whereas in the Shiraz it is frequently of cotton.

The pears are the favourite design, and, like those in Sarabends, extend over the field in orderly array; but they are much larger and consist of an assemblage of bright colours isolated from one another, yet grouped gracefully in a way that might readily suggest the origin of crown jewels sometimes ascribed to them. Frequently the ground is a dark blue, and the pears are of red, blue, green, and ivory. Violet and yellow are also employed. In other types, less usually seen, the field is covered with a lattice-work pattern containing small figures. The typical border has a broad central stripe of vine and flower, with narrow guards of simpler vine or reciprocal trefoil. Barber-pole stripes are also characteristic of the borders.

Type Characteristics. Colours, principally blue, red, yellow, green, and ivory. *Knot*, Ghiordes. Knots to inch horizontally six to eleven; perpendicularly, seven to fifteen. The rows of knots are not closely pressed down, so that at the back the warp is noticeable and the weft conspicuous. *Warp*, wool; one of the two threads encircled by a knot is depressed below the other at back and frequently doubled under the other. *Weft*, wool of medium diameter, generally dyed red. A thread of weft crosses twice between every two rows of knots. *Pile*, wool, of medium length. *Border*, generally of three stripes, sometimes as many as seven. *Sides*, a heavy double overcasting in a barber-pole stripe or in short lengths of different colours, such as red, blue, green, yellow, and black. *Both* ends, a broad web of coloured stripes, one row of knots, and loose warp fringe. *Texture,* loose. *Weave* at back is of slightly coarse grain. *Usual length,* four to seven feet. *Usual width,* three quarters to four fifths length.

FERAGHANS. — Stretching eastward from the base of Mt. Elwund is the plain of Feraghan. Its length does not exceed forty-five miles, nor its breadth ten or fifteen, yet here are clustered several hundred villages. On account of its altitude of seven thousand feet, the ground is covered with snow in winter, and the people are then huddled in their low mud houses, and the flocks and herds are gathered within the village walls. But in the spring the men are cultivating the fields, and the sheep are grazing on the banks of numerous streams. It is a plain of fertility and industry. For generations it has been productive of large numbers of fine rugs, and it is still possible among its villages to find some of those old pieces that have been regarded by the Persians themselves as the best examples of the textile art.

When the characteristic patterns of Feraghans have once been carefully observed, they are never forgotten; yet it is surprising to note the many distinctions observable in a large collection. These patterns may conveniently be divided into two groups, namely: one in which the field is entirely covered with diaper designs, and the other in which the field contains a central medallion surrounded by uniform colour. Probably nine tenths of these rugs fall within the first group, which is divisible into three sub-groups: those in which the field is covered with the Herati design; those in which the field is covered with the Guli Hinnai design; and those in which the field is covered with some other small diaper design.

The Herati design is the one most frequently seen, and is found in the very oldest of existing Feraghans. As a rule, the crumpled leaf does not exceed a length of four or five inches, and the rosettes are proportionally small, so that the ground colour is almost entirely concealed, and at a short distance is not distinguishable; but there are other pieces in which the leaf is over a foot in length, and the figures less closely clustered, so that the ground enters prominently into the colour scheme. The prevailing colour of the leaf and rosette is generally rose red, which gives a distinctly reddish tone to the rug; though the small designs have shades of green, yellow, white, and light blue. The ground is usually a rich, dark blue; but occasionally red or even ivory is used. In very few other rugs are the corners separated from the field, unless there is a central medallion; but in almost all Feraghans small triangular-shaped corners, with colours contrasting with those of the field, are separated from it by lines bearing teeth or serrated edges.

Surrounding the field is a border that has from five to seven stripes. The main stripe is about three times as wide as any other, and may have a ground colour of red, blue, or ivory white; but in many of the best pieces it is moss green, with blue, yellow, or red appearing in the overlying pattern. Of different but corresponding shades is the colour of the ground and designs of other stripes. Probably three fourths of the Feraghans now seen have the well-known turtle design in the main stripe; but it is sometimes replaced by the rose design shown in Plate E, Fig. 12 (opp. Page 156), or by an undulating vine with rosette or palmettes. On the innermost stripe, which is very narrow, is invariably represented some reciprocal figure, as the trefoil or sawtooth; and on the other stripes are undulating vines, with floral or quasi-floral figures.

The Feraghans with fields covered with Guli Hinnai designs instead of the Herati show a difference in both drawing and colouring, though the general effect is much the same. In place of crumpled leaves and rosettes of reddish hue are the star-like flowers of the Hinnai plants that brighten the mountains surrounding the Feraghan plain with their large yellow or ivory coloured petals. The pattern, as a whole, is slightly more prominent, and the prevailing colour tone, which is rich, is less red and more yellow. There is, however, a very noticeable difference in the pattern of the third sub-group, though specimens are not frequently seen. In these the small figures of conventionalised flowers sometimes have geometric shapes and are arranged in diagonal or perpendicular rows. Moreover, they generally lack the rich colouring of the preceding sub-groups.

The central medallion is found not only in modern but also in old Feraghans. It is generally of diamond or hexagonal shape, with serrated edges and with pendants. Almost invariably Herati figures cover its surface, and not infrequently some lattice-work design with small conventionalised leaves or flowers appear faintly on the field of uniform colour surrounding it. As a rule, pieces of this group are of a more striking and handsome appearance than those in which the entire field is covered with numerous minute figures of equally rich hues that blend and produce, when viewed at a distance, an undefined colour. The border designs are similar to those of the other group. All of the old pieces were stoutly woven; and though the nap was short, many of those that remain are still serviceable.

Type Characteristics. *Colours*, principally red and dark blue, with minor quantities of yellow, light blue, green, and white. *Knot*, Sehna, rarely Ghiordes. Knots to inch horizontally eight to thirteen; perpendicularly, seven to eighteen. The rows of knots are pressed down, so that the warp is usually concealed at back. *Warp*, cotton; each of the two threads encircled by a knot is equally prominent at back. *Weft*, cotton, occasionally dyed blue or pink. A thread of weft of fine or medium diameter crosses twice between every two rows of knots, or occasionally a thread of coarse diameter with much slack crosses only once, so that the transverse warp produces a quincunx effect. *Pile*, wool, clipped short. *Border*, three stripes. *Sides*, a double overcasting in dark colour. *Lower end*, a web. *Upper end*, a web and warp fringe. *Texture*, firm. *Weave* at back is of slightly coarse grain. *Usual length*, four to twelve feet. *Usual width*, three fifths to two thirds length.

HAMADANS. — A little to the northeast of Elwund and at an altitude that overlooks a small, well-cultivated valley adjacent to the Feraghan plain is the city of Hamadan. On this site was the ancient city of Ecbatana, capital of Media; and here guarded by Jews is a tomb, which tradition declares is the burial place of Esther and Mordecai. Within the encircling walls are gardens, bazaars, and mosques; yet the present city of forty thousand inhabitants with its general misery and squalor has little to remind one of the magnificence of that former capital which for a short period was mistress of the world.

Like Yezd, Hamadan is famous for its namads; and like Yezd it once produced, according to tradition, most beautiful silk carpets, though no longer are any woven there. But its looms have been busy for the last few generations weaving rugs of wool and camels' hair, which have such marked individuality that they bear unmistakably on their face the stamp of identification. The few old rugs that remain are sterling pieces, which are stoutly woven and of excellent dyes. They come in many sizes; some are simply mats,

PLATE 28. BERGAMO PRAYER RUG

PLATE 29. GHIORDES PRAYER RUG

others sedjadehs, and an unusually large number are runners. The typical pattern of the mats and smaller sedjadehs consists of a central diamond-shaped medallion, surrounded by a field of contrasting colour, from which are set off the triangular-shaped corners. In the large sedjadehs and in the runners, which are sometimes twenty feet or more in length, are often three or more pole medallions, though the pole device may be omitted. These medallions and corners are covered with small, carefully drawn geometric figures, or more frequently with floral designs such as appear in Feraghans, and as a rule are defined by serrated lines or are fringed with hooks or comb-like teeth. The colour of the surrounding field is unobtrusive. In some pieces it is void of pattern, and its monotonous tone is broken only by slight variations of shade; yet not infrequently it is marked with faint lines of slightly darker or lighter tint, like a delicate tracery. Not only are the borders wide, but a broad edging, which is at least one half and sometimes two thirds as wide as all the coloured stripes combined, surrounds them. As it is usually of camels' hair and without pattern, it is a very noticeable characteristic. The main stripe has an undulating vine with conventionalised flowers, and the two guard stripes have a simpler vine, or, more frequently, the reciprocal trefoils.

To this general type, however, are many exceptions. Sometimes the figures of the medallion and corners are more geometric; sometimes the corners are omitted; the outside edging may be decorated with large conventionalised floral or geometric figures; and occasionally a camel or some other animal is represented in the field or border. A few of the old rugs were strikingly handsome. Dr. George Birdwood refers to a large Hamadan that formerly hung in the India Museum in these words: * "An irregular lozenge form, a little island of bright clustering flowers, of which the prevailing colours are red and blue, adorns the centre; while the wide extended ground of yellow, in irregular shades, surrounds it with a rippling amber sea; and there are blue pieces in the corners, within the broad blue border worked in arabesques. It is a carpet not to be laid on a floor, but to be hung in a gallery, to be looked at like a golden sunset. It was a sacrilege to remove it from the mosque where it evidently was once spread under the great dome. *Beati possidentes.*"

Most of the old pieces have disappeared, and in their places are

* In "Industrial Arts of India."

modern products with pile of wool or goat's hair often dyed in garish colours. There are also many nondescript rugs, which were gathered from wandering tribes or surrounding villages and taken to Hamadan, since for a long time it has been one of the great rug markets of Persia. When exported from there they were often classed as products of that city.

Moderately old Hamadans contain more camel's hair than any other class of rugs, since in very many of them it forms the pile of both field and outer edging, where its soft tones of pale chestnut colour contrast with the bright shades of blue, red, and yellow yarn used in other parts of the field and border. This lavish use of camel's hair, the broad encircling edging, the cotton warp, and a single thread of coarse weft passing once between two rows of knots, distinguish them from all other rugs.

Type Characteristics. *Colours*, principally the chestnut of camel's hair with red and blue. *Knot*, Ghiordes. Knots to inch horizontally, six to nine; perpendicularly, eight to twelve. The rows of knots are firmly pressed down. *Warp*, cotton; each of the two threads encircled by a knot is equally prominent at back. *Weft*, generally cotton, frequently wool; of coarse diameter. A thread of weft crosses only once without slack between every two rows of knots, so that the white spots of transverse cotton warp exposed at back have a quincunx appearance. *Pile*, in old rugs, mostly camel's hair and some wool; in recent rugs, mostly wool clipped short. *Border*, wide, generally of three or four stripes, and a broad outer edging of camel's hair. *Sides*, overcast, generally in brown or red. *Lower end*, a narrow web and warp loops. *Upper end*, a narrow web turned back and hemmed. *Texture*, very firm. *Weave*, at back is of moderately coarse grain. *Length*, three to twenty-four feet. *Width*, two fifths to three quarters length.

IRANS. — Although neither a city nor district of Persia is called Iran, a well-defined class of rugs is known to the trade by that name. They are woven by some of the old Iranian stock dwelling principally in the province of Irak-Ajemi. These people follow no particular pattern or colour scheme of their own, but to a large extent copy those of a few well-known Persian classes; yet in other respects their rugs have a noticeable individuality. They are woven with a Ghiordes knot and so loosely that if the rug be observed from the front, as it is bent backward in a plane parallel to the direction of the weft, the foundation threads of warp and weft, which are of cotton, will show distinctly between the knots. Each of the two threads of warp encircled by a single knot are equally prominent at the back. Ordinarily the threads of weft cross twice between the rows of knots, but occasionally they cross only once, as in Hamadans. Many of the fabrics regarded as Sarabends, Feraghans, and even Hamadans are in reality Irans, which on account of their inferior workmanship are much less valuable.

Type Characteristics. Colours, principally blue and red, with minor quantities of ivory, yellow, green, and brown. *Knot,* Ghiordes. Knots to inch horizontally, six to eleven; perpendicularly, seven to eleven. A half knot as it appears at back is frequently longer, measured in the direction of the length of the rug, than wide. The rows of knots are not pressed down closely, so that the warp is noticeable at back. *Warp,* cotton; each of the two threads encircled by a knot is equally prominent at back; they are not closely strung, so that each half knot stands out distinctly. *Weft,* cotton; a thread of weft of coarse diameter as a rule crosses twice between each two rows of knots, and only rarely crosses but once. The weft is conspicuous between the knots at front when the rug is bent backwards. *Pile,* wool of medium length. *Border,* generally four to six stripes. *Sides,* a heavy double overcasting that is generally brown or black, but sometimes red. *Lower end,* a narrow web. *Upper end,* a narrow web and loose warp fringe. *Texture,* loose. *Weave* at back is of coarse grain. *Usual length,* five to ten feet. *Usual width,* two fifths to three quarters length.

SAROUKS. — Towards the western end of the Feraghan plain and at an altitude of seventy-five hundred feet is the mud-walled village of Sarouk. Here, shaded by poplars, are clustered one hundred and fifty houses, with floors, roofs, and sides of mud that has dried and cracked until it admits the wind. The sun and light enter through the open doors, for there are no windows. Nor are there chimneys, but simply openings between the rafters to permit the escape of smoke from the open fireplace in the floor below and the entrance of more wind. At times the atmosphere is not only oppressive with smoke, but is laden with odours that arise from the pens beneath and beside the houses, where fowls, sheep, and goats are huddled. During the winter and early spring snow lies on the ground; a little later a hot summer follows. Yet amid these depressing surroundings and under these adverse conditions lived weavers who gave the name of their little village to some of the most beautiful rugs made in all the East.

Now and then is seen an old piece with surface like velvet and with mellowed tones of perfect harmony that has come from these huts or surrounding hills; but probably not one in a score, perhaps not one in a hundred, of the Sarouks now offered for sale in this country was woven there, as most of them are made in the workhouses of larger cities, though they follow essentially the general appearance and technique of old and genuine pieces, even if lacking some of their best qualities. Nevertheless, the modern pieces are of handsome colour, of graceful pattern, and are well woven. Some of them, which were made two or three decades ago, had large designs of the cypress, willow, or the tree of life, as well as realistically drawn animals represented in the fields; but the great majority of those now seen invariably follow a pattern consisting of a large medallion with pendants, or of two or more concentric medallions resting on the field, from which are set off the four corners. Defining the edges of both medallions and corners are lines that are most artistically irregular, yet correspond with one another.

Between each part is the greatest co-ordination, for the designs of field, corners, medallions, and borders are similar. On long delicate stems that bend and interlock like carved tracery are leaves, buds, and flowers, suggesting the craftsmanship of the best days of old Iran. The borders generally have only three stripes: a broad main stripe on which appears an elaborately drawn undulating vine with pendent flowers, and a narrow guard stripe on each side. Sometimes the guards are ornamented with only a simple vine, but more frequently with a reciprocal pattern, which, however, is so well drawn as to conflict in no wise with the harmony of the floral forms. In the drawing of the borders the weavers exercise greater latitude than in any other part of the rug; for occasionally they add a narrow outer edging of dark colour, place the reciprocal figure next to the innermost stripe as a fringe to the field, or increase the number of stripes to seven. Rarely is the medallion wanting in modern pieces, but now and then the pendants are replaced by bunches of flowers, and in some pieces the corners extend along the sides in undulating lines until they meet near the centre.

All of these pieces are so closely woven that the fine bluish weft is hardly discernible at the back. Very few other rugs have such short-cut wool, which has a velvety appearance, rendered more effective by the soft, rich colours that are always in perfect harmony and excellent taste. As a rule they are dark. Ever present in the ground colours are deep blues and reds, suggestive of the hues of the so-called "Ispahans;" while olives, delicate greens, and ivory represent with consummate dignity of tone and design a lavish tracery of leaves and foliage motives.

Type Characteristics. Colours, principally dark blue and red, with minor quantities of green, olive, buff, and ivory. *Knot,* Sehna. Knots to inch horizontally twelve to eighteen; perpendicularly, twelve to twenty. The rows of knots are pressed down, so that the warp is concealed and the weft is partly hidden at back. *Warp,* cotton, rarely linen; one of the two threads encircled by a knot is almost always doubled under the other; in a few pieces it is only depressed. *Weft,* cotton, of small diameter, dyed blue. A thread of weft of fine diameter crosses twice between every two rows of knots. *Pile,* wool, short and velvety. *Border,* generally of three stripes but sometimes as many as seven. Occasionally there is an outer edging of dark colour. *Sides,* a tightly wound double overcasting of red, blue, or black wool. *Both ends,* a narrow web, or web and short warp fringe. *Texture,* very firm. *Weave* at back is of fine grain. *Length,* four to twelve feet. *Width,* two thirds to three quarters length.

KASHANS. — Near the centre of the province of Irak-Ajemi, on the ancient and well-travelled highway between Ispahan and Teheran, is the city of Kashan, from which, according to an old tradition, the three Wise Men of the East followed the Star of Bethlehem. Like many of the cities of Persia it is now largely in ruins; its homes are infested with scorpions; for many months of the year the heat, which in a measure is due to the proximity of the great salt desert that extends far into Khorassan, is unendurable; yet in spite of these inconveniences, for which perhaps familiarity has in a measure lent contempt, forty thousand people live there. In the past it has produced some of the greatest artists and artisans of weaving. It was once the home of Maksoud, whom Shah Ismael I ordered to weave the famous carpet of the Mosque of Ardebil, which, ranking among the greatest woven products that still exist, bears unmistakable evidence of the wonderful technique and artistic skill then practised in Kashan. Without a doubt other textile masterpieces of the XVI and XVII Centuries were woven there, for it would be unreasonable to believe that the city where Maksoud had learned his art was not at that time a prominent rug-producing centre.

According to Persian tradition many of the antique silk carpets came from Kashan. At any rate, it has been for a long time customary to take the raw silk from other places to be spun and dyed there. Some of it is woven into rugs, which are considered among the best of modern pieces, though the demand for them is small.

On the other hand, the woollen pieces are now found in every market, though it is only within recent years that they have been generally known. Occasionally they are defined as a higher grade of Sarouks, on account of the striking resemblance in texture, colours, and designs; yet there are certain distinctions: the warp is often linen, the nap is a little shorter, the texture slightly firmer, and there are a great number of border stripes. A feature that is more frequently found in these two classes than in any other is the fringe of hooks or short comb-like teeth that border the innermost stripe and extend into the field. Without doubt Kashans are among the most perfect as well as the most expensive woollen products of the modern Persian looms. Their velvet-like surface and rich sheen give them an appearance that to those unfamiliar with rugs seems like that of silken pieces. The fine wool is dyed with rich, deep tones of blue, olive, red, and brown; the perfectly balanced pattern is artistic as well as ornate; and on account of the very short nap the drawing of each minute detail is clear. In place of bold designs accentuated by masses of colour are delicate tracings of floral and foliage motives, of graceful arabesques and foliated stalks, so expressed in rhythmic lines and harmonious tones as to give a sense of the greatest refinement. Even though these rugs be modern and chemically washed, their wealth of artistic workmanship and exquisite colour make them exceedingly handsome.

Type Characteristics. Colours, principally dark blue, red, and yellowish brown, with minor quantities of light blue and green. *Knot,* Sehna. Knots to inch horizontally sixteen to twenty; perpendicularly, sixteen to twenty-four. The rows of knots are firmly pressed down so that the warp is concealed and the weft almost hidden at back. *Warp,* generally cotton, rarely linen; one of the two threads encircled by a knot is doubled under the other. *Weft,* generally cotton, of small diameter, dyed blue; rarely linen. A thread of weft crosses twice between every two rows of knots. *Pile*, wool, very short and velvety. *Border*, generally of seven stripes. *Sides*, a tightly wound double overcasting in dark red, blue, or brown. *Lower end*, a narrow web. *Upper end*, a narrow web and short warp fringe. *Texture*, very firm. *Weave* at back is of very fine grain. *Usual length*, six to ten feet. *Usual width*, three fifths to three quarters length.

SARABENDS. — Standing on the top of lofty Elwund, that rises on the boundary between the provinces of Ardelan and Irak-Ajemi, in Northwestern Persia, one would see within a radius of ninety miles as prolific a centre of rug weaving as anywhere exists. Just within this distance to the northwest are Sehna and Bijar, to the southeast is Sultanabad, to the southwest is Kermanshah; and skirting the mountain on the eastern side are the high plains where lie the districts of Hamadan, Feraghan, and Sarawan, as well as the village of Sarouk and less important centres of weaving.

Among the valleys of the Sarawan district, that lies on the northern flanks of mountain ranges extending as far as Ispahan, are made the rugs which, by a corruption of the word Sarawan, are known as the Sarabends. No other rugs of Persia have a pattern that is so simple, and that for generations has been followed with so little variation. Nor are there any other modern rugs that have changed less from the old styles in respect to colour and quality. The typical pattern of the field consists of rows of pear designs arranged in transverse lines, with the smaller ends pointing in different directions in alternate lines. The pears of the field show great diversity of shape, but those of the borders are long, narrow, and most angular; yet they never assume the rectilinear figures found in Baku rugs. Only very rarely is there any departure from this pattern; though in a few old pieces is an adaptation of the Herati design, and now and then is seen a geometric figure, or human form, or the date when the piece was woven.

The ground colour of the field may be blue, red, or white. If blue, it is so largely covered with pinkish or rose-coloured pears that the prevailing hue, when the pieces are viewed from a distance, is light red. If, on the other hand, the field is red, the pears are mostly blue; and if the field is ivory white, the pears are red and blue. In all old pieces the blue has rich, deep tones, the red has mellowed into soft rose or delicate pink, and the white has turned to ivory. This pleasing effect is increased by shades of yellow and green, which are added to the other colours of the pears.

With few exceptions the borders have a large number of narrow stripes, of which the central is about one third the aggregate width. Its ground colour is ivory white, but the angular vine and pendent, narrow pears have the same colours as those of the field. On each side of it is usually a stripe with ground colour corresponding to that of the field and with an undulating vine and rosette. Almost invariably there is an outer stripe of reciprocal trefoil in red and blue, which may be balanced by a reciprocal sawtooth adjoining the field. It is not unusual to see large pieces with two white stripes, and very rarely one is seen with three.

The best of these pieces are made in the town of Mirabad, which signifies the "city of Mir," and are accordingly called Mir-Sarabends. They can be distinguished from others, known to the trade as Royal Sarabends, by the fact that in tying the knots the yarn is so twisted that one thread of warp is doubled under the other; and in the latter each of the two threads appear with equal prominence at the back. Neither of them should ever be mistaken for Iran imitations, in which the pile is of much looser texture and is tied with the Ghiordes knot. For durability, there are very few modern pieces that will give the satisfaction of Sarabends; for as a rule they are stoutly and closely woven, and though there is monotony in the pattern, those coloured with vegetable dyes will grow more beautiful with age.

Type Characteristics. Colours, principally red or blue, with minor quantities of ivory, yellow, and green. *Knot*, Sehna. Knots to inch horizontally eight to thirteen; perpendicularly, nine to thirteen. The rows of knots are firmly pressed down, so that the warp does not show at back. *Warp*, cotton. In Mir-Sarabends one of the two threads encircled by a knot is doubled under the other at back. In Royal Sarabends each is equally prominent. *Weft*, cotton, of fine diameter, and dyed red or blue. A thread of weft crosses twice between every two rows of knots. *Pile*, wool of short or medium length. *Border*, five to seven stripes, and occasionally even more. *Sides*, a red double overcasting. *Lower end*, a web, or web and short warp fringe. *Upper end*, a web and short warp fringe. *Texture*, firm. *Weave* at back is of moderately fine grain. *Length*, five to eighteen feet. *Usual width*, two fifths to two thirds length.

BURUJIRDS. — About sixty miles to the west of Sultanabad and forty to the south of the Sarawan district is the city of Burujird. It is in a rich, well-watered valley and is surrounded by numerous hamlets. Most of the population are engaged in agriculture; and only a small part, who are stimulated by the increased prices occasioned by the rug industry of Sultanabad, are weavers. They produce pieces that resemble closely the Sarabend rugs, as the field is generally occupied with pear designs; but on account of the Ghiordes knot and cotton warp and weft, they might be mistaken for Iran rugs.

SULTANABADS. — Southeastward from the plain of Feraghan is the city of Sultanabad, which in recent years has become important as the centre of a great rug industry controlled by Europeans and Americans. Higher prices, resulting from the constantly increasing Western demand for Persian rugs, have stimulated the native weavers to more persistent efforts. Those who are too poor to purchase wool and dyes * are supplied by the companies. Others, who are more dependent, are paid regular wages. Thus it happens that not only large numbers of looms are constantly at work in the city, but a hundred hamlets and villages that lie within a day's journey produce rugs that are marketed there. But while the output has been increased the true artistic spirit has been suppressed, and patterns favoured or supplied by foreign purchasers only are in demand. Most of the rugs are well woven, though there is a difference in grades. Some take the name of the city, others are called Savalans, from a range of mountains that lie to the north, and others are known as Mahals. Most of them are large pieces, rather coarsely woven.

MUSKABADS. — In the district of Muskabad, a short distance to the northwest of Sultanabad, are produced rugs very similar to the Mahals. They come in the same large carpet sizes and nearly square shapes; they have almost the same harmonious colour scheme of unobtrusive red, yellow, blue, green, and ivory; they have the same cotton warp and weft, the same finish of sides and ends; but as a rule they are less closely woven. The patterns are varied. Occasionally they have large figures such as are seen in Gorevans,

* Sidney Churchill in the Imperial Vienna Book says that "the dyes of Sultanabad have perhaps the most extensive colour scheme in Persia."

though these are more usual in Mahals. In some of them the field is covered with conventionalised leaf and floral form. But the usual type has two or more concentric medallions of different colours covered with the small Herati designs so distinctive of the Feraghans. When such is the case, the border has usually the turtle pattern in the main stripe and some stiffly drawn vine and floral pattern in the smaller stripes. But the velvety appearance, the elegant finish of old Feraghans, is always lacking. The nap is of soft wool of medium length, but the surface of the back displays coarse texture. These pieces lack the artistic qualities of most Persian rugs; but on account of their excellent quality of material and stoutness of weave they are very serviceable.

Type Characteristics. *Colours,* principally red, blue, and ivory, with minor quantities of green and brown. *Knot,* Ghiordes or Sehna. Knots to inch horizontally seven to fourteen; perpendicularly, eight to twelve. The rows of knots are not firmly pressed down. *Warp,* cotton; one of the two threads encircled by a knot is generally depressed at back, and frequently nearly doubled under the other. *Weft,* cotton, of medium to coarse diameter. A thread of weft crosses twice between every two rows of knots. *Pile,* wool, of medium length. *Border,* three to five stripes, with a narrow outer edging. *Sides,* a double overcasting. *Lower end,* a very narrow web and short warp fringe. *Upper end,* short warp fringe. *Texture,* moderately firm. *Weave* at back is of very coarse grain. *Length,* ten to eighteen feet. *Width,* two thirds to seven eighths length.

JOSHAGHANS. — Lying to the southeast of Sultanabad and to the north of Ispahan is a district where a century ago were woven some of the best carpets of Persia, known as Joshaghans or Djushghans. Even long before then it was noted for its textile fabrics; but during the reign of Nadir Shah, who removed many of the best artisans from the central to the northwestern part of Persia, the carpet weaving received a new impulse, and continued to flourish there until nearly the middle of the last century. Since that time it has almost ceased, so that the genuine Joshaghans of rich, deep colour and skilfully drawn pattern are all sixty or more years of age. They may still be found scattered throughout the country, and should be carefully preserved; for they merit the high esteem accorded to them by the Persians themselves.

In a few of these pieces are seen the Shah Abbas pattern. In other

PLATE 30. GHIORDES RUG

PLATE 31. KULAH PRAYER RUG

pieces the field is covered with scrolls, or with a lattice-work pattern in which small floral forms are the motives.   Again it is occupied by pear designs encircled by small rounded figures, which combined form the outlines of a larger pear, while in the intervening spaces are small floral forms.   The principal border stripe generally consists of floral designs, which not infrequently are some form of the Herati pattern. The secondary stripes often contain floral vines.

Whatever the pattern of the field, the effect is always striking and beautiful; for the lines are never harsh, and the colours are rich. The ground is very frequently a rose tint, but is sometimes dark blue; and the overlying designs are rose, yellow, green, and ivory. The colours of the border are generally the same as those of the smaller designs, so that the effect is always harmonious.   These rugs are excellently woven; and the soft lustrous wool of the pile, which is usually longer than that of Sarabends and Feraghans, has often an appearance like plush.

Type Characteristics.   Colours, principally red and blue, with lesser quantities of yellow, green, brown, and ivory.   *Knot,* Ghiordes. Knots to inch horizontally seven to eleven; perpendicularly, eight to thirteen.   The rows of knots are not always firmly pressed down, so that the warp may be seen at back.   *Warp,* usually cotton, occasionally wool; one of the two threads encircled by a knot is usually depressed below the other at the back.   *Weft,* wool, sometimes dyed red, brown, or reddish brown, but frequently of natural colour. A thread of weft generally crosses twice, but sometimes three times between every two rows of knots.   *Pile,* wool of short or medium length.   *Border,* usually three stripes.   *Sides,* a double overcasting that is generally brown or black.   *Lower end,* a web.   *Upper end,* a web and warp fringe.   *Texture,* moderately firm.   *Weave* at back is of moderately fine grain.   *Usual length,* eight to sixteen feet. *Usual width,* two fifths to two thirds length.

SEHNAS. — Seldom has prophecy been more precisely fulfilled than the one made a decade ago that the old Persian rugs would rapidly disappear from the market.   Nor is it better exemplified than in the case of those woven before the middle of the last century in Sehna, capital of Ardelan, for to-day it is exceedingly difficult to obtain any of them.   Nevertheless, there are still many looms among the four or five thousand families of the city, where true to early traditions are woven modern fabrics that maintain the same

floral Persian patterns, the same colour, the same general character
of weave; but they lack the fine technique of the older pieces.
It is, indeed, surprising that these modern pieces so closely resemble
the old in all save quality, when it is considered that Sehna is distant
only fifty miles from the western border of Persia; that it is surrounded by Kurdish tribes who for generations have woven rugs
with nomadic features; and that it is not far distant from other important rug centres.

To one familiar with the leading characteristics it is possible at
once to distinguish these rugs. Their nap is exceedingly short, and
the weave is so distinctive that with eyes closed an expert will generally recognise them after rubbing the hand across the front and
back. Their patterns, also, conform to well-established types, yet
have sufficient variety to be always interesting. They may be
conveniently divided into two groups: one represents the entire
field covered with floral designs, and the other represents a field
of uniform colour with a medallion at the centre, or with two or
more concentric medallions. The former, which is undoubtedly
the older group, has generally a small diaper pattern of the Herati
design or floral figures daintily drawn. To obviate too great monotony, a number of the old pieces have the leaves and flowers so
adjusted that the ground conveys the effect of lattice work, or less
often have small trees of cypress regularly placed amid the other
floral designs. Again, the field may be covered with large pear designs placed in rows. Of modern pieces the most beautiful pattern,
as a rule, consists of a field of rich, uniform colour, as ivory or red,
containing at its centre a single medallion of contrasting ground
colour, which is generally dark blue or even black. The four corners
of the field have serrated edges and are covered with floral designs
similar to those of the medallion. The borders, which are invariably narrow, usually consist of three stripes, but sometimes of only
two. With very few exceptions they are floral, and in the main one,
that has a ground colour of yellow or red, are represented designs
which are also similar to those of the medallion. Some of the old
Sehnas had borders that were less floral than more modern pieces,
and the turtle design so common to Feraghans was often used. Isolated and adventitious designs, such as are seen in all nomadic rugs,
are never found in these pieces, nor are the floriated scrolls that are
peculiar to Sarouks, Kashans, and Kermanshahs.

As is seldom the case with modern rugs, occasionally both linen

and silk are used for the warp, and silk for overcasting, but generally
the warp is cotton and the overcasting is of wool.   The city of Sehna
has given its name to the kind of knot with which almost all the
rugs of China and Turkestan as well as many of the rugs of India
and Persia are tied; yet strange as it may seem, its own weavers
have been inconsistent in its use.   To be sure, most of its rugs have
the Sehna knot, but a surprisingly large proportion of both recent
and comparatively old pieces have the Ghiordes knot.   Only a
few other rugs ever adopt the same style of weaving; for a thread
of weft passes between two rows of knots but once, so that at the
back only alternate threads of white cotton warp appear between
these knots and thus give to the weave a checkered appearance or
quincunx effect.   Moreover, the yarn of the knots is not drawn
tightly against the warp, so that in whatever direction the hand is
rubbed the surface feels like a file.   Very few other rugs are so closely
woven, as four hundred knots to the square inch are not uncommon;
and in very old pieces nearly double that number are now and then
met with.   Since both warp and weft are of fine threads and the nap
is very short, these rugs are exceedingly thin and, accordingly, are
not well adapted for floor use.

Some old saddle-bags are still to be found, rich in their fields of
deep blues and floral forms of brighter tones, but unfortunately
they are somewhat marred by the long slit in the centre made to
fit the saddle.

Type Characteristics.   Colours, principally dark blue, red, and
ivory, with lesser quantities of green, light blue, and yellow.   *Knot*,
Sehna, often Ghiordes.   Knots to inch horizontally eleven to twenty;
perpendicularly, twelve to twenty-four.   The rows of knots are
closely pressed down, but the yarn of knots is not drawn tight against
the warp.   *Warp*, generally cotton, occasionally linen, rarely silk.
Each of the two threads encircled by a knot is equally prominent
at back.   *Weft*, generally cotton, occasionally wool or linen, rarely
silk.   A single thread of small diameter crosses only once between
every two rows of knots, so that the white spots of transverse warp
exposed at back have a quincunx appearance.   *Pile*, wool clipped
very short.   *Border*, three stripes.   *Sides*, a tightly wound double
overcasting.   *Lower end*, a short web, or web and warp loops, or web
and short warp fringe.   *Upper end*, short web and fringe.   *Texture*,
very firm.   *Weave* at back is of fine grain but very rough.   *Length*,
three to seven feet.   *Width*, two thirds to three quarters length.

BIJARS. — One hundred miles beyond Hamadan, on the road to Tabriz, is the city of Bijar, capital of the district of Gehrous. It is surrounded by barren mountains that rise out of high table-lands, where for miles scarcely a habitation or bush breaks the monotony, and where not even a blade of grass or flower brightens the cracked and sun-parched earth, except for a short season of the year. As is the case throughout nearly all Persia, the spirit of desolation has crept into the city; the grapevine climbs over ruined walls; the shade of poplars and willows falls alike on decaying palace and crumbling houses. Yet there still remain caravansaries, schools, and mosques, as well as a population of five thousand people. Without doubt the importance of the city is partly due to the regiment of soldiers that the governor maintains to keep in subjection the bands of robbers and fierce Kurds who, in large numbers, live throughout the surrounding country. Nor are they the only tribes of fierce foreign blood dwelling in this region; for it is stated that during the invasions of the Timurids, a body of Turkomans from the fortress town of old Saraks, where the corners of Persia and Afghanistan meet Turkestan, followed the conqueror westward and settled here. After them is named a small river that flows a short distance to the north and finally empties into Lake Urumiah; and it is not unusual to apply the name Saraks to the rugs woven about Bijar, though they have none of the Turkoman characteristics.

By adopting some of the best qualities of both Persian and Kurdish rugs, the Bijar weavers have produced pieces of unusual merit. The foundation is generally of wool; but unlike almost all other rugs with nomadic features one thread of warp to each knot is doubled beneath the other in the process of weaving, so that it is almost or entirely concealed. Bijars are accordingly pieces of great firmness and durability. Moreover, their threads of warp and weft are of coarse diameter, so that they are invariably thick even when the nap is not long. They are also distinctive in the effective massing of bright and strong colours. Perhaps the association with ranges of treeless hills, with salt wastes, with vast plains where rainless months leave the grass parched and the flowers withered, has deadened the Persian love for the brilliant, joyous colours so acutely cherished in other parts of Asia; but by the weavers of Bijar it is not unusual to discard many of the Persian colours, which, however rich, are subdued and sombre, and adopt the brighter hues seen in some of the rugs of Asia Minor. Yet, as is not always the case with the latter, there is no sense of outraged taste; and though crimson reds, deep blues, or tawny camel's hair be brought in relief against a field of strongly contrasting colour, the effect, except in modern pieces of poor dyes, is never displeasing.

In the pattern much latitude is exercised, but only in the oldest pieces are found the gracefully flowing lines suggestive of the highest Persian art. In many pieces a central medallion and triangular-shaped corners, separated by a field of plain or slightly shaded colour, is a favourite pattern. But the defining lines are severe, and lack the delicate drawing characteristic of Kermanshahs and Sarouks. Or the field may be covered with a lattice-work pattern that contains small repetitive forms, consisting of slender stems supporting one or more flowers. Frequently a rug is covered with a medley of designs composed of conventionalised flowers, crudely drawn trees, as well as birds, animals, or human beings. The borders generally consist of an outer edging of plain colour, and three stripes, on which are often represented purely geometric forms, but more frequently the undulating vine and pendent leaves, such as are common to most Persian rugs. Fortunately many sterling pieces still remain that have none of the earmarks of factory-made rugs, but are beautiful with their soft wool and lustrous colours, as well as interesting with their blending of Persian and Kurdish features.

Type Characteristics. Colours, principally red, also blue, ivory, green, yellow, and chocolate. *Knot,* Ghiordes. Knots to inch horizontally six to ten; perpendicularly, eight to twelve. The rows of knots are pressed down, so that the warp is concealed at back and the weft partly hidden. *Warp,* wool; one of the two threads encircled by a knot is doubled under the other. *Weft,* wool, of medium or coarse diameter, frequently dyed red. A thread of weft crosses twice between every two rows of knots. *Pile,* of medium length, usually wool, but frequently partly of camel's hair. *Border,* of three stripes, often with an outer edging. *Sides,* a double overcasting in red or purple. *Lower end,* a web that is occasionally coloured or a narrow braided selvage. *Upper end,* a web with loose warp fringe and sometimes a braided selvage. The webbing is occasionally turned back and hemmed. *Texture,* very firm. *Weave* at back is of coarse grain. *Length,* six to sixteen feet. *Width,* one quarter to three fifths length.

KERMANSHAHS. — On an ancient highway between Bagdad and Teheran is the city of Kermanshah. As it is situated near the frontiers of northwestern Persia, facing the Turkish provinces, and is surrounded by mountains where once wandered bands of homeless marauding Kurds who recognised no government, it was formerly a most important stronghold of defence. A century ago Robert Kerr Porter, who visited the city, referred to the luxurious gardens and orchards that surrounded it, and to the villages of the vicinity in which were made "carpets of most beautiful colour and fabric." Within later years the moat has filled with rubbish, the encircling walls have crumbled, and the deserted bazaars and caravansaries show that its present population of about twelve thousand is but a small part of what it has been. With its decline in political importance followed a decline in industrial activities; yet for a long time it remained a rug-producing centre of importance. In 1880 Sir George Birdwood wrote that "the finest Oriental rugs of our time, which at the Vienna Exhibition astonished all beholders, are those made in the palace of the Governor of Kermanshah, in Kurdistan, and are only disposed of as presents.* And in 1890 a traveller † spoke of the weaving as follows: "It is a process carried on in homes, hovels, and tents by women and children. . . . The vegetable dyes used are soft and artistic, especially a wonderful red and the various shades of indigo. The dull, rich tints, even when new, are quite beautiful. The women pursue their work chiefly in odds and ends of time, and in some cases make it much of a pastime."

From this city and the surrounding hills are still obtained large quantities of rugs, which follow the same patterns that for years have been characteristic of this district. Yet most of the modern Kermanshahs are made elsewhere in the workhouses of exporting companies. So noticeable is the resemblance in drawing and colouring of some of them to the Kirmans of Southeastern Persia, that they are offered now and then by dealers as real Kirmans, though they lack the fine technique and artistic merit of the latter. They possess, however, the same wealth of floral expression, for throughout border and field are sprays of flowers on delicate vines and foliate stalks. Most of the pieces now seen contain at the centre of the field a large medallion, which may have serrated or lobed edges, be oval or of diamond shape, and with or without pendants. The corners are

* "Industrial Arts of India."
† Mrs. Elizabeth Bishop in "Journeys in Persia and Kurdistan."

defined by lines that do not always conform to those of the medallion; and the borders have always several stripes, of which the main one is usually but little wider than the others. In all these different parts are floral and foliage motives that find expression in sunflowers, roses, tulips, daisies, and many simpler forms, supported by delicate branching sprays and vines.

There are, however, other patterns less frequently met with, as it is not unusual to see elaborate pear designs, and sometimes the cypress or the palm tree naturalistically drawn. Covering the field of a rare old Kermanshah recently seen were thirty large panels, which like so many small rugs contained central fields that were alternately coloured blue and ivory. Surrounding each of these little fields, on which were represented the arch of a temple and the tree of life, were borders wherein were woven verses from the Koran, and at the intersections of the borders were floral designs like roses. Encircling all the panels was a wide border containing escutcheons in which were woven other verses. Without doubt this rug was used for sacred purposes. In fact, a larger proportion of Kermanshahs than almost any other Persian rugs have prayer arches as well as verses from the Koran inscribed in some part of them, but with very few exceptions they are recently woven and bear no evidence of devotional usage.

The general colour scheme is distinctive, for the tones are much lighter than those of most other Persian rugs. Frequently a field of ivory surrounds the central medallion, though sometimes a light rose red is used. Other colours are light blue, green, and buff, which are softened by the floccy quality of the excellent and moderately short-clipped wool. One feature common to almost all of them is the narrow edging of pinkish red that surrounds the border. This edging, the foliate scrolls, the soft light tones, and the rather coarse weaving, that leaves the white or sometimes pinkish weft exposed at the back, are characteristics by which these rugs may readily be distinguished. As they come in all sizes from small mats to large carpets, and have tones that harmonise with almost any surroundings, they are a most popular class with those who care little for association and ignore the fact that they are chemically washed.

Type Characteristics. *Colours*, principally light rose and ivory, also blue, green, and buff. *Knot*, Sehna. Knots to inch horizontally twelve to eighteen, perpendicularly eleven to eighteen. The rows of knots are pressed down, so that the warp is concealed at back, but the weft is conspicuous. *Warp*, cotton; one of the two threads encircled by a knot is doubled under the other. *Weft*, cotton, of medium diameter, sometimes dyed pink. A thread of weft crosses twice between every two rows of knots. *Pile*, wool, soft and of medium length. *Border*, frequently of three stripes of almost equal width, but sometimes many stripes; also an outer edging that is generally red, but occasionally blue. *Sides*, a double overcasting in same colour as edging. *Lower end*, a narrow web and warp loops, or short warp fringe. *Upper end*, a narrow web and short warp fringe. *Texture*, firm. *Weave* at back is of moderately coarse grain. *Usual length*, four to fourteen feet. *Usual width*, three fifths to four fifths length.

WESTERN KURDISTANS. — Within the land lying between the Anti-Taurus and Zagros mountains, where the Euphrates and Tigris rivers have their sources, dwell a people almost as untamed as when in the dawn of history they were designated the "Warriors;" or centuries later, under the name "Carduchis," opposed the retreat of Xenophon and his ten thousand Greeks. Now they are known as "Kurds," of whom large numbers, wild, brave, and hospitable, live a nomadic life among table-lands partly covered with sycamores and oaks, or follow their sheep over lofty pine-crowned mountains, that for long months are enveloped in snow. Doubtless the cheering influence of green hillsides and the rich vegetation of innumerable valleys, where streams flow perennially, is in a measure responsible for their more sprightly aspect when contrasted with that of the Persians. They recognise no law but the will of their chief, to whom they maintain strictest fealty. "There was up to a recent period no more picturesque or interesting scene to be witnessed in the East than the court of one of these great Kurdish chiefs, where, like another Saladin, the bey ruled in patriarchial state, surrounded by his clansmen with reverence and affection, and attended by a body-guard of young Kurdish warriors, clad in chain armor, with flaunting silken scarfs, and bearing javelin, lance, and sword, as in the time of the Crusades." *

Large numbers, also, are settled in Persia, where they cultivate the soil of small tracts of land, or live in villages of stone houses. Many of them are scattered around Lake Urumiah. Others have made their homes in the district of Kermanshah, and not a few have

* Encyclopedia Britannica.

PLATE 32. MELEZ PRAYER RUG

PLATE 33. MELEZ RUG

wandered as far as Khorassan. But wherever they may be, they are distinguished by their appearance; for the men are bold and handsome, and the young women, whom custom permits to appear unveiled in public, are beautiful as well as graceful.

There is no racial distinction between the Kurds who live the pastoral life and those who dwell in villages, or between the Kurds of Asiatic Turkey and those of Persia; yet environment has produced a marked difference in their textile fabrics. Those woven by the tribes that live among the mountains that encircle Lake Van and extend to the north of Diarbekr embody the wild characteristics of the weavers. They are strong and coarse, with close weave, long nap, and bold patterns, that suggest Caucasian influence devoid of artistic feeling. In some of them is a large central diamond or lozenge surrounded by latch-hooks, as well as floral forms so conventionalised as to be purely geometric; now and then Arabic symbols and letters are scattered over the field. Moreover, the colours lack the delicate shades of Persian rugs, but possess rich, strong hues obtained from native dyes that applied to the excellent wool give it a warm, lustrous appearance. Brown is very largely used. There are also dark reds and blues brightened by dashes of white and yellow. Only the Kazaks, Tcherkess, and one or two Asia Minor weaves are trimmed with such long nap, which, together with the deep colours and long shaggy fringe, give these pieces a semi-barbaric appearance possessed by no other rugs. Sometimes they are confused with the Mosuls; but as a rule the pile is longer, and they are more coarsely woven. In fact, the yarn is so coarse that it is not unusual to see pieces with only thirty or forty knots to the square inch. Like the Persian-Kurdish rugs, they rarely come in large, almost square shapes, and are frequently decidedly oblong. They may, however, easily be distinguished from them by their cruder patterns, darker colours, coarser texture, and the fact that each of the two threads of warp encircled by a knot is equally prominent at the back.

Type Characteristics. Colours, principally brown, red, and blue, with minor quantities of yellow, green, and white, and the natural colour of the undyed wool. *Knot,* Ghiordes. Knots to inch horizontally four to seven; perpendicularly, six to nine. A half knot, as it appears at back, is as long as, or longer than, wide. The rows of knots are closely pressed down. *Warp,* wool; each of the two threads encircled by a knot is equally prominent at back. *Weft,*

wool, of coarse diameter, and often dyed a reddish colour. A thread
of weft crosses twice between every two rows of knots. *Pile*, wool,
occasionally camel's or goat's hair clipped long. *Border*, generally
of three stripes. *Sides*, a heavy double overcasting, usually in brown
or black, occasionally in several different colours. *Lower end*, a
narrow web, through which runs a coloured cord, and warp loops.
Upper end, a narrow web, one or more rows of knots and long,
coarse warp fringe. *Texture*, very stout. *Weave* at back is of very
coarse grain. *Length*, five to sixteen feet. *Width*, two fifths to two
thirds length.

PERSIAN KURDISTANS. — Nowhere is the influence of association among weavers more evident than in the Kurdish rugs woven
by the tribes settled in the rich valleys of Northwestern Persia,
as is apparent in weave, colours, and pattern, which differ widely from
those seen in the Kurdish rugs of Asiatic Turkey. The warp is only
rarely of coarse goats' hair, and is generally soft, brown wool. The
pile is much shorter, so that the drawing is clearly defined. Likewise, the colours are more varied and of more delicate tones so as to
include lighter shades of green, rose, and ivory with the darker reds,
blues, and browns. But the chief distinction consists of the more
artistic pattern. The medallion in the centre of the field with corner
pieces in which appear some form of repetitive pattern is most common. Instead of large figures are often the more dainty Herati designs
borrowed from the Feraghans and the Sehnas, or the pear design
from the Sarabends. Now and then is seen a rare old piece with
field completely covered with drawings of the tree of life and strange
floral conceits; but the pattern that is pre-eminently typical of this
type of Kurdish pieces is the Mina Khani, though it is occasionally
adopted in other rugs. The white and yellowish flowers, connected
by a lattice work sub-pattern of brown or olive, rests on a ground
of dark blue, that in accordance with a feature peculiar to rugs
of Kurdish weaves varies from one end of the field to the other, so
as to suggest that their wandering life often made it difficult to obtain the roots and herbs necessary to produce similar shades. As
is rarely the case with other patterns, the naturalistic flowers that
are pendent from the undulating vine of the main stripe and the
flowers of the field have nearly the same drawing. The two remaining stripes of the narrow border have most simple vines.

Almost without exception rugs of this class are stoutly woven.

To assure firmness, one thread of warp is depressed below the other in tying the knots; and the weft that is thrown across for filling is of fair quality. On account of the firm texture, excellent wool, and good colours it is still possible to obtain moderately old pieces, that as objects of utility as well as ornament are desirable for their sterling qualities.

A similarity exists between the Persian-Kurdish, Mosul, and Bijar rugs; but a precise, even if easily overlooked, difference in the weave serves to distinguish one from the other. As may be seen by examining the backs of typical specimens, in Mosuls every thread of warp lies in the same plane parallel with the surface of the pile; in the Persian Kurdistans one of the two threads of warp encircled by a knot is depressed at an acute angle to that plane; and in Bijars one of the two threads of warp encircled by a knot is doubled under the other so as to be at right angles to that plane.

Type Characteristics. *Colours*, principally red and blue, also yellow, green, and white. *Knot*, Ghiordes. Knots to inch horizontally seven to ten; perpendicularly, eight to twelve. A half knot, as it appears at back, is no longer than wide and is frequently not so long. The yarn is loosely woven, so that each separate ply is distinct. The rows of knots are pressed down, so that the warp is largely concealed and the weft partly hidden at back. *Warp*, wool; one of the two threads encircled by a knot is generally much depressed below the other at back; but sometimes each is equally prominent. *Weft*, wool, of medium diameter. A thread of weft usually crosses twice between every two rows of knots, only rarely once. *Pile*, wool, and occasionally some camel's hair of medium length. *Border*, three to four stripes. *Sides*, a heavy double overcasting in dark colour. *Lower end*, web crossed by a parti-coloured cord, and warp loops. *Upper end*, web crossed by a parti-coloured cord, and loose warp fringe. *Texture*, very firm. *Weave* at back is of coarse grain. *Usual length*, six to twelve feet. *Usual width*, five eighths to two thirds length.

KARAJES. — Dwelling near Hamadan, in the northwestern part of Persia, are tribes who weave rugs that are known in the markets as Karajes. In their colour scheme, length of nap, and texture they resemble many of the Kurdistans; but in the technicalities of weave they show a marked difference. As a rule, a single thread of weft crosses only once between two rows of knots, or in a few pieces two threads of weft pass side by side as though one. In this particular they resemble Hamadans; but the alignment of their knots at the back is more regular, their weft is inserted with some slack, their warp is of wool, and their weft is almost always of wool. They are generally runners, with long nap of soft, lustrous wool, with rich colours, and with border of three stripes. The pattern is Iranian, and very often consists of a small bush or sprig of leaf and flower disposed in formal array throughout the field. Sometimes the floral forms are placed within the diamonds formed by a trellis pattern, but more frequently they are arranged in rows like the pear designs of Sarabends. In some pieces they are very much conventionalised and suggest similar figures seen in rugs of Southern Caucasia; and in others stem, leaf, and flower are very realistic. Another pattern frequently followed consists of three or four large diamond-shaped medallions extending from one end of the field to the other. The borders are moderately narrow, and an undulating vine of well-known Persian character generally appears in one or more of the stripes. As these pieces are almost always comparatively old, the vegetable dyes that were used for colouring have mellowed, and have a richness of tone that is accentuated by the depth of pile and softness of wool. The prevailing tone of many is a deep plum colour.

Type Characteristics. Colours, principally dark blue or plum and red, with minor quantities of yellow, brown, and white. *Knot,* Ghiordes. Knots to inch horizontally six to twelve; perpendicularly, seven to twelve. A half knot, as it appears at back, is as long as wide, and occasionally is longer. The rows of knots, which have even alignment at back, are not firmly pressed down. *Warp,* wool, rarely cotton; each of the two threads encircled by a knot is equally prominent at back. *Weft,* wool, rarely cotton; a single thread of medium diameter crosses once between every two rows of knots; but in parts of the same rug two, three, or even four threads of small diameter will cross side by side as a single coarse thread. Occasionally a thread of weft crosses three or four times. The filling of weft stands up as high as the knots at the back, giving an even surface. *Pile,* wool, of medium length or moderately long. *Border,* of three stripes. *Sides,* a heavy double overcasting. *Lower end,* web and warp loops. *Upper end,* web and short fringe. *Texture,* moderately loose. *Weave* at back is of coarse grain. *Usual length,* eight to fourteen feet. *Usual width,* three eighths to one half length.

TABRIZ. — Although Tabriz, capital of the province of Azerbijan, is situated in a remote corner of Persia, from the earliest times it has been one of the most important centres in the Orient for the production of carpets. They were well known in the days of the Caliphs; and some of the earliest masterpieces that now remain were woven there during the reign of Shah Tamasp, who extended to this industry his royal patronage. This city has been for a long period on the great routes of caravans passing to Trebizond and Tiflis from the country to the south and east, so that it has become the principal mart of Persia for the export of rugs gathered from surrounding regions. Nevertheless, it still continues to produce its own pieces; but the weavers are in the employ of foreign companies who prescribe the character of workmanship. As a consequence, the rugs are of good material, excellently woven; and though many of the old dyes are no longer used, the colours as a rule are fair; yet on account of the mathematical exactness of their formal patterns the truly Oriental spirit is largely lacking.

Since the rugs are made solely to meet the requirements of Western buyers, the patterns are various. Most of them consist of a large central medallion surrounded by a broad field of ivory, blue, or red that extends to the sides and ends. In others, a small diamond occupies the centre and is surrounded by a series of concentric medallions. Although in these respects they correspond with Kermanshahs, Sarouks, and Kashans, the patterns of their fields lack the long scrolls and interlacing branches, and consist frequently of short, slender stems supporting fronds, leaves, flowers, or the pear designs arranged so as to present almost the appearance of lace-work. Sometimes the drawing is a delicate tracery representing intertwining arabesques. A field completely covered with the small designs peculiar to Sehnas, or containing the disjunct forms of nomadic rugs, is never seen; and yet it is not improbable that many of the early Tabriz weavers were Kurds. Sometimes the flowers are similar to the roses of Kirmans, or are realistically drawn *compositœ* surrounded by delicate leaves on graceful stems; sometimes the small designs are as formal as the palmettes of old Ispahans, from which they were doubtless copied; again, the naturalistic and conventional may be blended together in an harmonious whole. But whatever the pattern, the different parts show the perfect balance so frequently seen in the antique pieces of three or four centuries ago. Nevertheless, to these types are many exceptions, since the weavers will produce for hire any class of rug or copy any coloured drawing.

The borders differ from those of Kermanshahs, with which these rugs are frequently compared, in the fact that in their central stripe the continuous vine of leaf and flower is less conspicuous; and in its place are often palmettes, pears, shrubs, or formal trees separated by foliated scrolls. Not infrequently the smaller stripes, also, have a repetitive pattern of leaf and flower, though in some of the many stripes is usually a well-drawn vine. Again, the border may consist of a series of cartouches that have been copied from much older rugs and contain verses of the Koran or of Persian poets. Within recent years this tendency among the Tabriz and Kermanshah weavers to imitate not only borders but also fields of old masterpieces is increasing.

A feature peculiar to a very large number of these rugs is the adoption of very finely spun linen for the warp; though cotton, which is used for the weft, is sometimes substituted. The knots are carefully tied, and the closely woven texture presents an appearance at the back similar to that of Sarouks; but the almost concealed weft is generally either white or pink. The weave compared with that of Kermanshahs is finer, but the wool of the closely shorn nap is neither so soft to the touch nor so silky, the colours are harsher, and the patterns more formal. These rugs are made in all sizes, though most are large and almost square.

Type characteristics. Colours, principally red, blue, and ivory. *Knot*, Ghiordes. Knots to inch horizontally twelve to twenty; perpendicularly, ten to twenty-two. The rows of knots are pressed down, so that the warp is hidden and the weft partly concealed at back. *Warp*, generally cotton, frequently linen; one of the two threads encircled by a knot is doubled under the other. *Weft*, as a rule, is cotton, occasionally it is wool or linen, of fine diameter, and frequently dyed pink. A thread of weft crosses twice between every two rows of knots. *Pile*, wool, clipped short and harsh to the touch. *Border*, from five to eight stripes and an outer edging. *Sides*, a two-cord selvage. *Both ends*, a narrow web and loose warp fringe. *Texture*, firm. *Weave* at back is of fine texture. *Usual length*, nine to eighteen feet. *Usual width*, two thirds to four fifths length.

GOREVANS. — Of the many rugs now made in Persia and designed primarily for use, few are of such moderate price as the Gorevans, which, during recent years, have been imported in large numbers from the province of Azerbijan in Northwestern Persia. A hasty glance suggests Occidental craftsmanship, but in every essential they are distinctly Oriental. Their stout weave, large size, and nearly square shape place them in the class of Persian pieces often called carpets, to which belong the Kermanshahs, Muskabads, Mesheds, and rugs of Tabriz. Yet they are frequently larger than any of these, and are readily distinguished from them by their colours and patterns. It is true that they have the same light shades, but the tones are in a distinctly different scale, consisting principally of dull brickred, light terra cotta, buff, dark blue, dull green, yellow, and ivory, which, when once recognised, are rarely mistaken for those of any other rugs. Nor are the colours distributed in patches so small as to blend when viewed at a short distance, but are of sufficient masses to be separately observed and analysed.

The patterns are equally distinctive. The field is generally covered with a number of concentric hexagonal-shaped medallions, of which the longer sides of the largest are often marked with conspicuous indentations such as are not seen in classes made in other districts. All of the medallions are covered with large designs, in which the artist has departed from the usual forms of vine, leaf, and flower, that poorly imitate the splendid examples of so-called "Ispahans," and in many instances has represented them in the archaic drawing of the oldest remaining Persian carpets. Hard, straight lines with angles replacing graceful curves define the medallions, corners, stems, leaves, and flowers. And not infrequently the formal treatment shows a European influence, as when all semblance of leaf and flower has disappeared in the extremely conventionalised forms that are placed with set regularity in the field. A very noticeable feature of these rugs is the manner in which the designs are coloured, as it is not unusual to represent a large figure in two strongly contrasting colours, as blue and pink separated by a stiffly drawn line.

The designs of the corners are similar to those of the central medallions, but the designs of the borders are dissimilar. The small stripes are marked with Persian vines of well-known floral and leaf forms that show nothing of the drawing characteristic of the field. The main stripe occasionally has cartouches and star medallions, but in most instances has the turtle pattern, though its treatment differs from the usual form seen in Feraghans. A co-ordination in colour exists between field and border. The ground of both the main stripe and one of the medallions is often a dark blue or a red, while the ground of the other stripes corresponds with those of other medallions.

All of the Gorevans are modern pieces, and so lack the interest of those that follow traditional patterns; but their stout weave, warm colours, and archaic designs make them both serviceable and pleasing.

Type Characteristics. Colours, principally dull red, dark blue, and buff, with minor quantities of green, yellow, and white. *Knot,* Ghiordes. Knots to inch horizontally six to eight; perpendicularly, six to ten. The most conspicuous half of a knot, as it appears at the back, is, as a rule, longer than wide. The rows of knots are some-what pressed down, but the warp is rarely entirely concealed at back. *Warp,* cotton; one of the two threads encircled by a knot is usually depressed below the other at back; sometimes both threads are equally prominent. *Weft,* cotton, of coarse diameter, sometimes dyed blue. A thread of weft crosses only once between every two rows of knots, or frequently twice. *Pile,* wool, of medium length. *Border,* generally of three stripes, occasionally four or five. *Sides,* a two-cord double selvage. *Both ends,* a short warp fringe. *Tex-ture,* rather loose. *Weave* at back is of very coarse grain. *Usual length,* ten to sixteen feet. *Usual width,* three fifths to three quarters length.

BAKSHIS. — A close relationship exists between the Gorevans, which are a comparatively modern product, and several other less known sub-classes of earlier origin that are woven in small towns in the east central part of the province of Azerbijan. One of these towns, located fifty miles to the southeast of Tabriz, is Bakshis, which formerly produced rugs that were highly esteemed by the Persians, before the weavers were corrupted by a spirit of commer-cialism. Those which are exported to-day are of little artistic value, are poorly coloured, and carelessly woven. The patterns are inferior copies of other well-known classes.

SERAPIS. — The rugs known as Serapis are named after the village of Sirab in the mountainous district between Tabriz and Ardebil; but they are made not only there, but also in the country farther to the east. The large sizes are frequently mistaken for Gorevans, as

PLATE 34. RHODIAN RUG

PLATE 35. KONIEH PRAYER RUG

they are of similar shape and have similar finish of sides and ends, yet as a rule they are better woven. Many of them follow the same patterns of concentric medallions, but the lines of others are more artistically drawn. Although the borders lack the gracefully symmetric vines of old Iranian pieces, the drawing is interesting in its individuality and is in harmony with that of the field. All the colours are cheerful. A field of ivory or some light shade of buff usually surrounds the central medallions, on which appear soft and pleasing tones of smaller designs. Yet on the whole there is a tendency to employ richer and deeper tones than those of Gorevans. The smaller pieces often contain more elaborate patterns, but there are always the same pleasing and unobtrusive shades of colour.

Type Characteristics. Colours, principally red, blue, and ivory, with minor quantities of green and yellow. *Knot*, generally Sehna, frequently Ghiordes. Knots to inch horizontally six to ten; perpendicularly, seven to twelve. The rows of knots are firmly pressed down, so that the warp does not show at back. *Warp*, cotton; one of the two threads encircled by a knot is generally much depressed below the other at back, and frequently doubled under the other. *Weft*, cotton, of coarse diameter. A thread of weft crosses twice between every two rows of knots. *Pile*, wool of medium length. *Border*, three stripes. *Sides*, a double selvage of two cords, or double overcasting attached figure-eight fashion to the sides. The selvage or overcasting is usually in red or buff. *Lower end*, a narrow web and warp loops or short warp fringe. *Upper end*, a narrow web and warp fringe. *Texture*, stout. *Weave* at back is of coarse grain. *Usual length*, ten to eighteen feet. *Usual width*, two thirds to three quarters length.

HEREZ. — The city of Herez is in the extreme eastern part of the province of Azerbijan, where for a long time the weavers steadily adhered to the sterling values of early fabrics and produced pieces that were followed with slight modification in many of the former Gorevans. In a measure the rugs of Tabriz also are reflected in the medallion pattern of some of these pieces, but for their gracefully flowing lines are substituted more rectangular ones; and in place of many colours are few, of which blue and a reddish copper are particularly noticeable. Another well-known and interesting type consists of a field of white, on which, with formal precision, are represented, in delicate shades of red, blue, yellow, and green, archaic leaves and flowers supported by stems and tendrils that are so conventionalised as to form geometric lines and angles. At regular intervals the branching tendrils assume the shape of arches, of which in larger pieces there are frequently one or two dozen; and so closely do they resemble prayer arches that these rugs are sometimes mistaken for namazliks. The borders usually consist of three stripes. The outer and inner are narrow guards containing some simple floral figure, and the broad central stripe has often a continuous vine with formal leaves and a conspicuous design suggestive of the cloud-band. The tones are never harsh; many of the pieces are large and almost square, and the wool of the pile is generally excellent.

Type Characteristics. *Colours*, principally ivory, light blue, and reddish brown, also some yellow and green. *Knot*, Ghiordes. Knots to inch horizontally five to ten; perpendicularly, six to twelve. The most conspicuous half of a knot, as it appears at the back, is longer than wide. The rows of knots are only slightly pressed down, so that the weft is noticeable at back. *Warp*, cotton; one of the two threads encircled by a knot is depressed below the other at back, or each thread is equally prominent. *Weft*, of cotton, seldom of wool, of moderately coarse diameter. A thread of weft crosses twice between every two rows of knots. *Pile*, wool of medium length. *Border*, generally of three stripes. *Sides*, a two-cord double selvage. *Lower end*, a very narrow web and short warp fringe. *Upper end*, a short warp fringe. *Texture*, loose. *Weave* at back is of very coarse grain. *Usual length*, nine to fifteen feet. *Usual width*, two thirds to seven eighths length.

SUJ-BULAKS. — About fifty miles to the south of Lake Urumiah and the same distance from the western boundary of Persia is the old Kurdish capital of Suj-Bulak. Kurds still largely predominate in the district and comprise most of the population of the city, to the discomfort of the much smaller number of Persians, for whose protection a large garrison was formerly maintained. Accordingly, the rugs made in this vicinity are strongly characteristic of Kurdish pieces in the strong texture, the excellent quality of wool, the rich, dark colours, the finish of sides and ends. The patterns also are largely Kurdish, but frequently show the influence of Persian association.

In typical old pieces deep reds and blues are largely used. One of them is generally the ground colour of the central field, and shows the Kurdish influence by a gradual shading from end to end; the other appears in the overlying pattern, which partakes of a floral character. The drawing sometimes represents flowering plants, such as the rose bush, arranged in perpendicular rows and brightened by tints of white, green, or yellow. Detached flowers not infrequently line the edges of the field. The wide borders also, as a rule, have vines and floral forms.

Type Characteristics. Colours, principally dark red and blue, with minor quantities of brown, green, yellow, and ivory. *Knot,* Ghiordes. Knots to inch horizontally seven to ten; perpendicularly, eight to twelve. The rows of knots are, as a rule, pressed down, so that the alignment of each half knot is very uneven; but frequently this feature is not regularly maintained in all parts of the same rug, so that here and there the warp is noticeable at back. *Warp,* wool; each of the two threads encircled by a knot is generally equally prominent at back, but occasionally one is depressed below the other. *Weft,* wool, of medium diameter. A thread of weft crosses twice between every two rows of knots. *Pile,* wool of medium length. *Border,* of three to four stripes. *Sides,* a double selvage of two or three cords in blue, red, or brown. *Lower end,* a web through which runs a parti-coloured cord, and a warp fringe. Frequently there is a braided selvage in addition to the web. *Upper end,* the same as lower, excepting that the web is occasionally turned back and hemmed. *Texture,* moderately loose. *Weave* at back is of slightly coarse grain. *Usual length,* six to seven feet. *Usual width,* two fifths to three fifths length.

KARADAGHS. — In the extreme northwestern part of Persia, between the city of Tabriz and the river Aras, is a mountain range called Kara Dagh, which signifies the "Black Mountain." On its slopes and in the adjoining valleys rugs have been woven for at least several hundred years, and at one time were well known in Europe, but few have reached this country. Most of them are produced for home use, so that they are, as a rule, well woven, of good material, and of vegetable dyes. They resemble in colour scheme, weave, and finish of sides and ends the rugs of Karabagh, which immediately adjoins this district on the north. Indeed, in no other rugs of Persia are the traditions of Iranian weavers so much disregarded and Caucasian ideas so closely followed.

The field of many of these rugs is completely covered with conventionalised flowers of several different colours, so arranged that diagonal lines are of similar colours. Sometimes it is covered with a pattern of hexagonal-shaped figures containing geometric forms or conventionalised floral designs. Again, it may contain the Herati pattern or one similar to the Mina-Khani. In fact, some repetitive pattern of small design is the usual type; but now and then some form of pole medallion, which the weavers have learned from their more southern neighbours, is substituted. The patterns of the borders are either mechanically drawn vines or contain geometric figures characteristic of Caucasian pieces. For guard stripes the reciprocal trefoil is constantly used.

The colour scheme is generally bright and pleasing. A favourite colour for the field is blue or a camel's hair yellow; sometimes rose is seen. The nap of modern pieces is medium long and of old pieces is short. The weave of the latter is excellent, so that the closely pressed knots and stout threads of weft make at the back an even surface unlike the coarse appearance of many rugs.

Type Characteristics. *Colours*, principally blue, red, yellow, green, and white. *Knot*, Ghiordes. Knots to inch horizontally seven to eleven; perpendicularly, seven to eleven. The rows of knots are not firmly pressed down, so that the warp appears at back, and the weft is prominent. *Warp*, wool; each of the threads encircled by a knot is equally distinct at back. *Weft*, wool, of coarse diameter, occasionally dyed. A thread of weft crosses twice between every two rows of knots. *Pile*, wool, of moderate length. *Border*, three to six stripes. *Sides*, a double selvage of two or three cords. *Both ends,* a narrow web and short warp fringe. *Texture*, moderately firm. *Weave* at back is of rather coarse grain. *Usual length*, five to nine feet. *Usual width*, two fifths to two thirds length.

MOSULS. — Near the ruins of ancient Nineveh, on the bank of the Tigris, is the city of Mosul. Once it was not only an important mart for wares carried up and down the river, and for vast caravans from east and west, but it became noted for its textiles from which was derived the name "muslin." At length on account of pestilence, misrule, and the sack of armies its population and industries have dwindled; though it is still the capital and commercial centre of a district that lies between the high table-lands surrounding Lake Van and the low plains of Bagdad, and that extends across the Mesopotamian valley to the mountain ridges bordering Western Persia. Within this extensive area are large stretches of rich pasture, where Abraham once fed his flocks, and where each year Kurdish nomads from the north drive their sheep when the winter snows cover their own hillsides. Arabs, Turks, Armenians, Jews, and Christians likewise mingle with the natives, so that the population is as mixed as can be found anywhere in the Orient.

Thus it happens that the rugs marketed in the city of Mosul are made by different races and show great diversity of character. It would, indeed, be often difficult to distinguish them if the weave were disregarded; for though they are prone to yellow and russet hues, and the long wool is floccy as well as lustrous, there is no pattern that can be considered truly typical. Many of them borrow Caucasian designs, such as stars, latch-hooks, diagonal bands, and barberpole stripes. Others have patterns adopted almost bodily from Kurdish pieces. But however much the nomadic rugs are copied, a Persian influence is always shown by the way in which the severer features are softened. In fact, a very large percentage of rugs that come from Mosul are made by the tribes that wander as far east as the great mountain divides along the borders of Western Persia, and adopt patterns and colour schemes current in Azerbijan and Ardelan. It accordingly happens that medallion patterns resembling those of Bijars, but with bolder and less graceful outlines, are seen. More frequently the field is covered with small figures common to Feraghans, as well as with the well-known pear designs; but the former are coarsely drawn, and the latter lack the gracefully rounded lines seen in Sarabends and are often as geometric as those of the Baku rugs. Somewhere in almost all these pieces appears evidence of some conventionalised floral form; but now and then a rare old piece is found which was woven in the plains of Mesopotamia, with field completely covered with a naturalistically drawn tulip that grows on the banks of the Tigris and Euphrates. Its bright flowers and leaves, supported by a delicate stalk, constitute one of the most beautiful designs seen in any rug.

The borders are rarely wide, and generally consist of three stripes, one of which usually has some simple vine, and the others some well-known geometric pattern. It is, also, not unusual to find an outer edging surrounding the border. In a few of these pieces camel's hair is used even to the extent of occupying the whole field; and goat's

hair or sheep's wool, dyed to a similar colour, is constantly employed.
One of the most usual colours is some shade of yellow. Reddish
hues also prevail. These rugs frequently have the same pleasing
effect of slightly graduated changes so common in the ground colour
of Kurdistans, but as a whole the colour scheme is lighter. On
the other hand, they follow the shading adopted in Persian rugs,
which in a measure eliminates the sudden transition between adjacent areas of strongly contrasting colour so noticeable in nomadic
pieces. On account of the present remoteness of the Mosul district
from important highways of travel, many excellent pieces, which
with careful use should acquire the rich tones of those now old,
are still woven there.

Type Characteristics. Colours, principally yellow and brownish
red, with minor quantities of blue, green, and white. *Knot,* Ghiordes.
Knots to inch horizontally five to seven; perpendicularly, seven to
nine. A half knot, as it appears at back, is as long as wide and
frequently longer. The yarn is not drawn tightly against the warp.
The rows of knots are firmly pressed down, so that the warp is concealed at back. *Warp,* almost always wool, rarely cotton; each of
the two threads encircled by a knot is equally prominent at back.
Weft, generally of wool, of coarse diameter and frequently dyed
red or orange, but occasionally of cotton. As a rule, a thread of weft
crosses twice between two rows of knots, but sometimes crosses
only once; or two or three threads cross side by side, as in Karajes.
Pile, wool and occasionally camel's hair, of medium length. *Border,*
of three stripes with frequently an outer edging of solid colour.
Sides are generally a heavy double overcasting, but in a few pieces
there is a two-cord weft selvage or double selvage. *Lower end,* a web.
Upper end, a web and warp fringe; occasionally there is a heavy
braided selvage, or the web is turned back and hemmed. *Texture,*
moderately firm. *Weave* at back is of coarse grain. *Usual length,*
six to ten feet. *Usual width,* two fifths to three quarters length.

Now and then are seen comparatively scarce rugs, such as the
Teheran, Gulistan, Kara-Geuz, Bibikabad, Afshar, and Gozene,
that were woven within the Iranian boundaries. Some of them
are no longer produced, and others are woven in such small numbers
that but few are exported.

The Teherans were formerly made in the present capital of Persia.
The typical pattern consists of the Herati design or some floral

form occupying the central field, which is two or three times as long as wide. The weave resembles that of Irans, since the knot is Ghiordes, each of the two threads of warp that it encircles is equally prominent at the back, and both warp and weft are cotton. The borders are wide, and the sides are finished with a two-cord selvage.

Gulistan is the Persian name for a flower garden, and the rugs known by that name were once made in a district not far from Kashan, where rose bushes bloomed profusely. The fields may be covered with conventionalised floral and leaf patterns, or again they may contain roses naturalistically drawn with extended petals, as if viewed from above. The most striking characteristic is the opulence of colour, such as red, blue, and yellow softened by shades of brown and green. Even the weft and the webs of the ends are red, blue, or brown. The sides have a two-cord selvage, warp and weft are usually of cotton, and one thread of warp to each knot is depressed at the back. These rugs, which formerly came in large sizes, are no longer made.

Only a short distance to the northeast of Hamadan is the district of Kara-Geuz, which is occupied by a large tribe, who in the past have furnished some of the best of Persian cavalry. The people are industrious, and not only cultivate the land but engage in weaving. Some of their rugs closely resemble the Kurdish pieces, and others correspond with the Irans. In the technique of weave they often follow the Hamadans. On the outskirts of this district is the town of Bibikabad, where, also, rugs are woven for market.

For a number of generations the country adjoining Lake Urumiah on the west and stretching into the Turkish domain has been partly occupied by a powerful race of brave and active people who are known as Afshars. They are regarded as a branch of the Yuruks of Asia Minor, and the rugs of both tribes have many points of similarity. The wool of the nap is generally the coarse product of the mountain sheep. The patterns incorporate some of the floral features of Persian rugs, though they display many Caucasian characteristics. These Afshars bear a close resemblance to the Kazaks, from which they may be distinguished by observing a fold as they are bent backwards, which will show the fibres of the yarn of a knot standing out at front as a unit, while in Kazaks they have a greater tendency to blend. Also at the back, each half of a knot is no longer than wide, nor is it drawn closely against the warp, while in Kazaks each half of a knot is often double its width and is drawn closer.

In the country about Gozene, in the watershed of the Euphrates river, are made a few rugs for local use, though they occasionally reach Western narkets. The pattern, which is very simple, usually consists of some small diaper figure of brown or grey colour, or of dull tones of maroon. Many of this class have a double foundation of warp; and frequently, at the back, the knots do not form regular lines parallel with the length, as is the case with other rugs. This is due to the fact that any thread of warp may be encircled by both the left half of some knots and the right half of others. Occasionally, also, a knot is tied about four threads of warp. In other rugs of this class which have a single foundation of warp the weave resembles that of Mosuls.

BORDER STRIPES

The most noticeable feature of Persian border stripes is their floral character, which is very frequently represented by a vine winding from side to side with pendent flowers marking each flexure. Some of these vines have been evolved from arabesques, and others from naturalistic tendrils, but all are graceful. In a few pieces the stripes contain rows of detached flowers, rosettes, or pears, expressed in rich yet unobtrusive colours, that are always in perfect harmony with those of the field. Rarely is the pattern geometric. Accordingly, with the exception of the Indian and some of the Chinese, they are the most elegant, pleasing, and artistic of all border stripes. Moreover, some of them follow almost the same patterns that were in use centuries ago.

Primary Stripes.—In Plate E, Fig. 1 (opp. Page 156), is represented a typical Herat stripe derived from some of the XV and XVI Century carpets. It shows close relationship to the pattern of conventional rosette and pair of attendant leaves so frequently seen on the fields of such rugs as the Feraghans and Sehnas. In this stripe the angular and serrated leaves are extended to form a vine.

One of the best known Khorassan stripes, shown in Plate E, Fig. 2, bears a resemblance to the Herat stripe; and it is not unlikely that they had a common origin, since they were designed in adjoining and freely communicating districts. The enlargements of the vine at the centre of each flexure are doubtless leaves, but they occasionally resemble the heads of birds.

PLATE E.   PRIMARY BORDER-STRIPES OF PERSIAN RUGS

PLATE 36. KIR-SHEHR PRAYER RUG

The so-called turtle pattern, Plate E, Fig. 3, has probably been
derived from the interlacing arabesques that appeared in rugs at
least as early as the beginning of the XV Century, as is indicated
on Page 79. The rosette and attendant leaves between adjacent
"turtles" suggest the Herati pattern. This stripe is found principally in Feraghans, Irans, Sehnas, and Muskabads. One that is
similar, but more mechanically drawn and with wider spreading
arms, is typical of Gorevans and Serapis.

A stripe found in Joshaghans, representing a row of floral bushes,
is shown in Plate E, Fig. 4. It is also seen in some of the old rugs of
Northwestern Persia. Another Joshaghan stripe, which also suggests
the Herati pattern, is represented in Fig. 5.

A single row of pears (Plate E, Fig. 6) is a characteristic Lar-
istan stripe.

The dainty pattern of Plate E, Fig. 7, in which the vine has been
abandoned and serrated leaves nearly surround a floral device,
shows a not unusual Herez stripe.

As a rule the drawing of Persian-Kurdish stripes is never crowded,
and represents a simple vine with bright pendent flowers. A
stripe commonly seen in this class is represented in Plate E, Fig. 8.
It is also seen in the Bijars.

On account of the geographic position of the Karadagh district,
which is separated only by the Aras river from Caucasia, its stripes
show a combination of floral and geometric design not usual in other
Persian pieces. Plate E, Fig. 9, represents one of these stripes with
a rosette, and the serrated leaf so common among the Shirvans.
Plate E, Fig. 10, represents another stripe of the same class with
eight-petalled star-shaped flowers pendent from an angular vine.

A beautiful stripe, representing a vine and pendant flower, which
is frequently seen in some of the Persian-Kurdish rugs, is shown in
Plate E, Fig. 11.

In Plate E, Fig. 12, is illustrated a very dainty pattern of vine and
roses that now and then is seen in old Feraghans; and in Fig. 13
are also represented vine and roses as they occasionally appear in
old rugs of Northwestern Persia.

The very mechanically drawn double vine shown in Plate E,
Fig. 14, is sometimes seen in stripes of Hamadans. In fact, simplicity of border is a characteristic of this class.

Mosul and Kurdish stripes show a similarity, but the former are
often more mechanically drawn than the latter. In Plate E, Fig. 15,

is a stripe from an old and beautiful Mosul with conventionalised vine and King Solomon's eight-pointed star.

Undoubtedly the most typical of any class of Persian stripes is the well-known Sarabend pattern of formal vine with pendent pear on white ground. It is very rarely that a rug of this class is without this stripe (Plate E, Fig. 16). Its presence at once indicates that the piece is either a Sarabend or an Iran copy.

In Plate E, Fig. 17, is the well-known pear pattern of a Meshed stripe. The graceful form, resembling in a measure the Indian drawing, is peculiar to these stripes.

The Kirman stripe (Plate E, Fig. 18) invariably contains red roses naturalistically drawn, surrounded by a profusion of leaves and stems. This is one of the most beautiful of Persian border patterns.

Somewhat similar, but far more formal, is the Kermanshah stripe, one of which appears in Plate E, Fig. 19, with mechanically drawn flowers, leaves, and vines.

The formal pattern (Plate E, Fig. 20) of octagons surrounded by latch-hooks is now and then found in borders of Shiraz rugs, and indicates how great a concession their weavers at times make to nomadic influences.

The main stripe of Sehnas is always narrow and contains some floral form, though frequently much conventionalised. One of these stripes is shown in Plate E, Fig. 21.

Very few Persian rugs have such wealth of floral ornamentation in the borders as the Sarouks and Kashans. A stripe typical of the former is represented in Plate E, Fig. 22.

Secondary and Tertiary Stripes. — The ornamentation of a large proportion of secondary stripes of Persian rugs consists of running vines, which fall within two divisions, according to the absence or presence of pendants.

Plate F, Fig. 1 (opp. Page 158), taken from an inner stripe of a Kermanshah, shows one of the simplest vines with budding tendrils at each flexure.

In Plate F, Fig. 2, is a simple stripe seen in such rugs as Gorevans. Similar stripes are very common. As there is no pendant, the character of the vine depends upon the form it assumes in alternating flexures, one of which in this instance is an eight-petalled star.

In many of the Karadaghs is seen the Caucasian stripe (Plate F,

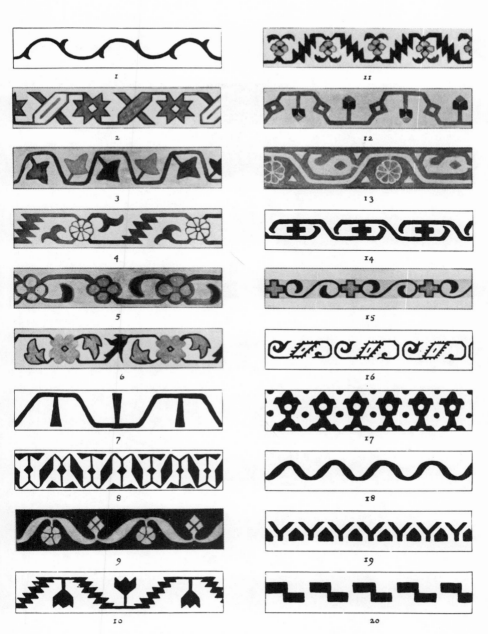

PLATE F. SECONDARY BORDER-STRIPES OF PERSIAN RUGS

PLATE 37. ANATOLIAN PRAYER RUG

Fig. 3) consisting of an angular vine, from each flexure of which spring small designs like three-leaf clover.

Another type peculiar to some rugs of Northwestern Persia, as the Bijars and even Sehnas, is shown in Plate F, Fig. 4. Here one flexure is a serrated leaf, and the other is a small rosette with short curving tendrils.

A simple vine of somewhat similar order appears in Plate F, Fig. 5. At each flexure is a flower of four petals, and from alternating flexures spring tendrils of colour different from that of the vine. Stripes of similar drawing appeared in Persian carpets as early as 1350 A.D. A further stage in the development of the same pattern is illustrated in Plate F, Fig. 6.

One of the simplest forms of a vine with pendant is shown in Plate F, Fig. 7. It appears in Asia Minor carpets woven during the XIII Century, and also in some of the earliest Iranian carpets. Now and then it is seen in modern Persian rugs.

A very common form of a vine with pendant is shown in Plate F, Fig. 8. This pattern is seen in a large number of Persian rugs, such as Mosuls, Bijars, Kurdistans, and Hamadans. Each flexure of the vine is enlarged to almost the form of a leaf, and between them is a branching pendant.

In another stripe (Plate F, Fig. 9), taken from a Feraghan, there is no particular enlargement to the vine, and the alternating pendants are buds and flowers of four petals.

A more geometric form that appears in such rugs as Muskabads is shown in Plate F, Fig. 10. In this the vine represents serrated leaves, and suggests one of the Shirvan patterns.

A very similar stripe (Plate F, Fig. 11), taken from a Sehna, should be compared with those of Figs. 8 and 10, as it serves to illustrate the evolution of vine patterns. In fact, if a very large number of stripes were arranged in proper order, they would show almost imperceptible gradations from one type to another.

One of the simplest vines with pendant, adopted by the Kurdish tribes, is shown in Plate F, Fig. 12; and in Fig. 13 is another vine with pendent pear alternating with a rosette.

Not all the patterns, however, are vines. In Plate F, Figs. 14 and 15, for instance, is represented the same secondary stripe as it appears at the sides and the ends of some moderately old Persian rugs. The former pattern bears a resemblance to the one in Fig. 5, and each illustrates a series of connecting links.

A graceful pattern that is seen in Bijars, Hamadans, and other rugs of Northwestern Persia is represented in Plate F, Fig. 16. It was probably derived from an old form of leaf and tendril.

The reciprocal trefoil (Plate F, Fig. 17) which is constantly used in a tertiary stripe, is probably a degenerate form of an ornate floral design. It is more widely used for a border stripe than any other pattern, as it is found not only in such Persian rugs as Sarabends, Bijars, Sarouks, and Kashans, but in many of the Indian and Beluchistan rugs, and in almost all of the Caucasian group. It was commonly used in Persian rugs as early as the year 1500.

In many of the rugs of Persia and Asia Minor is seen as a tertiary stripe the simple ribbon pattern (Plate F, Fig. 18). Its origin is lost in the dim past, and it is not improbable that once it had a symbolic meaning.

A very interesting tertiary stripe, because of its well-authenticated age, contains the "Y" pattern shown in Plate F, Fig. 19. It is found in some Persian carpets that were woven as early as 1550.

One of the simplest guard stripes, shown in Plate F, Fig. 20, is frequently found in modern Persian rugs, as well as in Iranian carpets woven six centuries ago.

TECHNICALITIES IN THE WEAVE OF PERSIAN RUGS

PERSIAN	G=Ghiordes	S=Sehna	Knot Horizontally	Knot Perpendicularly	Warp w=wool	Warp c=cotton	Warp s=silk l=linen	At back e=each equally prominent	At back d=1 to knot depressed	At back h=1 to knot doubled under	Weft w=wool	Weft c=cotton	Weft l=linen s=silk	No. of times crossing bet. two rows of knots	Sides O=overcasting	Sides S=Selvage	Lower End W=web S=selvage	Lower End K=rows knots	Lower End L=warp loops	Lower End F=Fringe	Upper End W=web S=selvage	Upper End K=rows knots	Upper End T=turned back and hemmed	Upper End F=Fringe	Nap	Weave	Texture
Bijar	G		6-10	8-12	w					h	w			2	O		W [S]				W [S]			F	m	m	f
Feraghan	[G]	S	8-13	7-18		c		e	d			c		2	O		W				W			F	s	m	m
Gorevan	G		6-8	6-10		c		[e]				c		1-2		S	W		L				T	F	m	c	l
Hamadan	G		6-9	8-12	[w]	c		e		h	[w]	c		1	O		W		L		W				m / s	m	f
Herat	G	[S]	8-11	6-12	[w]	c			[d]		[w]	[c]		[3-4]		S	W			F	W			F	m	c	f
Herez	G		5-10	6-12		c		[e]	d		[w]	c		2	O		W			F	W			F	m	c	l
Iran	G		6-11	7-11		c		e				c		2 [1]	O		W				W			F	m	c	l
Mod. Ispahan	G		6-9	8-11	w	c		e			w			1-2	O		W				W	[K]		F	m / s	m	f
Joshaghan	G		7-11	8-13	[w]	c		e	d		w			2	O		W				W		[T]	F	m	f	f
Kashan		S	16-20	16-24		c	[l]	e				c	[l]	2	O		W				W			F	m	m / c	m / f
Karadagh	G		7-11	7-11	w	c		e			w	c		2	O		W				W			F	s	f	l
Karaje	G		6-11	7-12	w	[c]		e		h	w	[c]		1 / [3-4]		S	W		[L]		W			F	m [1]	c	l
Kermanshah		S	12-18	11-18		c				h	w	[c]		2	O		W				W			F	m	c	f
Khorassan		S	8-13	12-20		c				h	[w]	c		2 [6-8]	O		W				W			F	m	m / f	m / f
Kirman		S	11-20	11-20		c				h	w	[c]		2	O		W				W			F	s	f	f

[ ] indicates the less frequent condition.

TECHNICALITIES IN THE WEAVE OF PERSIAN RUGS

PERSIAN	KNOT G=Ghiordes	KNOT S=Sehna	Number to inch — Horizontally	Number to inch — Perpendicularly	WARP w=wool	WARP c=cotton	WARP g=goat's hair / l=linen	WARP back e=each equally prominent	WARP back d=1 to the knot depressed	WARP back h=1 to the knot doubled under	WEFT w=wool	WEFT c=cotton	WEFT l=linen / s=silk	WEFT No. times crossing bet. two rows of knots	SIDES O=overcasting	SIDES S=selvage	LOWER END W=web / S=selvage	LOWER END K=rows knots	LOWER END L=warp loops	LOWER END F=fringe	UPPER END W=web / S=selvage	UPPER END K=rows knots	UPPER END T=turned back and hemmed	UPPER END F=fringe	NAP	WEAVE	TEXTURE
Persian Kurdistan	G		5-9	6-13	w			e	d		w			2	O		W		L		W			F	l	c	f
Western Kurdistan	G		4-7	6-9	w			e			w			2	O		W	[K]	[L]		W	[K]	T	F	l	c	f
Mahal	G	S	7-12	6-12		c		e	d			c		2	O		W			F	[W]			F	m	c	m/f
Meshed	[G]	S	8-15	12-17	[w]	c				h	w	c		2	O		W			F	W			F	m	m	m/f
Mosul	G	S	5-7	7-9	w	[c]		e			w	[c]		2 [1]	O	[S]	W				W / [S]		[T]	F	m	c	m/f
Muskabad	G	S	6-11	6-11		c			d	[h]		c		2	O		W			F	[W]	K		F	m	c	m/f
Niris	G		6-11.	7-15	w				d	[h]	w			2	O		W	K		F	W	K		F	m	l	l
Sarabend		S	8-13	9-13		c		e		h		c		2	O		[W]			F	W			F	m/s	m/f	f
Sarouk		S	12-18	12-20		c			[d]	h		c		2	O		W			F	W			F	s	f	f
Sehna	G	S	11-20	12-24		c	[l]	e				c		1	O		[W]				W			[F]	s	m	m
Serapi	[G]	S	6-10	7-12		c	[l]		d	[h]		c		2		S	W		L	[F]	W			F	m	c	f
Shiraz	[G]		7-12	8-12			[g]	e	[d]		w			2	O		W		L		W			F	m	m	l
Suj-Bulak	G		7-10	8-12	w			e	[d]		w			2		S	W			F	W		[T]	F	m	m/c	m/l
Tabriz	G		12-20	10-22	w	c	[l]			h	[w]	c	[l]	2		S	W			F	W			F	s	f	f

[ ] indicates the less frequent condition.

CHAPTER X

ASIA MINOR RUGS

LL rugs that are woven in the Turkish provinces of Asia are frequently grouped together and called "Turkish" rugs; but a more natural classification is to distinguish between those made to the east and those made to the west of a line drawn from the Gulf of Iskenderoon to Trebizond, deflecting slightly in its course so as to follow the ridges that divide the watershed of the western forks of the Euphrates river from the plateau of Anatolia. With the exception of the very few pieces that come from Syria or other southerly districts, those woven in the Turkish provinces east of this line show such a relationship to those of Persia that they are more properly classed with them; while on the other hand, with the exception of the rugs of the wandering Yuruks, those woven to the west of this line and in the neighbouring islands of the Mediterranean conform so closely to a common type that they fall naturally into a separate group. It is better, therefore, to treat them separately and to call them the Asia Minor Rugs.

Though a certain glamour attaches to all that comes from Persia, the Indes, or Far Cathay, in no part of the Orient are rugs woven on more classic ground than are the Asia Minor pieces. They are still made in the shadow of the walls where Crœsus lived and among villages where Homer trod. Their yarn is spun with crude distaff by the shepherd who still drives his flock along the same road where Artaxerxes marched, across the bridges that Roman legions built, and over the green slopes of Mt. Ida. In fact the names of some of them call to mind pictures of the Crusades, the journey of Paul, the march of Alexander's conquering army, and of cities founded before the beginning of history.

When analysing the rugs of Asia Minor, it is necessary to make a distinction that has been previously noticed in the case of Persian rugs, though with them it is less important. From the time when there arose a large demand in the markets of Europe and America for the rugs of the East the natural supply decreased, and, as a consequence, the price of those that remained increased. To meet this deficiency, and because of the higher prices, there was established a system by which large numbers of women and children were constantly employed; although many worked in their own homes, using such material as was furnished by their employers and receiving fixed daily wages. In the western and southern parts of Asia Minor, which are connected by railroads with seaports, are a number of communities where this system is in vogue. One of these is at Demirdji in the province of Smyrna, where there are a small number of looms; others are in the districts of Ghiordes and Kulah, which together have about one thousand looms; and Oushak, the principal rug-weaving centre of Asia Minor, has as many more.* Almost all rugs produced at such places are now shipped to Smyrna, which itself has but very few looms, or to Constantinople, whence they are reshipped to Western markets. These products lack much of the oldtime artistic spirit and individuality of character, on account of the dependence of the weavers on their employers, who demand the largest output consistent with fair quality. Furthermore, the weavers are frequently required to reproduce Western patterns. The result is that most of these rugs possess little of the firmness of texture, the harmonious relations of designs, and the excellent colour of old fabrics. Since, then, they represent in a measure European influences, and are subject to further changes to meet the demands of a fluctuating foreign taste, it would be of little use to describe them, especially as all their original characteristics exist in the old pieces.

The striking features of Asia Minor rugs woven over fifty years ago are the colour schemes, main patterns, and the separate designs, which may be either independent of the pattern or constitute part of it. The colour effect of Asia Minor rugs is as a rule brighter than that of the Central Asian, Indian, or Persian groups; for the reds, blues, and yellows are less subdued. Some of their tones never appear in Chinese rugs, and on the whole they most closely resemble those of the Caucasian pieces; yet it is not unusual to see such colours as mauve, lavender, and canary yellow, that rarely appear even among these. Moreover, in a few of them masses of strongly con-

* It is also to be noted that within the last few years large numbers of pieces bearing resemblance to old Oriental rugs have been woven about Constantinople.

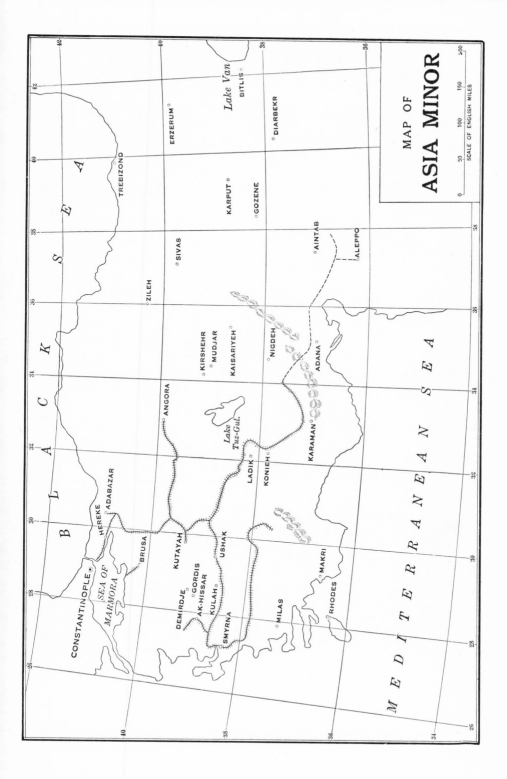

MAP OF
ASIA MINOR

SCALE OF ENGLISH MILES

0   50   100 150 200

BLACK SEA

MEDITERRANEAN SEA

SEA OF MARMORA

CONSTANTINOPLE

HEREKE
ADABAZAR
BRUSA
DEMIRDJE
KUTAYAH
GORDIS
AK-HISSAR
KULAH
USHAK
SMYRNA
MILAS
RHODES
MAKRI
LADIK
KONIEH
ANGORA
Lake Tuz-Gul.
KIRSHEHR
MUDJAR
KAISARIYEH
NIGDEH
KARAMAN
ADANA
ZILEH
SIVAS
AINTAB
ALEPPO
GOZENE
KARPUT
ERZERUM
TREBIZOND
DIARBEKR
BITLIS
Lake Van

PLATE 38. MUDJAR PRAYER RUG

trasting colours are placed beside one another without the customary
shading of Persian rugs or the artificial device of Caucasian latch-
hooks to soften the effect of harsh combinations.

The difference, nevertheless, between the Asia Minor rugs and
those of other groups is less apparent in the colour schemes than in
the main patterns, for in the Asia Minor rugs is evidence of an independent inspiration and development. There are lacking the rigid
octagonal figures of the Central Asian groups; the frets and floral
sprays distinctive of Chinese; the naturalistic floral treatment of
the Indian; the delicate tracings, rhythm of movement, and wealth
of foliage motives that characterise the Persian; as well as the
severely geometric forms and conventionalised motives of the Caucasian. Instead of gracefully flowing lines we find strong rectangular ones; instead of flowers realistically balanced on interlacing,
foliate stalks, they are arranged separately in formal rows. But
if their patterns lack the fertility of invention or the refinement
of Persian and Indian pieces, they excel them in the strength of
their clear definition, accentuated by massing of colour. It is, however, in the prayer patterns, which appear in the majority of Asia
Minor rugs, that the weavers attain their best results; for in such
work they have the inspiration of a high religious as well as artistic
spirit. In these patterns, which differ from those of any other group
of rugs, is often manifest singular beauty and grace, as well as
delicate sentiment derived from worship in Moslem chapels; for
in many is represented the burning lamp that, projected against a
background of sacred green, hangs from the column-supported arch,
above which is spread a spandrel of blue typifying the vaulted
heavens.

Likewise many of the small designs that are found in other groups
of rugs are rarely, if ever, seen in this one; as, for instance, animals, birds, fishes, and human beings are never employed, on account
of the religious prejudice of the Sunnite Mohammedans, who prevail
in the country. Nor, with very few exceptions, is the Herati design,
so characteristic of Persian rugs, nor the pear design, so characteristic
of both Persian and Indian rugs, ever seen. Furthermore, the reciprocal trefoil, that is used as a motive for a small border stripe in all
Caucasian and many Persian rugs, is very rarely found in Asia
Minor pieces woven during the last two centuries, though it appears
in some of an earlier era. But in its place are the water motive and
ribbon, which are less frequently employed by the weavers of any

other country. There are also many small floral motives that appear only in Asia Minor rugs, and that will be noticed in connection with the separate classes.

These characteristics of colour, pattern, and design are not the result of a spontaneous growth unalloyed by foreign influences; for a natural art never existed in Asia Minor, which has never enjoyed a national existence; but they are the results of artistic movements that at different times have swept over that country. Thus, as an heirloom of dynasties that once flourished farther east, are the Cufic characters that appear in some of the early border patterns; and as a relic of the Mongol and Timurid invasions are the dragon and other designs found in the oldest pieces. In Oushaks, as well as others, are seen the evidences of Persian treatment; while the drawing and colour schemes of the prayer rugs forcibly suggest Saracenic, Grecian, and Christian ideas. In fact, the rugs of Asia Minor, while possessing co-ordination of colour and design, are in a measure composite. They never reach the high artistic development of Persian rugs, because the latter were produced under the fostering care of great kings whose royal magnificence could secure from years of patient labour suitable furnishings for palaces and mosques; yet they are none the less interesting subjects for speculation and study.

BERGAMOS. — In the valley of the Caïcus and twenty miles from the Ægean Sea is the city of Pergamus, that gives its name to the Bergamo rugs. It is of unknown antiquity, and may have stood when Agamemnon was warring with the house of Priam before the walls of that other city of the same name. In turn, Persians, Macedonians, Thracians, Syrians, and Romans had taken possession of it before the Apostle Paul founded there one of the seven churches of Asia. Greek sculptors chiselled its monuments, philosophers taught beneath the shade of its trees, and scholars gathered there the library that rivalled that of Alexandria. Partly encircled by mountains and enclosed by the wall of this old city, that was wellnigh destroyed during the Turkish wars, is the modern city of some fifteen thousand inhabitants. It is to-day one of the flourishing cities of the Levant, yet only in the surrounding ruins is there any reminder of its former greatness and splendour. But in these crumbling relics of the past and in the excellence of its woven fabrics of more recent times are traces of the artistic spirit that once prevailed there.

It is still possible to obtain many good specimens of Bergamos representing the craftsmanship of fifty or more years ago, when aniline dyes and European patterns were unknown east of the Hellespont. Almost without exception they are sterling fabrics that glory in a wealth of colour accentuated by depth of pile and sheen of soft lustrous wool. An observer is at once impressed by the tones of deep blue and madder red that a few lines or patches of ivory white bring out more clearly, and forms a favourable estimate of the value of these pieces independently of the drawing, which seems subservient to the part of giving spirit and quality to the colour scheme. In fact, it is to the genius of the dyer who applies his knowledge to the tinting of carefully selected wool, and to the pains of the weaver in constructing the foundation of warp and weft rather than to his skill in arranging artistic designs, that these pieces command as high a price as old Kirmans of similar age.

In two particulars Bergamos differ from most Asia Minor rugs: in shape they are nearly square, and prayer rugs are the exception rather than the rule. Nor do all the prayer rugs follow the same general pattern, as is usually the case with other classes. They may have low tent-shaped arches like those of Daghestans, high triangular arches with stepped sides and a panel above the spandrels as in the Kir-Shehrs, or they may have shapes unlike those of any other class. Moreover, the pieces not used as prayer rugs also have great diversity of pattern; but as a rule some large figure, as a medallion, occupies the centre of the field. Very frequently it is of hexagonal shape, with the sides at upper and lower ends of the rug serrated or fringed with latch-hooks. As is not the case with many of the Persian rugs, the field surrounding the medallion is almost always covered with small designs, arranged with careful precision so as to show a perfect balance with reference to the centre. Eight-pointed stars and other geometric figures are frequently used, but there is a leaning to floral designs, which, however, are often so conventionalised as almost to lose their identity. Most prominent of these is the Rhodian lily and the pomegranate; but the lily never shows such graceful drawing or such dainty colouring as in the Kulahs, and in some pieces even loses all resemblance to a floral form. The pomegranate, which suggests the Ladik, is more frequently seen in the main border stripe. Undulating vines do not find favour among the Bergamo weavers, and small isolated geometric designs are largely employed in the narrow border stripes, while larger, more complex figures often replace the floral in the main stripe.

In no other class of rugs are so many and such painstaking devices to avert the spell of the evil eye. Should an unexpected visitor surprise the weaver while at work, he may be required to part with a bit of his frock, which is then attached to the wide web of the end; should a similar occurrence of ill omen follow, another bit of different material and colour may be sewn upon this; and as a crowning talisman, a button may be affixed to both. Small cowrie shells from the Ægean shores are often used for such purposes; and now and then may be seen a woollen tassel dangling from the centre or from one of the ends of the rug.

Type Characteristics. Colours, principally red and blue, with minor quantities of yellow, white, and green. *Knot*, Ghiordes. Knots to inch horizontally five and one half to nine; perpendicularly, seven to eleven. The rows of knots are pressed down, so that the warp is concealed at back. *Warp*, wool; each of the two threads encircled by a knot is equally prominent at back. *Weft*, wool of fine diameter, dyed red. A thread of weft crosses from two to six times between every two rows of knots. *Pile*, wool; generally of medium length but frequently long. *Border*, from one to four stripes; most frequently of three. *Sides*, a weft selvage of two, three, or four cords, coloured red or blue, with occasionally some green or yellow. *Both ends*, a web, that is sometimes six or seven inches wide, coloured red and crossed by broad longitudinal stripes, which are generally blue, but may be black, white, brown, or yellow. Some device to avert the evil eye is frequently attached to the webs. Beyond the web is a tasselled warp fringe. *Texture*, moderately firm. *Weave* at back is of fine grain. *Usual length*, three to seven feet. *Usual width*, three quarters to nine tenths length.

GHIORDES. — Whether, as has been maintained, the town of Ghiordes, that lies a day's journey to the east of Pergamus, is on the site of the ancient Gordium where tradition says the father of Midas dedicated his chariot to Jupiter, and Alexander severed the bark which bound the pole to the yoke, it claims attention from the fact that the rugs woven there one and two centuries ago not only excelled similar products in all other parts of Asia Minor, but equalled the best fabrics woven in Persia during the same period. Indeed, a few connoisseurs would rank them still higher; yet with reference to technique of weave and delicacy of colour and drawing, very few should be classed with those woven in the previous century by the protégés of Tamasp and Shah Abbas.

So essentially do the modern rugs of the Ghiordes district differ from the old pieces in weave, colour, and pattern, and so great is their inferiority, that they have little interest; but fortunately it is still possible to purchase pieces from seventy-five to one hundred and fifty years of age, and others still older are in the hands of collectors or in museums.   In determining their age the colours and drawing, as well as weave and pattern, are important indices.   For instance, the reddish tones of the fields of pieces less than a century old have a pinkish or even magenta tinge, while in the oldest the red is of rich, deep colour.   Similarly, in the case of blues, greens, yellows, and even the ivories that rarely occupy the field, a riper and richer colour marks the greater age.   Likewise with the drawing, greater painstaking and higher artistic skill are apparent in the older rugs; though in some of the oldest the designs are less ornate than in those of a subsequent period.   This is also true of the patterns as a whole; since the best types are found in rugs that are probably from one hundred and fifty to two hundred and fifty years old, whereas in the extremely old pieces there is an approach to archaic forms.

The difference between the odjaliks and namazliks, which are the kinds most frequently seen, is most noticeable.   The colours, to be sure, are much the same, though as a rule lighter and duller tones predominate in the odjaliks.   Their borders show a greater tendency to use geometric figures, some of which are profusely fringed with latch-hooks suggestive of Caucasian influences.   They also contain archaic designs believed to be associated with sun worship, as well as many floral forms common to the prayer rugs.   It is, however, in the fields that the distinction is most noticeable; since the large masses of uniform colour that make the namazliks so effective are wanting, and instead are frequently seen hexagonal-shaped medallions that are fringed with large rounded latch-hooks and contain a lozenge or other geometric design in the centre.   At both ends of the fields are sometimes narrow panels containing quasi-floral forms, and stiff conventions occupy the intervening corner spaces.

In striking contrast to these odjaliks are the old Ghiordes prayer rugs, with the rich tones of solid colour in the fields and the delicate drawing of the borders.   No doubt they were made with unusual care, since they were intended for religious purposes.   The pattern represents an entrance into a mosque; and it is not improbable that some of the earliest rugs were copied directly from archways, many of which still exist in Mohammedan countries.* Near the base of all Ghirodes arches, at each side, is a shoulder, which in old pieces was supported by a single pilaster or a pair. Sometimes these were ornamented with scroll work or floral forms, but finally many of them degenerated into floral devices that bore slight resemblance to columns, and in other rugs they have entirely disappeared. In some very old pieces the shoulders and the mihrab were rounded, but as a rule the shoulders are flattened at a very obtuse angle; and the mihrab is either plain or has stepped sides that culminate in a blunted apex. To further suggest the sacred purposes of the rug a lamp is often suspended from the niche, though floral forms may take its place, and not infrequently these too are wanting. Almost without exception some reminder of the tree of life, such as the small floral sprig or the Rhodian lily, is projected from the inner side of the arch and from all sides of the border against the field. In the spandrel, also, is almost invariably some floral or leaf form; though these may be very much conventionalised or even supplanted by geometric figures. Above the spandrel is a panel, which may contain some floral form, scroll device, or verse from the Koran; and another panel, though generally with different design, is almost invariably placed beneath the field. A scroll resembling a large S (Plate O, Fig. 9, Page 291) frequently appears in these panels. Its resemblance to forms found in Armenian dragon carpets of earlier centuries is very noticeable.

The border surrounding the field is as characteristic of this class as is the prayer arch. There are invariably a number of stripes, which generally consist of a wide central one, two secondary, and two or more small guard stripes. The drawing is distinctly floral, yet is widely different from the Persian. A design (Plate G, Fig. 1, opp. Page 192) frequently seen in the central stripe represents a large palmette or rosette partly surrounded by leaves, suggestive of the Herati

* One of the most interesting is at Sivas, where are the remains of a most beautiful Seljuk gateway, with architectural lines that might well have been taken for a weaver's model. As in many prayer rugs, the engaged columns support a high arch over which a panel rests above a figured spandrel. The outlines of each of these parts suggest most forcibly the drawing of the prayer rug, and the resemblance is carried even further; for corresponding with the border stripes is the chiselled masonry that once rested above the panel and still extends to the foot of the entrance at each side of the arch.

design, and connected by tendrils with more delicate flowers or leaves. But the more usual design (Plate G, Fig. 3) consists of flowers and fruits that are arranged in quadrangular shape, so that the alternate units face in different directions as they extend around the border. Though it is far from naturalistic, its delicate lace-like drawing with clear definition and its tones in harmony with the central field, contribute largely to the beauty of the rug. The secondary stripes have generally repetitive leaf forms; and running through the guard stripes is a simple vine, ribbon, or wave design. Occasionally, however, the typical Ghiordes border is replaced by one borrowed from the near district of Kulah, and instead of the broad central stripe are several narrow parallel stripes studded by perpendicular rows of small floral figures (Plate G, Fig. 12). An unusual feature of these rugs is the linen nap which is sometimes used in the field instead of wool, for the reason that it retains its colour while wool darkens with age; and another is the silken fringe which is often seen at the corners of fine specimens. The nap is always short, and the rugs are closely woven.

Type Characteristics. Colours, principally red, blue, yellow, and white. *Knot*, Ghiordes. Knots to inch horizontally seven to twelve; perpendicularly, eight to sixteen. The rows of knots are pressed down, so that the warp is concealed and the weft is partly hidden at back. *Warp*, wool or cotton and in a few pieces raw silk. One of the two threads encircled by a knot is usually slightly depressed below the other at the back. *Weft*, wool or cotton. A thread of weft crosses twice between every two rows of knots. *Pile*, wool, and occasionally some cotton, clipped very short so as to be harsh to the touch. *Border*, six to nine stripes. *Sides*, a weft selvage of two or three cords, or only infrequently an added selvage of silk. *Both ends*, a narrow web and warp fringe. A few pieces have an added silk fringe at the corners. *Texture*, firm. *Weave* at back is of very fine grain, but slightly rough. *Usual length*, five to seven feet. *Usual width*, two thirds to three quarters length.

KULAHS. — About fifty miles from Ghiordes, in a southeasterly direction, is the Turkish village of Kulah. Both places are surrounded by the same general character of hills and plains, and for the last several centuries the people of each have been subject to the same influences of race and religion. They have undoubtedly visited, intermarried, and become familiar with the arts and crafts of one another. It is not, therefore, surprising that some of their rugs should have similar technique of weave, and that a few resemble one another in general pattern and small designs. Moreover, such a close correspondence exists between many of the old rugs of both districts, that even the most experienced are sometimes at a loss to distinguish between them. In fact it is surprising that there is so marked a distinction between most of them. In the Kulahs the border designs are not so elaborately drawn, nor are the prayer arches so high. They have rarely the fringe that adorns the corners of some Ghiordes rugs, or more than one panel. The field usually contains floral figures, arranged in formal order; the spandrel is almost always extended in two narrow stripes, one at each side of the field; and the colours are always subdued. These and other characteristics of each class make it possible to distinguish between most of them.

As is the case with Ghiordes rugs, sedjadehs are almost unknown; but it is not unusual to see odjaliks. These resemble prayer rugs in the following respects: the borders are almost identical; the central fields contain the same floral figures resting on a similarly coloured ground; both ends of the hexagonal-shaped field resemble a mihrab; and the space between the field and border is covered with designs peculiar to the spandrels of the prayer rugs.

On account of their artistic drawing and soft colours the prayer rugs are favourite pieces with all collectors. It is true that the arch is flatter than that of any other rug of this group, and is defined either by plain sloping lines, or more frequently by stepped edges, so that it lacks the classic beauty of the Ghiordes type; but on the other hand the Rhodian lily and other floral forms characteristic of these pieces are delineated with a realism and graceful delicacy that are unequalled in any other Asia Minor rugs. Arranged on slender sprays along each side of the field, hanging as long clusters from the niche in place of a lamp, or placed on the panel in formal rows, they accentuate with their bright tones the subdued richness of the ground colours. Sometimes, however, these simple field designs are replaced by more formal drawings that represent a plat of land with a tomb shaded by a tall cypress and other trees with many leafy branches. Rugs with these designs are not uncommon in Germany, whither large quantities of Asia Minor prayer rugs were shipped many years ago, and where they are known as "Friedhofteppiche," or "Grave Rugs."

The most pleasing features are in the fields, but the most distin-

PLATE 39.   DAGHESTAN PRAYER RUG

PLATE 40.   KABISTAN RUG

guishing features are in the borders, which are invariably of several stripes. Instead of the large central stripe with floral and repetitive designs common to most rugs is a series of parallel bands, from five to ten in number and about an inch in width, that contain rows of minute floral forms. These narrow bands are a distinguishing feature of the Kulahs, though they have occasionally been copied by the Ghiordes weavers. Nevertheless, they are sometimes replaced by the broad stripe containing rows of geometric-shaped designs, as in Plate G, Fig. 13 (opp. Page 192), which also are peculiar to these rugs. Strange as it may seem, these designs have doubtless been derived from leaf forms by successive degradation, as will be seen by comparing Figs. 13a, 13b, 13c, and 13d of Plate O (Page 291). There is still another border design that is so constantly found in the secondary stripe of these pieces and so rarely in any others that it might well be designated the "Kulah stripe" (Plate H, Fig. 10, opp. Page 194). The design consists of a repetitive figure suggestive of some Chinese device, but is in reality a degraded form of a vine, as will be seen by observing some of the very old border stripes. Between the inner secondary stripe and the field is usually a narrow stripe containing a continuous ribbon design, or a simple vine-like form, as in Plate F, Fig. 18 (opp. Page 158). Often a part of each succeeding undulation of the vine has been omitted and the remaining parts have been compressed, so as to leave small detached figures like a row of "f's," as in Plate H, Fig. 2. It is not unusual to see both vine and detached figures in the same rug.

Diversity prevails in the colours of field, spandrel, panel, and borders. In the field is generally a mellowed red, or a yellow tint that is described both as golden brown and apricot; blue also is occasionally seen, and white is very rare. But whatever the colour of the field, that of the spandrel is generally a light blue, indicative of the sky, and the overlying panel is frequently a dark blue. Green and brown often appear in the border, as well as a canary yellow peculiar to Asia Minor rugs. Moreover, a few of these pieces have a single small area of red or blue, that was doubtless inserted to avert the evil eye, since it shows no more relation to the surrounding colours than spilt ink might have; yet in spite of these contrasts and the fact that the nap lacks the lustre peculiar to many other classes, some of them are as beautiful as Ghiordes.

Between these old fabrics and the modern, which factory-like are produced in large quantities to meet the demands of a Western market and taste, is the most noticeable difference, for the latter are inferior to the former in patterns, weave, and dyes. Furthermore, with the wool of many is mixed mohair, so that rapid deterioration follows slight usage.

Type Characteristics. Colours, principally red, brownish yellow, and blue, with minor quantities of green, dark brown, and white. *Knot*, Ghiordes. Knots to inch horizontally five to ten; perpendicularly, seven to twelve. The rows of knots are not firmly pressed down. *Warp*, wool; one of the two threads encircled by a knot is noticeably depressed at the back. *Weft*, in most rugs, of wool of medium diameter, sometimes dyed yellow. A thread of weft crosses twice between every two rows of knots. In other rugs, even very old, the weft consists of a coarse thread of jute crossing once between two rows of knots and alternating with a small thread of jute and another of wool crossing side by side once between the next two rows of knots. *Pile*, wool, of short or medium length. *Border*, six to nine stripes. *Sides*, a coloured mixed selvage of two, three, or four cords. *Both ends*, a coloured web and warp fringe. *Texture*, loose. *Weave* at back is of moderately coarse grain. *Usual length*, five to seven feet. *Usual width*, three fifths to three quarters length.

OUSHAKS. — Fifty miles eastward from Kulah is the city of Oushak, famous during the XV and XVI Centuries for the carpets exported thence to Europe to adorn the halls of cathedrals and thrones of monarchs. But with the subsequent decadence in Asiatic art its glory ebbed, so that half a century ago it was but a small mudhoused city known for the excellence of its dyes and the wool which was taken there from the interior to be washed, spun, and then sold to the weavers of the surrounding country. Since then, however, its population has steadily grown, and the weaving industry has thrived, until now it is one of the most populous cities of Asia Minor, with looms more numerous than those of any other city. The weaving is done entirely by women and girls, most of whom are Mohammedans. Though they live principally in private houses, they are under the direction of large firms, who furnish the wool as well as the patterns, which are in accordance with European and American demands.

Important distinctions exist between the different grades of these rugs. Some are known as "Turkish Kirmans," in which Persian designs are frequently introduced, others are of still finer workmanship, but the oldest and coarsest pieces were formerly known as "Yapraks." These are distinguishable by their strong colours of red, green, and blue, of which only two as a rule are seen in a single rug, and are massed to produce striking effects. Their foundation of warp and weft, which are dyed in the same colours, is loosely woven and often of an inferior grade of wool. Many of them are too large and heavy for domestic use, but are well adapted for salons and public halls.

With such slight variations in pattern and none in colour, Oushaks would be of little interest were it not that their prototypes were striking pieces woven by artisans whom Sultan Solyman the Magnificent brought from the northwestern part of Persia, when he conquered it in the XVI Century. Some of them appear in the paintings of old masters, and when contrasted with the modern fabrics indicate how great is the decline in the craftsmanship of the weavers. Of the beautiful well-balanced designs once represented in the fields, only large stars and diamonds, defined by less pleasing lines and placed with less regularity, remain. All of the graceful arabesques and dainty floral motives that appeared as sub-patterns are omitted. As works of art, the modern products are little esteemed; but their durability, depth of pile, and wealth of colour make them excellent objects of utility.

Type Characteristics. Colours, principally red, blue, and green. *Knot*, Ghiordes. Knots to inch horizontally four to eight; perpendicularly, four to nine. A half knot, as it appears at back, is longer than wide. The rows of knots are not closely pressed down. *Warp*, wool. Each of the two threads encircled by a knot is equally prominent at back, or one is slightly depressed below the other. *Weft*, wool of medium diameter and generally dyed red. A thread of weft crosses twice between every two rows of knots. *Pile*, wool, clipped long. *Border*, usually of three stripes. *Sides*, generally a double overcasting, occasionally a selvage. *Both ends*, generally a web coloured red and a warp fringe. *Texture*, very loose. *Weave* at back is of moderately coarse grain. *Length*, carpet sizes. *Usual width*, two thirds to four fifths length.

AK-HISSAR. — Almost seventy-five miles by rail from Smyrna and a short distance to the west of Ghiordes is the Turkish town of Ak-Hissar, the White Citadel. Even before the building of the railroad rugs were woven in this district; and in recent years the work-house system has been established, and large quantities, that bear some resemblance to the modern products of Kulah and Oushak, have been exported.

DEMIRDJI. — Half a century ago the town of Demirdji was almost uninhabited; but as a result of the Occidental demand for Oriental rugs and the disappearance of old pieces, it has grown to be an important manufacturing centre. Many of its weavers learned their trade at the historic Ghiordes, which is about twenty-five miles distant; but the fabrics are more closely woven and the wool is more carefully selected than is the case with the modern Ghiordes.

KUTAYAH. — On the main railroad that will eventually connect the Bosphorus with the Euphrates is the town of Kutayah. As it is on the edge of the Anatolian plateau, wool and goat's hair have been for a long period important articles in its trade. Both of them are now used in the local manufacture of rugs, which in a measure resemble the products of Oushak.

SMYRNA. — The location of Smyrna on a magnificent harbour and its connection by rail with all the important rug districts of the interior, have made it the principal centre for the export trade in Asia Minor rugs. Many of the people are also largely engaged in the industry of weaving, but almost all weavers are now in the employ of large companies who furnish the materials and patterns. As a result, the Smyrna rugs are mere copies of well-known types of other Turkish pieces, or, as is generally the case, of stereotyped patterns that have been evolved to meet the requirements of European and American tastes. Many of the rugs, to be sure, are well woven and serviceable, but they lack individuality of character.

MELEZ. — About seventy-five miles to the south of Smyrna and twenty from the Mediterranean Sea is the town of Melassa, or Melez. It is now little known, but was once the market place of an important rug-producing district, which included a large part of the classic province of Caria. Accordingly, the pieces that came from there were sometimes called Carian, but are more generally known as Melez.

On their face they show a close relationship to the Anatolians, and also, though in a less degree, to many other Asia Minor rugs; yet as is to be expected of the products from one corner of the country, they have a distinct individuality in both pattern and colour. Occasionally an old piece is seen, in which the border is very narrow and the whole field is covered with parallel stripes on which are systematically arranged geometric and semi-floral forms; but as a rule the fields are not much wider, and often less wide, than each of the adjacent borders. Within this central space are frequently arranged prominent designs, which are widely different from the designs of any other rugs, and are suggestive of Chinese ornament, but were doubtless derived from floral or tree forms (Plate O, Fig. 12, Page 291). Moreover, projecting in regular order from the alternate sides of the narrow border stripe, next to the field, are sometimes seen thumb-like figures, that fit against one another like the cogs of a wheel (Plate H, Fig. 15, opp. Page 194). Each of these features, though not always present, is peculiar to this class.

Of the several border stripes, the central is generally as wide as the remainder and not altogether dissimilar to that of the Ladiks. Very frequently it consists of a row of palmettes between which are conventionalised leaves and flowers on slender stems; but now and then the palmettes are replaced by eight-pointed stars or other geometric figures, and the intervening spaces filled with corresponding designs. The secondary stripes are of a pronounced Caucasian type; and almost invariably in a smaller tertiary stripe is represented a waving line or the reciprocal sawtooth.

The prayer rugs are equally characteristic. In typical examples the lines defining the mihrab descend from the niche to meet the sides of the narrow field at an angle of forty-five degrees, and are then deflected towards its centre, to return again to its sides. The resulting drawing shows two equilateral triangles on each side of the field at the base of the mihrab, which in conjunction with the upper sides of the triangles has the appearance of an incomplete diamond. This effect, moreover, is frequently accentuated by a perpendicular row of diamonds extending from just below the niche to the base of the field. The sides of mihrab, field, and central designs are, as a rule, fringed with small geometric or conventionalised floral forms; and in the spacious spandrel are more realistic floral designs arranged on a trellis-like sub-pattern.

This individuality of pattern is accompanied by a less marked yet noticeable individuality of colour scheme. As is the case with many Bergamos, the principal tone is a dark red, which generally appears in the central field, and is also used almost without exception in the broad end webs, the side selvages, and the threads of weft. Ivory white for the spandrel, some yellow and green for the borders, are common colours; but the one that rarely appears in any appreciable quantity in other rugs is a characteristic tone of lavender or mauve, which is present in almost every old Melez. Not always are these tones pleasing, as many of the rugs have been poorly dyed; but there are other pieces, now rapidly growing scarce, of which the colours are exceedingly rich and harmonious.

Type Characteristics. Colours, principally red, with minor quantities of blue, yellow, white, and some mauve. *Knot*, Ghiordes. Knots to inch horizontally five to eight; perpendicularly, six to eleven. A half knot, as it appears at back, is as long as wide or slightly longer. The rows of knots are not closely pressed down, yet the warp does not show at back. *Warp*, wool; each of the two threads encircled by a knot is equally prominent at back. *Weft*, wool of small diameter, dyed blue or red. A thread of weft generally crosses four times between every two rows of knots. *Pile*, wool, of medium length and sometimes short. *Border*, wide, from three to seven stripes. *Sides*, a selvage of two to four cords, usually coloured red. *Lower end*, a red web and loose warp fringe. *Upper end*, a red web, a braided selvage, and loose warp fringe. *Texture*, moderately loose. *Weave* at back is of slightly coarse grain. *Usual length*, four and one half to six feet. *Usual width*, three fifths to three quarters length.

ISBARTA. — In the town of Isbarta in the southern part of the province of Konieh are woven rugs which are sometimes known to the trade as "Spartas." Like many other pieces made to meet the Western demand, they lack spontaneous individuality, but are often of excellent quality and coloured in delicate tones, arranged harmoniously.

RHODIAN. — Even at a very early period the people of the islands bordering the southwestern coast of Asia Minor produced textile fabrics that rivalled many of the best products of the mainland. None of them were more beautiful or more interesting than those which came from the Island of Rhodes, where were blended the vigorous Grecian and the more subtle Oriental arts. Here was the inspi-

ration of the sea, cloudless skies, luxuriant vegetation. Here was
felt the deep influence of the Mohammedan and Christian religions,
as well as an early pagan mythology; and there is little doubt that
the cathedral walls and picturesque church of the valiant knights
of St. John made an impression on the weavers. It is not surprising,
therefore, that the fabrics should be of deep, rich colour full of suggestion, and that the drawing of the long central panels should
remind one of cathedral windows.

Of the many beautiful rugs formerly woven in Rhodes only a
few now remain, and these are generally in the hands of collectors.
Some are odjaliks, some namazliks, some sedjadehs; but all, with
the exception of a few crude and coarsely woven pieces, have colours
and weave that bespeak a ripe age, amounting in many instances to
one hundred years or more. On the field of odjaliks are represented
as a rule the usual hexagonal figure with two sides at each end forming a triangle; and on the fields of the namazliks are prayer arches
which, though characteristic, never equal the graceful drawing
seen in Ghiordes rugs. It is the sedjadehs that awaken the greatest
interest, as they have some striking peculiarities rarely seen in rugs
of the mainland.

Their field is divided into two or three panels that extend almost
the full length of the field, and terminate at one end in flat and
often serrated arches. The spandrels are small; and placed transversely above them is a low panel, that contains designs of mechanically drawn leaves, vandykes resembling those of Ladiks, and other
figures common to Asia Minor rugs. In fact, these pieces at once
suggest prayer rugs containing two or more prayer arches, but
the pattern is generally regarded as a representation of cathedral
windows. Both colouring and designs give force to this idea. In
each of the principal panels is a different ground colour, as red, blue,
or green, which is never gaudy, yet exceedingly rich on account
of the depth of pile; and in the overlying figures there is often a
strangely contrasting splendour of brighter colouring. Furthermore,
one of the most usual of these designs, arranged like pole medallions,
consists of large eight-pointed stars with effulgent rays of brilliant
hues. As we look at some of the rare old pieces with this pattern,
cathedral windows almost appear before us with bright sunshine
streaming in golden rays through the stained glass and brighten-
ing the interior with its more sombre tones of "dim religious
light." Sometimes the pole design is modified so as to suggest a

tree of life extending from one end of the panel to the other. An equally common design represents six very mechanically drawn leaves assembled in the form of a medallion (Plate O, Fig. 15, Page 291). Each of these leaves has two straight edges meeting at right angles and containing at the corner a small rectangular spot; but the remaining sides that form the circumference of the medallion are deeply serrated, so as to produce much the same effect as the rays of effulgent stars. In the fields are also frequently seen latch-hooks, and occasionally checkerboards with different colours for separate squares.

Between field and border is a close correspondence in both colours and small designs. The latter consist principally of geometric and semi-floral forms, as eight-pointed stars, the octagonal disc, and the geometric leaf that is typical of Kulah rugs. No other design is more prevalent than the last, which may be found in all parts of these rugs. Sometimes it is drawn most realistically so as to resemble the flower forms so common in spandrels of Kulahs; but again the outlines are most conventional with square-like projections at the edges and a bar of underlying field of contrasting colour crossing the face diagonally, as in the border stripe of Plate G, Fig. 13, (opp. Page 192), which shows the foliate origin of the latter.

The name "Makri" is frequently applied to these rugs, since they were often bought in the city of that name, which is one of the harbours of Southwestern Asia Minor nearest to Rhodes.

Type Characteristics. Colours, principally red and blue, also considerable yellow, green, and white. *Knot*, Ghiordes. Knots to inch horizontally five to eight; perpendicularly, seven to nine. The rows of knots are not firmly pressed down, so that the warp shows in places at back. *Warp*, wool; each of the two threads encircled by a knot is equally prominent at back, occasionally one to each knot is slightly depressed below the other. *Weft*, wool, of medium diameter, coloured red. A thread of warp usually crosses twice between every two rows of knots, rarely only once, and sometimes as many as four times. *Pile*, wool, clipped long. *Border*, two to three stripes. *Sides*, a double selvage of two, three, or four cords, usually coloured red or blue. *Lower end*, a web, either red or of several colours, and long warp fringe hanging loose or braided. *Upper end*, a web, either red or of several colours, beyond which is often a heavy braided selvage; also a long warp fringe hanging loose or braided. *Texture*, moderately loose. *Weave* at back is of slightly

PLATE 41. KUBA RUG

PLATE 42. CHICHI RUG

coarse grain. *Length*, four to seven feet. *Width*, three fifths to four fifths length.

BROUSSA. — At the base of Mt. Olympus and distant only twenty-five miles from the Sea of Marmora, with which it is connected by rail, is the city of Broussa. By reason of this location and its proximity to Constantinople, it is an important commercial centre; and on account of the excellence of the wool and silk obtained in the surrounding country, rugs are woven here for foreign markets. The fabrics are stoutly made and compare favourably with those of Smyrna.

HEREKE. — In the town of Hereke, on the Sea of Marmora, is a Turkish factory, where large numbers of silk rugs are manufactured. Most of the silk is obtained in the immediate neighbourhood and from the country about Mt. Olympus. As the early weavers were brought from Kirman to instruct the artisans of the Sultan, and the patterns have been largely copied from old Persian and Asia Minor pieces, it is not surprising that many of the fabrics compare favourably with the silk rugs of Persia.

KONIEHS. — At the base of Mt. Taurus and overlooking the salt desert of Central Asia Minor is the city of Konieh. Within its present walls is all that is left of the ancient Iconium that opened its gates to Xenophon, Cyrus, and Alexander, but drove forth the Apostle Paul. Finally it surrendered to Seljukian conquerors, who, realising the importance of its situation on one of the great highways between east and west and in an oasis of well-watered fields, orchards, and gardens which face a great barren plain, established there a Mussulman capital, that became noted for its opulence and culture. In later years it successfully resisted the assault of Frederic Barbarossa; but subsequently it declined, until now the only remaining vestiges of its former importance are several colleges, one hundred mosques, and the famous green tower surmounting the tomb of the whirling dervishes.

In few other cities of Asia Minor were greater inducements offered to the rug weavers. Surrounding them lay hills and plains that produced sheep with soft, fine fleeces. On the oaks that grew not far to the north lived the kermes, from which were obtained the vermilion dyes famous even through Persia. The political and com-

mercial importance of the city, as well as the religious fanaticism
of the people, aided them. Accordingly a great many choice pieces
were formerly woven there, but on account of the remoteness of
the city from the markets that supplied Europe, few found their
way into channels of trade.

Large numbers were used solely for religious purposes, but other
kinds are as frequently seen. All of them contain both geometric
and floral forms. The geometric forms resemble designs prevalent
in Eastern Anatolia and in Caucasia, such as latch-hooks, eight-
pointed stars, and barber-pole stripes; and the floral forms consist
of mechanically drawn palm leaves and the tree-of-life design.

Probably in no other Asia Minor rug is such latitude in the drawing of the prayer arch. Sometimes it begins below the middle of
the field and rises at a sharp angle to a point near the upper end;
again it may be exceedingly flat; but generally it has the same pitch
as the arches of Kulahs, and, like them, the sides, as a rule, are
stepped or serrated. Furthermore, it is not unusual to see latch-
hooks projecting from each step or serration into the spandrel,
which is filled with small floral and geometric forms. From the niche
is occasionally suspended a lamp; and arranged against the border,
on each side of the field, is a row of conventionalised flowers, or small
sprigs which resemble three triangular-shaped petals at the end of
a straight stem. These floral or foliate designs are one of the
most constant features of this class. The borders are more geometric than those of almost any other Asia Minor rugs, and even
when vines are represented they are drawn with stiff formality.

Whatever may be lacking in artistic drawing is frequently atoned
for by the excellence of the colour scheme, which occasionally rivals
that of the Ghiordes and Kulahs. Rich reds or blues are almost
invariably found in the fields, where there is sufficient depth of nap
to enhance their richness; and the borders are brightened by attractive tones of yellow, green, and white. Contrasted with these
old pieces, the modern rugs of Konieh have little artistic merit, but
are large pieces desirable solely for their durability.

Type Characteristics. Colours, principally red and blue, with
minor quantities of yellow, green, and white. *Knot*, Ghiordes. Knots
to inch horizontally five to eight; perpendicularly, six to ten. The
rows of knots are not very firmly pressed down. *Warp*, wool; each
of the two threads encircled by a knot is equally prominent at back.
Weft, wool, of medium diameter, dyed red. A thread of weft crosses

twice between every two rows of knots. *Pile*, wool, of medium length. *Border*, from two to five stripes, with frequently an outer edging. *Sides*, generally a selvage of two or three cords, but occasionally an overcasting. *Both ends*, a web and warp fringe. *Texture*, only moderately firm. *Weave* at back is of slightly coarse grain. *Usual length*, four and one half to six feet. *Usual width*, three fifths to three quarters length.

LADIKS. — On the ruins of ancient Laodicea is the mud-walled town of the village of Ladik, once the centre of an important rug industry. Among the surrounding hills are still woven pieces which resemble in pattern, though they poorly imitate in weave and colour, the early prototypes that have been classed among the masterpieces of Asia Minor. Few of these old rugs remain, and they are often badly worn in spots; yet they display tones mellowed by the touch of more than a century, and rival the Ghiordes in beauty of design.

As is the case with other classes of rugs woven in Turkish countries, the sedjadehs and odjaliks lack the interesting details of the namazliks, from which they widely differ. On the central fields of many of them are oblong hexagonal-shaped medallions, often three in number, that contain designs of stars or other geometric figures. Between the fields and the borders of the ends are generally spacious panels, on which are represented rows of vandykes. These figures are one of the most permanent characteristics of this class of rugs; and though their origin is uncertain, it is not improbable that they are derived from arrowheads, which were one of the emblems of the Chaldean deity Hoa, the reputed inventor of Cufic writing. The borders are also geometric, consisting, as a rule, of three stripes, of which the central contains an angular vine that in different pieces may be very simple or very ornate. One of the central stripes often adopted is represented in Plate G, Fig. 10 (opp. Page 192) and shows a vine with conventionalised leaf. Latch-hooks are common in the sedjadehs, and when floral forms are present the fact is generally disguised by the harsh, mechanical drawing.

In contrast with these pieces, the namazliks with their interesting arches and dainty drawing are most pleasing. In a large number of them the central fields occupy about one half the space within the border, the spandrels extend for a considerable distance above the arch, and the panels are larger than in any other prayer rug. Occasionally arches resembling those of the Ghiordes or Kir-Shehrs

are seen; but they are to be regarded merely as copies, since the
typical arch differs widely from any other and gives to this class
one of its greatest charms.   Instead of rising to the apex in lines of
many serrations, each side of the arch rises from the border and falls
in one large serration, then rises again to form the niche.   The arch is
often fringed with latch-hooks, and extending above the apex of each
serration and the niche are perpendicular devices that may, also,
be a development of the latch-hook, since they have not been traced
to any other satisfactory origin.   But whatever their origin may be,
their shape as well as that of the arch at once suggests Saracenic
mosques.   In the spandrel are constantly seen serrated leaves,
rosettes, and designs peculiar to the Ladik.   The large panel is
equally typical, and consists of reciprocally drawn vandykes, from
which rise perpendicular stems supporting leaves and pomegranates.
These are generally five in number, and are so gracefully and naturalistically drawn that it seems surprising that the vandykes, from which
they spring, are ornamented with a profusion of latch-hooks.   The
central fields are sometimes without ornament, but as a rule they
contain some suggestions of the tree of life either in the central design or in the three-leaf sprigs arranged about the borders.   The
latter are as characteristic as any other part of the rug, and consist
of four stripes separated by dotted lines.   The main stripe most
frequently contains a row of delicately drawn lilies alternating with
rosettes, though occasionally a very formal vine with conventionalised leaf is substituted for it.   In the stripes at each side are very
angular vines with three-cleft leaves, and in the narrow inner-most
stripe is generally a ribbon pattern.

All of the drawing has clear definition accentuated by rich and
strongly contrasting colours.   The fields of the namazliks, like
those of the Ghiordes, are entirely occupied by masses of unshaded
blue, red, or brown, that are relieved only by the colours of superimposed designs.   But as is not the case with Ghiordes, there is often
a strong contrast between the colours of centre and ends; yet the
tones are always in perfect harmony.   Other rugs may have more
delicate drawing or more exquisite finish; but in the barbaric arrangement of strong colour and in the uniqueness of graceful designs,
none exceed the old prayer Ladiks.

Type Characteristics.   Colours, principally red and blue, with
minor quantities of green, yellow, and brown.   *Knot,* Ghiordes.
Knots to inch horizontally nine to twelve; perpendicularly, ten to

thirteen. A half knot as it appears at back is longer than wide. The rows of knots are pressed down so that the warp is concealed at back. *Warp*, wool. One of the two threads encircled by a knot is generally depressed below the other at the back. *Weft*, wool of fine diameter, generally dyed red. A thread of weft crosses twice between every two rows of knots. *Pile*, wool, of medium length. *Border*, three to five stripes. *Sides*, a red added selvage of two or three cords. *Both ends*, a narrow web and warp fringe. *Texture*, moderately firm. *Weave* at back is of medium grain. *Usual length*, four and one half to seven feet. *Usual width*, three fifths to two thirds length.

KIR-SHEHRS. — To the north of the great salt desert and in the southern part of the province of Angora is the town of Kir-Shehr. It stands between two mountain ranges, on which are raised sheep with fine fleeces, and is on the branch of the Kizil Irmak, whose waters are well suited for preparing wool for the dyes obtained in the surrounding country. On account of the excellence of wool, water, and natural dyes, as well as the remoteness of the town from main highways of travel, many of the old rugs were excellent pieces, free from the taint of Western influences, and possessing the charm of individuality. It was due, moreover, to the fact that its three or four thousand inhabitants, and the Turkomans who roamed the surrounding country, rarely felt the influence of larger cities that they were so untrammelled by conventionalities. Unhesitatingly they grouped together large spaces of red, yellow, and blue, as well as grass-coloured green, for which they had a particular fondness and employed to a greater extent than almost any other weavers; yet in the case of these old pieces the artistic sense is rarely shocked, since the individual colours are good and the tones are harmonious. Furthermore, the patterns show an unusual blending of floral and geometric forms.

Most of the pieces come in moderate sizes; some are mats, others small sedjadehs, but the choicest are the prayer rugs. The serrated sides of the arch, which rise at a steep angle from the centres of each side of the rather narrow fields, are formed of several parallel lines of different colour. In a not unusual rug, for instance, eight narrow lines separating the spandrel of grass-green from the inner field of brick-red appeared in the following order: red, black, white, yellow, lavender, yellow, red, and blue. The inmost line is frequently fringed with tri-cleft floral forms, which, as in Koniehs, extend in a row along the sides of the field. From the niche is usually suspended the design of an inverted tree of life, and above it are projected latch-hooks or similar devices. It is not unusual to see two arches, and there are sometimes as many as four, placed one within the other. The spacious spandrel that is continued in narrow stripes along the borders to the bottom of the field is covered with geometric or conventionalised floral forms; and the horizontal panel, which may be placed at either end of the field, contains designs in harmony with the remaining parts.

On the whole, the wide borders have some of the most characteristic features; for, as a rule, not only are one or two of the stripes of a peculiar cherry red and one a rich yellow, but three or four of the narrow stripes next to the field are similar in width and ornamentation to those of the Kulah. When contrasted with them the broad central stripe and the outer one seem lacking in harmony, for they are distinctly floral and suggestive of Persian influences.

On account of the quality of their wool and weave, these rugs are soft and flexible. They resemble in some minor details others of the Anatolian plateau, yet they can be distinguished by the presence of grass-green colour and the shape of the prayer arch. The nap of these old pieces, like that of Kulahs and Ladiks, is of medium length; though in modern pieces it is often longer, and the weft and webs are coloured as are those of Bergamos.

Type Characteristics. Colours, principally red and green, also some blue, brown, and white. *Knot*, Ghiordes. Knots to inch horizontally five to nine; perpendicularly, five to ten. A half knot as it appears at back is as long as, or longer than, wide. The rows of knots are not firmly pressed down, so that in places the warp shows. *Warp*, wool; each of the two threads encircled by a knot is equally prominent at back, or occasionally one is slightly depressed. *Weft*, wool, of medium or coarse diameter and generally of different colours in the same rug. A thread of weft crosses from two to six times between two rows of knots, varying in the same rug. *Pile*, wool, of medium length. *Border*, from five to eight stripes. *Sides*, a weft selvage of two, three, or four cords of different colours. *Lower end*, web and warp loops. *Upper end*, a web and warp fringe. *Texture*, loose. *Weave* at back is of coarse grain. *Usual length*, four to six feet. *Usual width*, two thirds to four fifths length.

ANATOLIANS. — To all of Asia Minor was once applied the term "Anatolia," which signifies the Land of the Rising Sun; so that any product of this country might well be called Anatolian, just as any product of Persia might be called Iranian. In fact, many of the less known classes, as the Nigde, Tuzla, Mudjar, and even the Kir-Shehr, Melez, and Konieh, are often called Anatolian. But as there is a special type of rugs known as Iranians, so is there a special type known as Anatolians. They are, however, a mixed lot, that come from parts of a wide stretch of territory, extending over the interior table-land to the home of the Kurds, and incorporating ideas received from many districts. It is, accordingly, difficult to define them as a type; but, as a rule, they are small pieces that are often used for mats and pillows, with moderately long nap of soft, floccy wool, with narrow borders, and a colour scheme that inclines to bright and sometimes garish colours.

Doubtless the best of them come from the provinces of Angora and Konieh, lying within a radius of one hundred miles of Lake Tuz Gul. Here can be obtained the best of wool and dyes; and in some of the old pieces appears the artistic drawing of the more important rug centres farther to the west, but with a strange blending of geometric and floral forms. Eight-pointed stars as well as latch-hooks are seen everywhere, and a very old design with the shape of ram's horns is frequently used. In many of the prayer rugs the arches are of the Kir-Shehr order, though the panels may contain vandykes suggestive of Ladiks. There is the greatest latitude in the width of the borders, which occasionally are their most noticeable feature and again are most insignificant; but in either case they rarely contain more than three stripes, and not infrequently only one. Red, blue, green, and brown are the usual colours, but pink and canary yellow are sometimes used.

Farther to the east, among the foot-hills of the Anti-Taurus mountains, is woven a coarser type by the Kurdish tribes. With the exception of wool and dyes they have little to their credit; for their usual unsymmetric shapes, crude geometric designs, long uneven nap, and braided fringe of warp at the ends are lacking in all elegance.

Type Characteristics. *Colours,* principally red, blue, green, brown, and white. *Knot,* Ghiordes. Knots to inch horizontally five to nine; perpendicularly, six to twelve. A half knot, as it appears at back, is generally as long as wide, or longer. The rows of knots are not firmly pressed down, yet the warp is frequently concealed at back. *Warp,* wool; each of the two threads encircled by a knot is equally prominent at back. *Weft,* wool, of medium or coarse diameter and usually dyed. A thread of weft crosses two, three, and four times between two rows of knots frequently varying in the same piece. *Pile,* wool, of medium length. *Border,* one to three stripes, and occasionally an edging. *Sides,* a weft selvage of two or three cords. *Both ends,* a web and warp fringe. *Texture,* loose. *Weave* at back is of coarse grain. *Usual length,* two and one half to six feet. *Usual width,* one half to two thirds length.

KARAMANS. — At the foot of Mt. Taurus and overlooking the plain that stretches northward into the heart of Asia Minor is the city of Karaman. Before its subjection in the XV Century by Bajazet II and the removal of the capital to Konieh, that lies sixty miles to the northwest, it was the seat of a Turkish government extending to the Mediterranean Sea; but to-day the only reminder of its early importance are several Saracenic mosques covered with rich arabesques. Of the rugs woven there during the early period almost nothing is known, but, on account of the former importance of the city, it is not improbable that they compared favourably with the rugs of other parts of the Turkish Empire. On the other hand, some of the modern products are among the poorest rugs of the East, and contain little artistic merit. A feature peculiar to many of them is the use of natural wool of reddish brown colour, obtained from sheep which live on the mountain ranges to the south of Karaman. The pile is long, the weave is never very firm, and at each end is a coloured web.

SIVAS. — In the city of Sivas, at the eastern end of Anatolia, and in the villages of the surrounding plain, girls and women have woven rugs from time immemorial; but on account of the difficulties of transportation few of them reach this country. The carefully finished sides and ends, the formal character of the pattern, and the almost harsh effect of the strongly contrasting colours of many of them are unlike what are found in the nomadic rugs made farther to the east and west. In the weave is a hint of Persian influence; for not only are both warp and weft of cotton, but the warp is of small diameter and well spun, and one of the two threads to which a knot is tied is depressed below the other. The pattern, on the other hand, is distinctly Turkish. One of the best known types consists

PLATE 43.   TCHERKESS RUG

PLATE 44. BAKU RUG

of a large hexagon that reaches to the sides and ends, and contains within it a medallion on which are designs similar to those seen in Bergamos. On the white field surrounding the medallion are often small rosettes and floral figures. The corners of the field may be fringed with running latch-hooks or a row of formal T's, and contain a rosette at their centre. The borders are rarely wide, and often consist of a single stripe that contains some conventionalised floral form. Although these rugs are well woven, their crude blending of floral and geometric figures, as well as their formality of drawing, which is accentuated by the shortness of the nap, are most suggestive of Occidental conventions.

Type Characteristics. Colours, principally red and white; also dull blue, green, and light yellow. *Knot*, Ghiordes. Knots to inch horizontally seven to eleven; perpendicularly, nine to fifteen. A half knot, as it appears at back, is not as long as wide. The rows of knots are pressed down, so that the warp does not show at back. *Warp*, cotton, well spun and of small diameter. One of the two threads encircled by a knot is depressed below the other at back and sometimes doubled under the other. *Weft*, cotton, of medium diameter. A thread of weft crosses twice between every two rows of knots. *Pile*, wool of short to medium length. *Border*, narrow, one to three stripes. *Sides*, an added selvage of four or five cords attached in places, and with weft encircling inner cord of selvage. *Both ends*, narrow web and loose warp fringe. *Texture*, firm. *Weave* at back is only slightly coarse. *Usual length*, three and one half to six and one half feet. *Usual width*, two thirds to four fifths length.

MUDJARS. — Near the river Kizel Irmak in Central Asia Minor is the city of Mudjar, which produces rugs that occasionally reach this country. They are often classed as Anatolians, but their colour scheme covers a wider range, including red, yellow, green, blue, mauve, and pink, all of which may be seen in the same piece. In fact no other rug of Asia Minor contains as a rule so many colours, which appear in the broad borders of old, well-woven pieces with glistening wool almost like mosaic work. Many of this class are namazliks with arches very similar to the arches in the rugs of Kir-Shehr, which is distant only twenty-five miles to the north; and in the panels above the spandrel are not infrequently designs of vandykes borrowed from the Ladiks. Some suggestion of the tree of life often appears in the field, and again rows of flowers may extend into it from the sides. Some of the best examples are very handsome.

Type   Characteristics.   Colours, principally red, yellow, blue, green, and ivory, also mauve and pink. *Knot*, Ghiordes. Knots to inch horizontally six to nine; perpendicularly, seven to twelve. *Warp*, wool. Each of the two threads of warp encircled by a knot is frequently equally prominent at the back, but generally one is depressed below the other. *Weft*, wool, of medium to coarse diameter dyed red or brown. A thread of weft crosses twice between every two rows of knots. *Pile*, wool of medium length. *Border*, broad, of three to four stripes. *Sides*, a three-cord selvage, frequently red. *Both ends*, coloured webs and fringe. *Texture*, loose. *Weave*, moderately coarse. *Usual length*, four to six feet. *Usual width*, two thirds to three quarters length.

NIGDES. — Near the base of the Anti-Taurus mountains in the eastern part of the province of Konieh is the city of Nigde, which is little known in this country as a rug-producing centre, though its fabrics reach Europe. Many of them are namazliks, that are distinguished by their high geometric arches. The borders often show the influence of the Kurdish tribes, and contain patterns common in the Mesopotamian valley; but their colour scheme of red, blue, and yellow more closely resembles the Anatolian. Most of them are of small size and are poorly woven.

TUZLAS. — Another class of Asia Minor rugs rarely seen are the Tuzlas. They are generally regarded as Anatolians, but are made by people who live about Lake Tuz Gul in the province of Konieh. Some of them are well woven, and have soft woollen pile and attractive patterns. The prayer arch of the namazliks bears some resemblance to the arch of the Kir-Shehrs; the panel is relatively high; and not infrequently the borders have rosettes similar to those of Bergamos. The principal colours are red, blue, green, and ivory.

KAISARIYEH. — One of the few Asia Minor centres for the manufacture of silk textiles is the city of Kaisariyeh, the ancient Cæsarea, near the eastern part of Anatolia. Formerly rugs of excellent quality were made there; but the modern products are, as a rule, inferior both in workmanship and material to those of Hereke. Frequently their dyes are aniline and the colours garish. Many of them are prayer rugs with arches resembling the Ghiordes pattern, but their borders are more conventional. Woollen rugs which are copies of other well-known Asia Minor pieces are also woven there.

YURUKS. — Suggestive of gipsies, yet widely unlike them, are the tribes of Turkoman descent known as Yuruks. This term means "Wanderers;" and they are well named, since throughout the western part of Asia Minor they follow their sheep, cattle, and camels from the rich pastures among the mountain tops of the interior, where they live in summer, to the fertile, sunny plains bordering the seashore in winter. Even near Smyrna and the slopes of Mt. Olympus may be seen their black goat's-hair tents, where the unexpected guest is always welcome.

In their rugs is the reflection of their untrammelled lives, unaffected by the refinements of cities; and as their lives are different from those of all other inhabitants of Asia Minor, so are these rugs entirely distinct, resembling more than anything else the work of the wild Kazaks of the Caucasus. In them will be recognised the same long nap, the same massing of colour, the same profusion of latch-hooks, and other simple designs. The colours, however, are less brilliant, bright reds and yellows being more sparingly used; but on the other hand the depth of floccy nap gives a subdued richness to the dark metallic madder, blue, green, and brown, such as is rarely seen in any Kazak. The patterns show the usual diversity of nomadic rugs. The fields may contain crude, unrelated figures, or diagonal stripes on which are small geometric designs. Again from the Kurdish tribes to the east may be adopted the pear designs as well as floral forms, but the drawing is always far from realistic.

Most of the modern rugs have fine wool coloured with vegetable dyes, and stout warp and weft woven to give flexibility; but their patterns show a want of all artistic feeling. Now and then, however, comes to light a piece that has stood the wear of more than a century, showing the touch of a higher craftsmanship, and with colours softened by each succeeding year.

Type Characteristics. Colours, principally brown, red, and blue, with minor quantities of yellow, green, and white. *Knot*, Ghiordes. Knots to inch horizontally five to seven; perpendicularly, six to nine. The rows of knots are not closely pressed down, yet the warp does not show at back. *Warp*, wool or goat's hair; each of the two threads encircled by a half knot is equally prominent at back. *Weft*, wool of medium diameter. A thread of weft crosses two, three, or four times between every two rows of knots, varying in the same rug. *Pile*, wool, clipped long. *Border*, from four to six stripes, occasionally with an outer edging. *Sides*, generally a heavy double overcasting, but occasionally a double selvage of two or three cords. *Lower end*, a coloured web through which generally runs a parti-coloured cord, and warp loops; or the warp threads may be knotted and hang loose. *Upper end*, a coloured web through which generally runs a parti-coloured cord, a braided selvage, and a warp fringe; or the warp ends may be braided together at short intervals. *Texture*, loose. *Weave* at back is of moderately coarse grain. *Usual length*, four to nine feet. *Usual width*, two fifths to two thirds length.

ASIA MINOR BORDER STRIPES

Regarded as a whole, the borders of Asia Minor rugs show but slight relationship to either the geometric patterns of the Caucasian, or the floral patterns of the Persian; for as a rule the geometric features either are subordinate or suggest an origin by degradation from floral designs, and the floral features generally are represented by an orderly arrangement of disjunct forms rather than by continuous vines with pendent flowers. Yet there is no doubt that some were copied by Caucasian weavers, and that many were derived from Persian patterns. They are frequently, however, more artistic than the former, more interesting than the latter, and rival both in beautiful colouring and delicate drawing.

Primary Stripes. — Several different stripes peculiar to Ghiordes prayer rugs are illustrated in Plate G, Figs. 1, 2, 3, 4, and 5 (opp. Page 192). The first of these is probably the oldest. It is so strikingly suggestive of the Herati design of rosette and attendant leaves that there can be little doubt of its Persian origin. The seed-like processes of the alternate rosettes are noticeable. The second, which is found in many of the Ghiordes rugs, shows the same pattern more conventionalised, with the rosette resembling an open pod and with the leaves almost octagonal-shaped. The third is a still greater evolution of the same pattern in which leaves and rosettes of nearly equal shape and size are placed at three angles of a quadrangular space. The last, which is a very elaborate pattern somewhat similar to the first, is found in a few old rugs. Besides these, a number of parallel lines

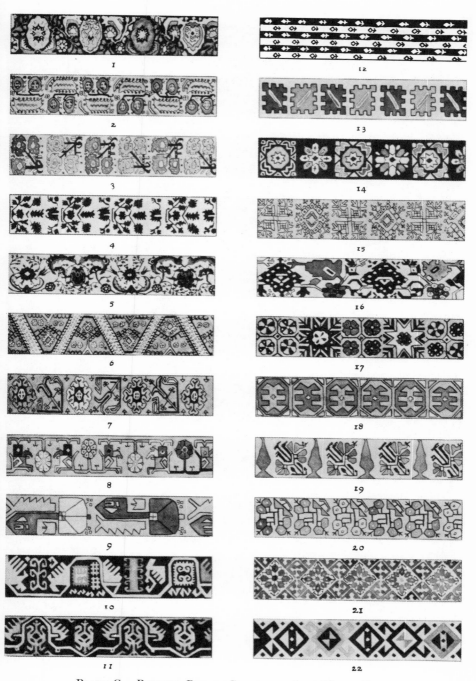

PLATE G. PRIMARY BORDER-STRIPES OF ASIA MINOR RUGS

PLATE 45. SHIRVAN RUG

similar to those of Kulah rugs (Plate G, Fig. 12) are sometimes seen in the Ghiordes.

One of the best known Ghiordes stripes found in odjaliks and sedjadehs is shown in Plate G, Fig. 6. It is a broad stripe with wide, vine-like bands covered with rows of small flecks or flowers. Between each flexure of the band are designs probably symbolic of early sun worship.

In Plate G, Fig. 7, is represented the most usual and beautiful stripe of the Ladik prayer rugs. The principal motives are Rhodian lilies, and rosettes identical with Persian forms, that are probably conventionalised roses. Another stripe, in which the lily is replaced by a conventionalised vine, is shown in Plate G, Fig. 8. Both these stripes are found only in Ladik rugs. Other stripes seen now and then in Ladik and Melez sedjadehs are illustrated in Plate G, Figs. 9, 10, and 11, each of which shows a conventionalised leaf.

One of the most typical Kulah stripes is seen in Plate G, Fig. 12. It might in fact be regarded as a number of parallel stripes, but as will be evident by observing a large series of Kulahs it serves the function of a single broad stripe. Often the separate bands are replaced by a ground of uniform colour marked by parallel rows of minute flowers of regularly varying colour. Occasionally this stripe is copied by Ghiordes weavers.

In Plate G, Fig. 13, is a well-known stripe that appears both in Kulah and Rhodian rugs. As previously explained, its origin is probably floral, though the drawing is geometric. A formal stripe found in Bergamos, and consisting largely of diamonds and eight-pointed stars, is represented in Plate G, Fig. 14.

Figs. 15 and 16 of Plate G illustrate the border stripes of Melez rugs. Each contains regularly spaced rosettes, separated by conventionalised leaf forms. A much more geometric Melez border, in which the rosettes are replaced by eight-pointed stars and the leaves by discs, is shown in Plate G, Fig. 17.

A geometric stripe of uncertain origin that is found in some Koniehs is shown in Plate G, Fig. 18.

In Plate G, Figs. 19 and 20, are represented two stripes characteristic of Kir-Shehrs. The former is a dainty pattern consisting of a row of bushes separated by the lily design. It is occasionally found in the Melez also.

A typical Mudjar stripe in which the geometric patterns are subdivided into small and richly coloured mosaic work is seen in Plate G, Fig. 21.

In Plate G, Fig. 22, is illustrated a Yuruk border stripe such as is frequently seen in modern pieces.

Secondary and Tertiary Stripes.—In Plate H, Figs. 1 and 2 (opp. Page 194), are illustrated two secondary stripes frequently seen in Ghiordes and Kulah rugs. The first is most suggestive of a running vine, and the second has doubtless been derived from it.

A more ornate pattern, which generally accompanies the broad band of perpendicular lines peculiar to Ghiordes and Kulah rugs, is shown in Plate H, Fig. 3. The arrangement of three leaves in angles of quadrangular spaces suggests relationship to the primary stripe of Plate G, Fig. 3 (opp. Page 192).

Two other secondary stripes found in Ghiordes rugs are seen in Plate H, Figs. 4 and 5. The former, which is also found in Kulahs is a vine and flower subject to many modifications.

A tertiary stripe containing a ribbon-like vine is very usual in Ghiordes and Kulah pieces. One of these, which is very graceful, is shown in Plate H, Fig. 6.

Another angular vine with pendent flower, that appears as a secondary stripe of a large number of Ladik prayer rugs, is illustrated in Plate H, Fig. 7. This resembles a few Persian stripes, but the drawing of the pendent leaf is characteristic of Asia Minor.

Figs. 8 and 9 of Plate H represent two tertiary stripes often seen in Ladiks and Kulahs. They illustrate the evolution of patterns; for in the same stripe of a rug will sometimes be seen the first of these and the simple ribbon pattern of Plate F, Fig. 18 (opp. Page 158), and also in the same stripe of another rug will sometimes be seen the second of these and a continuous row of "*ff*" designs, as in Plate H, Fig. 2.

The most typical of all Kulah secondary stripes, though it is also seen in Rhodian rugs and occasionally in an old Ghiordes, is illustrated in Plate H, Fig. 10. A somewhat similar stripe is shown in Plate H, Fig. 11. The design looks like a Chinese motive, but that it is evolved from a vine will be seen by comparing these stripes with those in Figs. 4 and 12. All of them are Asia Minor border stripes.

In Figs. 13 and 14 of Plate H are illustrated the swastika and

PLATE H. SECONDARY AND TERTIARY BORDER-STRIPES OF ASIA MINOR RUGS

PLATE 46. SOUMAK RUG

S stripe, which are seen now and then in Asia Minor rugs, such as Kulahs, and also in Caucasian rugs.

One of the most typical of Melez secondary stripes, representing processes like cogs projecting in a row from alternating sides of the stripe, is shown in Plate H, Fig. 15. The stripes shown in Figs. 16 and 17 of Plate H, representing a row of small rosettes and a row of octagonal discs, are also occasionally seen in Melez rugs.

The very angular vine shown in Plate H, Fig. 18, is sometimes seen in Koniehs.

A very unusual secondary stripe (Plate H, Fig 19), found in a few Anatolians, represents a fret pattern, which was probably copied from some monument.

The chain pattern (Plate H, Fig. 20) is occasionally seen as a tertiary stripe in the Ghiordes. It appeared in Asia Minor rugs of several centuries ago, and has been copied by the weavers of Caucasia. Sometimes the lines are angular, and again the S's are separated by small round or square dots.

TECHNICALITIES IN THE WEAVE OF ASIA MINOR RUGS

ASIA MINOR	KNOT G=Ghiordes	KNOT S=Sehna	No. to inch Horizontally	No. to inch Perpendicularly	WARP w=wool	WARP c=cotton	WARP s=silk / g=goat's hair	WARP e=each equally prominent	WARP d=1 to the knot depressed	WARP h=1 to the knot doubled under	WEFT w=wool	WEFT c=cotton	WEFT j=jute / s=silk	WEFT No. times crossing bet. two rows knots	SIDES O=overcasting	SIDES S=selvage	LOWER END W=web / S=selvage	LOWER END K=rows knots	LOWER END L=warp loops	LOWER END F=fringe	UPPER END W=web / S=selvage	UPPER END K=rows knots	UPPER END T=turned back and hemmed	UPPER END F=fringe	NAP	WEAVE	TEXTURE
Anatolian	G		5-9	6-12	w			e			w			2-4		S	W			F	W			F	m	c	l
Bergamo	G		5-9	7-10	w			e			w			2-6		S	W			F	W			F	m l	f	m
Ghiordes	G		7-12	8-16	w	c	[s]	e	[d]		w	c	[s]	2	O	S	W [S]			F	W		T	F	s	f	m
Karaman	G		6-9	8-13	w				d		w			2	O	S	W [S]		L		W			F	l	c	l
Kir-Shehr	G		5-9	5-10	w			e	[d]		w			2-6		S	W [S]		L		W			F	m	c	l
Konieh	G		5-8	6-10	w			e			w		[j]	2		S	W			F	W			F	m	m c	m f
Kulah	G		5-10	7-12	w			[e]	d		w			2 [1]		S	W			F	W			F	m s	m c	l
Ladik	G		9-12	10-13	w			[e]	d		w			2		S	W			F	W			F	m	m	m f
Melez	G		5-8	6-11	w			e			w			4		S	W			F	W S			F	m [s]	m c	l
Rhodian	G		5-8	7-9	w	c		e	[d]		w	c		2 [1-4]		S	W			F	W S			F	l	m c	m l
Sivas	G		7-11	9-15	w				d	[h]	w			2		S	W			F	W			F	m s	m c	f
Youruk	G		5-7	6-9	w		[g]	e			w	c		2-4	O	[S]	W	[K]	L	F	W	K	[T]	F	l	c	l

[ ] indicates the less frequent condition.

CHAPTER XI

CAUCASIAN RUGS

SIDE from the facts that the Caucasus is rugged, that during the Middle Ages it was ruled by the illustrious Tamara, and that till recently the physical charms of its women made them favourites in the slave markets of Constantinople, the character and history of that country are to-day almost as unknown to the average reader as they were when the bards of ancient Greece bound Prometheus to its rocks and hung the Golden Fleece from its oaken boughs. Yet it is a country of wonderful interest. Above its gorges, rivalling those of the Himalayas, rise mountains higher than the Alps. On the southwestern slope are combined the luxuriant vegetation of tropical lowlands with virgin forests of fir and pine, and in meadows and beside shaded brooks grow flowers of strange beauty. Beneath the ground is undeveloped wealth of ores and mineral oil. The river Phasis is the natural home of the pheasant; the crags are the resorts of ibex; and in secluded glens sharing solitude with bear, wolf, and boar are hidden the wild aurochs.

Moreover, the philologist, ethnologist, and historian can here follow his favourite pursuit with as much zest as the Alpine climber, botanist, mineralogist, and sportsman; for within the confines of this region are spoken some seventy languages by as many distinct clans, each of remote origin. Some are the descendants of the early dwellers; some are the Aryan stock that found its way to Europe before the beginning of history; still others are but the offspring of the flotsam and jetsam which recurring waves of Asiatic conquerors, surging westward in ancient times, left stranded here. Nevertheless, for so many generations have the present inhabitants remained among their mountain strongholds, unabsorbed and unassimilating, that they have been regarded as a type sufficiently pure and characteristic to give its name to the great Caucasian race.

Though enjoying greater isolation than surrounding countries, the Caucasus at different times and in different ways has felt their influences. During the Augustan age of Tamara's rule she attracted by her brilliancy, taste, and industry foreign courtiers and artisans. Hardly was she dead before Genghis Khan's horde of conquering Mongols poured over the land; and rival suitors, enraptured by her daughter's beauty, pressed their claims by invading it with their Mohammedan armies. For long succeeding years Persia struggled with Turkey for the mastery of the country, and was about to take it when Russia grasped the prize, but only after Shamyl with a few brave thousands had defeated vast armies.

Each of these foreign guests or foes left some impression on the native art; so that Caucasian rugs show traces of Turkoman, Turkish, and Persian influences. It is rarely, excepting in a few small geometric figures, that there is any evidence of the Turkoman influence; but it is not unusual to see border stripes and field designs adopted from the Turkish rugs. Some of these stripes represent both geometric and floral patterns, either copied directly or derived with slight modifications from rugs woven three or four centuries ago in Asia Minor or Armenia. The Persian influence is apparent only in the floral forms. It doubtless inspired the stripe of dainty carnations so common in a large number of Caucasian pieces, the pear design inseparable from Baku rugs, as well as many other figures that first appeared in the rugs of Persia.

Nevertheless, these rugs have their own distinct characteristics, which have a boldness and virility that are to be attributed in a measure to grand and rugged scenery as well as to centuries of struggle for independence, since in art the influence of environment is most apparent. They lack something of the sobriety, artistic drawing, and delicate colouring of those woven in vast deserts, amid the monuments of fallen empires, and in the gardens of the East; they contain on the other hand, both in line and colour, the forceful expression of untrammelled thought. The patterns are largely geometric; the tones of colour, in which clear red, blue, green, and yellow predominate, are strong. On the whole, they possess an individuality of character that is not surpassed by the rugs of any other group.

DAGHESTANS. — In no part of Caucasia have better rugs been woven than in Daghestan, "the mountain country." Nor is it sur-

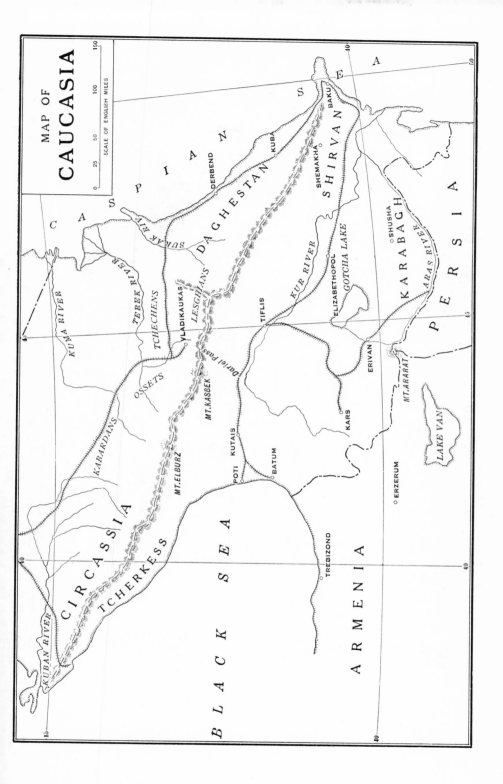

MAP OF
CAUCASIA

SCALE OF ENGLISH MILES
0   25   50   100   150

C A S P I A N   S E A

C

KUMA RIVER

TEREK RIVER

SULAK RIVER

DERBEND

KABARDANS

CIRCASSIA

TCHERKESS

OSSETS

TCHECHENS

VLADIKAUKAS

LESGHIANS

Dariel Pass

MT. KASBEK

MT. ELBURZ

DAGHESTAN

SHEMAKHA

KUBA

SHIRVAN

BAKU

KUR RIVER

ELIZABETHPOL

GOTCHA LAKE

TIFLIS

KUTAIS

POTI

BATUM

ERIVAN

KARS

MT. ARARAT

SHUSHA

KARABAGH

ARAS RIVER

P E R S I A

B L A C K   S E A

KUBAN RIVER

TREBIZOND

A R M E N I A

ERZERUM

LAKE VAN

PLATE 47. KAZAK PRAYER RUG

prising that this province should produce distinctive types, when it is considered that it has a length of over two hundred miles; that its topography is diversified by glaciated mountains, barren steppes, and fertile valleys; and that it is occupied by numerous clans, many of whom differ in origin as well as religion. Some of the rugs come from the city of Derbend on the Caspian Sea; some come from Kuba in the southeastern corner; others, called Kabistans, are produced in the country about Kuba; a few are made by the Lesghians who live among the lofty mountains; and in other parts of the province are woven pieces which formerly were sent in large numbers to Europe and America, where they soon became known as Daghestans.

Though their resemblance to the Kabistans is so great that it is often difficult to distinguish between them, the rugs which acquired the trade name of Daghestans are different from almost all other Caucasian pieces. This is largely because the province is bounded on three sides by a sea and a nearly impassable mountain range, which render communication with surrounding territory difficult, and create a natural isolation, where in the course of many generations a distinct type was developed. Moreover, these same physical conditions have impeded both the introduction of aniline dyes, so that even among modern pieces spurious colours are not frequently seen; and also the adoption of new designs, so that the patterns of two or three centuries ago are still largely used.

It is among the oldest rugs of the Daghestan weave that are found many of the best examples of Caucasian textile art. The dark, rich reds and blues of the fields, which are brightened by the ivory, light blue, green, and yellow of the small designs, resemble the fine colouring of choice Persian carpets. But the patterns are totally dissimilar; for it is only in a few rare old pieces, in which are copied some designs such as the lotus, or the running vine with leaf and bud, that there is any likeness to the realism of Persian floral ornamentation.

The drawing, however, is never crude, and on account of the short nap and strongly contrasting colours always appears with clear definition. With the exception of conventionalised pears, the three-leaf sprig, which is commonly seen in the field, and the narrow border stripes of carnations, almost all of the figures are geometric; and are so carefully drawn, so closely clustered, that they represent an appearance frequently compared to mosaic work.

Even when the patterns represent large medallions or stars, they contain smaller concentric forms, or are divided and redivided into smaller stars, diamonds, or tessellated figures, so that the effect is the same.   In some form or other the latch-hook is seen in almost all these pieces.   Of small designs, the octagonal disc is almost invariably found;   and animals, human beings, and the pear are not infrequently seen.

As the population of the province is largely Mohammedan, namazliks as well as sedjadehs are made;   but with the exception of the unobtrusive arch of the namazlik, which is represented in Plate C, Fig. 9 (Page 61), there is little difference between them.   There is never any panel as in Asia Minor rugs;   nor is there a noticeable spandrel, since the space above the arch contains designs similar to those on the rest of the field.

As a rule, the borders consist of three or four stripes separated by coloured lines.   Only in the secondary stripes are any floral forms employed;   and these, with the exception of the carnation design, are rare.   The reciprocal trefoil is most characteristic as an outer stripe;   the serrated line is also employed;   and it is not unusual to find next to the field a broad stripe of diagonal barber-pole bars, on which are small dotted lines.

Type Characteristics.   Colours, principally blue, red, and ivory, with minor quantities of green and yellow.   *Knot*, Ghiordes.   Knots to inch horizontally seven to twelve;   perpendicularly, eight to fifteen. A half knot, as it appears at back, is as long as wide and occasionally longer.   The rows of knots are not firmly pressed down, so that their alignment is even and the warp shows at back.   *Warp*, wool; each of the two threads encircled by a knot is equally prominent at the back;   occasionally in old pieces one thread is slightly depressed below the other.   *Weft*, wool of medium diameter.   A thread of weft crosses twice between every two rows of knots.   *Pile*, wool, clipped short.   *Border*, three to five stripes.   *Sides*, a selvage of two, three, or four cords, or occasionally a weft-overcasting.   *Both ends*, a web, one row of knots or more, and loose warp fringe.   Occasionally there is also a narrow braided selvage.   *Texture*, moderately firm. *Weave* at back is of fine grain.   *Usual length*, five to ten feet.   *Usual width*, one half to two thirds length.

KABISTANS. — Within recent years most of the rugs shipped from the southern part of Daghestan have become known in Western markets as Kabistans, though the distinction between them and the type that takes the name of the province is so slight that it is determinable only by the strictest analysis. In fact, Kabistans are merely a variety of Daghestans. Both have short nap and occasionally adopt the same colour scheme and patterns, so that many of each class are indistinguishable from one another.

On the other hand, there are a few interesting points of difference between the best types, which are largely attributable to geographic environment. As the only easy access to this province from the south is by the shore of the Caspian, where the great mountain wall that forms an almost impassable barrier between Northern and Southern Caucasia descends to the plain, the district adjacent to this entrance on the line of travel would naturally feel and show a foreign influence, while the remote and more inaccessible parts of the province would be unaffected. Accordingly, the designs of Kabistans are more varied, and it is not surprising to find in them evidences of Persian influence not so apparent in the Daghestans. In some, for instance, are pear designs, like those occasionally seen in Shiraz pieces; and the rich tones, that are usually more subdued than those of the Daghestans, suggest the finest dyes of the Feraghans. There is also a slight difference in weave. Both display the two threads of warp encircled by each knot with equal prominence at the back; but in the Daghestans the alignment of the two halves of the knot, as they appear at the back, is more regular; while in the Kabistans one extends beyond the other in the direction of the length of the rug, as is the case with the Shirvans woven in the adjoining country to the south. Frequently the weft of Kabistans is of cotton; and the filling is not as wide as that of Daghestans, which is of wool. Moreover, the Kabistans may be either overcast or have a selvage at the sides, but the Daghestans have almost always a narrow selvage. Among the modern pieces there is a tendency for both classes to follow the side finish of the Shirvans.

A well-known type of old Kabistans, that is also sometimes repeated in Daghestans, has a dark blue field on which are spaced in regular order white bracket-like designs, in which the perpendicular arms are usually connected (Plate O, Figs. 18-a and 18-b, Page 291). Their origin is unknown; but when their shape and their position in reference to the rosettes or effulgent stars that are placed near them are considered, the thought is at once suggested that in them is reproduced after a long process of slow change a conventionalised form of the Herati design. Other small harmonious designs are properly spaced throughout the fields, and in the main stripe of the border, on a cream-coloured ground, is frequently seen the beautiful pattern of Cufic origin represented in Plate J, Fig. 19 (opp. Page 228). Old pieces of this pattern, which are now growing rare, represent in weave, colour, and design the masterpieces of Caucasian textile art.

Another pattern consists of diagonal stripes with small geometric figures, or of small floral forms arranged in rows, so that those of similar colour fall in diagonal lines. Again, the entire field may be covered with rectangular pears like those of Baku rugs. Oblong odjaliks are often seen with fields of dark colour, at each end of which are large geometric figures symmetrically balanced with reference to the centre. But they are so fringed with latch-hooks and so subdivided into smaller devices, which are accentuated by the shortness of the nap, that they have the effect of an assemblage of smaller designs.

Type Characteristics. *Colours*, principally blue, also some red, ivory, green, and brown. *Knot*, Ghiordes. Knots to inch horizontally seven to twelve; perpendicularly, eight to sixteen. A half knot, as it appears at back, is as long as wide and occasionally longer. The rows of knots are not firmly pressed down; their alignment is less even than in Daghestans, yet the warp may be seen at back. *Warp*, wool; each of the two threads encircled by a knot is equally prominent at back. *Weft*, wool or cotton, of medium diameter. A thread of weft crosses twice between every two rows of knots and occasionally three times. *Pile*, wool, of medium length. *Border*, three to five stripes. *Sides*, generally a weft-overcasting, or a two-cord weft selvage; occasionally a double overcasting or selvage. *Lower end*, a narrow web, not infrequently a fine braided selvage and warp loops. *Upper end*, a narrow web, occasionally a fine braided selvage and warp fringe. *Texture*, moderately firm. *Weave* at back is of medium grain. *Usual length*, five to twelve feet. *Usual width*, one half to three quarters length.

KUBAS. — Not far from the southeast corner of the province of Daghestan, in a plain watered by streams that debouch from the Caucasus, is the small town of Kuba. It is on the site of an old Persian fort, about which in the course of time sprang up a town sufficiently important to be the residence of a Khan. For a long period previous to the treaty of Gulistan, in 1813, the influence of the Persians had been predominant in this part of the country; and it is not improbable that some of the oldest Kuba rugs now existing are the work of their weavers. Many, on the other hand, have few foreign characteristics either of weave or design, and show a relationship to the work of the Shemakha tribes, who inhabit an adjoining district in Shirvan.

In some of this class the floral form receives more elaborate treatment than in any other Caucasian rug. One of the patterns of undoubted Iranian inspiration represents a large oval panel or medallion, with graceful outlines resting on a field of deep blue and sable brown, streaked with waving lines of gold. Within the medallion is a lavish display of large flowers *en masse*, and not detached from one another or arranged in set form, as is the case with most floral patterns. In each corner is a rose with spreading petals that equals the largest seen in nature, and with colour that suggests the beauty of a Duchess or Marechal Niel. Surrounding all is a narrow dainty border of some well-known Persian vine. The most recent copies of this pattern, that has been followed for at least a century and a half, are so crude as to resemble but slightly the oldest, which suggest the work of some early Kirman weaver and are unsurpassed in beauty and artistic elegance by any other Caucasian rug.

Other patterns are more distinctly representative of the native art. The field of some is occupied by large, irregular, octagonal-shaped figures defined by serrated edges and subdivided by mosaic work, at the centre of which is some well-known design. One of the most pleasing patterns consists of a field on which with mathematical precision are placed large effulgent stars. At their centre is often a much smaller star enclosed by a diamond from which extend broad rays directed towards the eight principal points of the compass. When softened by time the different shades, such as light blue, ivory, and deep red of the enveloping rays, contrasted with other shades at the centre and with a dark blue of the ground, are exceedingly beautiful.

The Kubas and Shemakhas have similar tones of colour, consisting principally of blues, reds, sable brown, and yellow, to which the soft, velvety character of the wool of the best examples gives a quality of richness that is distinctive. The finish of their sides and ends, which is usually similar to that of the Soumaks, is also identical, so that they are frequently mistaken for one another, and can only be distinguished by a difference of pattern and a slight difference of weave.

Type Characteristics. *Colours,* principally blue, red, and brown, occasionally some green. *Knot,* Ghiordes. Knots to inch horizontally six to nine; perpendicularly, seven to thirteen. The rows of knots are pressed down, so that the warp is almost hidden at back. *Warp,* fine wool; the two threads encircled by a knot are equally prominent at back. *Weft,* wool of fine or medium diameter. A thread of weft crosses twice between every two rows of knots. *Pile,* wool of medium length. *Border,* one to three stripes. *Sides,* a blue double selvage of two or three cords. *Both ends,* a narrow blue web of "herring-bone" weave, a knotted selvage or several rows of knots, and short warp fringe. *Texture,* slightly loose. *Weave* at back is of moderately fine grain. *Usual length,* four to nine feet. *Usual width,* one half to two thirds length.

DERBENDS. — Near the great walls built by Alexander on the Caspian Sea, where mountains rise abruptly so as to leave only a narrow pass, is one of the oldest cities of Caucasia. It was known by the Romans as Albana, and was renamed by the Persians of the VI Century "Derbend," which in their language signifies a gateway. No other city of Caucasia has been visited by more foreign foes. Tartar tribes passed that way when entering Europe; Mongolians captured it as late as the XIII Century; Russians and Persians in turn held it. Moreover, the sea has offered an easy approach to the Turkoman tribes dwelling to the east. It is therefore somewhat surprising that there is so little evidence of artistic foreign influence in the weavings; but this is due, perhaps, to the fact that pieces with an authentic age of over two centuries no longer exist, and such old rugs as remain are very scarce; whilst the modern pieces are derived largely from the mountainous districts that find a market in the city.

Occasionally, however, there comes to light a very old piece that reaches the standard of the finest Kabistan. The field of such a one may be filled with elaborately drawn pears like those seen in many of the Niriz rugs. Again, it may be covered with a checkered or lattice-work pattern that contains within the diamonds geometric or semi-floral mosaic designs. Surrounding this field are three or four stripes, of which the outer has a reciprocal pattern. The nap is of fine wool of moderate length. At the back of these older rugs is sometimes displayed finely spun reddish dyed threads of woollen weft pressed closely together between lines of knots carefully tied to brownish threads of woollen warp; but not infrequently cotton is used for both warp and weft. Such designs and technique suggest the rugs woven much farther to the south.

In contrast with these beautiful but rare pieces, the modern products are sad commentaries on the retrogression in weaving; for those that are ordinarily found in the market are like poor imitations of inferior Daghestans. They are of slightly larger size, and have longer nap, looser weave, and cruder colours. Moreover, they show evidences of Turkoman influences; for not infrequently the warp is of brown goat's hair, and at each end is a reddish brown web like what may be seen in the rugs of Yomud tribes living on the eastern shores of the Caspian. Still other nomadic characters, resembling the workmanship of Kazak tribes, appear in the large starlike or diamond-shaped figures which, fringed with latch-hooks and coloured with bright tones of red, blue, or green, are often placed in simple array on a field of strongly contrasting colour. There is nothing, however, offensive in the colour scheme, excepting when aniline dyes are used. With wear the nap of many of them acquires the soft and pleasing effect of Beluchistans. Furthermore, they are both flexible and durable, though entirely lacking in artistic qualities.

Type Characteristics. Colours, principally blue, red, and ivory, with minor quantities of green, yellow, and brown. *Knot*, Ghiordes. Knots to inch horizontally five to nine; perpendicularly, six to twelve. Each half knot is about as long as wide, and occasionally longer. The rows of knots are generally pressed down, so that the warp is concealed at back. *Warp*, generally wool, occasionally cotton. The separate threads are not strung closely together. Each of the two threads encircled by a knot is equally prominent at the back. *Weft*, generally wool, but often cotton. In some pieces a thread of weft of medium diameter crosses twice between every two rows of knots; not infrequently it crosses both twice and three times in the same piece; rarely a thread of coarse diameter crosses only once. *Pile*, wool of medium length. *Border*, three stripes. *Sides*, a double selvage of two or three cords, or occasionally a double overcasting. *Both ends* have a web, frequently a knotted selvage, and a warp fringe. *Texture*, moderately loose. *Weave* at back is of medium grain. *Usual length*, five to seven feet. *Usual width*, one half to two thirds length.

LESGHIANS. — On the northern flank of the high mountain ranges that extend eastward from Kazbek into the province of Daghestan, live the numerous tribes classed as Lesghians. Their different dialects and languages would indicate unrelated origins; but their common religion, mode of life, and struggle for liberty have established between all of them strong bonds of sympathy. They are nominally Christians, but essentially Mohammedans. Most of them live in almost inaccessible spots, beneath the snow covered, glaciated ridges, and beside fierce flowing torrents, where on occasions they have converted their homes into almost impregnable fortresses. These are the people who united with the Circassians in the long-continued struggle against the Russian Empire, and followed Shamyl to repeated victory among the mountain defiles.

It might naturally be expected that the rugs of such people would partake of a character totally distinct from those woven in the sunny atmosphere of Kirman, amid the sacred influences of Meshed, or among the peaceful hills of Ghiordes. Such, in fact, is the case, since both patterns and colouring display extreme simplicity, as well as strength and beauty. Large numbers of these rugs are of moderate size and slightly oblong; and are flexible yet stout. Both warp and weft are of fine brown wool; and as is rarely the case with any other Caucasian rugs excepting the Shushas, one of the two threads of warp encircled by a knot is often almost doubled beneath the other. The knotted fringe of the ends suggests the work of tribes living further westward, but the selvage of the sides shows relationship to the Daghestans.

The patterns of some of these rugs are not unlike those of rugs woven south of the Caucasus; and not infrequently the fields contain unrelated designs such as the lozenge fringed with hooks, the octagonal disc, eight-pointed stars, and S forms. The borders usually consist of two or three stripes, on which is some geometric pattern. The colours are few and characteristic. Blue and yellow are generally present, and frequently red and brown. On the whole, these pieces have an interesting individuality unlike that of any other rugs.

Type Characteristics. Colours, blue, yellow, red, brown, and ivory. *Knot,* Ghiordes. Knots to inch horizontally six to nine; perpendicularly, six to eleven. The rows of knots are firmly pressed down, so that the warp is almost hidden at back. *Warp,* brown wool;

one of the two threads encircled by a knot is depressed below the other at back, or doubled under the other. *Weft*, wool of medium diameter. A thread of weft crosses twice between every two rows of knots. *Pile*, wool of medium length. *Border*, usually three stripes. *Sides*, an added selvage, which is generally wool but occasionally cotton, of two, three, or four cords. Both ends, a web, two or three rows of knots, and a warp fringe. In some pieces there is also a braided selvage. *Texture*, firm. *Weave* at back is of slightly coarse grain. *Usual length*, five to eight feet. *Usual width*, one half to two thirds length.

CHICHIS. — On the lower slope of the Caucasus, extending down into the valley of the Terek are the homes of the Tchechens, the weavers of pieces so often spoken of as Chichis. Beyond them to the north are great stretches of Russian steppes, and to the south is the land of the hardy Lesghians. Nevertheless, their rugs show little relationship to the work of the latter or of any other tribes to the north of the mountain chain; but resemble more closely the work of the Shirvans in the valley of the Kur, so that not infrequently they are mistaken for them. Indeed, their general character is remote from anything barbaric, and is more in keeping with the pleasing effect of the Persian sense of harmony. All floral forms are conventionalised, but the geometric designs have a delicacy of drawing, a refinement of detail, from which every jarring note is eliminated.

Like almost all weavers, the Tchechens adopt different patterns. On the field of some of the rugs is a plentiful array of small devices surrounding two or three large geometric figures; or again the field may be covered with pear designs arranged in regular order; but most of the rugs now seen follow a common type. In this the field resembles a floor inlaid with beautiful mosaic work, formed of carefully cut stones of various hues, studiously arranged in the form of small diamonds, eight-pointed stars, or rosettes. Not infrequently the rosettes are outlined by a fret device surrounding a central star. They are invariably arranged in lines parallel to the ends of the rugs, and this horizontal effect is sometimes accentuated by inserting between each row narrow bands composed of conventionalised leaves. The colours of these small designs are generally ivory, light blue, pale yellow, or red; and appear more pronounced by contrast with the underlying ground of light blue. Now and then the nomadic instinct of the Tchechen tribes, who lead their flocks regularly from the green pastures of the ridges to the valley of the Terek, crops out in unrelated devices such as combs and S forms, which they weave in the field. But they usually arrange them so as to harmonise with the main pattern, or else place them near the sides and ends, which are almost invariably fringed with either a serrated line or a row of reciprocal trefoils projecting from the border into the field. This feature of a reciprocal trefoil employed as a fringe to the edges of a field independently of the lines of a stripe, is seen in very few other classes.

Often the borders, which contain a large number of stripes, are as wide as the central field, with which they harmonise both in colour and design. There is something chaste in the simplicity of the geometric figures of the secondary stripes and of the conventionalised floral drawing of the main stripe. The latter, as represented in the type generally seen (Plate I, Fig. 6, opp. Page 226), consists of a row of about eight rosettes, connected by an angular vine drawn with such breadth and regularity as to resemble a number of parallel bars diagonal to the sides. In fact, this pattern would be entirely geometric were it not for the three-cleft leaves, which spring from opposite sides of the rosettes. Of the secondary stripes, the outer almost invariably has the reciprocal trefoil, and one has frequently a continuous line of eight-pointed stars. The arch of the prayer rugs is similar to that of Daghestans.

Type Characteristics. Colours, principally ivory, blue, and red, with minor quantities of green and brown. *Knot*, Ghiordes. Knots to inch horizontally seven to ten; perpendicularly, eight to twelve. The rows of knots are not firmly pressed down, so that the warp may be seen at back. *Warp*, wool; each of the two threads encircled by a knot is equally prominent at back. *Weft*, wool, of medium diameter. A thread of weft crosses twice between every two rows of knots. *Pile*, wool, of short or medium length. *Border*, three to five stripes. *Sides*, generally a double overcasting, but occasionally a double selvage of two or three cords. *Both ends*, a web, one row of knots or more, and a warp fringe. *Texture*, moderately firm. *Weave* at back is of medium grain. *Usual length*, four and one half to six and one half feet. *Usual width*, five eighths to three quarters length.

TCHERKESS. — The narrow strip of fertile and beautiful country that reaches from the Kuban valley southward along the shore of the Black Sea for a distance of two hundred miles is occupied by a people known to the western world as Circassians. In their own land they are called "Tcher-Kesses," a Tartar term for "cutter of roads" or highwaymen; and they have been in the habit of speaking of themselves as "Adighies" or Nobles. In fact, there has been no prouder Caucasian race, even though their homes were often log huts and their daughters were sold in the markets of Constantinople. These are the people, who half a century ago finally yielded after a long, fierce struggle for independence; but a hundred thousand families, preferring exile to submission to the Czar, migrated to Armenia and Asia Minor, where they intermarried with other races, and are rapidly losing their identity.

Very few of the Circassian or Tcherkess rugs have been woven by those who left their country. The best were made before the exodus; and on account of the hardships and poverty of the people, many that have come to the market within recent years are greatly inferior to the excellent pieces of former times and are often mistaken for the work of nomadic tribes. Not only so, but crude and foreign devices have crept into some of them. It is, therefore, to the older pieces that we must turn for a better understanding of this class.

Something of the ruggedness of lives spent in struggles with men and nature found expression in the fabrics, which show firmness of texture, boldness of design, richness of colour. In fact they resemble the Kazaks so closely in their long nap, and finish of sides and ends that they are constantly mistaken for them; yet they may be distinguished from all classes by the large amount of brownish red or tawny colour of the field and their stereotyped patterns. These usually consist of diamond-shaped figures sometimes called "sunbursts," that are often regarded as crude copies of the Russian coat of arms; but there is little doubt that they have been derived from the medallions of some old Armenian rugs of the XIV and XV Centuries, in which also appear the same tri-cleft leaves so common in both this class and the Soumaks. These patterns are sufficiently large to occupy the full breadth of the field; and there are seldom less than two and occasionally as many as four or five extending from one end to the other. The strong contrast between the blue and ivory of the figures and the red or tawny colour of the ground is softened by the depth of pile, which in turn adds warmth and richness. The borders are always of three stripes. The main one almost invariably has the tarantula design and is enclosed by guards with the serrated sawtooth design. Many of these old pieces are excellently woven and have a dignity of pattern and wealth of harmonious colour rarely seen in nomadic rugs.

Type Characteristics. Colours, principally red and tawny yellow, with minor quantities of blue and white. *Knot*, Ghiordes. Knots to inch horizontally six to nine; perpendicularly, seven to ten. A half knot, as it appears at back, is as long as wide or longer. The rows of knots are firmly pressed down, so that the warp does not show at back. *Warp*, wool; generally each of the two threads encircled by a knot is equally prominent at back, occasionally one is depressed below the other. *Weft*, wool of medium diameter. A thread of weft usually crosses only twice between every two rows of knots, but in some pieces as many as four or six times. *Pile*, wool of medium length. *Border*, three stripes. *Sides*, a two-cord double selvage. *Both ends*, as a rule have a web, a heavy braided selvage, and knotted warp fringe; occasionally either web or selvage may be omitted. *Texture*, very firm. *Weave* at back of medium grain. *Usual length*, five to ten feet. *Usual width*, one half to two thirds length.

BAKUS. — No other rugs of Caucasia have greater individuality of colour and design than the Bakus. This, perhaps, is partly due to the fact that the district from which they come is dissimilar to any other. It consists largely of the peninsula of scanty vegetation, where the great mountain chain extends to the dreary Caspian, leaving at its base the narrow strip of land now famous for its immense accumulations of mineral oil. Hither, during the past, the followers of Zoroaster have come from all directions to worship in the temple of the Guebres, where day and night the priests watched the blue flame that rose perpetually from the ground, and once in long intervals spread over the waters like a sea of fire. This sacred spot has been owned in turn by Saracens, Persians, Turks, Russians, and the Princes of Shirvan; so that the influences of different religions and different races have been felt here.

The most noticeable feature of many of these rugs is their dull colours, that give the impression of being partly bleached or having faded. There are subdued tones of light blue, tan, pale ocherous yellow, and black, as well as light, medium, and dark brown colours of natural wool; but in the rugs woven a century ago the colours were much richer. None of them are used in large masses excepting for the underground; nor are there striking contrasts, so that the effect is somewhat monotonous.

An equally important characteristic is the large number of pear designs, which are unlike those of any other rug. These designs (Plate O, Fig. 6b, Page 291) are so rectangular that they have lost all resemblance to floral drawing; and to add to their formality, each is placed in the field with studied regularity and often surrounded by a delicate hexagonal shaped sub-pattern giving a diaper effect. Sometimes, also, they appear in the border between an array of other designs, to which they show no relation; but they never constitute the sole feature of the rug as they do in Sarabends.

At the centre of the field is often a star-shaped design surrounded by a large diamond or other figure fringed with radiating lines. These lines suggest the effulgence of light; and it is not improbable that their origin lay in the mysticism of fire worship. In sedjadehs the corners are set off by quadrants of octagons, of which the diagonal sides are serrated and frequently fringed with radiating lines like the central medallions. Throughout both corners and fields often appear eight-pointed and effulgent stars, the three-cleft leaf, S designs, crude human and animal forms, and other small geometric devices like those seen in Daghestans and Shirvans. But more noticeable than any of these are the realistic but mechanically drawn birds, which are represented in larger numbers and more frequently than in any other rugs woven within the last century.

The borders contain from three to five stripes, of which one at least is always geometric; and another, as a rule, has some suggestion of floral form. Often it is only the carnation in profile; but now and then it is a running vine with leaf or flower, adopted without modification from Persian rugs. This is not, however, surprising, when it is remembered that during the reign of Shah Abbas, Baku belonged to Persia, which for centuries had been the home of devout Parsees, some of whom undoubtedly made pilgrimages to the sacred temple.

These rugs can at once be recognised by their short nap, and their characteristic colours and designs. They are always interesting on account of their marked individuality and the still unsolved symbols of Zoroastrian mysticism they may contain; but in spite of the careful delineation of the design and the delicate mosaic effect of the central medallions, very few, excepting the old pieces, are handsome.

Type Characteristics. Colours, principally brown, tan, blue, yellow, and black. *Knot*, Ghiordes. Knots to inch horizontally

six to nine; perpendicularly, seven to eleven. The rows of knots
are firmly pressed down, so that the warp does not show at back.
Warp, wool; each of the two threads encircled by a knot is generally
equally prominent at back, occasionally one is depressed slightly
below the other. *Weft*, usually cotton, sometimes wool, of medium
diameter. A thread of weft crosses twice between every two rows
of knots. *Pile*, wool, clipped short. *Border*, three to five stripes.
Sides, a weft overcasting or a narrow weft selvage. *Both ends*, a
web, one row of knots or more, and a warp fringe. *Texture*, moderately firm. *Weave* at back is of slightly coarse grain. *Usual length*,
six to nine feet. *Usual width*, one half to two thirds length.

SHIRVANS. — Between the rugs of Shirvan and Daghestan is a
relationship easily accounted for by the fact that they are adjoining
provinces, and that almost the only approach to Daghestan for the
Asiatic races among whom the art of weaving reached its highest
development was through Shirvan. Both districts, therefore, received ideas from the same sources; but since Shirvan has been at
times more completely under the sway of Persia, it has yielded more
readily to the influence of the Persian weavers, as is observable in
the flower and foliate forms which are used more frequently and are
drawn more realistically in its rugs than in those of Daghestan. On
the other hand, the technique of weave as well as finish of sides and
ends in the Shirvans lacks something of the refinement observable
in the Daghestans.

The oldest existing Shirvans are absorbingly interesting. In
them the foliate forms are more noticeable than in almost any
other Caucasian rugs, though they may in a measure be disguised
by formal treatment. Sometimes they appear as large figures covering a great part of the field and acting as sub-patterns for superimposed smaller devices; but they are most frequently found in the
borders. Other old pieces contain lattice-work of hexagonal-shaped
diaper patterns, within which may be designs abounding in latch-
hooks and figures strongly suggestive of Chinese devices. Such patterns, however, are unusual; as the fields of most old Shirvans
are covered with large medallions, stars, and diamonds similar to
those of Daghestans, although the drawing inclines to greater simplicity of outline and detail; and they have greater diversity of
colour, as tones of blue, red, green, and brown in a field of ivory
are not unusual.

PLATE 48. KAZAK RUG

PLATE 49. KARABAGH PRAYER RUG

The patterns of the more modern rugs have become corrupted into a mere mechanical copying of conventional forms lacking all artistic spirit. Some of them resemble those found in both Daghestans and Kabistans, but generally the designs are drawn less clearly in Shirvans. This is partly because, as a rule, they are not so closely woven and the nap is not quite so short. Now and then the large medallions so common to Soumaks are seen; and not infrequently the field is covered with diagonal parallel stripes on which are small geometric devices.

There is, however, one pattern peculiar to Shirvans that rarely, if ever, is adopted in any other class. It has somewhat the appearance of pole medallions and consists of a panel that occupies nearly the whole field and contains broad incisions at each side, which nearly divide it into three or four rectangular sections. Within each of them are octagonal figures, and an octagonal shape is given to both ends of the panel so as to leave small corners to the field. Each part often contains small designs such as latch-hooks, octagonal discs, S forms, eight-pointed stars, and combs, as well as crudely drawn dogs and other animal or human forms. With slight modifications this pattern is sometimes repeated in the prayer rugs (Plate C, Fig. 11, Page 61), but the section at one end is more completely an octagon, and the remainder is an oblong rectangle. A more usual pattern for prayer rugs has the same form of arch that is common in Daghestans.

Whatever the fields of these rugs may lack in delicacy of drawing is amply compensated for by the diversity and beauty of some of their borders, which have a well balanced harmony of colours. They have seldom less than three, nor more than five stripes, of which the secondary are often as interesting as the primary. The best known is the one with serrated leaf and wine glass, represented in Plate I, Fig. 1, opp. Page 226, which is found in such a large percentage of Shirvans that it is almost typical of them. If the figures of the field contain latch-hooks, they are very apt to be expressed in some form in the primary stripe. Such a one appears in Plate I, Fig. 2; and the beautiful Georgian pattern (Plate J, Fig. 9, opp. Page 228) is also occasionally seen. A very much rarer stripe, which is shown in Plate J, Fig. 8, is only used when the field has a large central panel with a corresponding pattern. Now and then appears a stripe with no other ornamentation than a formal row of pear designs. Of the secondary stripes, the one with the designs of carnations (Plate K, Fig. 1, opp. Page 230) is very frequently seen, but its beauty depends largely upon the delicacy of its drawing and colour scheme. On the whole, the Shirvan dyer displays a wider scope in the selection of colours than his Daghestan neighbour, but the tones are not always so rich or harmonious.

Type Characteristics. Colours, principally blue, red, and ivory. *Knot,* Ghiordes. Knots to inch horizontally seven to twelve; perpendicularly, eight to twelve. The rows of knots are firmly pressed down, so that the transverse warp does not show at back. *Warp,* wool; each of the two threads encircled by a knot is equally prominent at back. *Weft,* generally wool, occasionally cotton, of medium or coarse diameter. A thread of weft crosses twice between every two rows of knots. *Pile,* wool, of short or medium length. *Border,* three to five stripes. *Sides,* generally a weft selvage of two or three cords or a double selvage, occasionally a double overcasting. *Both ends,* a web, one row of knots or more, and a warp fringe. *Texture,* slightly loose. *Weave* at back is moderately coarse. *Usual length,* four to six feet. *Usual width,* one half to four fifths length.

SOUMAKS. — Seventy miles to the northwest of Baku, and about the same distance to the south of Kuba, where the high ranges of the Caucasus begin to descend to the sea, is the city of Shemakha. It was almost destroyed by Nadir Shah, but recovered sufficiently within the last century to become the capital of Shirvan and a manufacturing centre of silks. It is the market place for many tribes from the mountains of Daghestan and the valley of the Kur, who take thither their rugs, from which its own weavers often borrow patterns. By a corruption of the name of the city, their fabrics are called Soumaks, though they are more popularly known as Kashmirs, because ends of yarn hang loosely at the back, as is the case with the beautiful shawls of the noted valley of India.

It is, of course, the finish at the back and the absence of pile that make them so different from all other rugs and place them in a class by themselves; but even apart from these characteristics, they are as distinct a type as any in Caucasia. On the fields of most of them are three or four diamond-shaped medallions, that occupy nearly the full width of the field and extend from one end to the other. Almost without exception thay are slightly hexagonal, and are incised on the diagonal sides to represent crosses. These patterns are doubtless derived from very old Armenian rugs; and it is possible that once the crosses had a religious significance, as it is claimed that the earlier weavers of this type were a Christian sect; but the present weavers are mostly Mohammedans. At the centre of the medallions and in the triangular spaces at the sides are flattened octagons, which are generally ornamented with some star-shaped devices. Superimposed on these larger patterns and surrounding them on the field, are also many small designs, which as a rule are grouped with a regularity suggestive of the mosaic. Some are common to other Caucasian pieces; but a few are more frequently seen in this class than in any other, as for instance, the knot of destiny (Plate O, Fig. 17, Page 291), and the tri-cleft leaf, drawn like a bird's claw, which appeared in Armenian rugs at least five centuries ago. Sometimes the medallions and octagons are replaced by smaller and more ornate figures, but the geometric character is seldom entirely lost.

There are also some old pieces with a totally different pattern, and with fine colours that are most pleasing in the rich harmony of tones. They may contain geometric, foliate, or floral designs. One recently examined had a field of rose red completely covered with diagonal rows of innumerable dainty figures, which were evidently the conventionalised forms of small flower bushes. Not a single other design appeared in the field, yet the richness of colour and chasteness of pattern made it exceedingly beautiful.

The patterns of the border stripes, that number from two to five, are generally distinctive; though occasionally they follow well known Caucasian drawing. The outer one has so frequently the running latch-hook that it is almost typical. As a rule, it has the simple form shown in Plate K, Fig. 20 (opp. Page 230); but now and then the more elaborate drawing of the Georgian stripe (Plate J, Fig. 9, opp. Page 228) is followed. Sometimes this is replaced by the reciprocal trefoil, which is used also for the inner stripe; and a running vine and rosette, such as the one in Plate K, Fig. 4, is not infrequently used for a secondary stripe. The primary stripes, on the other hand, although most dissimilar to those of other rugs, differ so widely among themselves, that no one is typical. Separating these primary and secondary parts of the border are frequently narrow lines with the barber-pole device.

The old pieces are of fine texture and excellent wool, which even in the warp displays a silky character. The dyes are faultless, though the colours never acquire a lustre. Red and blue are largely employed, but they are partly replaced by brown in the more modern pieces; and in both old and modern is usually an orange yellow that rarely appears in other Caucasian rugs.

Type Characteristics.   Colours, principally red, blue, brown, some yellow, and white. *Knot,* flat stitch. Knots to inch horizontally eight to fourteen; perpendicularly, six to sixteen. *Warp,* wool; each thread is equally prominent at the back. *Weft,* wool, of fine or medium diameter. A thread of weft crosses twice between every two rows of knots in old rugs, and between every second and third row in modern rugs. *Border,* two to five stripes. *Sides,* generally a double selvage of several cords, occasionally an overcasting. *Both ends,* narrow web, one or more rows of knots and fringe; sometimes heavy added selvage. *No nap. Usual length,* five and one half to twelve feet. *Usual width,* one half to three quarters length.

SHEMAKHAS. — Flatly woven Soumaks are not the only rugs of the Shemakha tribes. Some of the same people, who dwell among the ranges of the Caucasus a short distance to the north, make rugs of pile that occasionally surpass in quality of material and beauty of colour scheme the best of Daghestans, and are sometimes spoken of by dealers as "Royal Daghestans;" yet they are seldom seen and little known. In fact, they are frequently mistaken for Persian fabrics on account of the subdued richness of their deep reds, blues, greens, yellows, and browns, and the patterns which are largely floral.

Very often the principal border stripe is the well-known Georgian pattern, that occurs in so many Soumaks, even though the secondary stripe be some Persian pattern. These rugs also resemble the Soumaks in the coloured woollen selvage of the sides, and in the narrow coloured web of "herring-bone" weave and knotted fringe of the ends. In some, the field is divided by diagonal bars into large diamond-shaped figures containing conventionalised flowers; in others, it is merely a background over which are strewn more realistically drawn floral forms; and in all is expressed an artistic perception of design and colour not frequently found in Caucasian pieces.

Type Characteristics.   Colours, principally blue, red, and brown. *Knot,* Ghiordes. Knots to inch horizontally seven to eleven; perpendicularly, seven to thirteen. The rows of knots are pressed down, so that the warp is almost hidden. *Warp,* wool; one of the two threads encircled by a knot is depressed below the other at back.

Weft, wool, of fine or medium diameter. A thread of weft crosses twice between every two rows of knots. *Pile*, wool, of medium length. *Border*, two to three stripes. *Sides*, a blue selvage of two or three cords. *Both ends*, a narrow blue web of "herring-bone" weave, a knotted selvage or several rows of knots, and short warp fringe. *Texture*, slightly firm. *Weave* at back is of moderately fine grain. *Usual length*, four to eight feet. *Usual width*, two fifths to two thirds length.

TIFLIS. — When it is considered that for centuries Tiflis has been the Georgian capital, where culture and art received more encouragement than in the provinces; that it was in constant communication with the rug-producing countries on all sides; and was on one of the great highways between Persia and Europe, it is surprising that what has been written hitherto about Caucasian rugs has contained almost no reference to a type peculiar to this city and district. This is undoubtedly due to the fact that within recent years hardly any rugs have been produced there, and that the old pieces are few and but little known.

Nevertheless, now and then come to light beautiful old rugs which are dissimilar to those of all other classes. The wool of their moderately long nap has a silkiness that suggests a Shiraz or a Meshed; the colour scheme includes a very wide range of bright and positive tones, such as blue, green, rose, and ivory; the weave of delicate and fine threads is as close as that of old Bergamos. A glance at the ends and back helps to determine the type; for the warp is occasionally of cotton, which is a peculiarity not seen in many other Caucasian classes; the weft which crosses from three to five times is of very finely spun wool mostly dyed a brown or dull red, and strung with great exactness; and the knots are tied with care. There is also something distinctive in many of the patterns; for however interesting they may be, precision of drawing is often combined with discordance of detail. One part of the field, for instance, may consist of a well executed diaper pattern; another part may represent a number of stiff, perpendicular, parallel bars, occupying the full width of the field; and still another part may be entirely occupied by hexagonal-shaped pear designs. Adjoining these may be other pear designs of totally dissimilar shape as well as mystic symbols and other strange devices. Likewise, many different colours may be placed in close relation, yet the wool is so soft and the tones so delicate that the effect is not harsh. Some sort of tree-form is not unusual; but on the whole, the designs of both field and border are geometric.

Type Characteristics. *Colours,* principally blue and red, with minor quantities of yellow, green, and brown. *Knot,* Ghiordes. Knots to inch horizontally six to ten; perpendicularly, six to ten. A half knot, as it appears at back, is as long as wide or longer. The rows of knots are firmly pressed down, so that the warp does not show at back. *Warp,* generally wool, occasionally cotton; each of the two threads encircled by a knot is equally prominent at back. *Weft,* wool, of fine diameter, usually dyed red or brown. A thread of weft crosses from three to five times between every two rows of knots. *Pile,* soft wool of medium length. *Border,* three to five stripes. *Sides,* a double overcasting or narrow selvage. *Both ends,* a web and warp fringe. *Texture,* firm. *Weave* at back is of moderately fine grain. *Usual length,* six to eleven feet. *Usual width,* three eighths to two thirds length.

KUTAIS. — Among a large assortment of Caucasian rugs are occasionally seen a few pieces from Kutais, once famed as the home of Media, and now the capital of Imeritia. The gardens surrounding its homes, that line both banks of the river Rion, are fragrant with lilacs and roses; in the valley beyond the city, pink rhododendrons and yellow azaleas blossom beneath the oaks. Here is woodland scenery not found in other parts of Caucasia, and it might be expected that the weavings of the people would have a striking individuality of their own; but they are little known as a distinct class. In fact, they bear such a resemblance to the Kazaks that they are constantly mistaken for them; though as a rule they have a more oblong shape and somewhat shorter nap; they are less stoutly woven, less barbaric, and contain fewer crude, nomadic devices. Moreover, as this district was producing rugs before the Cossacks had settled permanently in Southern Caucasia, it is not improbable that some of its patterns were copied by them.

A peculiarity of this class is the drawing of the pear designs, which are found in a very large number of the rugs. The extension of the narrower end, instead of being a short, curved hook, is generally more developed, so that it may be as long as the major axis of the pear and frequently stands almost at right angles to it. Also attached to the sides of the pear are rectangular bead-like processes (Plate O, Fig. 6c, Page 291). In many of these rugs, the field is di-

PLATE 50. GENGHA RUG

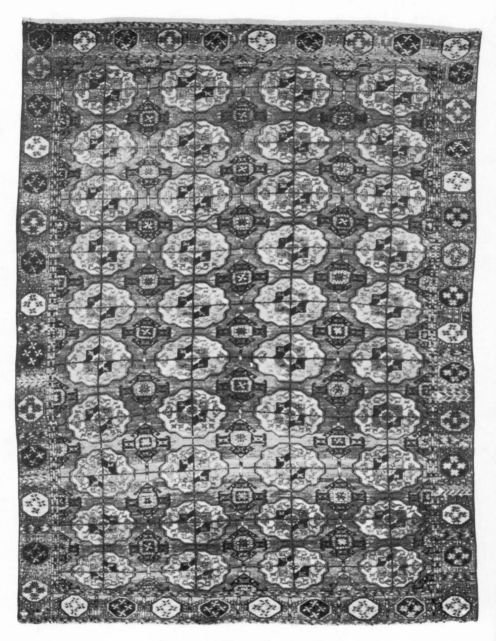

PLATE 51. ROYAL BOKHARA RUG

vided into a number of bands parallel with the sides; and through them run vines, from which the pears are suspended. Or the pears may be arranged in regular order on the field without the bands and vines. Sometimes the field is reduced to a very small space by a broad border consisting of a number of stripes, some of which are often of striking patterns. One of them is represented in Plate I, Fig. 15 (opp. Page 226), which suggests the grape vine common to the gardens of Kutais. Some form of the tree of life and floral forms are also seen in old pieces.

A resemblance exists between the weave of Kutais and Tiflis rugs, as in each the weft usually crosses several times; it is generally coloured blue or red, and is formed of fine threads of yarn. The wool of the nap is of the same fine quality; but the warp of the Kutais rugs, which is almost invariably of wool, frequently consists of a brown and white thread twisted together; and the knots are tied less evenly, so that the alignment at the back is a little more irregular, yet less so than in Kazaks.

Type Characteristics. *Colours*, principally red, blue, and white, with minor quantities of yellow, brown, and black. *Knot*, Ghiordes. Knots to inch horizontally five to nine; perpendicularly, six to eleven. A half knot, as it appears at back, is as long as wide or longer. The rows of knots are slightly pressed down. The alignment is more even than in Kazaks. *Warp*, generally wool, occasionally cotton; each of the two threads encircled by a knot is equally prominent at the back. *Weft*, wool, of fine or medium diameter. A thread of weft usually crosses three times, occasionally only once, and again four or five times. *Pile*, wool, of medium length or long. *Border*, three to five stripes. *Sides*, either a double overcasting, or a double selvage of two or three cords. *Both ends*, a web and warp fringe. *Texture*, moderately firm. *Weave* at back, generally of medium fine grain but occasionally coarse. *Usual length*, six to twelve feet. *Usual width*, one third to two thirds length.

KAZAKS. — Of the warlike Cossack tribes, which were once stationed along the southeastern border of Russia to protect it from the depradations of Caucasians, a number settled permanently in Circassia, and a few crossed the mountains to the high plateau lying between Lake Gotcha and Mt. Ararat. Here they adopted more sedentary lives; but there still lingers the inherited spirit that generations ago won for them the name Kazaks, which denotes to the Tartars, from whom many have doubtless sprung, a Marauder. All of these tribes weave; but the rugs seen in this country come principally from the southern district, where may also be found the fabrics of other races such as Armenians, Tartars, and the native people. Nevertheless, the Kazak weavings are of a most distinct type, to which even the smaller Kazakjes conform. They have bright, rich colours, of which a liberal amount of green is almost invariably present, though sparingly used in other Caucasian rugs. Only the Tcherkess vie with them in the length of the nap; and no other class has such noticeable patterns of incongruous sizes and shapes. They have, in fact, the most nomadic, unconventional patterns of all this northern group; and in their barbaric characteristics, they bear much the same relation to other Caucasian rugs as those of Western Kurdish and Yuruk tribes bear to Persian and Asia Minor pieces.

In marked contrast to the almost mosaic drawing of Chichis and many Daghestans, the Kazaks show a tribal fondness for large patterns. Sometimes the field is divided into three horizontal panels, which may be entirely plain except for a simple design fringing the edges; or as is more frequently the case, it may be occupied by large, slightly elongated octagons, within which are represented smaller figures. Occupying almost the entire field of other pieces are large patterns like medallions, perfectly balanced with reference to the centre and subdivided into small sections, each of which contains individual motives. A few of this class, also, have the "sunburst" pattern, so characteristic of the Tcherkess.

At least half the pieces now seen are without any formal pattern, but contain a heterogeneous lot of geometric designs characteristic of nomadic weavings; but even these are generally arranged with the idea of symmetrical balance. For instance, at the centre may be a large geometric figure surrounded at equal distances by pairs of smaller and similar figures. Not infrequently the drawing of the upper and lower half, or of the right and left side, shows an almost perfect correspondence, notwithstanding the many separate designs. The most common of these are eight-pointed stars, lozenges fringed with latch-hooks, and what are known as the "tarantula" device. Of the innumerable small figures, the octagonal discs and S forms are the most common; crude animal and human figures are also seen.

Excepting the addition of the arch, there is little distinction between namazliks and sedjadehs. It is small and less graceful than that of Asia Minor pieces, and follows stiff lines in harmony with the general pattern. It is, however, drawn in two different ways. Generally it has the shape of half an octagon, or of a wall-tent with apex flattened; but not infrequently it is square or slightly oblong. The narrow bands that form the arch are extended transversely from each side of the base to the borders; and occasionally they are continued down the sides of the field to form at the bottom a figure similar to the square-shaped arch. Now and then a comb, or small figure of diamond shape, on which to place the bit of sacred earth from Mecca, is outlined within the mihrab; and now and then crude palm-like figures, indicating where the hands are to be rested in the act of devotion, are represented at the sides.

However many stripes the border may contain, rarely are there more than one of any consequence; since the guard stripes have generally only the reciprocal sawtooth or trefoil patterns, the barber-pole or dotted lines. The absence of important secondary stripes, however, brings out more prominently the drawing and colouring of the main one. The most common pattern is what is known as the "tarantula" represented in Plate I, Fig. 8 (opp. Page 226). Very similar is the crab pattern (Plate I, Fig. 7), which was undoubtedly derived from the double vine of some Persian rug, as the crab-like figure may be resolved into a rosette to which are attached four conventionalised leaves. Another pattern, which is also seen in Kutais rugs, is the crude but striking vine shown in Plate I, Fig. 15, which, when represented in bold, rich colours on an ivory field, makes a most effective and beautiful border stripe. Other border stripes frequently employed in these rugs appear in Plate I.

Unfortunately, during recent years, many inferior rugs of other tribes have been sold as Kazaks, which in a measure they often resemble though they lack their spirit and character. The very modern Kazaks, also, are often of poor quality, but those made two generations or more ago were carefully and stoutly woven, with silky wool dyed with the best of vegetable colours. There is always something interestingly barbaric in their long, almost shaggy nap, their masses of rich red and green, their bold designs surrounded by smaller nomadic figures, all of which collectively find no counterpart in any other Caucasian rugs.

Type Characteristics. Colours, principally red, green, and yellow, also some blue, white, and brown. *Knot*, Ghiordes. Knots to inch horizontally six to nine; perpendicularly, seven to ten. The rows of knots are pressed down, so that the warp is hidden at back. *Warp*, wool; each of the two threads encircled by a knot is equally prominent at back. *Weft*, wool, of coarse diameter, usually dyed red or brown. A thread of weft generally crosses only twice between every two rows of knots, but occasionally three or four times. *Pile*, wool, clipped long. *Border*, three to five stripes. *Sides*, a double overcasting attached in figure-eight fashion to the sides, or a double selvage having from three to five cords. *Lower end*, a red or brown web and warp loops, or a braided selvage and fringe. *Upper end*, a red or brown web, occasionally a braided selvage or several rows of knots, and a warp fringe. *Texture*, stout. *Weave* at back is of very coarse grain. *Usual length*, five to twelve feet. *Usual width*, one third to three quarters length.

KARABAGHS. — To the southeast of Lake Gotcha and north of the river Aras, that divides Caucasia from Persia, is the district of Karabagh, a name signifying "Black Vineyard." On account of its geographic position, it has been subject to the Shahs for long periods, during the many struggles between the two countries. It is, moreover, separated from the rug-producing district of Karadagh by the river only; and its southern border is less than eighty miles distant from the city of Tabriz, to which many of its rugs are taken. For these reasons it would be only natural to expect that the weavings of Karabagh would show more of the Persian influence than those of any other part of Caucasia. Such, indeed, is true, when applied to the oldest pieces; but it is not at all true in the case of a large percentage of the modern products.

Within recent years large numbers of these coarsely made and wretchedly dyed rugs have reached the Western markets. Some of them resemble Kazaks in their geometric figures; but differ from them in their workmanship, since one of the two threads encircled by a knot is depressed; they are much more loosely woven; they are not so large; nor for the most part are they so heavy. Other pieces often lack the symbolic and other small designs that render nomadic rugs so interesting. Occasionally the central field is almost figureless, or there may be large expanses of white or some raw colour such as startling red, yellow, or blue, on which appear stiffly and crudely drawn nondescript devices.

It is a relief to turn from these poor pieces to those woven half a century ago, with less obtrusive colouring and more chaste patterns. Many of the old pieces are oblong sedjadehs, which have often a length almost twice the breadth; though the more modern pieces incline to smaller and nearly square sizes. There are also namazliks that do not always religiously follow the usual pattern; for now and then one is seen with an arch of several steps, rising from near the middle of the sides, and with a diamond for the sacred earth or pebble from Mecca, as is shown in Plate C, Fig. 12 (Page 61). The particular piece from which this was drawn was over fifty years old and was three fourths as wide as long. Scattered over the main field, which was yellowish brown, and the spandrels, which were white, were geometrically shaped flowers with long angular stems tinted with blue, green, and pinkish red.

The borders show as great diversity as the fields, but one stripe usually contains a concession to the Persian and another to the Caucasian tradition. For instance, the primary stripe may be of Iranian character flanked by the running latch-hook; or it may be the well-known crab pattern, while the adjacent stripe may be a running vine of simple form.

Many of these old pieces are very handsome and equal in artistic finish the best of Caucasian rugs; the drawing is carefully executed; the colours are rich; the weave is fair; but like the rare old rugs of Daghestan and Tiflis, are now seldom seen.

Type Characteristics. Colours, principally red, blue, yellow, and white. *Knot*, Ghiordes. Knots to inch horizontally six to ten; perpendicularly, seven to ten. The rows of knots are only slightly pressed down, yet the warp is generally concealed at back. *Warp*, wool; one of the two threads encircled by a half knot is depressed below the other at back. *Weft*, wool, of medium or coarse diameter, sometimes dyed red. A thread of weft crosses twice between every two rows of knots. *Pile*, wool, of short or medium length. *Border*, three stripes. *Sides*, generally a double selvage of two or three cords, in lengths of different colours; occasionally a double overcasting attached figure-eight fashion. *Lower end*, a web and warp loops, or a braided selvage, one row of knots or more, and a warp fringe. *Upper end*, a web, a web turned back and hemmed, or a braided selvage, one row of knots or more, and a warp fringe. *Texture*, loose. *Weave* at back is of coarse grain. *Usual length*, four to nine feet. *Usual width*, one half to three quarters length.

SHUSHAS. — About seventy miles to the southeast of Lake Gotcha is Shusha, capital of Karabagh. Nearly two centuries ago, it was built by Nadir Shah on an almost inaccessible mountain side to guard the northern boundary of Persia, which had been extended to the Caucasus. It has now about twelve thousand inhabitants, and is the market place for numerous tribes that are scattered over the dry plains as far as the Aras river. In this city and in the suburbs are woven rugs that are frequently imported to this country and sold under several names, yet are of a distinct type. They resemble the Karabaghs of the surrounding country but differ from them in their richer and more subdued colours as well as in the stoutness of weave. One thread of warp to each knot is doubled beneath the other, whereas in the rugs of the desert tribes it is only depressed.

Type Characteristics. Colours, principally dark blue, red, and brown, with minor quantities of green and yellow. *Knot*, Ghiordes. Knots to inch horizontally seven to twelve; perpendicularly, six to eleven. The rows of knots are only slightly pressed down, so that the warp shows at back. *Warp*, wool; one of the two threads encircled by a knot is much depressed below the other at back, and frequently doubled under the other. *Weft*, wool, of medium diameter, generally dyed red. A thread of weft crosses twice between every two rows of knots. *Pile*, wool of medium length. *Border*, three stripes. *Sides*, a double selvage of two or three cords, often attached to the sides in figure-eight fashion. *Lower end*, a narrow web and warp loops. *Upper end*, a web that is sometimes turned back and hemmed, and a warp fringe. *Texture*, moderately firm. *Weave* at back is of slightly coarse grain. *Usual length*, four to nine feet. *Usual width*, one half to three quarters length.

GENGHAS. — Over the land lying between lakes Gotcha, Van, and Urumiah, in Caucasia, Armenia, and Persia, tribes of mixed origin wander back and forth, but frequently gather at the yearly fair of Elizabethpol. During the period when the Persian rule extended over the country, it was the residence of a Khan and an important centre of trade. As it was then known as Ganja or Gengha, the weavings of these nomads, which were marketed there, acquired that name.

Naturally they are a heterogeneous lot containing ideas incorporated from many sources; but they resemble the Kazaks more than anything else, and are frequently mistaken for them. Yet some of the distinctions are very marked: they have a more oblong shape; the nap is shorter; and they are less stoutly woven. In the Kazaks a thread of weft, as a rule, crosses only twice between two rows of knots, which are firmly pressed down; but in these rugs a thread of weft crosses from four to eight times between two rows of knots, which are not firmly pressed down, so that the narrow filling of weft is sometimes even four times as wide as a row of knots and presents a bead-like appearance. In the colour scheme of numerous pieces, which in many respects resembles that of Karabaghs, is often a preponderance of ivory white. There is no characteristic pattern. The field may be covered with diagonal stripes as in some Shirvans; it may consist largely of lozenges fringed with latch-hooks and tarantula devices; again, it may have some large central figure surrounded by a motley lot of emblematic as well as apparently meaningless devices, or crudely drawn human, animal, or floral forms. The borders, likewise, include a wide scope of patterns. It is, therefore, largely by the character of the weave, quality of material, and finish of sides and ends, that these pieces can be distinguished from other nomadic products.

Type Characteristics. Colours, principally blue, red, and white, with minor quantities of green, yellow, and brown. *Knot,* Ghiordes. Knots to inch horizontally six to eight; perpendicularly, six to nine. A half knot, as it appears at back, is longer than wide. The rows of knots are not firmly pressed down, so that the warp shows at the back. *Warp,* generally wool, occasionally goat's hair; each of the two threads encircled by a knot is equally prominent at the back. *Weft,* wool, of medium diameter and usually dyed red. A thread of weft crosses twice between every two rows of knots, but generally three and frequently as many as six or eight times. *Pile,* wool of medium length. *Border,* three or four stripes. *Sides,* a double selvage of two, three, or four cords. *Lower end,* a web, usually coloured red, and warp loops. *Upper end,* a web to which a braided selvage is often added, and a warp fringe. *Texture,* very loose. *Weave* at back is of coarse grain. *Usual length,* five to nine feet. *Usual width,* two fifths to two thirds length.

BORDER STRIPES

Disregarding a very few floral secondary stripes that have been derived from Persian rugs, the Caucasian borders are characterised by geometric patterns, which distinguish them from other groups. But were it possible to trace them to their origin, it would doubtless be found that a very large number that are now strictly geometric have degenerated from leaf and flower patterns. Of the remainder, some are symbolic and others are crude copies of familiar objects. The more artistic and realistically drawn floral patterns appear in the less conspicuous secondary stripes; but on the other hand the primary stripes contain a number of unusually interesting patterns, which have been copied for centuries.

PRIMARY STRIPES. — The cup and serrated leaf pattern (Plate I, Fig. 1, opp. Page 226) appears so frequently in Shirvans as to be almost typical. It is also occasionally seen in Daghestans and Kabistans; but probably originated in Southern Caucasia or Armenia, since it is found similarly drawn in rugs woven in that district about 1500 A. D. It is a pattern that scarcely varies with time or locality except in the number of serrations to the leaf and in the shape of the cup.

Serrated leaf patterns, represented in Figs. 2 and 3, Plate I, are sometimes seen in Kazak and other nomadic rugs. It is not improbable that they have a common origin with the Shirvan cup and leaf pattern.

In the stripe represented in Plate I, Fig. 4, is a series of wine cup rosettes that are occasionally seen in the old rugs from the Shirvan district. In fact, the wine cup design is a favourite there.

Another stripe, in which a somewhat similar cup appears, is shown in Plate I, Fig. 5. This is an old nomadic pattern not frequently seen.

Fig. 6 of Plate I, represents the well-known Chichi border stripe, composed of rosettes separated by diagonally drawn ribbon-like bars. To the rosettes are attached tri-cleft leaves. This stripe suggests at once some Persian vine and flower.

What is known as the crab pattern (Plate I, Fig. 7), is seen in Kazaks and other Caucasian nomadic rugs, as well as in a few very modern Asia Minor pieces. Though its resemblance to a crab is noticeable, it is really a rosette to which are attached four crudely drawn leaves, that frequently contain smaller designs at their centres.

Slightly resembling the last is the so-called tarantula pattern (Plate I, Fig. 8), that was possibly derived from the stripe with an eight-pointed star (Plate K, Fig. 12, opp. Page 230); but it seems more

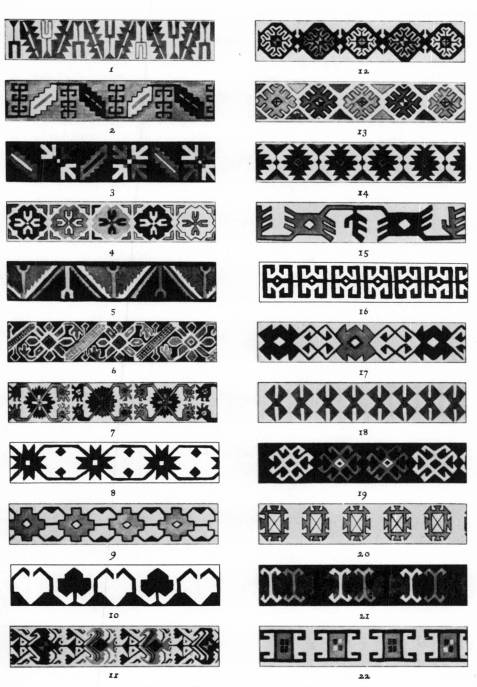

PLATE I.   PRIMARY BORDER-STRIPES OF CAUCASIAN RUGS

PLATE 52. PRINCESS BOKHARA RUG

probable that the inspiration is Iranian and that it is intended for rosette and double vine. This stripe is found in Kazaks, Genghas, Tcherkess, and other nomadic rugs.

Somewhat like the last is the stripe of Plate I, Fig. 9, that is now and then seen in old Tiflis and other rugs of Southern Caucasia. It suggests a geometric rosette and double vine.

Occasionally the dainty clover-leaf design, represented in Plate I, Fig. 10, is used by the nomadic weavers. It is almost the only reciprocal pattern found in a Caucasian primary stripe.

The repetitive urn-shaped pattern of Plate I, Fig. 11 is once in a while seen in old rugs of the Daghestan country.

On account of the resemblance between the stripes shown in Plate I, Figs. 12 and 13, they have probably a common origin. Both are found in rugs of the Daghestan and Shirvan districts, and the former is occasionally seen in rugs of Asia Minor. Sometimes smaller adventitious devices are placed at the sides of the stripes between the rosettes.

Resembling the last is the pattern shown in Plate I, Fig. 14, which is commonly seen in Shirvan rugs and kilims. It is purely geometric and resembles one used in Western Asia Minor rugs of the XV Century, from which it may have been derived.

Though greatly conventionalised, the pattern represented in Plate I, Fig. 15 is a vine and leaf derived from much more ornate forms, which may be seen in a XVI Century Asia Minor piece that is in the British Museum. It is now seldom copied, but was once a popular pattern for the Kazak and Kutais weavers.

Some form of the latch-hook appears in a large number of Caucasian stripes, but mostly in nomadic pieces. Figs. 16, 17, 18, 19, and 20 of Plate I, represent patterns found mostly in old Kazaks and kindred rugs. The last one is also occasionally used as a secondary stripe. The patterns shown in Plate I, Figs. 21 and 22 are from stripes sometimes seen in the Daghestan and Shirvan districts.

A much more interesting stripe because of its well authenticated antiquity, is the one shown in Plate J, Fig. 1 (opp. Page 228). It is found in rugs made in Southern Caucasia two centuries ago, and according to Dr. Martin has been used since the XII Century. Probably as the result of copying, the design appears reversed in many old rugs.* These stripes are seen in comparatively recent pieces, but principally

* One of these is represented in Dr. Bode's "Knupfteppiche," where it appears as a secondary stripe.

in those of the Daghestan and Shirvan districts.   Though the latch-hook is suggested by the small triangular parts, it is more probable that originally they were intended for leaves.   In a few stripes the design is elongated, and in place of a single crossbar there are several, forming a figure that slightly resembles a poinsetta, which is the term occasionally applied to it by weavers.

The stripe shown in Plate J, Fig. 2, which is found in Kazak and other nomadic rugs, is interesting as representing a vine of which the pendant flower is replaced by a T formed by latch-hooks.

In Figs. 3 and 4 of Plate J, are patterns of stripes found in rugs of the Shirvan and Daghestan districts.   As they are several centuries old, they may be derived from Armenian patterns, to which they show kinship.   Both patterns are at times reversed as the result of copying.*   A stripe also used in the same districts and probably of similar origin is seen in Plate J, Fig. 5.

Differing from any of these because of their utilitarian origin, are the separate designs, which arranged in perpendicular rows, form the "churn" stripe of Plate J, Fig. 6.   Each of them represents crude machines for churning milk, which were formerly used by the nomadic tribes of Southern Caucasia and Armenia, who constructed them out of logs with a length of about five feet, and placed the sharpened base in the ground.   Then hanging a goat's skin filled with milk over each of the sides, and seating themselves in the middle, they turned first one then the other.   As might be expected, these stripes belong entirely to nomadic rugs.

Figs. 7 and 8 of Plate J, represent stripes sometimes seen in Shirvans.   The latter is undoubtedly derived from the prayer patterns that are often used in these rugs.

What is known as the Georgian stripe is shown in Plate J, Fig. 9. It is found in Daghestans, Kabistans, Shirvans, Soumaks, She-makhas, and Kubas.   Though a primary stripe, it is rarely placed at the centre of the border, but at the outer or the inner side, or at both sides with a less ornate stripe between.   As a rule it accom-panies only the more artistic rugs.

Generally the primary stripes of Soumaks are different from those of other rugs.   A few appear in Figs. 10, 11 and 12 of Plate J.   The last is interesting on account of the leaf-like forms of the octagonal designs.

* An intermediate pattern suggested by each is found in an old Asia Minor piece owned by Dr. Bode.

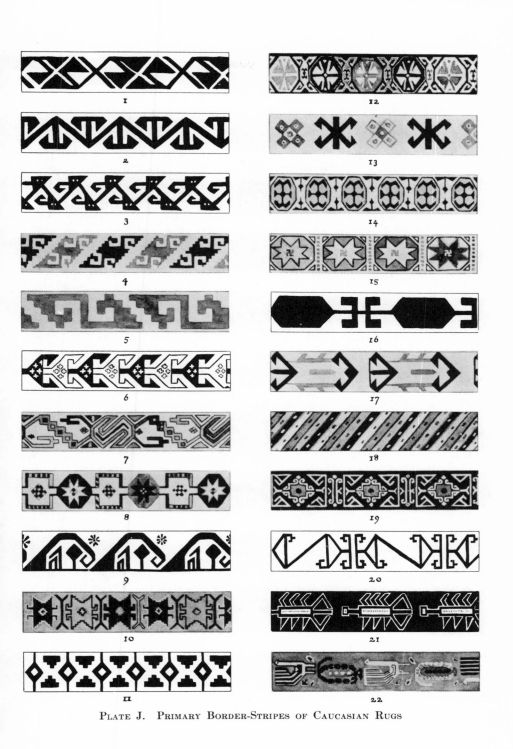

PLATE J.   PRIMARY BORDER-STRIPES OF CAUCASIAN RUGS

PLATE 53. TURKOMAN RUG WITH KATCHLI PATTERN

The stripes seen in Plate J, Figs. 13, 14 and 15 are found only in nomadic rugs. The last is interesting principally on account of the swastikas.

And old form now and then seen in the Daghestan-Shirvan classes appear in Plate J, Fig. 16. It is an archaic pattern copied from a most interesting Daghestan prayer rug.

The stripe shown in Plate J, Fig. 17 is sometimes adopted in rugs of Southern Caucasia, such as the Kutais and Kazak.

Another very old pattern found in the borders of the Daghestan-Shirvan classes is shown in Plate J, Fig. 18. Though it suggests the narrow tertiary stripes known as "barber-poles," it differs from them by being very much wider, and by containing bars of many different colours, as red, yellow, cream, blue, green, and brown, which generally contain short, oblong dashes.

A very interesting stripe, found almost exclusively in rugs from the districts of Daghestan and Shirvan, is the Cufic pattern of Plate J, Fig. 19. It is particularly characteristic of old Daghestans and Kabistans, but must have been introduced through Shirvan from Armenia, as it can be traced through a gradation of changes to stripes of Cufic characters used in Asia Minor rugs of the XV Century.

Plate J, Fig. 20 represents a "bracket-chain" pattern that probably originated in Asia Minor, but is occasionally found in the rugs of Caucasia.

In Plate J, Fig. 21 is a stripe representing scorpions, that is very rarely seen in Shirvans; and in Fig. 22 is a stripe representing birds, sometimes seen in Bakus.

SECONDARY AND TERTIARY STRIPES. — As the pattern shown in Plate K, Fig. 1 (opp. Page 230) shows in profile flowers representing carnations, it has been called the "carnation pattern." It is very common in Shirvans, Kabistans, and Daghestans.

Less frequently seen are the rectangular vine with a desiign lke a three-leaf clover, shown in Plate K, Fig. 2, and the very graceful vine with leaf and flower shown in Fig. 3, both of which are indiscriminately used in place of the carnation pattern in rugs with the same primary stripe. The latter is the most dainty and graceful Caucasian floral stripe. It is found in pieces of the Kabistan and Daghestan classes made over a century and a half ago, and is probably of Iranian extraction.

Another floral pattern from the same district is seen in Plate K, Fig. 4. It often accompanies the Georgian stripe of Daghestans and Soumaks, with which its stiff drawing harmonises.

Likewise, the stripe shown in Fig. 5 is found now and then in the same classes of rugs. Similar rosettes are sometimes represented in Persian stripes that show the influence of nomadic weavers.

Simple forms of the running vine which are seen mostly in the rugs of Southern Caucasia are represented in Plate K, Figs. 6, 7, 8, 9, and 10. All are old patterns. The third appears in an Asia Minor carpet woven about 1250 A. D. The fourth is found in some of the oldest remaining rugs from Southern Caucasia, that date back two and a half centuries; and a pattern similar to the last is seen in some Persian carpets made about 1650 A.D.

Plate K, Figs. 11 and 12 represent stripes sometimes seen in Chichis and a few other Caucasian rugs.

A very simple pattern, but one that at times is very attractive on account of its delicate colouring, is shown in Plate K, Fig. 13, and another is shown in Fig. 14. Both are used principally in rugs of Southern Caucasia.

The stripe represented in Plate K, Fig. 15, is found in very old rugs of the Daghestan and Derbend types; and there is a tradition among some of the native weavers that the designs originally represented boat hooks used by the sailors of the Caspian Sea. It is not unreasonable to suppose that the early weavers imitated objects of utility before those of mere ornament; but even if there is any basis for the tradition, it is equally probable that these designs are derived from the lily or other floral forms, and were introduced from Persia.

Somewhat similar to the last is the reciprocal trefoil, which generally appears with more simple drawing than is shown in Plate F, Fig. 17 (opp. Page 158). It is more widely used for a border stripe than any other pattern, as it is found in almost all Caucasian, in a large number of Persian, in Indian, and Beluchistan rugs. It was commonly used in Persian rugs as early as the year 1500.

The dainty Chain pattern of Plate K, Fig. 16 has a well authenticated antiquity, as it is found in Asia Minor carpets of the XV Century, from which it was probably derived. Without doubt it was a favourite pattern three centuries ago, as it appears in some of the early paintings in which Oriental carpets are represented.

PLATE K. SECONDARY AND TERTIARY BORDER-STRIPES OF CAUCASIAN RUGS

PLATE 54. TURKOMAN PRAYER RUG, WHICH ACCORDING TO A. BOGOLUBOW HAS
THE TYPICAL PINDÉ PATTERN

Not infrequently the right-angled corners are rounded so as to give it a more graceful form.

As the purely geometric pattern of Plate K, Fig. 17 is entirely lacking in ornamental features, it is used principally to separate more important stripes. Occasionally it is found in such rugs as the Chichis and Shirvans.

Another very simple pattern that is sometimes used as an inside stripe is seen in Plate K, Fig. 18. This is evidently an archaic form and is found principally in pieces of the Shirvan district.

The reciprocal sawtooth and the running latch-hook patterns (Plate K, Figs. 19 and 20) belong to the less important stripes of not only Caucasian but a number of Persian rugs. The former pattern appears constantly on the monuments of ancient Susa, and doubtless had once some symbolic meaning. The latter is seen in the corners of the Dragon and Phœnix carpet (Plate 20, opp. Page 87) which was woven about 1350 A.D.

TECHNICALITIES IN THE WEAVE OF CAUCASIAN RUGS

CAUCASIAN	Knot type	Knot No. Horizontally	Knot No. Perpendicularly	Warp (w/c/g)	Warp at back (e/d/h)	Weft (w/c)	Weft No. times crossing bet. two rows knots	Sides (O/S)	Lower End (W S / K / L / F)	Upper End (W S / K / T / F)	Nap (l/m/s)	Weave (f/m/c)	Texture (l/m/f)
Baku	G	6–9	7–11	w	e	w	2	O, S	W, K, F	W, K, F	s	m	m f
Chichi	G	7–10	8–12	w	e	w	2	O, [S]	W, K, F	W, K, F	m s	m	m
Daghestan	G	7–10	8–15	w	e, [d]	w, [c]	2	[O], S	W, K, F	W, K, F	s	f	m f
Derbend	G	5–9	6–12	w, [c]	e	w	2 [1]	[O], S	W, [K], F	W, [K], F	m	m	m l
Gengha	G	6–8	6–9	w, [g]	e	w	2–4 [6–8]	S	W [S], L	W [S]	m	c	l
Kabistan	G	7–12	8–16	w	e	w	2 [3]	O, S	W [S], L	W [S], [K], F	m	m	m f
Karabagh	G	6–10	7–10	w	d	w	2	[O], S	W [S], [K], L, F	W [S], [K], T, F	m	c	l
Kazak	G	6–9	7–10	w	e	w	2 [3–4]	O, S	W [S], L, F	W [S], [K], F	l	c	f
Kuba	G	6–9	7–13	w	e	w	2	S	W, [K], F	W, F	m	m	m l
Kutais	G	5–9	7–12	w, [c]	d	w	3 [1–5]	O, S	W, F	W, K, F	m	m	m f
Leghian	G	6–9	6–11	w	[e], [h]	w	2	S	W S, K, F	W, F	m	c	f
Shemakha	G	7–11	7–13	w	d	w, [c]	2	[O], S	W, F	W S, K, F	m s	m f	m f
Shirvan	G	7–12	8–12	w	e	w	2	S	W, K, F	W, F	m	m c	m l
Shousha	G	7–12	6–11	w	d, h	w	2	[O], S	W [S], L, F	W, F		m c	m f
Soumak	G	8–14	6–16	w	e	w	2	[O], S	W [S], K, F	W [S], K, [T], F		m	m
Tcherkess	G	6–9	7–10	w	e, [d]	w	2 [4–6]	[O], S	W [S], K, F	W [S], K, F	m	m	f
Tiflis	G	6–10	6–10	w, [c]	e	w	3–5	O, S	W, F	W, F	m	m f	f

[ ] indicates the less frequent condition.

Legend:
G = Ghiordes, S = Sehna.
Warp: w = wool, c = cotton, g = goat's hair. At back: e = each equally prominent, d = 1 to the knot depressed, h = 1 to the knot doubled under.
Weft: w = wool, c = cotton.
Sides: O = overcast, S = selvage.
Lower End: W = web, S = selvage, K = Rows knots, L = warp loops, F = fringe.
Upper End: W = web, S = selvage, K = Rows knots, T = turned back and hemmed, F = fringe.
Nap: l = long, m = medium, s = short.
Weave: f = fine, m = medium, c = coarse.
Texture: l = loose, m = medium, f = firm.

CHAPTER XII

CENTRAL ASIATIC RUGS

HE land that extends eastward about fourteen hundred miles from the Caspian Sea to the western boundary of the Chinese Empire, and northward for a similar distance from the Arabian Sea through Beluchistan and Afghanistan to the steppes of Western Siberia, is one of the least civilised parts of the eastern continent. Here until within a few recent years, the people lived the same untrammelled lives that their ancestors pursued for past centuries; and the encroachments of the Russian Empire on the north and the English on the southeast, have as yet made little impression on their uncultured natures. To these circumstances it is largely due that the rugs termed Central Asiatic, which come from this district, still possess to a large degree the originality of design, virility of character, and beauty of colour that are so rapidly disappearing from the woven products of countries more subject to the influence of Western civilisation.

These rugs may conveniently be divided into three natural subgroups, which include:

1. The Turkoman, consisting of what are known in this country as Royal and Princess Bokharas, the Tekkes, Yomuds, Khivas, and Beshires, all of which are made in Turkestan;* and the Afghan, of which part are made in Turkestan and part in Afghanistan.

2. The Turko-Chinese, consisting of the Samarkands, which

* A. Bogolubow, in his excellent work "Tapis de l'Asie Centrale," divides the Transcaspian Turkomans into two principal groups, the Salors and Yomouds, each of which includes subgroups. These are again divisible into many tribes, almost all of whom weave. As their rugs, though resembling one another, show different characteristics, they might properly be separated into numerous classes; but since only a few of them are known in this country, they alone will be described.

are made in Western Turkestan, and the Kasghars and Yarkands made in Eastern Turkestan.

3. The Beluchistans or Beluches, made principally in Beluchistan.

No other rugs adhere more strictly to uniformity of colour and design than the Turkoman. And, when it is considered that their prevailing tones and their simple, geometric designs are such as would readily be adopted by people with primitive ideas of ornamentation, it seems probable that they have been copied with only slight modification for a great many centuries, even though more gorgeous and elaborate carpets were woven during the short period when Samarkand was capital of the East. This is probably true, notwithstanding no other country in the world has been subject to more conquests than Turkestan or overrun by so many different races. For here, as we learn by the aid of philology, dwelt the Aryans even before the light of history had come to dispel the mists of antiquity. Two or three thousand years later it was overrun by Cyrus and added to the dominion of the Medes and Persians. In the V Century A.D., Tartar tribes conquered it; and in the following century Turks and Persians divided it between them. Still later it was again overrun by the Arabs, who, sword in hand, converted the vanquished to the creed of Islam. When a few more centuries had rolled away the Mongol hordes of Genghis Khan swept over it; and once again it suffered desolation under the iron hand of Tamerlane, "Scourge of Asia." But in spite of these waves of conquest and the minor struggles with Persians, Greeks, and Romans, that left their impress on the country, each of the several classes of Turkoman rugs, including even those made two centuries ago, show a remarkable conformity to definite types, however much may be their modification in small detail. Their nap is invariably short; in all of them some shade of dark red is the predominating colour; and in most of them some form of an octagon appears. They are, moreover, the best woven and the most beautiful of the Central Asiatic rugs.

Though the Turko-Chinese rugs are made in places subject to the influence of Turkomans and far removed from the culture of Chinese, they are unlike the rugs of the former and resemble those of the latter. Not improbably this is because Tamerlane had gathered at Samarkand noted artists and artisans from China, whose influence continued long after his death. And as traditional patterns have been transmitted for centuries, there is little doubt that some of the

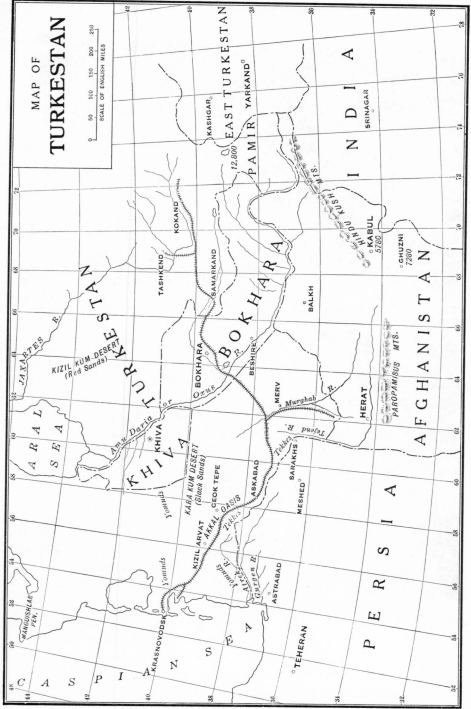

MAP OF
TURKESTAN

SCALE OF ENGLISH MILES
0 50 100 150 200 250

TURKESTAN

EAST TURKESTAN

PAMIR

INDIA

BOKHARA

AFGHANISTAN

PERSIA

KHIVA

ARAL SEA

CASPIAN SEA

KIZIL KUM DESERT
(Red Sands)

KARA KUM DESERT
(Black Sands)

JAXARTES R.

Amu Daria or Oxus R.

KASHGAR
YARKAND
12,800

SRINAGAR

HINDU KUSH MTS.

KABUL
5780
GHUZNI
7280

BALKH

PAROPAMISUS MTS.

HERAT

MERV
Murghab R.

Tejend R.

SARAKHS
MESHED

ASKABAD
Tekke R.

GEOK TEPE
AKKAL OASIS

KIZIL ARVAT

Yomuds

KRASNOVODSK

Atek R.
Gurgen R.

ASTRABAD

TEHERAN

MANGUISHLAK PEN.

KOKAND

TASHKEND

SAMARKAND

BOKHARA

BESHIRE

KHIVA

PLATE 55. TURKOMAN RUG OF THE SALOR TRIBES

modern rugs, even though falling far short of the standard of their early prototypes, more closely resemble them than they do any other rugs of Asia. In these pieces Turkoman simplicity of geometric figures is replaced by an elaboration of conventional floral forms and by designs associated with early philosophies; sobriety of colour yields to the bright and even gaudy tones not infrequent in modern textile fabrics.

The Beluchistans, which are regarded as a subgroup of the Central Asiatic rugs, show a closer relationship to the Turkoman rugs than to any others. A few of them have octagonal patterns suggestive of Bokharas, and all have the long webs at the ends and the heavy goat's hair selvage at the sides peculiar to Afghans and Tekkes. On the other hand, many of the patterns both of field and border resemble Persian workmanship; so that placing these rugs in the same group with the Turkoman and Turko-Chinese rugs, which are not made in an adjoining territory, is slightly arbitrary.

ROYAL BOKHARAS. — The best known district in Turkestan is the Khanate of Bokhara, which extends from the offshoots of the lofty Pamir mountains in the east to the desolate sandy plains beyond the Amu Daria, or Oxus river, on the west. Situated in its northern half and near the centre of a fertile valley is its capital, Bokhara, "The Noble." Though noted for its cruelty, it was once the intellectual centre of Asia, and still possesses nearly a hundred schools and innumerable mosques. These and its bazaars are almost all that remain of the splendour of those days when the great caravans that came from China, India, Persia, and Russia made it one of the great marts of the East.

On account of its commercial importance, the wild tribes of the Kirghiz steppes, the Turkomans from Kizil Kum,* the Afghans who dwell north of the Paropamisus range, and the fierce Tekkes and Yomuds from the west, came and bartered their rugs for other necessities. Many of these rugs were taken in caravans, that often numbered several thousand camels, and sold in the Russian market places of Astrakan, Orenburg, or Nijni Novgorod. Since they came from the same place, the term Bokhara was often applied to each of the different classes. Thus we hear of Royal Bokharas, Princess Bokharas, Tekke Bokharas, Yomud Bokharas, and Khiva Bokharas.

Of these five classes the Royal Bokharas, as a rule, not only are

* "Desert of Red Sands."

the best woven, but are made of the finest material; even the warp of many of them is of soft, silky white wool. The old rugs were made in the city and suburbs of Bokhara, where now only a few pieces are made. Both old and new are found only as sedjadehs. They have two well-known patterns, one of which consists of an octagon surrounding a quartered hexagon. Of these quarters, which are either plain or contain a small triangle of contrasting colour, a pair that are opposite are always white or cream coloured, and the other pair are of some shade of red. Small triangular figures are invariably seen above and below the hexagons, as well as small diamond, oval, or spear-shaped figures at each end of the major axis. In the other pattern the contour of the octagon is rounder; and the hexagon is replaced by an eight-pointed star, at the centre of which is a diamond containing a rectangle or occasionally a Greek cross. Projecting into the four corners from the star are small designs, that careful observation of a large number in many different kinds of rugs shows to be leaf forms. Between the diagonally placed octagons of both these types are stars or diamond-shaped figures, that are usually of the same design regardless of the shape of the octagon. In large rugs the centres of the octagons are generally joined by straight lines of dark blue colour.

It is uncertain why the term Royal has been applied to this class of Bokharas, but it is eminently befitting the old well-woven, velvet-like pieces. A few have small patches of pink or ruby coloured silk; and all have a prevailing tone of red diversified by deep blues and touches of lighter red and ivory, that convey an idea of opulence and dignity worthy of a king.

Type Characteristics. *Colours,* principally dark red, with minor quantities of blue, pink or orange, and ivory. *Knot,* Sehna. Knots to inch horizontally eight to twelve; perpendicularly, sixteen to twenty-four. The rows of knots are firmly pressed down, so that the warp is concealed at back and the weft is almost hidden. *Warp,* fine white wool; each of the two threads encircled by a knot is equally prominent at back. *Weft,* wool, of fine diameter. A thread of weft crosses twice between every two rows of knots. *Pile,* fine wool, or occasionally silk, clipped short. *Border,* three stripes divided by smaller coloured lines. *Sides,* a blue double overcasting. *Both ends,* a narrow web and short warp fringe. *Texture,* firm. *Weave* at back is of fine grain. *Usual length,* four to ten feet. *Usual width,* three fifths to four fifths length.

PRINCESS BOKHARAS. — The rugs known as Princess Bokharas are woven by the Mohammedan tribes who dwell in parts of the Khanate of Bokhara. They are nearly square and the field is divided into four equal sections by perpendicular and horizontal bands. Because of this pattern they are called "Katchlis," a word derived from the Armenian language signifying "like a cross." The bands generally have designs that are co-ordinate with those in part of the border; but not infrequently the designs of the horizontal band differ from those of the perpendicular one, and in a few rare instances consist of an octagonal figure. It is generally believed that the well-known Y-shaped motive characteristic of the field and the border is intended to represent the tree of life, but some native weavers suggest a different interpretation. To them the whole rug symbolises a mosque; the perpendicular arm of the cross is the entrance; the Y-shaped designs are benches; and the broad diagonal lines with serrated edges in the borders are groves of trees surrounding the mosque. A very large percentage of these pieces are namazliks. One of their peculiarities is the position of their unobtrusive tent-shaped prayer arch, which is in a panel entirely within their upper border.

Compared with Royal Bokharas their nap is rarely of as fine quality, the warp is usually of brown instead of cream white wool, and the weave is coarser. Also, the tones of colour are more sombre, and of browner shades; but in rare old pieces the rich mahogany and bronze hues of the ground, on which are represented small designs in shades of cream and dark blue, are exceedingly rich and pleasing. Unfortunately, within recent years large numbers of this class have been made solely for commercial purposes, and lack the finer qualities of their prototypes.

Type Characteristics. Colours, principally dark red or brown, with minor quantities of dark blue and ivory. *Knot*, Sehna. Knots to inch horizontally eight to twelve; perpendicularly, fourteen to eighteen. The rows of knots are firmly pressed down, so that the warp is concealed at back and the weft partly hidden. *Warp*, brown wool or goat's hair; each of the two threads of warp encircled by a knot is equally prominent at back. *Weft*, wool, of fine diameter. A thread of weft crosses twice between every two rows of knots. *Pile*, wool of short or medium length; occasionally some goat's hair is used. *Border*, three stripes, separated by narrow lines. *Sides*, a double overcasting or a double goat's hair selvage of three cords. *Both ends*, a web and warp fringe. *Texture*, stout.

Weave at back is of moderately fine grain.   *Usual length,* four and
one half to six feet.   *Usual width,* two thirds to four fifths length.

TEKKES. -- A little over two centuries ago there lived on the
peninsula of Mangishlar, on the eastern shore of the Caspian Sea,
an almost unknown tribe called the "Tekke," a term which is said
to denote a mountain goat, and was applied on account of the head-
long pace at which the men rode over rough mountain sides. About
the beginning of the XVIII Century they packed their *khibitkas,* *
and after moving southward to escape from the attacks of a more
powerful tribe, they met the Yomuds in the southwestern corner
of Turkestan and robbed them of their lands. Further eastward
they snatched the fertile oasis of Ak-kal from some Kurds, whose
ancestors a Shah of Persia had located there in earlier times to
protect his kingdom from fierce northern tribes. By irrigating and
cultivating the soil, they prospered and increased rapidly in population, until, about 1830, they numbered one hundred thousand.
One fourth of them then moved eastward; and after settling on
the banks of the Tajand, not far from the Persian town of Saraks,
they attacked the inhabitants of Merv and captured the city. Growing thus to be a powerful people, they occupied much of the country
between Persia and the Amu Daria.

Ever restless, they were constantly looking for weaker foes on
whom to fall; and when a leader would announce an intended raid,
hundreds or even thousands would meet at the appointed rendez-
vous prepared to blindly follow him. Sometimes it was through the
passes that looked down into the fertile valleys of Northern Persia.
Stealthily creeping through them they would fall unexpectedly upon
an unprotected village and dash away with young women and children. If pursued, they would stab their captives, and if necessary,
ride more than one hundred miles a day in flight. At other times,
they would attack caravans crossing the deserts and carry away
both camels and wares.

Their raids, however, were not viewed with complacence by the
Russians, who had been steadily advancing on the land lying between
the Caspian and the Amu Daria, and whose armies the Tekkes har-
assed. At length in January, 1881, came the final death struggle
in the memorable attack on the fortress of Geok Teppe, where
thirty-three thousand tribesmen and seven thousand women and
                     * A tent in which an average of five people live.

children had taken refuge. With the fall of that stronghold and the terrible punishment that followed, the power of the Tekkes was completely crushed; and a people whose ancestors for countless centuries had roamed the desert, recognising no master, yielded finally to the advance of civilisation.

These were the people whose wives and daughters wove the rugs generally known as Tekke Bokharas, of which large numbers with excellent weave and sterling dyes can still be found. As few of them were designed for mosques or palaces, it is very unusual to find pieces over one hundred years old, and even these are rare. Indeed, any that are now forty years old should possess great interest, as they were woven at a time when the Tekkes were still a fierce race. Very many have the Katchli pattern. The prayer arch, which is similar to that of Princess Bokharas, is in a panel exterior to the field and within the border. Not infrequently there are three arches in the same horizontal panel, which, as a rule, is above the field, but occasionally below it. In a great many of these rugs the three-leaf clover is found in some part of the field; and in the band of pile that extends beyond the border at one end are usually small conventionalised bushes with white and yellow flowers. The pattern shown in Plate L, Fig. 4 (opp. Page 250), appears almost invariably in the outer stripe.

There are other types, into one of which it would seem as if the very spirit of the desert had crept. Their dark ground colours are brightened by lighter tones that give an effect of strange yet not inharmonious beauty. A few would seem to speak of the early Zoroastrian faith, for in their fields are designs like stars with effulgent rays that suggest the burning altars of fire worshippers.

The shape or some peculiarity of the rug indicates the purpose for which it was intended. For instance, the rugs which were made for doors of the khibitkas have at the upper end a selvage with the web turned back and hemmed, and at each corner a heavy braided cord of about two feet in length, by which they were suspended. Other pieces have webs at both ends. Many beautiful pieces are made for use on horses or camels. Those intended for camels are of oblong shape with a field usually containing large octagons, between which are smaller octagons similar to those in Royal Bokharas.

Tekkes may be distinguished from the Princess Bokharas, which they resemble, by their goat's hair selvage at the sides, by one thread of warp to each knot being slightly depressed at the back, and by their coarser character. There is, however, a great similarity in the colours, though in the Tekkes tones of deep plum and rich red are not uncommon.

Type Characteristics. Colours, principally dark red, brown, or plum, with minor quantities of dark blue and ivory. *Knot*, Sehna. Knots to inch horizontally seven to twelve; perpendicularly, nine to fourteen. The rows of knots are slightly pressed down, but the warp shows at back. *Warp*, wool or goat's hair; one of the two threads encircled by a knot is depressed below the other at back. *Weft*, wool of fine or medium diameter. A thread of weft crosses twice between every two rows of knots. *Pile*, wool, or occasionally goat's hair of short or medium length. *Border*, three stripes, separated by coloured lines. *Sides*, a three-cord double goat's hair selvage. *Lower end*, a wide coloured web and long warp fringe. *Upper end*, a braided selvage turned back and hemmed, or occasionally a wide coloured web and long warp fringe. *Texture*, firm. *Weave* at back of moderately fine grain. *Length*, five to eight feet. *Usual width*, three fifths to four fifths length.

KHIVAS. — On the west bank of the Amu Daria, and stretching for two hundred miles above its mouth, is the plain of the Khanate of Khiva. Most of the people live in khibitkas, and either follow a nomad's life or raise from the alluvial soil, that is watered by innumerable canals, crops of cotton, corn, and rice, as well as melons, peaches, and pomegranates. A large population, also, inhabits the city of Khiva, which before the building of the Siberian railway, was on one of the direct highways between east and west. Caravans of nearly two thousand camels regularly passed through it en route to Orenburg in spring and to Astrakhan in fall, carrying wares from districts farther to the east as well as its own rugs and manufactured articles.

On account of the constant intercourse between the Khiva and Bokhara tribes, their woven fabrics show a close relationship in patterns and colours; yet they contain important differences. Those made by the Khiva tribes are cruder, and reflect the effect of constant struggles against the rigours of the desert and the fierce Kirghiz from the steppes to the north. The wool is also coarser and longer, and the knots are much fewer to the inch. Occasionally geometric as well as animal designs suggestive of Caucasian influence occur. Moreover, the brownish threads of weft that separate each row of knots, are noticeable at the back, whereas in other Turkoman rugs the weft is hardly perceptible.

Many of the old pieces were very handsome, as is shown by the following description of an antique goat's hair carpet from Khiva by Dr. Birdwood.* "The ground is of madder red, decorated with leaves and scrolls and lozenge-shaped forms in red, white, and orange, each lozenge being defined by a deep line of indigo blue. The ends terminate in a fringe. Professor Vambery says that these rich lustrous carpets are made entirely by the nomad women about Khiva, the head worker tracing out the design in the desert sand and handing out to her companions the dyed materials of different colours as required in the progress of weaving."

Type Characteristics. *Colours*, principally dark red, with minor quantities of blue and ivory. *Knot*, Ghiordes or Sehna. Knots to inch horizontally six to ten; perpendicularly, eight to fourteen. The rows of knots are but slightly pressed down, so that the warp shows at back. *Warp*, wool or goat's hair; each of the two threads encircled by a knot is equally prominent at the back. *Weft*, wool of medium or coarse diameter. A thread of weft crosses twice between every two rows of knots. *Pile*, wool of medium length. *Border*, generally three stripes. *Sides*, a double selvage of two or three cords, which is generally of goat's hair. *Both ends*, a web, one or more rows of knots and a warp fringe. *Texture*, stout. *Usual length*, four and one half to six feet. *Usual width*, three fifths to three quarters length.

YOMUDS. — When, in 1718, the Yomuds were driven by the Tekkes from their homes in the well-watered region about Kizil Arvat, they moved to a less fertile country to the north and west. Though now numbering about one hundred thousand, they have few villages; and regardless of the dreary sand storms, the biting cold of winter, or the terrible heat of summer, they wander with their sheep and goats from place to place in search of more favoured spots. Sometimes their khibitkas are seen along the border of the Caspian Sea as far south as Astrabad in Khorassan, or among the sandy trackless wastes of Kara Kum, nearly as far north as the Aral Sea.

Many of their rugs rival the Royal Bokharas in wealth of colour. The prevailing tone of the field is usually red or maroon, but is sometimes rose, plum, or dark brown; and the remaining shades

* In "Industrial Arts of India."

correspond with the blue, green, brown, and white of Tekkes. Contrasted with these is the ivory ground of the border, which, as a rule, has a much brighter colour than the field. Furthermore, the pile of the old pieces has a lustre that is due to the excellence of the dyes and the thick soft wool.

There are several distinct types, of which only one is well-known. Its pattern is clearly Turkoman, though the lesser designs show that there has been frequent intercourse with the weavers of Caucasia. Covering the field of these pieces are regularly placed diamond-shaped figures that suggest those of the Royal Bokharas, from which they may have been developed to the almost entire exclusion of the octagon; though the latter appears much less prominently in the centre of the diamonds. In the border occurs the running latch-hook, the barber-pole stripe, and a geometrically drawn vine. The webs of the ends, which are usually red and striped, are broad and have a fringe of goat's hair, sometimes braided into rope-like tassels, but more often hanging loose.

The saddle bags are of irregular shape resembling a flat walled tent, and contain in both field and border much brighter colour than the rugs. Their field is checkered with diamond-shaped figures rich in ivory colour and separated from each other by diagonal barber-pole stripes; their border contains the running latch-hook.

Type Characteristics. Colours, principally dark red and mahogany brown, with minor quantities of blue, green, and white. *Knot*, generally Sehna, occasionally Ghiordes. Knots to inch horizontally five to eight; perpendicularly, seven to ten. The rows of knots are pressed down, so that the warp is largely concealed at back. *Warp*, coarse wool or goat's hair; each of the two threads encircled by a knot is equally prominent at the back, or one is slightly depressed below the other. *Weft*, wool, of medium diameter, or occasionally wool mixed with goat's hair. A thread of weft crosses twice between every two rows of knots. *Pile*, wool, of medium length. *Border*, three stripes. *Sides*, either a two-cord selvage of red alternating with blue or brown, or a goat's hair double selvage of three or four cords. *Both ends*, a broad, reddish brown web through which, as a rule, run coloured lines or several narrow stripes, and a long warp fringe. *Texture*, stout. *Weave* at back is moderately coarse. *Usual length*, five to twelve feet. *Usual width*, two thirds to three quarters length.

BESHIRES. — On the Amu Daria and not far from Afghanistan is a small district from which the rugs known as Beshires now and then find their way to this country. As it is not far from several routes of caravans, these rugs show a relationship to the products of other Turkoman tribes. Their colour scheme is principally the dark red and brownish tones found in Bokharas, Yomuds, and Khivas. The ends, too, have the web crossed by several lines, such as blue, green, and yellowish brown, that are usual in Afghans. The patterns sometimes contain a suggestion of the geometric figures of the Yomuds and some Caucasian pieces; and yet they have a striking character of their own. Not infrequently the field is covered with broad, irregular scrolls or foliate forms, unlike anything seen in any other class of rugs. Again the field may be occupied with a trellis pattern, which divides it into diamond-shaped figures. Within these are smaller diamonds surrounded by eight-pointed stars and quasi-floral forms. The borders, as a rule, are narrow and have simple designs that incline to the geometric; but a few are of fair width and are ornamented with rosettes and conventionalised leaves. In namazliks, which are rarely seen, the prayer arch lies within the field. Almost all of this class found in this country are old rugs; and on account of their rich, harmonious colours and unobtrusive yet distinctive patterns, are always pleasing and interesting.

Type Characteristics. Colours, principally dark red and brown, with minor quantities of blue, yellow, and white. *Knot*, Sehna. Knots to inch horizontally seven to twelve; perpendicularly, seven to twelve. A half knot, as it appears at back, is as long as, or longer than, wide. The rows of knots are pressed down, so that the warp is almost hidden at back. *Warp*, generally goat's hair. Each of the two threads encircled by a knot is equally prominent at back, or occasionally one is slightly depressed. *Weft*, wool or goat's hair of medium or coarse diameter. A thread of weft crosses twice between every two rows of knots. *Pile*, wool, of medium length. *Border*, generally three stripes, occasionally only one. *Sides*, a goat's hair selvage of two to four cords. *Both ends*, a wide web, crossed with several coloured stripes. *Texture*, stout. *Weave*, coarse. *Length*, four to twelve feet. *Usual width*, two fifths to two thirds length.

AFGHANS. — One of the most distinctive classes of Turkoman rugs is known in this country both as Afghans and Khivas. Both of these

names are unfortunately applied; for their only title to be called
the latter is that many were formerly exported from the bazaars
of Khiva, and that they slightly resemble the rugs of that city.
Nor are they strictly Afghans, since they come from the territory of
mountain ridges and fertile valleys that stretches from the Hindu
Koosh Mountains northward across the eastern part of the Khanate
Bokhara, and are made by the tribesmen of both countries. In
fact, they differ considerably from the rugs of Central and Southern
Afghanistan, and bear no resemblance to those of floral pattern
woven about Herat.

Within the territory where these rugs are made the Aryan and
Teutonic races have met and blended; and across it have passed
the armies of the greatest conquerors of Asia. Here still exist some
of the most untamed races of the East, feeding their flocks on lofty
table-lands, or cultivating patches of valleys, through which flow
icy streams to form the Amu Daria. Here the rights of hospitality
are held sacred, but wrongs are revenged without recourse to any
tribunal.

When the antecedents, customs, and surroundings of the people
are taken into consideration, it is not strange that their rugs should
be strong and firm in texture, bold in design, positive and striking
in colour. Most of them are large and almost square in shape, though
mats are not uncommon. The traditional pattern consists of perpendicular rows, usually three in number, of large octagons, that
are almost in contact. Between these rows are much smaller diamond-
shaped designs, which consist in some pieces of a cluster of eight-
pointed stars, and in others of a geometric figure that is occasionally
fringed with hooks and contains within its centre an eight-pointed
star.

With a few exceptions the octagons, which closely resemble
those of Royal Bokharas, are symmetrical, and all their details are
drawn as regularly as if the rugs were factory woven. They are invariably divided into quarters which usually are marked with a small
figure like a three-leaf clover. The field contains but few adventitious designs and they are rarely animal, as the Afghans are Sunni
Mohammedans. One of the most common of these designs, which
appears also in the Tekkes and Yomuds, is probably intended to
represent part of the headstall of camel trappings. The pattern of
the border conforms to that of the field, but frequently has crudely
drawn floral forms and a conventionalised vine. The sides have

an added selvage of brown goat's hair; and the ends are finished with reddish brown webs, from which hang loose fringes of dark wool or goat's hair.

As characteristic as the large bold octagons are the colours, which however subdued are invariably of rich hues. Those of the field consist of dark red, maroon, or reddish brown. The quarters of the octagon are of a deep blue alternating with a red that is lighter than the field. In some pieces this red is blood colour, or nearly crimson, standing out in bold relief against the adjacent blue and a field of maroon. Lines of green, orange, yellow, and white often appear in the body of the rug; lines of dark blue and a checkered pattern in red and blue are frequent in the red webs of the ends.

Though these rugs are, as a rule, heavier and coarser in texture than most other Turkoman rugs, the old pieces have a soft plushy nap of fine wool and goat's fleece, as well as richness of tone, that is very attractive. They are exceedingly durable and moderate in price.

Type Characteristics. Colours, principally dark red and mahogany brown, with minor quantities of blue, green, yellow, and white. *Knot,* generally Sehna, occasionally Ghiordes. Knots to inch horizontally five to eight; perpendicularly, seven to ten. The rows of knots are pressed down, so that the warp is largely concealed at back. *Warp,* coarse wool or goat's hair; each thread encircled by a knot is equally prominent at back, or one is slightly depressed below the other. *Weft,* wool, of medium diameter, or occasionally wool mixed with goat's hair. A thread of weft crosses twice between every two rows of knots. *Pile,* wool, of medium length. *Border,* three stripes. *Sides,* a goat's hair double selvage of three or four cords. *Both ends,* a broad web of reddish brown colour through which run several narrow lines or several narrow stripes, and a long fringe. *Texture,* stout. *Weave* at back is moderately coarse. *Usual length,* five to twelve feet. *Usual width,* two thirds to three quarters length.

SAMARKANDS. — A little over one hundred miles east of Bokhara, and on the southern border of the desert of Red Sands, the river Zarafshan, "Strewer of Gold," has turned a plain of yellow loam into an oasis. Forty-three large canals bring its waters to fields of cotton; to vineyards; to orchards of apple, pear, peach, and pomegranate; and to gardens of fragrant flowers. Here is Samarkand, "The Mirror of the World." Few cities as old remain after passing through so many vicissitudes of fortune. Alexander forced his way through its gates, the Chinese Empire annexed it, and finally Tamerlane seized and made it the magnificent capital of one third of the known world. His tomb and other remaining monuments attest the grandeur of that time when there was fostered here the art, the luxury, and the splendour of the East.

The rugs known as Samarkands are woven in a district somewhat eastward from the city and are often called "Malgarans." They are not to be compared with the magnificent carpets that adorned the palaces and mosques of the capital of Tamerlane; yet they possess a special interest, as in them are combined features derived from both Eastern and Western Asia. Either because this city, known as Sa-mo-Kien, was once part of the Chinese Empire, or as is more probable, because it is on one of the great highways of caravan travel between China and Western Asia, the Chinese element is particularly notice-able. It appears in the colours that are in strong contrast; in the general pattern that shows little affinity for those of Persian or West Asian rugs; and even in the weave, in which silk is occasionally mixed with the wool of both warp and pile.

The ground colour of the field is usually some shade of red or madder, with blue and yellow appearing conspicuously in the prin-cipal designs and border stripes. Or again, the field may be blue, soft brown, gray, or tan, with which the colours of the designs and borders, that may contain red, yellow, and blue, invariably appear in strong contrast.

Few rugs have a more noticeable pattern, which consists princi-pally of rounded medallions. If there be but one, it is in the centre; and if there be many, one is at each corner. They are usually orna-mented with Chinese scrolls or some geometric design, as an eight-pointed star; but dragons, birds, or fishes are not uncommon. Occasionally, also, flowers of Persian design, with eight rounded petals, appear in the medallion, and others of larger size cover the field; or they may even exclude the medallion and constitute the principal motive. Some simple design in fretwork gives finish to the corners of the field, which is further covered with Chinese butter-flies, scrolls, or archaic flower forms. The borders are equally dis-tinctive, and unlike those of Chinese rugs are relatively wide and consist of several stripes surrounded by an edging of uniform colour. One of the stripes has generally a stiffly undulating vine; another a continuous swastika design; and a third is marked with frets, the barber-pole design, or a design which by some is regarded as the sacred Chinese mountain rising from the waves. In most pieces warp and weft are loosely woven, and the pile is of a medium grade of wool; but in very old pieces the wool is fine and lustrous.

Type Characteristics. *Colours,* principally red, blue, and yellow. *Knot,* Sehna. Knots to inch horizontally six to eight; perpendicularly, five to eight. Each half knot, as it appears at back, is as long as, or longer than, wide. The rows of knots are not firmly pressed down, so that the warp shows at back. *Warp,* generally cotton, occasionally wool; one of the two threads encircled by a knot is doubled under the other. *Weft,* generally cotton, occasionally wool, of coarse diameter and frequently dyed. A thread of weft crosses twice, between every two rows of knots, and occasionally three times. *Pile,* wool, of medium length. *Border,* three stripes with a pink edging. *Sides,* a red or pink overcasting. *Lower end,* web and warp loops. *Upper end,* web and warp fringe. *Texture,* moderately firm. *Weave* at back, rather coarse. *Length,* six to fourteen feet. *Usual width,* one half to three fifths length.

KASHGARS AND YARKANDS. — Among the foothill plains at the western end of the Chinese Empire, are the mud-walled cities of Kashgar and Yarkand, that were ancient even in the days when Marco Polo visited there. Situated in populous and fertile districts, each has been a city of political and industrial importance; but on account of the great divides that separate them from Western Turkestan, Persia, and India, their commerce has been principally with Thibet and China. Thus it has happened that only within recent years have any of their textile fabrics reached Europe and America, where they are still almost unknown. Yet even in the remote past, these cities gained a reputation for the culture of silk and the weaving of carpets. Moreover, at different periods they were centres of luxury, so that it may safely be assumed that many of their woven products were of a high order of excellence.

These rugs, to be sure, come from a district lying within the Chinese Empire; but it is so remote from the centres where the well-known Chinese rugs have been and are woven, and is so much nearer to West Turkestan and Afghanistan, that it seems best to place them in the Central Asiatic group.

As a rule, such pieces as reach this country show crude workmanship entirely lacking in graceful floral patterns or artistic drawing. Octagonal forms, animals, and even mythical creatures are often distributed over the fields so as to give them a decidedly Chinese character. The narrow border stripes ornamented with the swastika and fret forms are often similar to some of the Samarkand stripes. The colours, which lack the subdued richness of Persian pieces, are often light; but they occasionally consist largely of tones of dark blue and red which show Turkoman influences. Most of these rugs are interesting on account of their quaintness and individuality; but few compare in quality of material, weave, or artistic finish with other classes of this group.

BELUCHES OR BELUCHISTANS. — "When creating the world, the Almighty made Beluchistan out of the refuse" are the words of an old proverb, that refers to a land which formerly produced some of the most interesting rugs of the East. In fact, the thought is not surprising when the desolate character of the country is considered; for a sandy, waterless waste stretches over the greater part, and only in a corner to the northeast and in narrow strips, where streams from mountain sides water small valleys, is any cultivation. Across this sparsely settled land and farther westward into the southeastern part of Persia, untamed tribes of Beluches and Brahoes wander with their sheep, goats, and large numbers of camels. Their rugs, woven on crudely made looms, bear little resemblance to the more artistic floral pieces of the Indian weavers to the east or to those of Kirman to the west. Nor are they closely related to the Turkoman rugs with which they are usually grouped. In fact, they possess an individuality that once recognised is never forgotten; an individuality due to the isolated condition of a country that is protected from its nearest neighbours by barriers of deserts and mountain ridges, and is possessed by a still unconquered people. To these circumstances, also, it is due that the rugs are rarely coloured with aniline dyes, though many modern pieces have been chemically washed by dealers.

One of the most distinguishing features of Beluchistans are their tones of colour, that rarely depart from traditional usage. They are principally a red of the shade of madder, a blue with purple cast, and a dark brown that has sometimes a slight olive tinge, particularly when appearing in the webs. Frequently, too, dull tones of green are seen. Contrasting with these more subdued ground colours is almost invariably some ivory which appears as small detached figures in part of the border, or as outlines of principal designs. The patterns also show individuality and diversity. Most frequently they are geometric and represent some ill defined octagons suggesting Turkoman rugs. Or they may consist of a field covered with diagonal bands, with large lozenges, or medallions, all of which are decorated profusely with latch-hooks. Still others have some crudely drawn flower design, as the Mina Khani, that tells of Persian influences.

A fair proportion have the prayer pattern, consisting of a large rectangular shaped mihrab, which is as high as, and frequently higher than, wide. The borders, as a rule, consist of three or four stripes. The main stripe is geometric and in the guard stripes are running latch-hooks or the reciprocal trefoil, though occasionally they are replaced by some conventionalised vine or ribbon pattern.

Proportionally to their length few other rugs have such long webs at the end, though they are sometimes entirely worn away while the body of the rug is still serviceable. They are usually coloured in harmony with the colours of the field, and are marked with embroidered lines or simple designs. No other rugs have a surface with more lustrous sheen, due to the soft, fine wool of the pile, which in old pieces is short and closely woven, giving a play of colours, and velvety appearance unsurpassed by any other nomadic rugs. Many of the choicest pieces of Beluchistan weave now on the market are the small saddle bags, that are of rich yet subdued colours, and possess the character and sheen of very old rugs.

Type Characteristics. Colours, principally red, blue, and brown, with minor quantities of white. *Knot,* Sehna. Knots to inch horizontally six to nine; perpendicularly, seven to ten. The rows of knots are usually pressed down, so that the warp does not show at back. *Warp,* wool; each of the two threads encircled by a knot is equally prominent at back, or one is slightly depressed below the other. *Weft,* of coarse, wiry wool, of medium diameter. A thread of weft crosses twice between every two rows of knots. *Pile,* wool, and occasionally camel's hair, of medium length. *Border,* three stripes. *Sides,* a heavy goat's hair selvage of three or four cords. *Both ends,* a broad embroidered web with warp fringe. *Texture,* slightly loose. *Weave* at back is moderately coarse. *Usual length,* four and one half to six feet. *Usual width,* two thirds to three quarters length.

BORDER STRIPES

The border stripes of the Central Asiatic group are even more geometric than the Caucasian; for it is rarely that any floral forms are seen in them, though they may appear in the pile that extends beyond the borders of the ends. Even the vines are so angular as almost to lose their identity. Octagonal figures, stars, frets, and latch-hooks are common. In fact, the group as a whole, shows the influence of the Caucasian and Chinese groups more than the Persian.

PRIMARY STRIPES

The stripe shown in Plate L, Fig. 1 (opp. Page 250) is one of many found in the rugs known as Royal Bokharas. The eight-pointed stars, as well as the small tent-like designs, which may have been derived from the headstalls of horses, are almost always found in it.

A well-known stripe of Princess Bokharas corresponding with the pattern of the field, appears in Plate L, Fig. 2. It represents a continuous series of designs shaped like a Y, that were doubtless derived from forms of trees. More frequently the stripe (Fig. 3) of broad, serrated diagonal lines, that originally may have been intended to represent foliage, is seen.

Another stripe found in Princess Bokharas and also in Tekkes and Khivas is shown in Plate L, Fig. 4. It forcibly suggests the Chinese fret. Sometimes it is used as a primary but more frequently as a secondary stripe.

In Plate L, Fig. 5, is a stripe frequently seen in Tekkes, which is interesting on account of the eight-pointed stars and latch-hooks similar to those of Caucasian rugs. Without doubt this is only one of the many instances illustrating the migration of designs.

Plate L, Fig. 6 represents a stripe peculiar to Yomuds. The running vine is most mechanically drawn and fringed with latch-hooks, which are a constant feature of this class.

Another Yomud stripe with vine in which serrations take the place of latch-hooks is shown in Plate L, Fig. 7. Pendent from the vine are other hooks shaped like frets.

Very similar to an old Caucasian stripe is the one represented in Plate L, Fig. 8; but in this stripe the small designs are drawn so that the proportion of length to width is greater; and it is probable

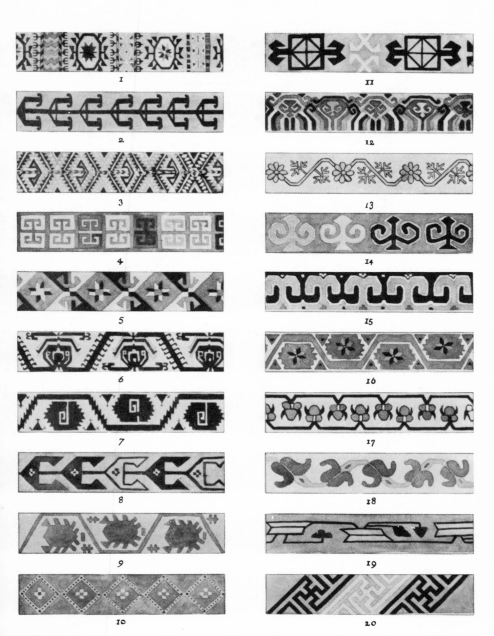

PLATE L. PRIMARY AND SECONDARY BORDER-STRIPES OF CENTRAL ASIATIC RUGS

PLATE 56. YOMUD RUG

that they were copied from a wreath of leaves. This stripe is very commonly seen in Beluchistans.

Plate L, Fig. 9 represents a mechanically drawn vine found in Beshires.

Well-known Afghan stripes are shown in Plate L, Figs. 10 and 11.

In Plate L, Figs. 12 and 13 are two of the most typical and interesting stripes of Samarkands and Yarkands. The first is supposed to represent the sacred mountain of Chinese lore rising out of the waves. The second is a vine with leaves and flowers, which suggest Persian influences.

A stripe with simple archaic pattern peculiar to Yarkands is seen in Plate L, Fig. 14.

SECONDARY STRIPES

In Plate L, Fig. 15 (opp. Page 250), is a well-known form of a secondary stripe found in Royal Bokharas.

A stripe seen in both Princess Bokharas and Tekkes is shown in Plate L, Fig. 16. It bears a slight resemblance to some conventionalised vines found in other groups.

Stripes of running latch-hooks (Plate K, Fig. 20, opp. Page 230) are frequently found in Yomuds, and occasionally in Beluchistans.

In Beluchistans the reciprocal trefoils, so well-known in Caucasian and Persian rugs, are very frequently used.

The pattern of a double vine, illustrated in Plate L, Fig. 17, is a Beshire stripe that suggests a Persian influence.

In Plate L, Fig. 18, is the narrow pear stripe that appears in a very large number of Afghans and in some Khivas.

Two well-known stripes that belong to Samarkands are shown in Plate L, Figs. 19 and 20. The pattern of the conventionalised vine speaks of Persian origin, and the swastikas suggest Chinese origin.

In Tekkes, Yomuds, Afghans, and Beluchistans the small barber-pole stripes are constantly employed.

TECHNICALITIES IN THE WEAVE OF CENTRAL ASIATIC RUGS

CENTRAL ASIATIC	KNOT				WARP						WEFT				SIDES		LOWER END				UPPER END				NAP	WEAVE	TEXTURE
	G=Ghiordes	S=Sehna	Horizontally	Perpendicularly	w=wool	c=cotton	g=goat's hair	e=each equally prominent	d=1 to the knot depressed	h=1 to the knot doubled under	w=wool	c=cotton	g=goat's hair	No. times crossing bet. two rows knots	O=overcasting	S=selvage	W=web S=selvage	K=rows knots	L=warp loops	F=fringe	W=web S=selvage	K=rows knots	T=turned back and hemmed	F=fringe	l=long m=medium s=short	f=fine m=medium c=coarse	l=loose m=medium f=firm
Afghan	[G]		5-8	7-10	w			e	d		w			2		S	W			F	W			F	m	m c	f
Beluchistan . . .		S	6-9	7-10	w			e	d		w			2		S	W			F	W			F	m	c	m l
Beshire		S	6-9	8-11	[w]	[c]	g	e	[d]		[w]	[c]	g	2 [1]		S	W			F	W			F	m	c	f
Princess Bokhara .		S	8-12	16-24	w			e	[d]		w			2	O		W			F	W			F	s	f	f
Royal Bokhara . .		S	8-12	14-18	w		[g]	e			w			2	O	[S]	W			F	W			F	m s	m f	f
Tekke Bokhara .		S	7-12	9-14	w		[g]	e	d		w			2		S	W	K			W			F	m s	m f	f
Khiva	G		6-10	8-14	w		[g]	e			w	c		2	O		W			F	W		[T]	F	m	m	f
Samarkand . . .		S	6-8	5-8	[w]	c				h	[w]	c			O		W		L		W			F	m	c	m
Yomud	[G]		7-12	9-17	w		g	e	[d]		w			2		S	W			F	W			F	m	m c	f

[ ] indicates the less frequent condition.

CHAPTER XIII

INDIAN RUGS

HROUGHOUT parts of India are woven rugs known as *Dari,* which are unlike the rugs of any other country. They are pileless cotton fabrics, that may represent an indigenous craft old as the Aryan migrations. Their designs are of the simplest order; usually no more than plain stripes of blue, red, and black, or only blue and white modified occasionally by simple geometric figures. Furthermore, their workmanship is poor, so that they possess little artistic merit. Some pieces of large size are exported, but they awaken but little interest compared with other kinds of rugs.

The weaving of pile carpets in India, on the other hand, does not appear to have been the result of spontaneous growth or to have flourished without artificial encouragement. It was probably introduced by the Saracens, but carpets of elaborate design and workmanship were not made till the reign of Shah Akbar, who imported Persian weavers. Under his patronage and the encouragement of his royal successors, the manufacture of pieces that rivalled those of Persia continued for a hundred years, but after the death of Shah Jahan, in 1658, the industry began to decline. Nevertheless, for nearly a hundred years longer excellent fabrics were produced as the result of the system that was maintained in all the provinces by lesser potentates. This system, which was also in vogue in parts of Persia, is described by Dr. George Birdwood as follows: "The princes and great nobles and wealthy gentry, who are the chief patrons of these grand fabrics, collect together in their own houses and palaces all who gain a reputation for special skill in their manufacture. These men receive a fixed salary and daily rations and are so little hurried in their work that they have plenty of time to execute private orders also. Their salaries are continued even when through age or accident they are past work; and on their death they

pass to their sons, should they have become skilled in their father's
art. Upon the completion of any extraordinary work, it is submitted
to the patron; and some honour is at once conferred on the artist
and his salary increased. It is under such conditions that the best
art work of the East has always been produced."

After the overthrow of the Mogul dominion by Nadir Shah,
in 1731, the production of carpets rapidly diminished and the quality
deteriorated. This was due to several causes. With the conquests
of the East Indian Company, that began in the middle of the XVIII
Century, and the extension of trade into every district, large quantities of antique carpets became the property of the Company or
of those in its employ. Many of them, including sumptuous pieces
that had adorned the palaces of the descendants of Tamerlane,
found their way to England. Thus were removed many of the masterpieces that had been an inspiration to the weavers. Moreover,
with the overthrow of native princes their patronage ceased; and
later, when looms were established in jails for the employment of
convicts, undesirable competition reduced the wages of free labour.
Still more pernicious was the introduction of aniline dyes, and the
elimination of individual taste by supplying patterns, that were
often of European origin, to be mechanically copied. Thus it followed that, in spite of the efforts of Mr. Robinson and of others,
for nearly half a century, to resuscitate the art and restore it to its
former condition, weaving in India, to-day, rests purely on a commercial basis; and the workmanship is almost as mechanical as the manufacture of machine-made carpets in Europe or America.

Yet to the cloud hanging over the weaving of India is a brighter
lining. European companies have established factories where
natives are employed making rugs that in quality equal the products
of Smyrna and Sultanabad. Some of them, indeed, are even more
firmly woven than the Persian products from which they are copied.
In many of the towns, also, are looms where the weavers, who are
mostly boys, enjoy more independence. Moreover, the companies,
realising that the future of their business depends on the quality
of the fabrics, are largely discarding aniline dyes. It is now possible,
therefore, to obtain Indian rugs of excellent workmanship and colours
at very moderate prices; but individuality, representative of native
character and temperament, is entirely lacking; and in its place
is simply a reproduction of Persian or European patterns.

Any arrangement of these rugs in subgroups must be arbitrary,

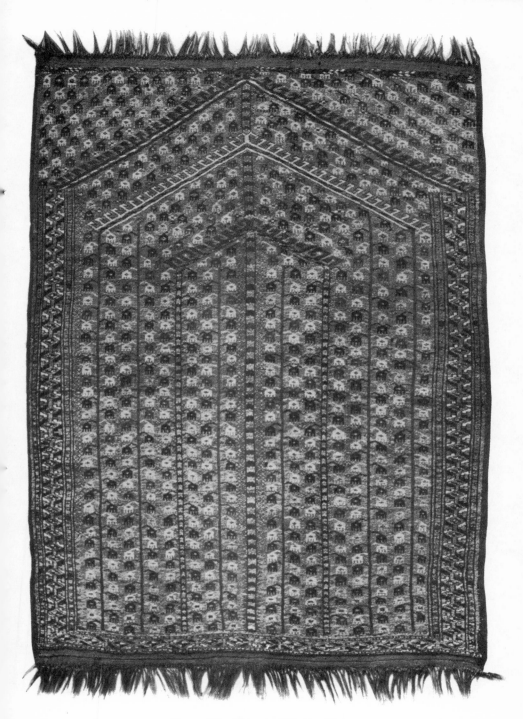

PLATE 57. BESHIRE PRAYER RUG

PLATE 58.   BESHIRE RUG

as similar conditions of early foreign influence, royal patronage, and the jail and factory systems, have prevailed throughout India. Yet since the northern part has been more directly under the influence of the courts and more intimately connected with Herat, which seems to have left a strong impress on the weavings of all the surrounding country, it is convenient to make a distinction between the rugs of Northern and Southern India.

The principal rug-producing centres of Northern India at present are Srinagar, Amritsar, Lahore, Multan, Allahabad, Agra, Mirzapur, Sindh, Jubbulpur, and Jaipur.

SRINAGAR. — From the extreme northern part of India come the rugs of Kashmir, which are often named after the capital of the province, Srinagar, the "City of the Sun." To a large extent, they resemble the far more famous shawls that were woven in the central valley, where winds the Jhelum, that some believe first suggested the pear design. The pieces woven before the British occupation of India were of excellent quality and contained delicate colour schemes, that were exceedingly pleasing; but the products of the last half century show deterioration. The colours are harsher, the mechanical drawing of the patterns show European influence, and the borders resemble too closely the central field to have distinct characters. Yet many of them are now dyed with vegetable colours, and are stoutly woven with the soft and silky wool for which this district is renowned.

AMRITSAR. — On account of famine and several other causes, a large number of the people of Kashmir migrated about the year 1840. Some of them settled at Amritsar, where they followed their former craft of making shawls, until a change of fashion, that occurred about the year 1870, deprived many of their occupation. These turned to rug weaving and thus gave an impetus to that industry.

Amritsar is now the most populous and wealthy city of the Punjab; and as some twenty thousand men and boys are employed at the looms, it is one of the leading rug-producing centres of India. Yet before the exhibition of Indian rugs at the World's Fair in Chicago, in 1893, there had not been any demand in this country for its rugs. For a long period it has been the home of weavers who found in the surrounding mountains and valleys the best of wool, but before the revival of the industry their patterns and workmanship were of an inferior character. Under the factory system, conducted by American and English firms, has been a marked improvement. Both dyes and wool are excellent, and the technique of weave equals what is found in the best of Persian products. To the square inch are frequently two hundred Sehna knots; and since when tying a knot one thread of warp is doubled under the other, as in Bijars, and the threads of weft are pressed down very firmly, the texture is unusually close. The nap is short; the sides are overcast; and as a rule, the lower end has a cotton web and the upper end a web and fringe. The moderate prices for rugs of such excellent dyes and workmanship are possible only on account of the wage of the weaver, which does not exceed one eighth what he would receive in this country.

There is nothing, however, in the pattern to distinguish these rugs from others; for in the drawing the greatest latitude is exercised. It may be a copy of a European carpet, or some Indian or Iranian antique. Of recent years, many well-known modern Persian patterns have been followed, so that not infrequently these pieces are mistaken for the products of Kermanshah or Sultanabad.

LAHORE. — About the year 1580, the imperial carpet factory of Shah Akbar was established at Lahore, the capital of the Punjab; where during the reign of the Mogul princes were produced many of the best examples of Indian weaving. It was here that, in 1634, was woven the well-known carpet now in the possession of the Girdler's Company of London. Some of the pieces that still remain show wonderful delicacy of drawing and brilliancy of colouring. At a much later period, under the British rule, the jail system of weaving was inaugurated, and rugs were made with both woollen and cotton foundation. Within more recent years the factory system followed; and on account of the nearness of Amritsar to the capital, some foreign firms have weaving establishments in both cities. It is not surprising, then, that there should be a resemblance in their products, which is seen in the finish of sides and ends and in the character of weaving, which usually shows one thread of warp to each knot doubled under the other; but as a rule the rugs of Lahore come in lighter shades and are woven with fewer knots to the square inch. In the guards of the border often appear geometric figures; but the patterns in other respects largely follow well-known

Persian drawing, though leaf and flower are more artistically portrayed and the designs are less crowded.

MULTANS. — One of the most ancient cities of the Punjab is Multan, which during the vicissitudes of centuries was more than once captured by early Mohammedan conquerors and also by Tamerlane. Its woven fabrics are of three types: the *Dari*, which are made almost exclusively in the jails; rugs of cotton pile, that have been made only within the last sixty years; and rugs of woollen pile, that have been produced for an unknown period. As the looms on which they are made are unlike those of other districts, and the weavers are but little affected by external influences, it is not surprising that the pile carpets not only display uniqueness of pattern rarely seen in other Indian pieces but also possess peculiarities of weaving as well as of material. Usually they are of moderate size, but some have a breadth of twelve feet. There are seldom more than one hundred knots to the square inch and occasionally only nine, so that the texture is coarse. Not infrequently a single knot encircles four threads of warp, and between two rows of knots is a single thread of weft. Almost all of the weavers are Mohammedans, who have a tradition that they originally came from Persia; yet their products contain few of the Iranian characteristics, since the field is usually occupied by geometric designs or crudely drawn floral patterns. As is seldom the case with weavers who dwell in cities, these dye their own wool, using both vegetable and aniline dyes. The principal colours are bold and strongly contrasting tones of red, yellow, and blue. Some of the cotton rugs, however, have a single colour of bluish shade. On the whole, the Multan rugs possess great individuality but little artistic merit.

AGRA. — Almost within sight of the minarets of the Taj Mahal are prison walls where convicts of Agra ploddingly weave. In 1891, Dr. John Hurst "saw a long row of prisoners for life, who were chained to each other by the feet, engaged in weaving a rug for Queen Victoria, and another for the ex-Empress Eugenie." Most of these pieces are of cotton foundation. Each thread of warp is equally prominent at the back, and the texture is looser than in Amritsars. The nap is short, and the fibres of the knots blend well together. Not infrequently the fields are monotones of delicate shades of blue, green, or fawn colour. As a rule, the rugs are very large and heavy; and it would seem that this has always been the case, as Mr. Robinson suggested that the reason for establishing looms at this place was the early demand for carpets too large to be imported on elephants.

ALLAHABAD. — Situated like Benares on the banks of the Ganges, and next to it the most sacred city of India to the faithful Brahman, is Allahabad, capital of the northwestern provinces. Its geographic and political importance, as well as the fact that each year half a million or more devotees visit it, have been important factors in the growth of its industries, one of which is the weaving of rugs. Yet the numbers produced have never been great. As a rule they are of large size, and are loosely woven with each thread of warp equally distinct at the back. Few of them equal the best examples of the Amritsar looms.

MIRZAPUR. — When it is considered that Mirzapur is the centre of a very populous cotton-producing district in the valley of the Ganges, to the west of Benares, and is the seat of important manufactures, it is not surprising that it is noted for its carpets. Those made half a century ago were well woven and dyed with fast colours, but largely on account of the employment of convicts, the texture of those made since then is coarse and loose, the patterns are poor, the colours crude. To a limited extent a higher grade of wool has been imported as a substitute for the harsh local product, but the result has not been satisfactory. These rugs accordingly find small favour among those who appreciate artistic qualities, and give little satisfaction where durability is the chief requisite. It should be noted, however, that within recent years efforts have been made to raise their standard.

JUBBULPUR. — Two hundred miles to the southwest of Allahabad is Jubbulpur, capital of a district of over half a million people. A century ago many beautiful rugs were woven there; but since the establishment of a School of Industry, in 1850, the character of weaving has retrograded rather than advanced. In 1880, Dr. Birdwood wrote of its rugs as follows: "The foundation, as now scamped is quite insufficient to carry the heavy pile which is a feature of this work; and is moreover so short in the staple as to be incapable of bearing the tension even of the process of manufacture. Jubbulpur carpets often reach this country (England) which will not bear sweeping, or even unpacking. I know of two which were shaken to pieces in the attempt to shake the dust out of them when first unpacked. The designs once had some local character, but have lost it during the last four or five years." Within recent years few have been exported.

SINDH. — Formerly good rugs were woven at Sindh, one hundred miles above the mouth of the Indus; but after the introduction of aniline dyes their colours, as well as patterns, deteriorated. In the poorest pieces the foundation was of cotton and hemp, and cow hair was frequently used for pile. Very few of them have been imported into this country.

JAIPUR. — In the palace of the Maharajah at Jaipur, the great commercial centre of Rajputana, are some of the most beautiful carpets that remain in India. Native appreciation is also apparent in the present workmanship of the district weavers. There is nothing crass or inelegant in the patterns which follow the pleasing drawing of Persian rugs. The vine, leaf, and flower, trees, and animals are faithfully portrayed. The texture of weave is excellent.

The principal rug-producing centres of Southern India are Madras, Marsulipatam, Ellore, Vellore, and Bangalore. Rugs are also woven in Hyderabad, Warangal, and Ayyampet in the Tanjore district.

MADRAS. — Only within a comparatively recent period have rugs been made at Madras, the early stronghold of the British in South India. Over half a century ago, native products, woven in the interior towns of the Dekkan, were shipped by way of Coconada to that city and were sometimes known as Madras rugs. Two of these pieces, which were sent by Mr. Vincent Robinson to the South Kensington Museum, differ widely in harmony of colours, beauty of design, and delicacy of workmanship from the present products of Madras. Yet the latter have much to commend them. Some are made in the jail, others in the School of Fine Arts, and others in the Anjuman Industrial School. All are made of good wool, coloured with vegetable dyes. Great diversity appears in the patterns, as some are copied from antique carpets represented in the "Vienna Carpet Book," others are copied from rugs of Northern India, Persia, and Asia Minor. As a rule, the fields are well covered with repetitive designs, that give them the appearance of factory-made carpets.

MARSULIPATAM. — Two hundred and fifty miles north of Madras on the Coromandel coast is the city of Marsulipatam, one of the earliest of the British settlements in India, from which the East India Company shipped rugs over two centuries ago. At that time they were among the finest produced in that country, but the demands of agents for articles that could be produced as cheaply as possible resulted in the use of inferior materials and in poorer workmanship. Most of the dyes are aniline. The patterns, that once were executed with marvelous beauty of detail, gave way to crude drawing until "these glorious carpets of Marsulipatam have sunk to a mockery and travesty of their former selves." * Few of them are any longer imported into this country.

ELLORE. — Not far from the delta of the Godavari river is the town of Ellore, where a few centuries ago some Persians settled, and where their descendants, faithful to early tradition, have followed the craft of weaving. Here in former times were produced some of the best rugs in Southern India; and even as late as 1883, Mr. E. B. Havell wrote that he had seen pieces woven to meet special orders which were equal in point of interest and material to the old specimens in the hands of connoisseurs of London or in native palaces. This is one of the few districts in Southern India where the industry exists outside of jails. In the town and surrounding country are about four hundred looms operated by some three thousand people, who are Mohammedans.

In the better class of rugs, in which vegetable dyes are still used, and the yarn is often a native product of wool obtained from sheep of the uplands and spun by shepherds, something of the old style of craftsmanship remains. On the other hand, a very large percentage of the rugs which are intended solely for export trade are of an inferior order, since many of their colours are obtained from aniline, their weaving is inferior, and their patterns are ordinary. Mr. Henry T. Harris, in his report on the Madras Industrial and Art Exhibition, 1903, said: "The exhibits of carpets sent from Ellore were poor in conception, weave, and colour. . . . The patterns in use were poor and often modifications of cheap Wilton, Kidder-

* Dr. Birdwood.

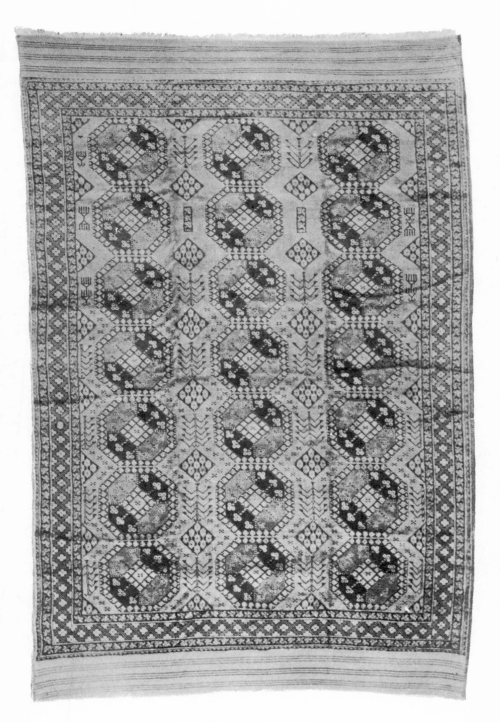

PLATE 59. AFGHAN RUG

PLATE 60. BELUCHISTAN PRAYER RUG

minster, and German power loom designs. Some of the old patterns are still with the weavers, but unfortunately there is no trade demand for this fine class of goods, the old dyes are being forgotten and have given place to cheap anilines unskilfully applied."

In length, the rugs are from a few feet to twenty-four feet. The warp is of cotton, and the weft is sometimes of jute or hemp. The pile is of an inferior quality, as it consists largely of the wool taken from a sheep after death, known as "dead" wool, or as "Chunam" or "limed" wool, since it is necessary to treat it with lime. Unfortunately vegetable dyes do not produce in it the same results as in "live" wool; and since the scarcity of wool in Southern India frequently necessitates its use, aniline dyes are for this reason alone often employed. The number of knots to the square inch is relatively small. The patterns show great diversity, as Persian features predominate in the older rugs; but both geometric and floral designs are employed in the modern.

VELLORE. — Almost a hundred miles to the west of Madras is the town of Vellore, where native weavers once produced fine woollen carpets on their own looms. A few specimens of these old pieces are preserved in the jail to serve as patterns for the convicts, who now weave the only rugs of the district. There are some fifty looms; and as the largest is about thirty feet wide, almost any size of rug may be obtained. The product rests on a commercial basis and depends on the market demands, restricted by the material available and the limitations of the weavers. According to the order, the rugs may be coloured with vegetable or aniline dyes; they may have warp and weft of cotton, jute or hemp; and they may have from six to sixteen knots to the inch measured horizontally and perpendicularly. In the patterns, which are as promiscuous as those of Ellore and often similar, the Herati design with a corresponding border is not infrequently used. Recently an effort has been made to exclude all but vegetable dyes and improve the craftsmanship.

BANGALORE. — The principal weaving industry in the Mysore state is centred about Bangalore, a city of about two hundred thousand inhabitants. Its founder, Hyder Ali, is said to have established looms and to have imported the first weavers. In 1908, the nine jail looms, of which the largest had a length of nearly thirty feet, were constantly occupied in making rugs to order. The number of knots to the square inch varied greatly according to the quality required; and the dyes were almost entirely aniline. In the city are employed a much larger number of weavers, who clean and spin the wool produced in the district, as well as dye it by secret processes, that they guard most carefully. The closeness of texture; the colouring by aniline or vegetable dyes; and the use of cotton, jute, or hemp, for warp and weft, are regulated by the requirements of the trade, which is conducted largely by two or three English firms.

HYDERABAD. — Splendid craftsmanship was once displayed in the rugs made in the cities of Hyderabad and Warangal, in the district of Hyderabad. The weave was exceedingly fine, and the colours were brilliant but harmonious. Now few rugs are produced in these cities, and they have poor patterns and wretched colours.

CHAPTER XIV

CHINESE RUGS

HE existence of Chinese rugs of age and merit was almost unknown to the Western world until the close of the last century, when a few pieces reached Europe, where they aroused the just admiration of art connoisseurs. About the beginning of this century a larger number, which were obtained during the Boxer revolution by reason of the spoliation of homes, temples, and palaces, that never before had been entered by foreigners, were exported to this country. In New York City, between the years 1908 and 1910, some of them were sold at public auctions for prices that stimulated collectors in China to search for more. But they have proved to be scarce when compared with other Oriental rugs, so that, as yet, the general public are only slightly familiar with them.

Moreover, little is known about their antecedents, for written records are exceedingly meagre. It has been suggested that many were made in Eastern Turkestan along the highways that extend to Persia and India. But it is more probable that they were woven in Eastern China, where other branches of art reached a remarkable development under the patronage of wealthy mandarins and the imperial court. Even if they are not the product of an indigenous growth, the knowledge of weaving may easily have been acquired from Western Asia; since it was not unusual several centuries ago to import weavers from one country to another to instruct native craftsmen. Furthermore, the features which at a glance differentiate these rugs from all others, proclaim their Chinese character. The diaper patterns that cover the fields of some of them, and the foliate and floral forms that appear in most of them, not only are unlike those of any other groups, but have well-known Chinese elements. A more distinctive feature are the colours, which are relatively few. Many of them, as tan, yellow, and blue, are of shades unlike what are seen in other rugs. Even more distinctive than these are the reds, which never have the primary colours found in other groups but resemble the tints of ripe apricot, peach, pomegranate, and persimmon. Similar tones are seen in old Chinese porcelain. The geometric and floral ornamentation also shows relationship to what is found in the products of other branches of Chinese art. More characteristic still are the small designs which are so related to the philosophic and religious thought of the people and to the industrial and social life that their Chinese origin is unmistakable.

Though it be granted that nearly all were woven in Eastern China, it is not possible satisfactorily to assign them to different classes based on locality; yet without doubt important distinctions, observable also in the early paintings and porcelains and resulting largely from differences of race and character of country, exist between those woven in Northern China, where the highest appreciation of art existed, and those woven in Southern China. It is probable, however, that such marked local distinctions as are found in other groups never existed in Chinese rugs. Such distinctions as do exist relate more to stages in development of the textile art, so that the natural classification is based on the successive periods when they were woven.

The absence of written and traditional history regarding the weaving of these periods is by no means an insuperable obstacle to such classification. By a careful examination of large numbers of rugs, it is possible to arrange them with reasonable accuracy in series that represent progressive forms of ornamentation and design from the archaic to the modern. A most important aid to this arrangement is the interdependence so conspicuous in the several arts of China; for designs of innumerable articles with well-established ages, especially of the ceramic art, have been copied by the weavers.

Technical peculiarities in weaving are also an aid in determining the period to which rugs belong. An important distinction, for instance, often exists in the manner in which the material is spun. If pieces of yarn be taken from old rugs and carefully examined, as they are untwisted, the simpler, cruder methods of spinning practised in former days are often apparent. In some of the oldest fabrics that remain the wool was very loosely spun. Irregularities in the size of yarn are also more noticeable in old than in modern pieces.

More important often in determining the relative age of a rug than either design or technical peculiarities of weaving, is the shade of colour; for however excellent were the original dyes and whatever care was exercised in their application, they slowly changed under the mellowing influence of time to tones that are obtained by no human process. Furthermore, as is the case with porcelains, certain colours were peculiar to certain periods. For instance, golden browns are seen mostly in pieces woven before the middle of the XVIII Century, and azure blue in pieces woven before the XIX Century. Yellow with a lemon or citron cast is found principally in pieces woven since the beginning of the XVIII Century; and green is rarely found in pieces woven before the middle of the XVIII Century. Aniline dyes were not introduced into China much before the year 1870. The time when a rug was woven may safely be regarded as not more remote than the period when the ornamentation and designs it contains were generally adopted; yet it may be much more recent, as the oldest designs were copied even after the adoption of newer ones. It is necessary, then, in determining the age of a rug to consider not only the evidence of the spinning, the weaving and designs, but also the evidence of colour.

Though Chinese rugs have features that distinguish them from other groups and divide them into separate classes; they also have many features in common. All are woven with the Sehna knot. In all but the earliest rugs the warp and weft are of cotton; each thread of warp is equally prominent at the back; and the weft, which is coarser than the warp, crosses twice between two rows of knots. The nap of both old and modern rugs is almost always wool or silk, and rarely, if ever, jute or cotton. The sides are finished by carrying the weft around the outer threads of warp, but never so as to form a wide selvage. The lower end, as a rule, has a very narrow web and warp loops; and the upper end has a narrow web and fringe. Compared with other groups they are generally more loosely woven. These and other features of resemblance and of distinction will be more fully noticed in considering the rugs of different periods.

In rugs of this group are constantly seen symbols intimately associated with the religious and philosophic thought of China. One of them is the Sacred Mountain rising out of the waves of eternity, which is an old Chinese emblem, though more frequently found in rugs of Samarkand and Yarkand. Others are the cloud-band and the Joo-e. There are also mythical creatures, as the dragon, emblem of imperial power; the Ky-lin, partly deer, partly unicorn;

the Fung-Kwang or phœnix; and the lion-dog. Still other symbolic and decorative designs are the figure Shou and the stork, emblems of longevity; the bat and butterfly, denoting happiness; the conch, wheel of law, and the two fishes, which are Buddhist emblems; and the lyre and chess board, which are symbols of the literati.

It is not improbable that rugs were woven during the Sung dynasty (960–1280 A.D.), when for nearly three centuries prosperity prevailed, literature and art flourished, and the court at Hang Chow was maintained with imperial splendour; but as far as is known, none of them exist. Nor do any remain that may have been woven during the Yuan dynasty (1280–1370) distinguished by the reign of the illustrious Mongol prince, Kublai Khan; though designs appearing in later rugs were used in kindred arts of these and preceding periods.

MING RUGS. — The oldest Chinese rugs that remain were probably woven near the end of the Ming period, or during the first half of the XVII Century. It may reasonably be assumed that they were superior in quality to those of any former period, since during this time Persia and India were producing their greatest woven masterpieces; and other branches of Chinese art were marked by an advance over the work that had preceded. Yet, on the whole, it was a period of ebb in the splendid accomplishments of intellectual and artistic effort that marked the Tang and Sung dynasties.

Such pieces as exist are distinguished by careful workmanship, archaic designs, and sobriety of colour. Most of the rugs were woven with warp and weft of cotton. Some, intended principally for wealthy mandarins or the imperial court, had pile of silk attached to warp and weft of cotton; and others were made entirely of silk. Fewer in number, but constituting the most sumptuous products of the Chinese weavers' art, were the rugs of silk woven on a web of metal threads.

The field of many of these early rugs contained all-over patterns. Sometimes the repeat designs are of octagonal shape and are arranged in horizontal and perpendicular lines, so as to leave small diamond-shaped spaces between diagonally placed octagons. Within these designs are often the emblems of happiness or longevity, floral motives, and sometimes archaic dragons. In another well-known pattern the field is completely covered with a swastika-fret and marked at regular intervals with diagonal rows of bats, emblematic of happiness. Occasionally a field of plain colour contains an irregular arrangement of objects used for sacrificial or sacred purposes. Again, it may be covered with an all-over pattern of small archaically drawn dragons resembling some of the earliest designs in Chinese decorative art, or of most conventionalised floral forms on mechanically drawn stems.

The essential feature, however, of a large number of these rugs, and one that probably antedates the all-over pattern, is a central medallion surrounded by a field that is either plain, that is marked with a subdued diaper pattern, or contains what is known as the "tiger skin" pattern, consisting of waving lines repeated throughout the field. The medallions may be either octagonal or, as is more frequently the case, rounded; but the defining lines are angular and generally represent frets. Sometimes they contain archaic dragons, which are so conventionalised in a few pieces that it is apparent that from them originated many of the Chinese scrolls. In other pieces, the shape of the central medallions and the designs which cover them suggest most forcibly that they were copied from old mirror backs. The corners of the fields may contain simple scrolls, but more frequently they correspond closely in drawing with the central medallions.

The borders are equally typical. They are invariably narrow, and generally consist of a single stripe which is figured and surrounded with a coloured edging. Probably over three quarters of the rugs of this period have a stripe with a pattern of swastika-frets. Two of these stripes, which are very old patterns, are illustrated in Plate N, Figs. 1 and 2 (opp. Page 274). Occasionally some form of the key pattern appears in the inner stripe, but almost all Chinese rugs that have two border stripes with figures belong to a later period. Many of the oldest borders are without figured stripes, and consist merely of one or more stripes of plain colour.

The few colours used in the rugs of this period have deep, rich tones. Undyed dark brown or blackish wool was occasionally used in the outer edging that surrounded the field or in the narrow border stripes; but more frequently the same colour effect was obtained by the use of corrosive dyes that in time have often eaten the wool almost to the foundation of warp and weft. Wools dyed with corrosive browns are also used in the fields and enhance the effect of designs of contrasting colours, which stand out in bold relief. Other colours, as soft dull yellow and shades of blue, are also seen

in the borders. The field is usually richer. In some pieces it is a
deep red; in others it is a soft yellow, golden brown or yellowish
tan, that shows the effect of time on what were originally several
shades of apricot. Dark and light blues, sky blue, and robin's
egg blue, as well as jade green and bottle green, are also found in
these old pieces. In the metal and silk rugs the glint of silver even
though tarnished, adds lustre to colours that have grown deeper and
richer with age.

KANG–HI. — During the first years of the Tsing dynasty, that
continued from 1644 to its recent overthrow, the country was so
occupied by wars waged between the conquering Manchoos and the
still resisting followers of the Ming dynasty that art was nearly at
a standstill. But during the reign of the illustrious Kang-hi, 1662–
1722, art revived and enjoyed one of the most splendid periods of
its history. There is, however, a noticeable difference between the
rugs that belong to the early and to the late part of this reign; so that
it is convenient to divide them into the early Kang-hi pieces, that
were woven during the last part of the XVII Century, and the late
Kang-hi pieces, almost all of which were woven at the beginning
of the XVIII Century. This division is also convenient; as many
rugs cannot be definitely assigned to the reign of a particular emperor,
and, accordingly, the broader distinction of assigning them to different centuries is frequently adopted.

In weaving, as in making porcelain, many of the products of
the late Ming were still copied during the early Kang-hi period, but
there was a freer use of colour and a more decorative ornamentation.
Many of the figures are still geometric. Frets are conspicuous in
the fields of large numbers of these pieces. The dragon also is a favourite motive; but in the scrolls that represent the legs and bifurcated
tail, and in the conventionalised head, the resemblance to the mythical monster is almost lost. Sometimes two or more of these constitute a medallion in the centre of the field, in which others are grouped
with regularity; while similar forms occupy the corners. Some of
the rugs in which the fields are covered with sundry objects, as
scrolls, vases, altar pieces, and sacred plants, also belong to this
period. The borders of these and late Kang-hi pieces have frequently
an outer edging of brown and a single border stripe with swastika-
fret. In a few pieces, the stripe has a well-balanced scroll which has
been developed from designs of conventionalised dragons and frets

that appear in the central medallion and in the corners of the field. Occasionally, however, there is an inner stripe with the key meander. The colour scheme of the late Ming, including the golden browns and deep blues, is largely employed in rugs of this period.

The same influences that resulted during the late Kang-hi period in the remarkable development of decorative art as applied to porcelains, produced a corresponding effect in the rugs woven at the same time. Manchurian ideas and taste gave renewed spirit to earlier Chinese style. The fields were not infrequently covered with sub-patterns of fret work, on which medallions appeared more prominently. The geometric figures were largely supplanted by foliate forms. Even when the central medallions and corner figures are of frets or stiffly conventionalised dragons, the fields are often covered with delicate scroll or foliate sub-patterns that support floral forms resembling the lotus or the peony. The drawing of some of these has a Western character, and there is little doubt that at this time the art of Persia had a strong influence on the weaving of China. In other pieces of this class, the foliate and floral forms no longer appear as sub-patterns but become the prominent feature in the decoration of the field; and the conventionalised flowers are arranged with precision in diagonal or perpendicular lines. To this period also belong rugs of a distinct type, in which the field represents a blending of pictorial and symbolic ideas, as, for instance, a homeward flight of swallows; or a grove where butterflies flit among the leaves, and deer with sacred fungus, emblematic of longevity, wander.

The employment of border stripes of uniform colour was still continued, but there was a tendency to employ more elaborate designs in many of the figured stripes. It is not unusual to see single or double vines with conventionalised flowers; and though the drawing is mechanical, the relationship to Persian art is apparent. Yet in most of these pieces the swastika-fret is used. A noticeable difference also exists in the colour scheme of many of the late Kang-hi rugs, which frequently display brighter colours. Much of the yellow, for instance, contains more red, giving it a golden hue known as the "imperial yellow."

YUNG–CHING. — During the short reign of Yung-ching (1722–1736), though many of the old patterns were followed, the tendency to adopt more ornate forms begun during the first part of the XVIII Century continued. Manchurian ideas were now a strong factor in Chinese art, so that the use of colours and ornamentation followed broader lines. To this period are assigned most of those rugs in which designs are defined by lines of contrasting colour that has been so treated that the lines are depressed and throw the designs into bold relief. It is very difficult, however, to definitely determine that any particular rug belongs to this period; since the transition in colour scheme and patterns was gradual; and the effect of time on dyes, one of the most reliable factors in determining age, depends somewhat on their exposure to the elements and to use. But broadly speaking, figures of leaf and flower were more frequently adopted than in preceding periods and designs became less conventionalised and more artistic. Lemon and citron shades of yellow, also, became more prominent during this period.

KEEN–LUNG. — The long reign of Keen-lung, lasting from 1736 to 1795, was one of the most prolific for Chinese art. To this period may safely be assigned most of the existing rugs made before the XIX Century, as well as many of the finest porcelains. The rugs partake of a more cosmopolitan character than those which had preceded; for not only are many of the designs and colours strictly Chinese, but others are of a Persian character, and others still suggest Mohammedan influences observable in the products of Turkestan and India. Moreover, many of the designs show a delicate shading that is not observable in the rugs made during the early part of the century. As a whole they are the most ornate of Chinese rugs. Woven after the inspiration of Persian masterpieces had left its strongest impress on Chinese weavers, and decoration in kindred arts had assumed a luxurious style, they represent in the drawing of leaf and flower, of birds, butterflies, and emblems of early philosophy and faith, and in the colours that blend with rare harmony, the most elaborate and voluptuous expression of native craftsmanship.

In the best examples the geometric, and many of the stiff conventional forms which continued through the XVII and the early part of the XVIII Century, disappeared. In their place was a greater refinement of design, a greater accuracy of drawing, which found expression in floral forms that reached their highest development at this time and became characteristic of it. Occasionally they are represented in profile as is usually the practice in Western Asia, but more often are represented as viewed from above. Some of them, as chrysanthemums, peonies, sunflowers, and orchids, are most dainty and naturalistic. The fields of many of these pieces are covered with such flowers carefully arranged in harmonious group-ings of leaf, bud and flower, but never with the formal and exact balance of old Persian carpets. Not infrequently mingled with them in the same piece are more conventional designs that belong to an earlier period; sometimes there is a single central medallion; and occasionally there are a large number of them. As a rule these medallions are entirely floral, and in rugs made during the latter part of this period they display elaborate ornamentation that dis-tinguishes them from earlier ones; but now and then they contain fabulous creatures, as the lion-dogs, by which in a few instances they are entirely replaced.

There are also many other well-known types of Keen-lung rugs. Surrounding the central medallion of some pieces are grouped the Taoist symbols; emblems of the literati, as chess boards, scrolls, and the lyre; as well as tripods, flower vases, fans of state, fruits of abundance, emblems of honours, and symbols of longevity and happiness. To this class also belong many of the pieces which have neither medallions nor corner pieces, but have fields completely covered with a pattern of continuous foliate stems and conventional flowers, repeated with exact precision of drawing. Likewise, in a few pieces the field is completely covered with an all-over pattern of small hexagonal or other geometric figures containing a convention-alised flower, strongly suggesting Turkoman influences. Some of the "Grain of Rice" rugs, also, were woven during this period.

The borders are as distinctive as the fields. Only in a few pieces is the swastika meander seen, but in its place is often the T pattern. The key patterns represented in Plate N, Figs. 7 and 8 (opp. Page 274), as well as the dotted line (Fig. 22), are also largely employed. Almost all of these rugs have two ornamented stripes, and occasion-ally three, to which is added an outer margin of plain colour. In a few pieces both stripes are geometric; but generally one is floral and one geometric, in which case the wider, that, with very few excep-tions, is the floral, is the inner one. Very rarely the border contains two floral stripes; and now and then Buddhist emblems and other devices are introduced.

The breadth of artistic conception expressed in designs is accom-panied by a wider scope of colour, in the use of which these rugs may conveniently be grouped in three subclasses. The first is the

Blue and White, with ground of ivory or ashy white and designs that have shades of light or dark blue. The second comprises those in which the ground is some shade of yellow. Sometimes it has a tinge of lemon, orange, or apricot. Again it is what is known as dull, golden, mandarin, or imperial yellow. The overlying designs may contain a different shade of yellow from that of the field, an ivory white, a blue, or a red. The third subclass comprises those in which the ground colour is some shade of red; such as persimmon, terra cotta, crushed strawberry, apricot red, or a deep salmon pink, which is rare. The overlying designs may be a shade of blue, ivory white, yellow, gray, and even green. Colours of both field and border are sometimes the same but are more frequently complementary. As a whole, the elaborate designs, delicate shading, and rich colours rank these rugs among the most beautiful products of the Chinese loom.

The rugs woven during the reigns of Kea-king (1796–1820) and Tao-Kwang (1821–1850), extending to the middle of last century, repeat with slight modification the patterns of the preceding period, though there is a tendency to use larger and coarser designs. The colours, too, are similar, yet they lack the deep richness that is matured only with the lapse of great time. Many of these rugs, as well as some woven still later, before the introduction of aniline dyes and factory processes, are beautiful; but as a rule the modern pieces lack the refinement of technique observable only in those produced before the beginning of the XIX Century.

MEDALLIONS

The study of medallions which occur in fields of Chinese rugs is not only interesting but is an important aid in determining their age; yet it should be remembered that approved patterns were often repeated even after the introduction of more elaborate styles. Many of the oldest medallions were copied from bronzes or mirror backs, and their drawing is geometric except as embellished by some conventionalised figures of the dragon. By a process of evolution these figures, in turn, were converted into scrolls, which in time were replaced by elaborate leaf and flower patterns.

In Plate M, Fig. 1 (opp. Page 272), is a "Shou" design of octagonal shape, copied from an old rug which was probably woven during the early part of the XVII Century.

PLATE 61. TURKOMAN SADDLEBAGS

Figs. 2, 3 and 4 of Plate M, represent fret-covered medallions, which also are found in rugs of the same period. The first is probably the oldest pattern; and the last, to judge by the panel surrounding it, was apparently copied from a bronze mirror back.

In Plate M, Fig. 5, is a copy of a medallion similar to the one shown in Plate M, Fig. 2, but with the dragons replaced by frets.

A medallion of greater interest is illustrated in Plate M, Fig. 6. It shows the evolution of scrolls from dragons, of which the heads alone betray their origin. Such medallions are found mostly in the earliest rugs.

By comparing Fig. 7 of Plate M with the preceding, it is apparent that its scrolls had a similar origin, but in this one the dragon heads have entirely disappeared. The design is characteristic of the early Kang-hi rugs.

In Plate M, Fig. 8, is represented a medallion that closely resembles some of the earliest period; but the more accurate drawing and clearer definition of lines shows that it is a later copy. It is found in late Kang-hi pieces.

To this period, also, belongs the geometric pattern with swastikas represented in Plate M, Fig. 9.

Another medallion with frets and dragon heads is shown in Plate M, Fig. 10. The particular rug from which it was copied was probably woven about the Yung-ching period; but there is little doubt that similar medallions appeared in older rugs.

In Figs. 11 and 12 of Plate M, are represented two medallions with foliate designs that were largely employed in the early Keen-lung period. A comparison of the first with Fig. 13 of Plate M, shows an interesting step in the evolution of the Chinese drawing.

A very different medallion pattern of the same age is shown in Plate M, Fig. 14, in which an encircling border consists of cloud-bands.

Also during the Keen-lung time first appeared medallions with accurately drawn flower designs. One of this period is shown in Plate M, Fig. 15. Wreath-like borders, such as are seen in this and the preceding one, are found in XVIII and XIX Century pieces.

CHINESE BORDER STRIPES

The knowledge that certain border stripes antedate others in definite sequence of time, is another aid in determining the age of

Chinese rugs. As was seen to be the case with medallions, the earliest stripes were purely geometric. In others, still very old, appeared forms of conventionalised dragons, which again were replaced by simple scrolls and these by ornate floral forms. But it should be remembered that earlier designs were often copied in later rugs, so that the evidence of age is merely contributory.

Stripes containing the swastika meander were used almost exclusively in the oldest rugs. Figs. 1, 2, and 3 of Plate N (opp. Page 274), represent three old forms, which rarely appear in any pieces woven since the Kang-hi time. The pattern of Plate N, Fig. 4, in which alternate swastikas are reversed, is also very old.

The usual drawing of the swastika stripe is shown in Plate N, Fig. 5. It is found largely in Kang-hi rugs, and if used in more recent fabrics, is often accompanied by a stripe with some other pattern. As illustrated here, the facing of the swastika is reversed in the middle of the stripe.

The shading of Plate N, Fig. 6, which is somewhat similar to Plate N, Fig. 4, is characteristic of the Keen-lung and subsequent periods.

In Figs. 7, 8, 9, and 10, of Plate N, are Key and T patterns, which are found in rugs of the Kang-hi and subsequent periods, but rarely in earlier pieces. When employed in rugs woven later than the middle of the XVIII Century they are often shaded. These meander and key-patterns are of great antiquity; and though the drawing is exceedingly simple, it is supposed that the figures from which they were derived once symbolised clouds and thunder.

A very interesting stripe derived from dragons is illustrated in Plate N, Fig. 11. The rectangular frets represent bodies of which conventionalised heads alone betray their origin. The graceful scroll in the middle was also probably derived from dragon forms. This stripe is seen in old Kang-hi rugs.

The rectangular frets and floral forms are combined in an unusual stripe (Plate N, Fig. 12) that appeared in rugs which were probably woven about the Yung-ching period. It shows the influence of older traditions on which are ingrafted the later inspiration.

Still more interesting is a stripe (Plate N, Fig. 13) seen in what are known as Buddhist rugs of the Keen-lung period. In different parts of the border appear the Buddhist emblems, the Joo-e, conch, wheel of law, and knot of destiny, separated by cloud-bands and foliate and floral motives.

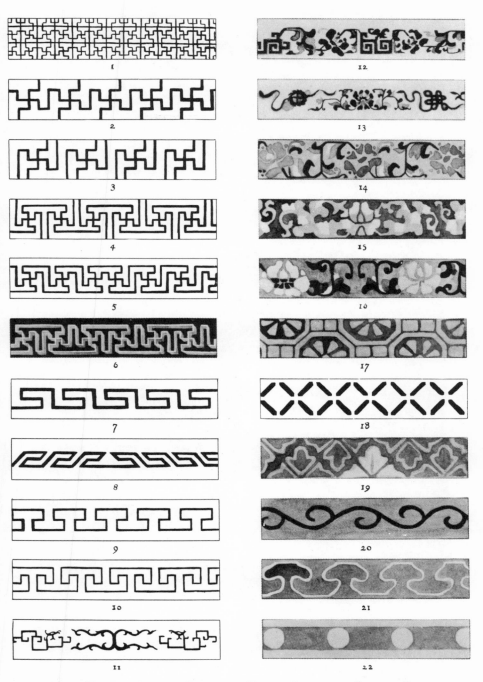

PLATE N.   PRIMARY AND SECONDARY BORDER-STRIPES OF CHINESE RUGS

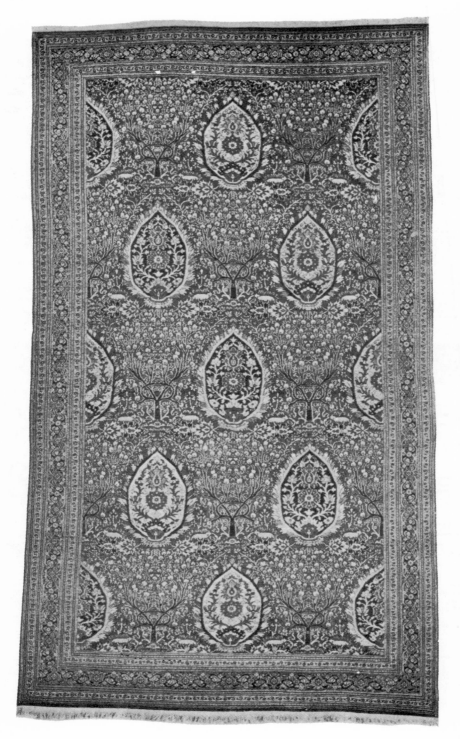

PLATE 62.   SRINAGAR RUG

The tendency to use more ornate forms in the Keen-lung and later rugs is shown in Plate N, Figs. 14, 15, and 16, which illustrate three stripes that with slight modifications are found in large numbers of Chinese rugs of the last half of the XVIII and the XIX Centuries.

The stripe illustrated in Plate N, Fig. 17, on which are represented halves of octagonal discs containing conventional flower forms, is found in some rugs woven as early as the first part of the XVIII Century, as well as in more subsequent pieces. The central fields of some rugs in which it is found have geometric Ming patterns, and others have floral conceits that suggest Persian influences.

In Figs. 18, 19, 20, and 21, of Plate N, are represented simple stripes found in XVIII Century rugs. The last of these, which is found in Keen-lung porcelain, shows a marked resemblance to the reciprocal trefoil so common in Persian pieces.

The simple dotted stripe (Plate N, Fig. 22) was rarely employed before the middle of the XVIII Century, but has been constantly used since then.

CHAPTER XV

KILIMS

ILIMS have a special interest apart from their beauty and utility, as some of them undoubtedly resemble the early fabrics of the Egyptians and Babylonians from which were evolved the more durable pile carpets. The different links in this evolution can only be conjectured. Yet it is not unlikely that such pieces as the nomadic kilims, which occasionally have little tufts of wool attached for ornament or loose threads of weft hanging from one side, first suggested the greater durability and warmth that would be derived from a woven fabric completely covered with tufts of yarn.

It is also certain that the most delicately woven kilims have likewise been evolved from cruder forms. In fact, the different steps in this evolution correspond to three separate styles of weaving still in vogue. The earliest products which were made subsequent to the primitive weaving of uncoloured warp and weft were doubtless similar to the simple fabrics now used to line the under side of saddle bags, and consisted of a warp and weft of uniformly coloured threads. A much more advanced style, induced by a desire for ornamentation, was the representation of patterns which required the use of different coloured threads of weft. As these threads were never carried beyond the edges of each pattern, their loose ends were at first allowed to hang at the back, giving an appearance somewhat similar to what is seen in Soumaks. The third and most finished style, representing much higher workmanship, was produced by deftly disposing of the ends of threads of weft so that they should be concealed and thus permit each surface of the kilim to be exactly the same.

Each of these kinds of weaving is constantly seen in the East. The first not only is used as a lining for saddle bags, but is frequently substituted for them. It is also sometimes used as the only floor covering, or again is laid as a protection beneath valuable carpets. It often replaces the heavier felt for tents, and indeed is utilised for all purposes requiring a strong material like canvas. The second is found among nomadic weavers, especially those of Asia Minor; who naturally waste no unnecessary labour in weaving kilims with a delicate finish, which would be quickly marred by the rough usage that they receive. The third, which is the more elegant product, is invariably not only of excellent finish but of carefully drawn patterns. In this country, the last two are used principally for portieres and couch coverings; but in the Orient they still serve, as they have from the remotest times, for floor coverings; and because of the custom of removing the shoes when entering a house, last for a great many years.

Though these three styles represent the principal variations in kilim weaving, there are a few pieces with embroidered pattern; and embroidered stitches are sometimes added to represent some simple design, or as is frequently the case in Shirvans, to make more prominent the separate horizontal compartments.

When weaving a kilim, the threads of warp are strung as in piled rugs, and number from six to eighteen to the inch according to the texture. There are generally about twenty threads of weft to the inch, measured at the front or back; but in pieces of the finest workmanship, there may be as many as fifty, and in the crudest only eight or nine. At the sides of the kilim, the threads of weft encircle the last thread of warp as at the sides of any pattern; but at the ends, the threads of warp are braided about a heavier added cord, or else are tied in knots, from which their loose ends are permitted to hang like tassels.

The patterns are usually geometric; and even when an attempt is made to copy floral figures, the drawing inclines to the rectilinear. If a straight line representing the side of a figure is horizontal, or in the direction of the weft, it will often be several inches in length; but a straight perpendicular line never exceeds an inch in length. This is because the threads of weft are never carried from one pattern to another or to the adjoining field, but are turned back at its defining edges, so that an opening is left, which would impair the strength of the fabric if it were of much length. Accordingly, if it is desired to represent a pattern with perpendicular sides, it is necessary that the edges be slightly uneven. But here necessity is turned to advantage, as this unevenness or fringing softens lines

that otherwise would be harsh.   Defining the outlines of many
figures is yarn of different colours, which either may be woven like
other threads of weft, or when it serves the purpose of closing the
space between adjacent threads of warp, may be attached by
stitches.   Borders find slight favour with kilim weavers, and in most
pieces they are entirely wanting or only present at one end.   Even
when they completely surround the field, there is generally some
difference in design or colour between the stripes of side and end.
Prayer arches are found in some of the kilims, but their outlines
rarely correspond closely with those of piled rugs.

The colours, by which alone the patterns are distinguished, are
largely responsible for the character of the kilim.   Threads of weft
of every hue that is seen in piled rugs are employed in these pieces;
yet the colouring never appears the same, since there are lacking the
lustre and deep wealth of tones due to the length of pile, in which
appears an almost imperceptible gradation from the ends that are
exposed to the light and have incurred the mellowing influence of
the elements to the part which retains more of the original colours
and seems darker, because it is more concealed.   Indeed, on account
of the lack of pile, the colours and patterns would seem harsh
were it not for the irregularities of perpendicular and diagonal
lines, the devices of latch-hooks, and other peculiarities that convey to the eye an impression of blending.   Moreover when the
designs are large, the effect of the colour is always severe; but
when the field is covered with innumerable small figures, it is greatly
softened.

As kilims are much less durable than rugs that have a pile to
protect the warp and weft, it is not surprising that few of great age
remain.   The oldest piece of which we have any knowledge is a
fragment obtained by Dr. M. A. Stein, the archæological explorer,
from the ruins near Khotan, in Eastern Turkestan, of an ancient
settlement, which was buried by sand drifts about the fourth or
fifth century *anno domini*.   The weave is almost identical with that
of modern kilims, and has about fourteen threads of warp and sixteen
threads of weft to the inch.   The pattern consists of narrow stripes
of blue, green, brownish yellow, and red, containing very small
geometric designs.   With this one exception, so peculiarly preserved,
there are probably very few over a century old.

Though kilims are now made in most of the districts where
piled carpets are woven, very few classes are recognised.   This

is because it is difficult to distinguish between most of them, and such differences as exist are with few exceptions unimportant. The best known classes are the Sehna, Shirvan, Karaman, Kurdish, Turkish, and Merv.

The Sehna kilims are usually of small size, and rarely exceed a breadth of four and a half feet and a length of seven. They are far superior to all others in the delicacy of colour, daintiness of design, quality of material, and character of workmanship. Their patterns, including border, are identical with those of the piled rugs; and the colours, to which at a short distance the small figures of the Herati design give the effect of blending, are the same. As is not the case with other kilims, the warp is of cotton or linen and there are generally from fourteen to sixteen threads to the inch. The weft is of wool, and to an inch there are often nearly fifty threads encircling a thread of warp as they cross and recross. The old pieces, like the rugs of which they are true copies, are rapidly becoming scarce. They resemble tapestries and are unfit for hard usage.

A large percentage of the kilims now sold in this country are Shirvans. Their fields are divided into a number of parallel horizontal compartments or bands a foot or more in width separated by narrower bands. Not infrequently the principal figures of the wide bands are hexagons surrounding smaller geometric figures; and through the more narrow bands runs a waving line or a parti-coloured cord. Another peculiarity, occasionally seen, are the ray-like projections of uniform colour fringing the edges of the sides. As a rule, there are no borders, but at each end are two or more narrow bands that give the effect of a border. In some pieces webs of plain colour extend beyond the bands; and the ends are fringed with loose threads of warp. The colours are always pronounced, because of lack of shading, and consist mostly of red, blue, and ivory. Yellow and green are also used. These kilims are much heavier than the Sehnas, and also larger, as the average size is about five by nine feet; and some are even seven by twelve feet.

From the district of Karaman in Southern Asia Minor, such a large number of kilims were formerly imported into Europe that the general name of Karamani was applied to all kilims. They are still made there by many of the tribes of Turkish or Turkoman origin, who wander over the Taurus mountains, and like all their fabrics are stoutly woven. Their average size is about four and a half by eight feet. In colours and patterns, they resemble many of the Kurdish kilims from the districts farther to the east.

A distinction similar to what exists in the piled rugs of the Kurds, and dependent on the district in which they are made, is observable in their kilims, as those which come from the Persian border have carefully drawn designs, that are generally lacking in others woven in the mountainous watershed of the Tigris and the Euphrates. Many of these are coarsely woven, and from the back hang the loose ends of threads of weft, that in more artistic pieces, are removed. Moreover, in modern pieces the colours are often crude or even garish. Some of the kilims have large diamond-shaped figures containing small designs; others have horizontal bands in which are woven embroidered devices suggestive of the so-called Bagdad portieres; in many are wide spaces without designs; but whatever the pattern, there is usually a parti-coloured cord running through the web at the end.

In many parts of Asia Minor are made kilims that are usually classed as Turkish. They are of large size, and since they are used mostly for portieres or curtains, are divided perpendicularly into equal halves, that at times are united by stitches. The tribes that make them also make large numbers of smaller prayer kilims with pointed arches suggesting the Ghiordes design. Some of them are beautifully woven, yet the finest workmanship is shown in pieces known as "Kis-kilims" or girl's kilims. These are made with the utmost care, since they are intended as a bride's gift to her husband; and a sentiment of romance, and the hope that her skill may weigh favourably in the estimation of her accomplishments, contribute to influence the weaver. Sometimes even a lock of hair is added as a charm, or coloured beads as a talisman.

The Christians who live permanently about Oushak, and are, accordingly, not under the necessity of making such small pieces as can conveniently be carried by wandering tribes, weave some of the largest kilims. Most of them are at least six feet in width and many are much wider.

The best known kilims from the Central Asiatic group are known as "Merv Kilims," since they are woven by Turkoman tribes who inhabit the desert near the old capital of Merv. The brilliant colours found in the products of more Western tribes are entirely wanting, and in their place are the few subdued, rich tones so characteristic of all Turkoman weavings. These pieces are stoutly woven, and since the pattern is represented by diagonal lines, there is no open work. The designs are largely of diamond-shape, and are arranged in parallel horizontal lines on a field that is usually surrounded by a border profusely ornamented with carefully drawn latch-hooks. A heavy embroidered selvage, from which hang loose threads of warp, often occurs at the ends. These kilims are noted for their durability, and are usually of large size.

In the city of Dera Ghazi Khan, four miles from the Indus river, are woven kilims in which warp and weft are of wool, as is not the case with almost all the rugs of India. They are made by the women in their own homes and display an individuality which also is rare in Indian textile fabrics. In a monograph on "Carpet Weaving in the Punjab," Mr. C. Latimer says: "The Dera Ghazi Khan rug, which belongs really to the kind of fabrics known as kilims, is woven in stripes, with designs between them, and it is interesting to notice that the patterns employed were by local tradition originally copied from the robes of the Pharaohs of Egypt."

Though all such Oriental weavings lack the precision of drawing and the delicacy of minutely varied colour so frequently found in piled rugs; though they never display high, artistic perception or poetic instinct, nevertheless some of the oldest pieces with designs suggestive of the workings of a primitive imagination untrammelled by the conventions of art, and with a chaste simplicity of colour that lends an atmosphere of dignity, possess a subtle charm that awakens an intense interest.

CHAPTER XVI

HOW TO DISTINGUISH RUGS

HE owner of an Oriental rug will find the pleasure to be derived from it will be greater if he knows where and by whom it was made. This is particularly true if it is one of those pieces of which the charm depends more on its individuality than on the masterly handling of line and colour. The study of classification, therefore, will well repay the effort; though unfortunately it is often discouraging, since it involves a consideration of the characteristics of a hundred different classes, almost all of which are found to have exceptions to the best known types. To add to the difficulty, the opinions of dealers in regard to the less known classes are very often erroneous; and detailed descriptions, even at the best, are unsatisfactory. Without a long personal experience in handling rugs, combined with careful study, it is impossible to become expert; but familiarity with one class makes it easier by comparison and a process of elimination to distinguish others.

The beginner should first learn to identify each of the six groups. Of these the Chinese can readily be distinguished by their well-known patterns, which are found in no other part of the Orient except in the rugs known as Samarkands, Yarkands, and Kashgars; and the Indian may generally be recognised by the realism and formal arrangement of their floral patterns. Relatively few of either group are found in the United States; and as about ninety per cent of the rugs belong to the other four groups, they alone will be considered in detail. Leaving out of consideration, then, the Chinese and Indian rugs, it should be remembered:

(a) That, as a rule, rugs from Persia have floral patterns; and rugs from Asia Minor, Caucasia, and Central Asia have geometric.

(b) That figures with latch-hooks belong principally to rugs of the Caucasian group and, to a limited extent, to the rugs of the Asia Minor group.

PLATE 63. XVIII CENTURY CHINESE RUG

PLATE 64. CHINESE RUG OF THE KEEN-LUNG PERIOD

(c) That fields covered with designs of octagonal or diamond shape belong to rugs of the Central Asian group.

(d) That about two thirds of the Persian group have cotton warp; and the remaining third, as well as the Asia Minor and almost all the Caucasian and Central Asian group have woollen warp.

(e) That about one third of the Persian group have one of the two threads of warp encircled by a knot doubled under the other so as to be hidden at the back; and that this is not the case with the remaining two thirds nor with almost all classes of other groups.

(f) That, with few exceptions, the Persian rugs have a side finish of overcasting; and the other groups have both overcasting and selvage.

(g) That the rugs from Persia and Central Asia have both light and dark colours which, though rich, are subdued and harmonious; that the rugs of Asia Minor and Caucasia have colours that are often gaudy and inharmonious; and that the rugs of the Central Asian group have dark tones of red, blue, and brown.

(h) That all of the rugs of Asia Minor and Caucasia have the Ghiordes knot; that the rugs of Central Asia, with rare exceptions, have the Sehna knot; that the rugs of Persia with woollen warp have the Ghiordes knot; and that those with cotton warp have either the Ghiordes or the Sehna knot.

(i) That the few classes of rugs which have very long end-webs belong to the Central Asian group. Of the classes with moderately long end-webs, several belong to the Central Asian and the Asia Minor groups, only two belong to the Persian group, and none belongs to the Caucasian group.

Excluding the Indian and Chinese rugs, it follows from the above statements that:

(1) A rug is from Persia or Central Asia, —
    If it has a Sehna knot.

(2) A rug is probably Persian, —
    If the patterns are distinctly floral;
    If the warp is cotton;
    If one of the two threads of warp encircled by a knot is doubled under the other.

(3) A rug is probably from Asia Minor, Caucasia, or Central Asia, —

If the pattern is geometric;

If the sides are selvaged.

(4) A rug is probably from Asia Minor or Caucasia, —

If the colours are gaudy or inharmonious.

(5) A rug is probably from Caucasia, —

If the designs are largely fringed with latch-hooks.

(6) A rug is probably from Central Asia, —

If the field is covered with octagons or diamond-shaped designs, and has dark tones of red, blue or brown;

If it has long webs at the ends.

Of these four groups the Persian has the largest number of classes, some of which can only with difficulty be distinguished from one another. They may, however, conveniently be divided into the following subgroups, depending on the technical peculiarities of the weaving and the material of the warp, so that the task of learning the class of a particular rug will be greatly facilitated by first determining to which of these subgroups it belongs, and then eliminating the others from consideration.

Cotton Warp	One thread of warp to each knot doubled under and hidden at back.	Sehna Knot (A)	Kashan. Kermanshah. Khorassan. Kirman. Meshed. Mir Sarabend. Sarouk.
		Ghiordes Knot (B)	Gorevan. Herat. Herez. Serapi. Tabriz.
	Each thread of warp equally prominent at back or one slightly depressed.	Sehna Knot (C)	Feraghan. Mahal. Muskabad. Royal Sarabend.
		Ghiordes Knot (D)	Gulistan. Iran. Joshaghan. Luristan. Sultanabad.
	Quincunx effect of weft at back.	Sehna Knot (E)	Sehna.
		Ghiordes Knot (F)	Hamadan. Ispahan (modern).

It should be remembered, when studying the foregoing table, that all classes of rugs are subject to occasional variations in the technicalities of their weave, as for instance, the Herats may have woollen warp and Sehna knots; the Tabriz very often have linen warp; some of the Feraghans, Mahals, Muskabads, and Sehnas have the Ghiordes knot and some of the Sultanabads have the Sehna knot; the Joshaghans may have woollen warp; and in modern Ispahans the weft sometimes crosses twice between two rows of knots.

Woollen Warp, Ghiordes Knot.	One thread of warp to each knot doubled under at back (G)	Bijar. Niris *
	Each of the two threads of warp to a knot equally prominent at back, or one slightly depressed (H)	Karadagh. Suj-Bulak Kurdistan. Afshar. Mosul. Shiraz.†
	Quincunx effect of weft at back (I)	Karaje.‡

With reference to size, these rugs may conveniently be divided as follows:

Rugs invariably of carpet size	Gorevan. Mahal. Muskabad. Serapi. Sultanabad
Rugs frequently, but not always, of carpet size	Bijar. Herat. Kermanshah. Khorassan. Meshed. Sarabend. Tabriz.
Rugs frequently seen as runners	Hamadan. Karaje. Kurdistan. Mosul.

Of the subgroups represented on Page 284, "A" includes those that have the closest and finest woven texture. In this respect the Kashans, Sarouks, and Kirmans are, in the order named, superior to the others; and the Kermanshahs are the coarsest and the least evenly woven. In subgroup "B" the Tabriz are the best woven and have the shortest nap. The Gorevans and Serapis have several concentric medallions, in which are designs of archaically drawn

* Sometimes Sehna knot.
† Sometimes one thread of warp to each knot is doubled under the other.
‡ Rarely Iran, Feraghan, Mosul, and Kurdistan.

leaves, and have generally the so-called turtle border. The Herats have the typical Herati border. Of the classes of subgroup "C," the Royal Sarabends are the closest woven. The Feraghans are slightly coarser and the Mahals and Muskabads are much coarser and have longer nap. The Luristans, Joshaghans, and Gulistans are the best woven of subgroup "D." At the back of Luristans each half knot is distinct from the other like a separate bead; and in a few Joshaghans each half knot is almost as distinct. Both Irans and Sultanabads are coarsely woven. Comparing subgroups "E" and "F," the weave of Sehnas presents a file-like appearance at the back; and in Hamadans the weft is of much coarser diameter than in the other two classes. The Bijars of subgroup "G" are much stouter than the Niris and have one of the two threads of weft to each knot more completely doubled under the other. The webs at the ends of the Niris are very much longer than those of Bijars. Subgroup "H" contains the Kurdistans, Suj-Bulaks and Mosuls, all of which are woven in territory where for generations the Kurds have held sway, and show Kurdish characteristics. The Western Kurdistans may easily be distinguished by their brown colours, nomadic character, and coarse warp and weft. The Persian Kurdistans are very stoutly and firmly woven, and usually have one of the two threads of warp encircled by a knot depressed below the other. The Mosuls have each of the two threads of warp encircled by a knot equally prominent at the back; and a characteristic feature is the coloured, crudely spun yarn of weft, which on account of the size of its diameter stands up as high as the yarn of the knots at the back. In a typical Suj-Bulak the alignment of knots at the back appears uneven or serrated. The Karadaghs have Caucasian characteristics; the Afshars have coarse, wiry wool for the weft, and threads of warp strung so that each half knot is distinct.

Although the technicalities of weaving are the most reliable evidence for determining the class to which a rug belongs, the patterns are important guides. It will be well, therefore, to remember that:

A Persian rug is probably a Shiraz, Karadagh, Karaje, Mosul, Kurdistan, or Afshar, if the pattern is partly geometric.

If the field has concentric medallions, the rug may be a Kermanshah, Sarouk, Kashan, Sehna, Gorevan, Herez, Tabriz, Mahal, Muskabad, or Sultanabad.

If the field is covered with pear designs, the rug may be a Sarabend, Burujird, Khorassan, Shiraz, Niris, Iran, Joshaghan, or Luristan.

If the field is covered with small Herati designs, the rug may be a Feraghan, Sehna, or an Iran.

If the field is covered with small designs of the Guli Hinnai plant, the rug may be a Feraghan.

If the field is covered with the Mina Khani pattern, the rug may be a Persian Kurdistan.

A Persian rug is usually a Shiraz, Niris, Mosul, or Kurdistan if the nap is long.

It is almost invariably either a Shiraz or a Niris if the webs of the ends are long, and the overcasting of the sides has a barber-pole design or has short lengths of different colours. The Niris resembles the Shiraz; but one thread of warp to each knot is more depressed, the ends generally have longer webs, and the field is more frequently covered with large pear designs. It is a Shiraz if short tassels or tufts project at regular intervals from the ends; and it is probably a Niris if it has a long end-web of different coloured stripes.

It is probably a Karadagh, Gorevan, Serapi, Herez, or Tabriz if the sides are finished with a selvage.

Many of these classes have features by which they can be distinguished at once from all others. For instance:

The Sarabend has a field completely covered with pear designs of moderate size facing in opposite directions in alternate lines; borders of several stripes, of which one or two are ivory white with an angular vine from which are suspended mechanically drawn pear designs, and one or two narrow stripes with reciprocal trefoils. Only two other classes are similar: the Iran copies, which are always woven more coarsely and have the Ghiordes knot, and the Burujirds, which are rarely seen.

Most Feraghans have fields that are completely covered with small Herati or Guli Hinnai designs, and have the turtle pattern in the border. The only other rugs that are similar are the Iran copies, which have the Ghiordes knot and are more coarsely woven.

Almost all Hamadans may be distinguished at once by the broad band of camel's hair surrounding the border, and the coarse weft crossing only once between two rows of knots so as to give a quincunx effect at the back.

Gorevans are invariably of carpet size. They have fields almost covered with central medallions on which are archaically drawn leaves, and a broad central border stripe with a large conventionalised turtle pattern. They have usually the same colour tones, which once seen are not forgotten. The Serapis are similar to Gore-vans but are usually older and of better colours.

The Kermanshahs have tones of ivory, pink, and light green, that are softer and lighter than those of almost any other rug. The fields have concentric medallions with dainty floral forms that are rarely seen in other classes except the Sarouks and Kashans; and the borders, that correspond in drawing and colouring with the field, have an outer edging that is almost invariably of pink, but sometimes dark blue. The drawing and colours, which are not easily described but quickly learned, at once distinguish these pieces from all others.

Some Mesheds resemble Kermanshahs, but the nap is more silky, uneven, and lustrous. The texture at the back is finer.

The rugs of Tabriz, which are usually made in carpet sizes, may be distinguished by their linen nap hanging in a short fringe at the ends. They are not likely to be confused with any classes but the Mesheds, Khorassans, and Kermanshahs; but the nap is shorter, and harsher to the touch; the knot is Ghiordes, and the drawing more formal.

Almost the only Persian rug that has small, geometric, adventitious designs and latch-hooks is the Shiraz. It is the only one that has small tufts of wool projecting from the sides; and with the exception of the Niris is the only one that, as a rule, has a barber-pole overcasting and a long web at the ends. It is also one of the most loosely woven.

The Sarouk and Kashan may be distinguished from all others by their short velvety nap; dark rich colours; fields of graceful foliated stalks and floral forms resting on concentric medallions; and the fine, firm, texture of the weave. A carefully drawn design of the running latch-hook appears in the borders; and the weft is usually some shade of blue. The Kashans are almost the same as Sarouks but have closer weave and finer texture. They very rarely come in large sizes.

Muskabads and Mahals are invariably made in large carpet sizes. Their texture is firm; they are very coarsely woven; and there is great irregularity in the size of the knots as shown at the back. Of the two, the Mahals are the better grade.

A large rug with woollen warp and with one thread of warp to each knot doubled under the other is almost always a Bijar.

Sehnas are always very thin rugs and of small or moderate size. With few exceptions the field is covered with Herati or pear designs.

They can be identified by the quincunx appearance of the fine cotton weft at the back and the file-like feeling of the weave.

The only Persian rug that has a side selvage and also shows evidence of Caucasian influence in the geometric drawing of the patterns is the Karadagh.

The Gozenes may be distinguished from other classes by their dull colours. In many of them each thread of warp is encircled by the right half of some knots and the left half of others.

The Asia Minor rugs have so many features in common that they cannot conveniently be divided into subgroups. For instance: almost all have a coloured weft, a coloured web with fringe at the ends, and a selvage at the sides; all, excepting the Ghiordes and a few modern pieces, have woollen warp and weft; and all have the Ghiordes knot. To be sure, a distinction may be made in the length of the nap, since as a rule the Bergamo, Rhodian, Karaman, Yuruk, and some of the Anatolians have a long nap; and the remainder usually have a short nap; and also in the weaving, as in the Bergamo, Ghiordes, Karaman, Kulah, and Ladik, one thread of warp to each knot is generally depressed, and in the remaining classes all threads of warp are equally prominent; furthermore, Anatolians, Bergamos, Karamans, Rhodians, and Koniehs, have rarely more than three stripes to the border; and Kir-Shehrs, Kulahs, Ladiks, and Ghiordes have seldom less than five; but these features are not always constant and pronounced. The patterns, therefore, and those smaller designs which frequently are peculiar to a single class are of considerable assistance in distinguishing one from the other. The arch of the namazliks is also an invaluable feature for identification since its shape is different in each class as will be seen by reference to Plates C and D (Pages 61 and 63).

Leaving out of consideration modern pieces, made to meet the demands of exporting companies, the Bergamo and Rhodian have certain points of resemblance. As a rule, they are almost square, and have long nap, long webs with coloured bands at the ends, a side selvage, and coloured weft. The Rhodian may generally be distinguished by their brighter colours and their panels, suggesting windows, placed parallel to the length of the rug. The Bergamos, which are more frequently seen, have rich, deep blue and red colouring, and more devices to avert the evil eye than any other Oriental rug.

Two panels, one above the arch and the other below the field, are almost invariably seen in the Ghiordes prayer rugs and occasionally in the Kulahs, but rarely in any other classes. The typical pattern of the central border stripe of Ghiordes prayer rugs, consisting of most conventionalised leaf and rosette, is not seen in any other rugs; nor is the pattern of the broad border stripe of the odjaliks and sedjadehs, consisting of an undulating band covered with small flecks and fringed with latch-hooks.

The most characteristic features in the pattern of Kulahs are the numerous narrow fleck-covered bands that occupy the centre of the border, and the secondary stripe with design like a Chinese device represented in Plate H, Fig. 10 (opp. Page 194).

The pomegranates at the end of the field, and the Rhodian lilies in the main stripe of the border, distinguish Ladik prayer rugs from all others. Figures of vandykes, which are seen in some Anatolians and Mudjars, are also a constant feature of Ladiks.

A characteristic feature of Koniehs is the row of sprigs with three triangular-shaped petals that project from the border against the field.

As a rule, the Kir-Shehrs contain in the field a larger amount of grass-green colour than any other rug.

The narrow border stripe of thumb-like processes that fit one another like cogs and the mauve or heliotrope colour are important aids in distinguishing Melez rugs.

On account of their long pile and their patterns of latch-hooks and other geometric figures, the Yuruks alone of all this group resemble the Caucasian rugs. They may also be distinguished from other Asia Minor rugs by the facts that the weft is of coarse, wiry wool, and the threads of warp are not strung closely together, so that at the back each half knot appears very distinct from the other.

A similarity prevails in the technique of most Caucasian rugs, as all have the Ghiordes knot, and almost all have warp and weft of wool, sides that are selvaged, and ends with a web and loose fringe. Moreover, classes that are in a measure geographically related show resemblances, as for instance: the Chichi, Daghestan, Kabistan, and Shirvan, which have short nap; the Tcherkess, Kazak, and Genghas which have medium to long nap; and the Soumak, Shemakha, and Kuba, which have a similar selvage at sides and ends. The only classes in which one thread of warp to each knot is depressed or doubled under the other are the Karabagh, Shemakha, and Shusha, from the southeastern part of Caucasia, and the Lesghian from the northern part.

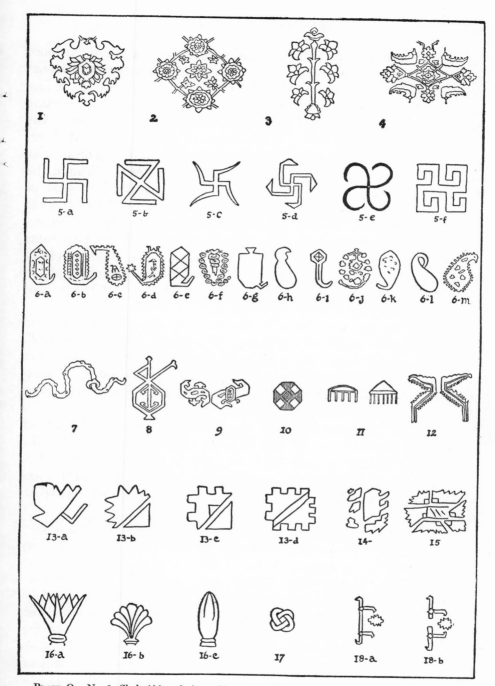

PLATE O. No. 1, Shah Abbas design. No. 2, Mina Khani design. No. 3, Guli Hinnai design.
No. 4, Herati design. Nos. 5-a, b, c, d, e, f, Swastikas. Nos. 6-a, b, c, d, e, f, g, h, i, j, k, l, m, Pear
designs. No. 7, Cloud-bands. No. 8, Pitcher. No. 9, Motives of Asia Minor and Armenian rugs.
No. 10, Octagonal disc. No. 11, Combs. No. 12, Motives of Melez rugs. Nos. 13-a, b, c, d, 14,
15, Conventionalised leaf-forms in Asia Minor rugs. Nos. 16-a, b, c, The lotus. No. 17, Knot of
destiny. Nos. 18-a, b, Motives of Daghestans and Kabistans.

The Soumak with its flat stitch and with ends of yarn hanging loose at the back is unlike all other rugs.   At the sides is a carefully woven selvage, and next to the nap at the end is a narrow selvage of fine spun threads.   The rugs of Shemakha, woven by some of the same tribes who dwell nearer the mountains, have similar selvages at the sides of blue or bluish green, similar ends of a narrow web of "her-ring-bone" weave and one or more rows of knots, and a medium long nap of rich blues, reds, yellows, browns, and greens.   The Kuba rugs are almost identical with them, except that each thread of warp is equally prominent at the back, whereas in the Shemakas one thread to each knot is depressed.   When once these selvages, the narrow end-webs of "herring-bone" weave, and the particular tones of colour characteristic of these rugs have been carefully observed, they are not forgotten.   The well-known Georgian stripe (Plate J, Fig. 9, opp. Page 228) is rarely found in any but these three classes.

The Baku rug may be distinguished by its geometric-shaped pear designs, and stiffly drawn birds.   If modern, the tones are dull.

Long, shaggy nap, strong colours, of which red and green are almost invariably present, and large designs surrounded by numer-ous small nomadic figures are the general features of a Kazak.   The Tcherkess has a striking resemblance to it, so that they are constantly mistaken for one another; but the Tcherkess is generally better woven and the pattern usually consists of what is known as the "Sunburst" resting on a field of dull red or a tawny shade.   The border is almost invariably of three stripes, of which the central has the tarantula design, and the two guards have a reciprocal sawtooth design.

The field of the typical Chichi has an all-over pattern of small geo-metric design; and its main border stripe has rosettes separated by diagonal ribbon-like bars, as shown in Plate I, Fig. 6 (opp. Page 226).

Rugs from the Karabagh district may frequently be recognised by the Persian influence in the drawing of their patterns.

Genghas may readily be distinguished from other classes of this group by the fact that the weft crosses more than twice and fre-quently many times, between every two rows of knots, which are not appressed, so that the weft, as it encircles the warp, appears at the back like a narrow beaded surface.

Daghestans, Kabistans, and Shirvans have so many different patterns that it is not always easy to distinguish the classes; but

PLATE 65. CHINESE RUG OF THE KEEN-LUNG PERIOD

Plate 66. Kurdish Prayer Kilim

it will be some assistance to remember that the border design of wine cup and serrated leaf (Plate I, Fig. 1, opp. Page 226) is found in about one half of the Shirvans, and that the bracket design (Plate J, Fig. 19, opp. Page 228) is peculiar to Daghestans and Kabistans.

The small Central Asiatic group is not only unlike other groups, but may naturally be divided into three subgroups, which are also distinct from one another and contain well-defined classes, viz.:

(a) Afghan, Royal Bokhara, Princess Bokhara, Tekke, Khiva, Yomud, and Beshire.
(b) Samarkand, Kashgar, and Yarkand.
(c) Beluchistan.

In the first subgroup the prevailing colours are dark reds and browns with minor quantities of blue, green, and ivory. The Afghans are almost always of large size, and may be recognised at once by the broad web of the ends and the large octagonal shaped figures placed in contact in perpendicular rows. The Royal Bokharas are smaller, the end webs are not so wide, the octagons are never in contact and are separated diagonally by diamond-shaped figures. The Princess Bokharas and many Tekkes have the Katchli pattern. The Yomuds resemble the other classes of this subgroup in colour; but in the fields, diamond designs have entirely replaced the octagons.

The rugs of subgroup "b" almost always have cotton warp; whereas the rugs of subgroups "a" and "c" invariably have woollen or goat's hair warp.

The Samarkands are somewhat similar in colours and patterns to Chinese rugs, but may be distinguished by the fact that they almost invariably have three border stripes, whereas the Chinese usually have only one or two. The Kashgar and Yarkand also show Chinese influence.

The Beluchistans with brown, blue, green, and claret colours may be identified at once by their long embroidered webs at each end.

In the determination of the class to which a rug belongs, the pattern first of all attracts attention; and if it be one peculiar to a single class, it is an important guide. But in the great majority of cases, this will not be sufficient. It is, therefore, desirable to observe if the designs be floral or geometric, if the colours be subdued or obtrusive, if the knot be Sehna or Ghiordes, if the warp be cotton or wool. The variations in finish of sides and ends are also an index of the class. The pattern and these few technical details are the only characteristics by which most dealers attempt to determine the different kinds of rugs. But in the case of half of them, such evidence is far from conclusive. The back should be even more carefully examined than the front; because here are shown those subtle, but nevertheless positive distinctions, relating to the manner of tying the knot and the treatment of warp and weft, which are the most permanent tribal characteristics of Oriental weaving. It should be noticed, then, if each thread of warp encircled by the yarn that forms the knot lies in the same plane parallel with the surface and is equally prominent; or if one to each knot be depressed below the other, or if it be doubled under the other so as to be concealed. It should also be noticed if the weft be coloured or uncoloured, of fine or of coarse diameter; and if a thread of weft crosses only once or two or more times from side to side between every two rows of knots. Furthermore, the knots themselves should be carefully scrutinised to see if each row of them is firmly pressed down upon the weft, if each knot has a length equal or exceeding its width, if the yarn of which they are formed is drawn tight against the warp, and if it is loosely or closely spun. Only by consideration of all these different points, and sometimes even more, such as the nature of the colours, the character of wool, and the manner in which it is spun, is it possible to determine doubtful cases of identification.

CHAPTER XVII

PURCHASING RUGS

S those who have expert knowledge of the value of Oriental rugs are exceedingly few, compared with those who admire and wish to own them, the object of this chapter is to make suggestions regarding a proper selection, when purchasing, and to point out some of the pitfalls that beset the inexperienced.

In estimating the value of any rug, three distinct qualities are to be considered: rarity, artistic beauty, and utility.

Rarity may depend on the age of a rug, the locality where it was woven, or its type. In determining the age, which as a rule is greatly exaggerated, a number of facts should be considered. One is the condition resulting from wear; though at times this is misleading, since of two pieces, one may have been handled with almost religious solicitude and the other exposed to the elements and to hard usage. Moreover, an artificial appearance of natural wear is sometimes counterfeited. Another is the pattern, since, as has been shown in the case of antique carpets, the character of drawing changed with succeeding periods. Even when the patterns of old carpets are copied in modern pieces, a distinction is usually discernible to a careful observer. The colours, too, play an important part in determining age; for not only are some characteristic of different periods, as particular shades of yellow and green of Chinese rugs and the blue of Persian; but the mellowing influences of time, acting through the agencies of exposure and wear, cause effects that cannot be produced by any artificial process.

Occasionally the time when a rug is made is recorded in Arabic numbers woven above a word denoting "year." If they are indistinct on account of the length of the nap, they may be more clearly read in reverse order at the back. In the following lines, each of them is represented below the one in our own notation, to which it corresponds.

0,   1,   2,   3,   4,   5,   6,   7,   8,   9

٠, ١, ٢, ٣, ٤, ٥, ٦, ٧, ٨, ٩

These numbers represent not the Christian but the Mohammedan year, which, dating from the time of the Hegira, began about the middle of July 622, or a little before the actual flight from Medina. It should also be remembered that the lunar and not the solar year is considered in Moslem chronology; which, according to our reckoning, gains about one year in every thirty-three and seven tenths years. To calculate, then, the year of our time corresponding with the year expressed in the rug, from the number should be subtracted one thirty-three and seven tenths part of itself, and then should be added six hundred and twenty-two. Thus, if the year 1247 was woven in the rug, our corresponding year would be A.D. 1247 less 37 (or 1210) plus 622, or 1832. When such dates appear in old rugs, they are generally to be depended on, but in modern ones they are more likely to be antedated to give the effect of greater age.

With reference to the time when woven, rugs may conveniently be divided into three broad classes; Antique rugs or carpets made over two centuries ago; old rugs made fifty or more years ago; and modern rugs made since the introduction of aniline dyes, or within the last fifty years.

The number of antique carpets that exist is undetermined, as it is impossible to estimate how many remain in Oriental mosques and palaces. Nor has any complete catalogue been made of those that are owned in Europe and America. They consist principally of the products of Persia, Asia Minor, Armenia, and China. Many belong to the museums and the remainder to sovereigns and wealthy collectors. Like rare porcelains and old paintings, their value increases with each passing year; and the prices received for them range according to the fancy and caprice of the purchaser. They are the most valued and the most costly of all rugs.

The number of rugs over fifty years of age, but not belonging to the previous class, is very large. A few are sufficiently prized to be placed in art museums, some belong to collectors, large numbers embellish the halls and drawing rooms of people of refinement, and others are yearly brought from the Orient; but dealers and the public already realise that their numbers are limited. Even now they are searched for in the remotest corners of every rug-producing country; and in a few years the last, now cherished as family heirlooms, will have been exchanged for western gold. Almost all are well woven, though some are too much worn to be trodden longer under foot. None are treated with aniline dyes, but the colours mellowed by time are exceptionally good and frequently contain rare tones characteristic of the first class. Moreover, large numbers contain emblems of a symbolism still shrouded in mysteries that increase their fascination. On the whole, this is the choicest stock from which to choose elegant carpetings for luxurious homes. When it is considered that rugs of this class are beginning to disappear from the market, the prices at which they may be purchased are moderate compared with the prices of more modern pieces.

The great majority of existing Oriental rugs have been woven within the last fifty years. A few of them, including many of the newest, have colours that compare favourably with those of older pieces; but a large number show the effect of aniline dyes. Some woven by nomads or dwellers in remote villages, without thought of sale, have designs and workmanship such as have characterised the fabrics of these people for past generations; but others, which are the products of the workhouse system, though well woven as a rule, lack the charm of spontaneous individuality. Age alone has little influence in determining the value of these modern rugs, since they have not yet become rare; yet even in them the wear of time affects their other qualities. Other things being equal, they cost less than the old and the antique rugs.

The locality where a rug was woven is also to be considered in determining its rarity and therefore its value. Of the countless carpets that once existed in Egypt, of the very early rugs of Caucasia and Turkestan, not a piece remains; but if one were to be found it would be almost priceless. The antique carpets of Syria, or of Kirman, Shiraz, and Tabriz, woven over three centuries ago, are more valuable than others of equally good workmanship, of which relatively large numbers remain. So, too, of the rugs classed as old, but falling short of the venerable age of the real antiques, those which are now difficult to be obtained on account of their scarcity, are more valuable than those which are being produced in larger numbers. Rugs such as the Joshaghan, Tiflis, and many others of sixty or more years of age, are no longer woven. Modern products from the same districts may adopt the old names, but they are not the same. Accordingly, it will be only a short time when they too will disappear from the market. Good examples of such pieces should therefore receive more careful consideration on the part of purchasers and collectors, as their value is increasing with each passing year.

Furthermore, the rarity of an old rug is often independent of its age or the locality where it was made, and is due to its peculiar type. For instance, the Ming Rugs of China with silver threads and the so-called Garden Carpets of Iran represent types rather than localities. Likewise the Hunting Carpets of Persia, the Holbein Carpets of Asia Minor, and the Dragon Carpets of Armenia, represent, as far as we know, the textile craft of no well-defined district of limited area, as is the case of modern rugs, but rather rare types. Such pieces are valuable, not alone on account of their age, but also because they represent these rare types.

A rug is also valued for its artistic beauty. The innumerable rugs which centuries ago were in daily use soon disappeared, and only those intended for palaces or temples have been preserved. It is but natural, then, that the antique carpets representing the highest art of their time should be not only rare but also beautiful. Yet even in them is often a distinction that affects their value. Fortunately, very many of the larger number of rugs of less age, but classed as old, likewise possess artistic beauty. This chiefly depends on the drawing and the colouring.

It will be noticed that almost without exception careful drawing accompanies workmanship of a high class. This is partly due to the facts that the more excellent the weave the easier it is to clearly define patterns; and that on shortness of nap, which as a rule is found in closely woven rugs, depends accuracy of delineation. The charm of rugs often depends, also, on the graceful flow of lines, the careful balance of different parts of patterns, and the proper co-ordination between border and field. Careful attention should accordingly be given to the drawing when selecting a rug.

The artistic beauty of Oriental rugs depends still more on the colouring, since, as has been elsewhere expressed, drawing, which is intellectual, finds its highest development in the Occident, and colouring, which is sensuous, finds its highest development in the Orient. It at once suggests sumptuous luxury. In all of the antique carpets that remain and in very many rugs over fifty years of age, all the colours employed in a single piece are in tones of perfect harmony, and are so placed with reference to one another that the effect is most agreeable. But in some of the modern pieces, such as are produced in parts of Asia Minor and Caucasia, are colours which, like discordant notes of music, grate harshly on the senses. The most pleasing effect is when colours of border and field are complementary, yet so in harmony as to accentuate the qualities of each.

There are also colours which, independent of their association, are in themselves good or bad. The best are found in the antique carpets woven when the art of the dyer was an honourable profession. The colours are also very good in still later pieces; but for a century now some of the finest have not been used, and even the secret of producing them has been lost. Here and there dyers and weavers cling to early traditions, so that among modern rugs are many examples of good colouring; but the most recent pieces, excepting when softened by artificial processes, often display harsh and garish colours. This distinction is in a measure due to the fact that old colours were largely produced by vegetable dyes and the modern are too often produced by aniline. Not infrequently both vegetable and aniline colours are used in the same piece, and sometimes the quantity of aniline colour is so small that it is scarcely objectionable; but as a rule it is best never to purchase a rug that is so tainted.

One objection to the use of aniline dyes is that by removing some of the natural oil of the wool they are apt to make it brittle, so that it is less able to stand wear. Another is that in time some of the dyes, which have been applied collectively to produce a single colour, will fade or even disappear, so that the final colour may be a most undesirable shade not in harmony with those that surround it. If the fibres are brittle and become harsher to the touch when wet with water, it is an indication that aniline dyes have been used. Another test is the application of weak vegetable acids, which will make the colour spread if produced by aniline dyes, but are not likely to affect it if produced by vegetable dyes. Many native weavers can distinguish by placing the wool in their mouths, when they experience a sweet or bitter taste, according as vegetable or aniline dyes have been used. It is a mistake, however, to assume that the dyes are aniline because the wool has a brighter colour at the surface of the nap than at the foundation; or because the colour spreads when wet with water; since in time even some of the vegetable colours will fade; and when fresh they will run during the first washing in water, but afterwards they are little affected either by water or weak acids.

Even when the same colours and the same kind of dyes were used, there is a marked distinction in the appearance of old and of recently woven rugs, which is due to wear as well as exposure to sun and weather. The effect of time, imperceptible at first, is shown in rich tones of remarkable softness and beauty, that add greatly to the value of a rug. It accordingly happens that artificial processes are adopted to create as far as possible the same results without the lapse of time. Some of these are as novel as were the efforts of the distinguished viceroy of King-te Chin, in the reign of Kang-hi, to produce antique porcelains.* Henry Savage Landor says † that "to manufacture 'Antique Carpets' is one of the most lucrative branches of modern Persian carpet making. The new carpets are spread in the bazar in the middle of the street, where it is most crowded, and trampled upon for days or weeks, according to the days required, foot passengers and their donkeys, mules and camels making a point of treading on them in order to 'add to age' in the manufacturer's goods. When sufficiently worn down the carpet is removed, brushed, and ordinarily sold for double or treble the actual price, owing to its antiquity."

Whatever may be their character, the methods employed to give softened effects to the colours are known as "washing." Most of those in vogue in the Orient, such as washing with lime water, do little real injury. In this country to artificially mellow the colours has become a regular business of firms, who guard the secret of their different methods. Some use ammonia, borax, and soap,

* It is stated that in the short space of a few weeks he created valuable antique porcelains to present to his noble friends by placing recent copies of old specimens in a vessel containing very greasy soup, where they were duly boiled for a month, and after that placing them in the " foulest drain of the neighbourhood," where they remained until seasoned.

† In " Across Coveted Lands, 1903."

which also do very little injury to the rug. Others use chloride of lime, boracic acid, vinegar, or oxalic acid, that remove some of the natural oils of the wool and accordingly impair its qualities for wear. In fact, pieces are occasionally injured to the extent that the wool has become brittle and may readily be plucked out. Nevertheless, it does not necessarily follow that all rugs washed with an acid solution have been seriously injured; but the colours never have the same richness as those which have been softened by natural processes operating for a long period of years. To be sure, rugs that have been washed are often more attractive than they were in their raw colours; but the older, more beautiful rugs with genuine tones mellowed by time are always to be preferred. Over ninety per cent of the Kermanshahs, Sarouks, Kashans, Tabriz, Muskabads, Mahals, and Gorevans, and a large percentage of all other modern rugs sold in this country, have been treated by some artificial process to soften their colours or give them the appearance of age. It is generally necessary, when selecting a large rug for a floor covering, to accept a washed piece; but when a smaller rug or a runner will meet the requirements, it is preferable to choose the older unwashed piece, which, as a rule, is more beautiful and costs but little more. In the case of most pieces, the tones of colour are sufficient to enable one who is experienced to distinguish between those that are artificially aged and those that are not. In the case of others, a simple test is to rub them thoroughly with a wet rag; when, if acid or chloride of lime has been used, it can generally be detected by the odour.

The artistic beauty of a rug also depends somewhat on the fineness of the nap; as the soft, floccy fibres of some wools acquire a velvety appearance, or give to the colours a sheen and a lustre compared with which other rugs look harsh and coarse. For instance, the rugs of Shiraz and Meshed, the Beluchistans, and many Bokharas are noted for the lustre of their colours; but on the other hand many of the rugs of Asia Minor and Caucasia have colours that are without lustre, and the rugs of India which are made of dead or "Chunam" wool, seem lifeless.

When selecting any rug, then, the purchaser should carefully observe if the patterns are well drawn and their different parts show a proper balance. He should observe if the colour tones are harmonious with one another, if each colour in itself is good, and if they have been softened by natural processes acting for a long time.

And he should notice if the wool is coarse, dead, and lustreless, or if it has a sheen and glint in the light of day; for these are the qualities that make up the artistic beauty of a rug.

The utility to be derived from rugs that properly belong to museums and collectors receives small consideration, though even with them the more perfect their condition the more valuable they are. But in case of the great majority of rugs, which are intended for use as well as for ornament, their utility is an important consideration to the purchaser. Rugs that have warp and weft of strong yarn and a close firm texture, will wear better than others. Also, such rugs as Bijars, in which one thread of warp to each knot is doubled under the other, will be found to wear better than such rugs as Mosuls which have each thread of warp equally prominent at the back. For durability, long nap is also to be preferred to short, since it protects the foundations of the knots from wearing and becoming loose.

Before purchasing an old rug, it should be spread on the floor to see if it lies flat and if its shape is regular. It should be examined by daylight and not by electric light, which gives a false impression of colour and sheen. It should be held up with the back turned to the purchaser, and carefully examined for weak spots through which the light may pass; since, when so held, many pieces which seem in good condition when lying on the floor, resemble a sieve. The foundation threads should also be carefully inspected, as sometimes they rot and will tear with slight tension. Moreover, as the selvage or overcasting of the sides and the webs of the ends are intended primarily not for ornament but for protection, it should be noted if they are in good condition. Sometimes the webs of the ends are entirely gone, so that continual fraying of the nap is prevented with difficulty. Sometimes the selvage or overcasting of the sides is broken and some of the threads of warp are injured. Or the sides may be well protected by a stout overcasting; but on examination it will be seen that it is not the original finishing, and that some of the border has disappeared. Again, it may have been overcast too tightly, so that the sides curl and turn under, and thus expose the border to injury when trodden on. Careful examination will often reveal surprises. In many old rugs the field is full of rents, that have been sewn together; in others entire pieces have been removed, so that they are no longer of their original length; or parts of the border are gone, or even the whole of it has been replaced by the border of another rug; yet all so deftly done that the changes are scarcely noticeable.

Nevertheless, old pieces, if otherwise meritorious, are not to be discarded on account of a few imperfections, since what can be accomplished in the hands of a careful repairer is remarkable. Broken threads of warp and weft can be mended; missing knots can be replaced with others of similar yarn; crooked pieces can be straightened by loosening here and stretching there; borders that curl can be flattened by removing the yarn and overcasting again more carefully. In fact, if the nap be not so worn that the foundation of warp and wept is exposed, it is far better to choose an old rug with some rents than a new one with garish aniline dyes. Nor should a piece be slighted, because the brownish black areas of wool dyed with iron pyrites are worn low; since often the most beautiful effects are obtained by a surface of brighter colours standing out in relief, on account of the worn blackish nap that surrounds it. Now and then a bargain can be had by buying a rug which, because of some imperfection that is not serious, has been passed by; and now and then a piece reeking with dirt has proved, when properly cleansed, to be a gem.

The foundation, consisting of the warp and weft, receives but little consideration from purchasers; yet it is one of the most important indices of the quality of a rug, and its strength is one of the most necessary conditions for utility. The warp is best observed at the ends. In most Chinese and Indian rugs and in some of the Persian, it is of cotton; in others it is of wool or goat's hair. In the Chinese rugs the diameter of the threads of warp is much smaller than the diameter of the threads of the weft, and has little strength, but in almost all other rugs it is at least as large and as stout. The weft may readily be observed at the back. In very many of the best rugs, it consists of fine spun wool; but in many modern ones, it is of coarse wool or cotton. The number of knots to the square inch does not of itself demonstrate the quality of texture, since a rug may have only a few knots of coarse diameter and be firmly woven, or it may have many knots of fine diameter and be loosely woven; but in the same class the better rug has generally more knots than a poorer one. When selecting a rug, then, the back should be most carefully observed; for here may be seen if the yarn that forms the knots is well spun, if the knots themselves are drawn tight and well pressed down, and if the threads of weft are carefully inserted and have a texture that indicates fine workmanship. Almost invariably it will be found that if the back of a rug shows good material, and has an appearance of firmness and skilful, painstaking weaving, the front will correspond with good colours and careful drawing.

The value of antique carpets, which depends to some extent on their size, and to a much greater extent on their rarity and character, is constantly increasing; for the reason that their number is limited and each year they are more highly appreciated. It is, therefore, impossible to affix even approximate prices; but the sums paid at the Yerkes sale in 1910, when some thirty pieces were sold at auction for an average of about $9,400, will serve as a guide. The following are some of the pieces sold and the prices realised:

Carpet, size 7 feet 4 inches by 5 feet 4 inches, attributed to Western Persia, at end of XVI Century, and purchased by the Metropolitan Museum of Art, N. Y. $5,600

Persian carpet, XVI Century, described on page 86 5,600

Polish silk carpet, XVI Century, size 6 feet 6 inches by 4 feet 7 inches . . 4,700

Polish silk carpet, XVI Century, size 6 feet 6 inches by 4 feet 7 inches . 3,500

Polish silk carpet, XVI Century, size 6 feet 11 inches by 4 feet 10 inches 12,300

Silk carpet, XVI Century, size 7 feet 2½ inches by 6 feet 5 inches, stated to have belonged to the Ardebil Mosque 35,500

Moorish carpet, XVI Century, size 10 feet 11 inches by 5 feet 10 inches, stated to have belonged to the Ardebil Mosque and purchased by the Metropolitan Museum of Art, N. Y. 15,200

Hispano Moresque Mosque carpet, size 34 feet 5 inches by 16 feet 8 inches, flat stitch 8,600

Carpet attributed to Western Iran, size 16 feet 4 inches by 11 feet 2 inches, and purchased by the Metropolitan Museum of Art, N. Y. . . . 19,600

Carpet similar to the Mosque carpet of Ardebil, XVI Century, size 23 feet 11 inches by 13 feet 5 inches 27,000

The value of rugs over fifty years of age but not sufficiently old to belong to the antique class also depends as much on the technique of weave, drawing, colouring, and rarity as on the size; yet even this must be taken into consideration. In proportion to their size the most expensive of these rugs are the Kirmans, Sehnas, and Niris from Persia; the Ghiordes and Ladiks from Asia Minor; the Daghestans and Kabistans from Caucasia; and the Royal Bokharas and Yomuds from Central Asia. Considering both utility and attractiveness the least expensive are probably the Sarabends and Mosuls from the Persian group, the Yuruks from Asia Minor, Kazaks and Tcherkess from Caucasia, and Afghans and

Beluchistans from Central Asia. As is the case with antique carpets, the prices of all old rugs in good condition are steadily advancing.

There is likewise a tendency for the prices of modern rugs to increase with each year, since on account of the gradual opening of Oriental countries to the markets of the world, and the greater demand for rugs, the wages of weavers are increasing. Some of them, as the Tabriz, Gorevans, Kermanshahs, Muskabads, Mahals, Sarouks, and Kashans, are now made almost exclusively under the direction of the work-house system, and are sold at prices that fluctuate but slightly. But in a short time the prices of all of them will doubtless be higher.

When a rug of carpet size is required, the Kermanshahs are generally preferred on account of their soft colouring and refined patterns, that harmonise with the furnishings of most reception rooms. Less expensive and more showy are the Gorevans, which are suitable for halls or dining rooms. In the Afghans, which are splendid rugs for a den, are combined durability with a moderate price. Within recent years some of the Indian rugs, as the Amritsars and Lahores, have been growing in favour, as they not only have good colours, artistic patterns, and exceedingly good texture, but are reasonable in price. Of smaller rugs required both for ornament and use, the Shiraz, Feraghan, Mosul, Bergamo, Tcherkess, Bokhara, and Beluchistan are desirable.

As is the case with other works of art, so much deception can be practised in the sale of rugs that a purchaser cannot use too much circumspection. Sometimes through ignorance or with intention, a dealer will declare that the wool of a rug which has been coloured with aniline dyes has been coloured with vegetable dyes only; that a rug washed with acid has matured naturally; that a new rug which has been artificially worn almost to the knot is an antique; or that a particular rug belongs to the class desired, as where a Shirvan is offered for a Shiraz or a Bijar for a Bergamo, which ordinarily are worth much more. It is, accordingly, discreet to buy only of such firms as have a reputation which is above reproach; and if for any reason it is difficult to learn the standing of a firm, the purchaser would do well to make an effort to test its reliability by inquiring about the qualities of some class of rugs with which he is familiar before purchasing others; and if there appears to be any intention to deceive, he should at once look elsewhere. In any event, he should take a guarantee that the rug purchased is as represented. Firms that have gained an honourable reputation by honest dealing deserve the patronage of the public, and will always be found ready to make restitution if any mistake has been made.

At times, the best rugs may be bought at auctions and at the fairest prices. Auctions such as the Yerkes, where estates are being closed or where firms are dissolved, occasionally occur, when every opportunity is given the purchaser to thoroughly examine in advance pieces which are sold without reservation to the highest bidder. On such occasions, rare pieces are sometimes bought at very moderate prices. But as a rule, unless the purchaser is a good judge and has previously carefully examined a coveted piece in broad daylight, it is better not to buy at auctions. During the sale it is impossible to properly examine a rug. The glare of electric light thrown upon it gives a too favourable impression of its beauty. The competitive bids of other real or fictitious purchasers and the words of the auctioneer too often lead beyond the dictates of good judgment. At such times one would do well to remember the old words *caveat emptor.*

INDEX

INDEX*

A

Abbas, Shah, 88, 89, 169, 211; pattern named after, 105; sent artisans to India, 111; rug industry declined after death of, 112.

Abraham, 23, 31.

Acacia used as a dye, 40, 41.

Accadians, 23.

Adighies, 209.

Afghan rugs, 293, 304, 305; geometric designs of, 62; technicalities in weave of, 51, 53, 56, 57, 235. Rugs described, 243, 244, 245; border stripes, 251.

Afghan tribes, 90.

Afghanistan, 41, 103, 233, 243, 244; camel's wool of, 32.

Afshar rugs, 100, 286; technicalities in weave of, 51. Rugs described, 155.

Aga Mohammed Khan pillaged Kirman, 113.

Agamemnon, 166.

Agra, 255, 257.

Agra rugs described, 257.

Akbar, Shah, 28; received assistance from Shah Abbas, 29; established rug weaving at Lahore, 94; imported Persian weavers, 253; carpet factory of, 256.

Ak-Hissar, 175.

Ak-Hissar rugs, 101. Rugs described, 175, 176.

Ak-kal, oasis of, 238.

Albana, 204.

Alexander the Great, 169, 181, 246; destroyed Shiraz, 115; built walls at Derbend, 204.

Alhambra, 25.

Ali Riza, Imam, 110.

Allahabad, 258.

Allahabad rugs described, 258.

Altai Mts., 29; original home of the Turks, 26.

Altman, Benjamin, 85.

Alum, used as a mordant, 40, 41.

Amritsar, 255, 258.

Amritsar rugs, 101, 257, 305. Rugs described, 255.

Amu Daria. See Oxus river.

Anatolia, 163, 182; the "Land of the Rising Sun," 187.

Anatolian rugs, 101, 176, 190, 289, 290; illustration of prayer arch of, 63. Rugs described, 187, 188, 189; border stripes, 195.

Angora, 27, 185, 187; goat's wool, 32.

Anilines. See Dyes.

Animal carpets, 86, 87.

Anjuman Industrial Art School, 259.

Anoschar, 76.

Anti-Taurus Mts., 140, 187, 190.

Arabia, 24, 29, 32.

Arabic features in rugs, 85; notation, 296; symbolism in Western Kurdistan rugs, 141.

Arabs, in Persia, 103; overran Turkestan, 234.

Ararat, Mt., 103, 219.

Aras river, 151, 157, 224.

Ardebil, Persian capital under Ismael, 28; mosque of, 82, 127.

Ardebil carpet, 15; described, 83, 84.

Ardelan district, 100, 129, 133, 153.

Armenia, 209; origin of some Caucasian border stripes of, 226, 228, 229.

Armenian rugs, 91, 170, 209, 220; designs derived from, 64, 65, 67, 209, 214, 215. Rugs described, 91.

Armenians in Persia, 103; in Mosul, 103.

Artaxerxes, 103.

Aryan races, in India, 28; in Persia, 103; in Caucasia, 197; in Turkestan, 234; floral ornamentation employed by, 62.

Asburg used as a dye, 41.

Astrabad, 241.

Astrakan, market for Bokharas, 235, for caravans from Khiva, 240.

Auctions, 306.

* All references of an unimportant character are indicated by the page number only.

Ispahan rugs, lotus design in, 69; made at Ispahan, 89; sombre tones of, 90; red fields of, 95; blues and reds of the antique, 127; palmettes of the antique, 145. Modern rugs described, 111, 112, 113.

J

Jahan, Shah, 28; builder of Taj Mahal, 94; Indian rug-weaving declined after death of, 253.
Jail system of India, 254.
Jaipur, 255, 259.
Jaipur rugs described, 259.
Japan, 17.
Jhelum river, suggested as origin of pear design, 70; Srinagar on the, 255.
Joshaghan district, 132.
Joshaghan rugs, 100, 286, 298; technicalities in weave of, 50. Rugs described, 132, 133; border stripes, 157.
Jubbulpur, 255, 258.
Jubbulpur rugs described, 258, 259.
Jute, used in weaving, 30, 33; in Kulaks, 174; in Vellore rugs, 261; in Bangalore rugs, 262.

K

Kaaba, 117.
Kabistan, 199.
Kabistan rugs, 101, 204, 290, 292, 293, 304; technicalities in weave of, 54; illustration of prayer arch of, 61; effulgent stars of, 91; Cufic borders of, 92; patterns of some Shirvans similar to those of, 213. Rugs described, 200, 201, 202; border stripes, 226, 228, 229.
Kain, 108.
Kaisariyeh, 190.
Kaisariyeh rugs described, 190, 191.
Kaiser Friedrich Museum, 79, 92.
Kang-hi rugs, 78, 101. Rugs described, 268, 269; border stripes, 274; medallions, 273.
Karabacek, Dr., quoted, 74.
Karabagh district, 222, 224.
Karabagh rugs, 101, 290, 292; technicalities in weave of, 51, 53; illustration of prayer arch of, 61; Karadaghs compared with, 151; Shushas compared with, 224. Rugs described, 222, 223.
Karadagh district, 151.
Karadagh rugs, 100, 286, 289. Rugs described; border stripes, 157, 158.
Kara-Geuz district, 155.
Kara-Geuz rugs, 100, 154. Rugs described, 155.

Karaje rugs, 100, 286; technicalities in weave of, 53. Rugs described, 143, 144.
Kara Kum desert, 241.
Karaman, 188.
Karaman rugs, 101, 289. Rugs described, 188. Kilims, 278, 279.
Kashan, 115, 127, 155.
Kashan rugs, 100, 285, 286, 288, 301, 305; technicalities in weave of, 35, 51, 55; illustration of prayer arch of, 61; pattern of Sarouks like that of, 134; correspondence of some rugs of Tabriz with, 145. Rugs described, 127, 128, 129; border stripes, 160.
Kashgar, 247.
Kashgar rugs, 101, 234, 282, 292. Rugs described, 247, 248.
Kashmir, 70, 255; goat's wool of, 32, 114.
Katchli, derivation of, 237; pattern used in Tekkes, 239, 293.
Kazak rugs, 101, 290, 292, 304; technicalities in weave of, 51, 53; illustration of prayer arch of, 61; Western Kurdistans compared with, 141; Afshars compared with, 155; Yuruks compared with, 191; Tcherkess compared with, 209; Kutais compared with, 222; Genghas compared with, 224. Rugs described, 219, 220, 221, 222; border stripes, 226, 227, 228, 229.
Kazakje, 220
Kea-king dynasty, 272. Rugs described, 272.
Keen-lung dynasty. Rugs described, 270, 271, 272; border stripes, 274, 275; medallions, 273.
Kenares defined, 97.
Kerim, Khan, 115; royal patronage of weaving at Shiraz under, 116.
Kermanshah, 83, 129, 138.
Kermanshah rugs, 134, 137, 147, 160, 285, 288, 301, 305; technicalities in weave of, 52; illustration of prayer arch of, 61; corners of Khorassans compared with those of, 109; Tabriz rugs compared with, 145, 146; Amritsars mistaken for, 256. Rugs described, 138, 139, 140; border stripes, 38.
Kermes used as a dye, 38.
Key pattern, 27.
Khali defined, 97.
Khibitkas, defined, 238; rugs made for doors of, 239.
Khiva, 110, 240, 241, 244.
Khiva rugs, 100, 233, 235, 242, 293; illustration of prayer arch of, 61. Rugs described, 240, 241; border stripes, 250, 251.

Dover Books on Art

Dover Books on Art

MASTERPIECES OF FURNITURE, Verna Cook Salomonsky.
Photographs and measured drawings of some of the finest examples of Colonial American, 17th century English, Windsor, Sheraton, Hepplewhite, Chippendale, Louis XIV, Queen Anne, and various other furniture styles. The textual matter includes information on traditions, characteristics, background, etc. of various pieces. 101 plates. Bibliography. 224pp. 7⅞ x 10¾.
21381-1 Paperbound $2.50

PRIMITIVE ART, Franz Boas. In this exhaustive volume, a great American anthropologist analyzes all the fundamental traits of primitive art, covering the formal element in art, representative art, symbolism, style, literature, music, and the dance. Illustrations of Indian embroidery, paleolithic paintings, woven blankets, wing and tail designs, totem poles, cutlery, earthenware, baskets and many other primitive objects and motifs. Over 900 illustrations. 376pp. 5⅜ x 8.   20025-6 Paperbound $2.50

AN INTRODUCTION TO A HISTORY OF WOODCUT, A. M. Hind. Nearly all of this authoritative 2-volume set is devoted to the 15th century—the period during which the woodcut came of age as an important art form. It is the most complete compendium of information on this period, the artists who contributed to it, and their technical and artistic accomplishments. Profusely illustrated with cuts by 15th century masters, and later works for comparative purposes. 484 illustrations. 5 indexes. Total of xi + 838pp. 5⅜ x 8½. Two-vols. 20952-0,20953-9 Paperbound $5.50

ART STUDENTS' ANATOMY, E. J. Farris. Teaching anatomy by using chiefly living objects for illustration, this study has enjoyed long popularity and success in art courses and home-study programs. All the basic elements of the human anatomy are illustrated in minute detail, diagrammed and pictured as they pass through common movements and actions. 158 drawings, photographs, and roentgenograms. Glossary of anatomical terms. x + 159pp. 5⅝ x 8⅜.   20744-7 Paperbound $1.50

COLONIAL LIGHTING, A. H. Hayward. The only book to cover the fascinating story of lamps and other lighting devices in America. Beginning with rush light holders used by the early settlers, it ranges through the elaborate chandeliers of the Federal period, illustrating 647 lamps. Of great value to antique collectors, designers, and historians of arts and crafts. Revised and enlarged by James R. Marsh. xxxi + 198pp. 5⅝ x 8¼.
20975-X Paperbound $2.00

Dover Books on Art

LANDSCAPE GARDENING IN JAPAN, Josiah Conder. A detailed picture of Japanese gardening techniques and ideas, the artistic principles incorporated in the Japanese garden, and the religious and ethical concepts at the heart of those principles. Preface. 92 illustrations, plus all 40 full-page plates from the Supplement. Index. xv + 299pp. 8⅜ x 11¼.

21216-5 Paperbound $3.50

DESIGN AND FIGURE CARVING, E. J. Tangerman. "Anyone who can peel a potato can carve," states the author, and in this unusual book he shows you how, covering every stage in detail from very simple exercises working up to museum-quality pieces. Terrific aid for hobbyists, arts and crafts counselors, teachers, those who wish to make reproductions for the commercial market. Appendix: How to Enlarge a Design. Brief bibliography. Index. 1298 figures. x + 289pp. 5⅜ x 8½.

21209-2 Paperbound $2.00

WILD FOWL DECOYS, Joel Barber. Antique dealers, collectors, craftsmen, hunters, readers of Americana, etc. will find this the only thorough and reliable guide on the market today to this unique folk art. It contains the history, cultural significance, regional design variations; unusual decoy lore; working plans for constructing decoys; and loads of illustrations. 140 full-page plates, 4 in color. 14 additional plates of drawings and plans by the author. xxvii + 156pp. 7⅞ x 10¾. 20011-6 Paperbound $3.50

1800 WOODCUTS BY THOMAS BEWICK AND HIS SCHOOL. This is the largest collection of first-rate pictorial woodcuts in print—an indispensable part of the working library of every commercial artist, art director, production designer, packaging artist, craftsman, manufacturer, librarian, art collector, and artist. And best of all, when you buy your copy of Bewick, you buy the rights to reproduce individual illustrations—no permission needed, no acknowledgments, no clearance fees! Classified index. Bibliography and sources. xiv + 246pp. 9 x 12.

20766-8 Paperbound $4.00

THE SCRIPT LETTER, Tommy Thompson. Prepared by a noted authority, this is a thorough, straightforward course of instruction with advice on virtually every facet of the art of script lettering. Also a brief history of lettering with examples from early copy books and illustrations from present day advertising and packaging. Copiously illustrated. Bibliography. 128pp. 6½ x 9⅛. 21311-0 Paperbound $1.25

Dover Books on Art

ART ANATOMY, Dr. William Rimmer. One of the few books on art anatomy that are themselves works of art, this is a faithful reproduction (rearranged for handy use) of the extremely rare masterpiece of the famous 19th century anatomist, sculptor, and art teacher. Beautiful, clear line drawings show every part of the body—bony structure, muscles, features, etc. Unusual are the sections on falling bodies, foreshortenings, muscles in tension, grotesque personalities, and Rimmer's remarkable interpretation of emotions and personalities as expressed by facial features. It will supplement every other book on art anatomy you are likely to have. Reproduced clearer than the lithographic original (which sells for $500 on up on the rare book market.) Over 1,200 illustrations. xiii + 153pp. 7¾ x 10¾.
20908-3 Paperbound $2.50

THE CRAFTSMAN'S HANDBOOK, Cennino Cennini. The finest English translation of IL LIBRO DELL' ARTE, the 15th century introduction to art technique that is both a mirror of Quatrocento life and a source of many useful but nearly forgotten facets of the painter's art. 4 illustrations. xxvii + 142pp. D. V. Thompson, translator. 5⅜ x 8.
20054-X Paperbound $1.75

THE BROWN DECADES, Lewis Mumford. A picture of the "buried renaissance" of the post-Civil War period, and the founding of modern architecture (Sullivan, Richardson, Root, Roebling), landscape development (Marsh, Olmstead, Eliot), and the graphic arts (Homer, Eakins, Ryder). 2nd revised, enlarged edition. Bibliography. 12 illustrations. xiv + 266 pp. 5⅜ x 8.
20200-3 Paperbound $2.00

THE HUMAN FIGURE, J. H. Vanderpoel. Not just a picture book, but a complete course by a famous figure artist. Extensive text, illustrated by 430 pencil and charcoal drawings of both male and female anatomy. 2nd enlarged edition. Foreword. 430 illus. 143pp. 6⅛ x 9¼.
20432-4 Paperbound $1.50

PINE FURNITURE OF EARLY NEW ENGLAND, R. H. Kettell. Over 400 illustrations, over 50 working drawings of early New England chairs, benches, beds, cupboards, mirrors, shelves, tables, other furniture esteemed for simple beauty and character. "Rich store of illustrations . . . emphasizes the individuality and varied design," ANTIQUES. 413 illustrations, 55 working drawings. 475pp. 8 x 10¾.
20145-4 Clothbound $10.00

Dover Books on Art

AFRICAN SCULPTURE, Ladislas Segy. 163 full-page plates illustrating masks, fertility figures, ceremonial objects, etc., of 50 West and Central African tribes—95% never before illustrated. 34-page introduction to African sculpture. "Mr. Segy is one of its top authorities," NEW YORKER. 164 full-page photographic plates. Introduction. Bibliography. 244pp. 6⅛ x 9¼.

20396-4 Paperbound $2.25

CALLIGRAPHY, J. G. Schwandner. First reprinting in 200 years of this legendary book of beautiful handwriting. Over 300 ornamental initials, 12 complete calligraphic alphabets, over 150 ornate frames and panels, 75 calligraphic pictures of cherubs, stags, lions, etc., thousands of flourishes, scrolls, etc., by the greatest 18th-century masters. All material can be copied or adapted without permission. Historical introduction. 158 full-page plates. 368pp. 9 x 13.

20475-8 Clothbound $10.00

A DIDEROT PICTORIAL ENCYCLOPEDIA OF TRADES AND INDUSTRY. Manufacturing and the Technical Arts in Plates Selected from "L'Encyclopédie ou Dictionnaire Raisonné des Sciences, des Arts, et des Métiers," of Denis Diderot, edited with text by C. Gillispie. Over 2000 illustrations on 485 full-page plates. Magnificent 18th-century engravings of men, women, and children working at such trades as milling flour, cheesemaking, charcoal burning, mining, silverplating, shoeing horses, making fine glass, printing, hundreds more, showing details of machinery, different steps in sequence, etc. A remarkable art work, but also the largest collection of working figures in print, copyright-free, for art directors, designers, etc. Two vols. 920pp. 9 x 12. Heavy library cloth.

22284-5, 22285-3 Two volume set $22.50

SILK SCREEN TECHNIQUES, J. Biegeleisen, M. Cohn. A practical step-by-step home course in one of the most versatile, least expensive graphic arts processes. How to build an inexpensive silk screen, prepare stencils, print, achieve special textures, use color, etc. Every step explained, diagrammed. 149 illustrations, 201pp. 6⅛ x 9¼.

20433-2 Paperbound $2.00

STICKS AND STONES, Lewis Mumford. An examination of forces influencing American architecture: the medieval tradition in early New England, the classical influence in Jefferson's time, the Brown Decades, the imperial facade, the machine age, etc. "A truly remarkable book," SAT. REV. OF LITERATURE. 2nd revised edition. 21 illus. xvii + 240pp. 5⅜ x 8.

20202-X Paperbound $2.00

Dover Books on Art

PRINCIPLES OF ART HISTORY, H. Wölfflin. This remarkably instructive work demonstrates the tremendous change in artistic conception from the 14th to the 18th centuries, by analyzing 164 works by Botticelli, Dürer, Hobbema, Holbein, Hals, Titian, Rembrandt, Vermeer, etc., and pointing out exactly what is meant by "baroque," "classic," "primitive," "picturesque," and other basic terms of art history and criticism. "A remarkable lesson in the art of seeing," SAT. REV. OF LITERATURE. Translated from the 7th German edition. 150 illus. 254pp. 6⅛ x 9¼.   20276-3   Paperbound $2.25

FOUNDATIONS OF MODERN ART, A. Ozenfant. Stimulating discussion of human creativity from paleolithic cave painting to modern painting, architecture, decorative arts. Fully illustrated with works of Gris, Lipchitz, Léger, Picasso, primitive, modern artifacts, architecture, industrial art, much more. 226 illustrations. 368pp. 6⅛ x 9¼.   20215-1   Paperbound $2.50

METALWORK AND ENAMELLING, H. Maryon. Probably the best book ever written on the subject. Tells everything necessary for the home manufacture of jewelry, rings, ear pendants, bowls, etc. Covers materials, tools, soldering, filigree, setting stones, raising patterns, repoussé work, damascening, niello, cloisonné, polishing, assaying, casting, and dozens of other techniques. The best substitute for apprenticeship to a master metalworker. 363 photos and figures. 374pp. 5½ x 8½.
    T183   Clothbound $8.50

SHAKER FURNITURE, E. D. and F. Andrews. The most illuminating study of Shaker furniture ever written. Covers chronology, craftsmanship, houses, shops, etc. Includes over 200 photographs of chairs, tables, clocks, beds, benches, etc. "Mr. & Mrs. Andrews know all there is to know about Shaker furniture," Mark Van Doren, NATION. 48 full-page plates. 192pp. 7⅞ x 10¾.   20679-3   Paperbound $2.50

ANIMAL DRAWING: ANATOMY AND ACTION FOR ARTISTS, C. R. Knight. 158 studies, with full accompanying text, of such animals as the gorilla, bear, bison, dromedary, camel, vulture, pelican, iguana, shark, etc., by one of the greatest modern masters of animal drawing. Innumerable tips on how to get life expression into your work. "An excellent reference work," SAN FRANCISCO CHRONICLE. 158 illustrations. 156pp. 10½ x 8½.   20426-X   Paperbound $2.75

Dover Books on Art

200 DECORATIVE TITLE-PAGES, edited by A. Nesbitt. Fascinating and informative from a historical point of view, this beautiful collection of decorated titles will be a great inspiration to students of design, commercial artists, advertising designers, etc. A complete survey of the genre from the first known decorated title to work in the first decades of this century. Bibliography and sources of the plates. 222pp. 8⅜ x 11¼.

21264-5 Paperbound $2.75

ON THE LAWS OF JAPANESE PAINTING, H. P. Bowie. This classic work on the philosophy and technique of Japanese art is based on the author's first-hand experiences studying art in Japan. Every aspect of Japanese painting is described: the use of the brush and other materials; laws governing conception and execution; subjects for Japanese paintings, etc. The best possible substitute for a series of lessons from a great Oriental master. Index. xv + 117pp. + 66 plates. 6⅛ x 9¼.

20030-2 Paperbound $2.25

PAINTING IN THE FAR EAST, L. Binyon. A study of over 1500 years of Oriental art by one of the world's outstanding authorities. The author chooses the most important masters in each period—Wu Tao-tzu, Toba Sojo, Kanaoka, Li Lung-mien, Masanobu, Okio, etc.—and examines the works, schools, and influence of each within their cultural context. 42 photographs. Sources of original works and selected bibliography. Notes including list of principal painters by periods. xx + 297pp. 6⅛ x 9¼.

20520-7 Paperbound $2.50

THE ALPHABET AND ELEMENTS OF LETTERING, F. W. Goudy. A beautifully illustrated volume on the aesthetics of letters and type faces and their history and development. Each plate consists of 15 forms of a single letter with the last plate devoted to the ampersand and the numerals. "A sound guide for all persons engaged in printing or drawing," Saturday Review. 27 full-page plates. 48 additional figures. xii + 131pp. 7⅞ x 10¾.

20792-7 Paperbound $2.25

PAINTING IN ISLAM, Sir Thomas W. Arnold. This scholarly study puts Islamic painting in its social and religious context and examines its relation to Islamic civilization in general. 65 full-page plates illustrate the text and give outstanding examples of Islamic art. 4 appendices. Index of mss. referred to. General Index. xxiv + 159pp. 6⅝ x 9¼.   21310-2 Paperbound $2.75

Dover Books on Art

THE FOUR BOOKS OF ARCHITECTURE, Andrea Palladio.
A compendium of the art of Andrea Palladio, one of the most celebrated architects of the Renaissance, including 250 magnificently-engraved plates showing edifices either of Palladio's design or reconstructed (in these drawings) by him from classical ruins and contemporary accounts. 257 plates. xxiv + 119pp. 9½ x 12¾. 21308-0 Clothbound $10.00

150 MASTERPIECES OF DRAWING, A. Toney. Selected by a gifted artist and teacher, these are some of the finest drawings produced by Western artists from the early 15th to the end of the 18th centuries. Excellent reproductions of drawings by Rembrandt, Bruegel, Raphael, Watteau, and other familiar masters, as well as works by lesser known but brilliant artists. 150 plates. xviii + 150pp. 5⅜ x 11¼. 21032-4 Paperbound $2.00

MORE DRAWINGS BY HEINRICH KLEY. Another collection of the graphic, vivid sketches of Heinrich Kley, one of the most diabolically talented cartoonists of our century. The sketches take in every aspect of human life: nothing is too sacred for him to ridicule, no one too eminent for him to satirize. 158 drawings you will not easily forget. iv + 104pp. 7⅜ x 10¾. 20041-8 Paperbound $1.85

THE TRIUMPH OF MAXIMILIAN I, 137 Woodcuts by Hans Burgkmair and Others. This is one of the world's great art monuments, a series of magnificent woodcuts executed by the most important artists in the German realms as part of an elaborate plan by Maximilian I, ruler of the Holy Roman Empire, to commemorate his own name, dynasty, and achievements. 137 plates. New translation of descriptive text, notes, and bibliography prepared by Stanley Appelbaum. Special section of 10pp. containing a reduced version of the entire Triumph. x + 169pp. 11⅛ x 9¼. 21207-6 Paperbound $3.00

LOST EXAMPLES OF COLONIAL ARCHITECTURE, J. M. Howells. This book offers a unique guided tour through America's architectural past, all of which is either no longer in existence or so changed that its original beauty has been destroyed. More than 275 clear photos of old churches, dwelling houses, public buildings, business structures, etc. 245 plates, containing 281 photos and 9 drawings, floorplans, etc. New Index. xvii + 248pp. 7⅞ x 10¾. 21143-6 Paperbound $3.00

Dover Books on Art

THE COMPLETE BOOK OF SILK SCREEN PRINTING PRO-DUCTION, J. I. Biegeleisen. Here is a clear and complete picture of every aspect of silk screen technique and press operation—from individually operated manual presses to modern automatic ones. Unsurpassed as a guidebook for setting up shop, making shop operation more efficient, finding out about latest methods and equipment; or as a textbook for use in teaching, studying, or learning all aspects of the profession. 124 figures. Index. Bibliography. List of Supply Sources. xi + 253pp. 5⅜ x 8½.

21100-2 Paperbound $2.75

A HISTORY OF COSTUME, Carl Köhler. The most reliable and authentic account of the development of dress from ancient times through the 19th century. Based on actual pieces of clothing that have survived, using paintings, statues and other reproductions only where originals no longer exist. Hundreds of illustrations, including detailed patterns for many articles. Highly useful for theatre and movie directors, fashion designers, illustrators, teachers. Edited and augmented by Emma von Sichart. Translated by Alexander K. Dallas. 594 illustrations. 464pp. 5⅛ x 7⅛.

21030-8 Paperbound $3.00

CHINESE HOUSEHOLD FURNITURE, G. N. Kates. A summary of virtually everything that is known about authentic Chinese furniture before it was contaminated by the influence of the West. The text covers history of styles, materials used, principles of design and craftsmanship, and furniture arrangement—all fully illustrated. xiii + 190pp. 5⅝ x 8½.

20958-X Paperbound $1.75

THE COMPLETE WOODCUTS OF ALBRECHT DURER, edited by Dr. Willi Kurth. Albrecht Dürer was a master in various media, but it was in woodcut design that his creative genius reached its highest expression. Here are all of his extant woodcuts, a collection of over 300 great works, many of which are not available elsewhere. An indispensable work for the art historian and critic and all art lovers. 346 plates. Index. 285pp. 8½ x 12¼.

21097-9 Paperbound $3.00

Dover publishes books on commercial art, art history, crafts, design, art classics; also books on music, literature, science, mathematics, puzzles and entertainments, chess, engineering, biology, philosophy, psychology, languages, history, and other fields. For free circulars write to Dept. DA, Dover Publications, Inc., 180 Varick St., New York, N.Y. 10014.

DATE DUE

MAY 8 '78	101007	
MAY 2 1 1980		
JAN 1 6 1982		
JUN 6 1983		
MAR 1 8 1984		
JAN 2 6 '87		
MAR 13 '89		
AUG 1 4 '89		
APR 0 3 92 MAY 31 '95		
JUL 31 '95 MAY 31 '96		
MAY 31 '98		
MAY 31 '98		
NOV 1 8 1997		PRINTED IN U.S.A.